THE ESSENTIAL GUIDE TO
PLANT
SELECTION

THE ESSENTIAL GUIDE TO
PLANT
SELECTION

HUGH WILLIAMS

CHANCELLOR
PRESS

First Published in 1988 by Hamlyn.
This edition published in 1996 by Chancellor Press
an imprint of Reed Books, Michelin House, 81 Fulham Road,
London SW3 6RB, England

ISBN 1 85152 9225

Reprinted 1996

Cover Photography
FRONT, main picture: Jerry Harpur; left (top to bottom): Photos
Horticultural, Hamlyn Publishing Group Limited, Photos
Horticultural, Harry Smith Horticultural Photographic Collection,
Photos Horticultural; right (top to bottom): Photos Horticultural, Pat
Brindley, Harry Smith Horticultural Photographic Collection, Photos
Horticultural, Hamlyn Publishing Group Limited/W.F. Davidson.
BACK, top row: all by Photos Horticultural; second row: Pat Brindley,
Harry Smith Horticultural Photographic Collection, Octopus Books
Limited/Jerry Harpur; third row: Photos Horticultural, Hamlyn
Publishing Group Limited/Anthony Martin, Harry Smith Horticultural
Photographic Collection; fourth row: Harry Smith Horticultural
Photographic Collection, Harry Smith Horticultural Photographic
Collection, Pat Brindley, Photos Horticultural.

Produced by Mandarin Offset
Printed and Bound in Hong Kong

Contents

Introduction

This book provides a simple, easy-to-use method of selecting the most suitable plant for a specific situation and set of requirements.

Both the absolute beginner faced with having a garden for the first time and the life-long experienced professional will gain considerable benefit from this selection system, for not only does it offer a quick way of choosing plants to suit a number of separate requirements, but also it will help to find which plants will be complementary to, and associate well with, each other.

For the beginner, it does not matter if you are not familiar with the names of many garden plants – all you need to know are the conditions of the site and your own preferences as to height, colour and plant characteristics.

Professional garden centre assistants who believe in freely giving the best advice to customers are often asked to suggest a plant to suit a particular situation. As a garden centre proprietor, I know how very difficult it is, when under pressure with other customers waiting for attention, to come up with the ideal answer with easy spontaneity.

It is as a direct result of this that I devised the system of plant selection used in this book, originally producing it privately as a small handbook featuring only hardy shrubs for use by my staff and myself. We found it invaluable, and we started lending copies to customers to take with them round our shrub lines. The customers were always delighted that they had managed so easily to locate the right shrub to suit their needs. At the same time the pressure on my staff was reduced.

Landscape gardeners and architects will also find the plant selection system of this book particularly useful when designing customers' or clients' gardens.

It is my hope that it will also prove a valuable handbook to experienced and knowledgeable gardeners, and keen amateurs.

An attractive summer display from hardy herbaceous perennials, roses and lilies ('Cobblers', Crowborough).

Permanent Plants for the Garden

Garden plants, for the purpose of this book, are those of a hardy, permanent or long-term status, and no mention, therefore will be made of bulbs, summer annuals for bedding, of biennials, or of perennials of such a tender constitution as to necessitate inside over-wintering. These plants do, however, have a valuable place as seasonal fillers.

The hardy garden plants that form the permanent planting framework of the garden as described here are divided into three sections.

Hardy shrubs, climbing plants and ornamental trees

These grow either on a short stem, or directly from the surface of the soil. They have woody stems, and may be either deciduous – those that lose their leaves in autumn – or evergreen – those that are in leaf all year round. In fact evergreens lose leaves throughout the year, but produce new ones at the same time.

A small group of shrubs are known as semi-evergreen, as they are prone to leaf loss in hard winters, but retain most of their leaves during mild ones.

The size of hardy shrubs can vary greatly, from low-growing, ground-covering ones to those of 4 or 5 m (13 or 16 ft). Similarly, they can vary greatly in spread.

There is tremendous variety to be had in leaf colour, size and shape and in flower colour, size, shape and season. Some shrubs have gloriously fragrant flowers while others provide startlingly beautiful autumn tints.

Ornamental trees are obtainable as full standards, growing on a single stem of at least 1.5 m (5 ft), or as half-standards, 1.2 to 1.5 m (4 to 5 ft). They are ornamental, either by virtue of their decorative flowers or their foliage, or a combination of both.

Some, such as *Prunus sargentii* and *Amelanchier lamarckii* are renowned for their exquisite autumn colour whilst also producing an impressive display of flowers in the spring.

Care must be taken when selecting a tree, for, though it may look charming and suitable when seen in the garden centre, it may quickly become too big for the garden. The golden weeping willow (*Salix × chrysocoma*) is a good example, often purchased on impulse to be regretted later.

Conifers

This term comes from the Latin, meaning 'cone bearing'. While the majority of conifers are evergreen, there are some, such as the larches, which are deciduous. There is a tremendous variation in height and spread from some of the dwarfs growing to no more than 30 cm (1 ft) to the massive redwoods of California which achieve the amazing height of 108 m (360 ft) in their natural habitat.

Generally speaking, conifers are not too choosy as to soil requirements, and many, especially the dwarf forms, will grow well on quite poor soils and in pots. Junipers (*Juniperus*) and yews (*Taxus*) will thrive on extremely chalky or lime soils.

However, it is my opinion that an extra brightness is always apparent, particularly in the case of gold and blue cultivers of Lawson cypresses (*Chamaecyparis lawsoniana*) when they are growing in neutral or acid soil.

Hardy herbaceous perennials and rock plants

These are soft-stemmed plants which, in general, require cutting back each autumn and lifting and dividing every few years. This means that there is usually nothing to look at in the winter and they do entail a fair amount of work.

However, a well planned and well maintained herbaceous border is enormously rewarding. A mixed border also works very well if carefully selected herbaceous perennials are used together with shrubs and conifers. Alpines are dwarf and compact plants which, in their natural habitats, spend a long rest-period, cosily protected from winds and kept dry under a blanket of snow. They do not always take kindly to wet and cold, but snowless, winters.

Above: *Skimmia japonica* 'Rubella'
Above, right: A formal double cultivar of *Camellia japonica*

Opposite, left: *Lupinus* 'Russell Hybrids'
Opposite, right: *Nyssa sinensis*

Key to the Book

This guide to plant selection consists of two main sections. First, there is a series of easy-to-follow charts, listing well over 1100 plants in a computer-sorted order of category seniority. It is divided into two sub-sections, firstly shrubs and conifers including climbing and wall shrubs and some ornamental trees, and secondly herbaceous and rock garden perennials. A key to the symbols can be found on page 11.

Part two of the book is an illustrated dictionary of the plants with full descriptive and cultural details.

Most people consider plant height to be of paramount importance, so five height groups head the categorization list. These are followed by five categories of flower colour, being second only to height as a main consideration. Thereafter follows leaf colour, then berry, fruit or cone colour, and then general environmental requirements such as light, soil type, moisture requirements and other essential information.

All the items have been sorted into an order which provides a unique plant selection system of unprecedented simplicity. It is not necessary to know the name of a plant or to have any particular one in mind. All you need to know are the basic requirements, that is, those that satisfy your own wishes, plus those that are determined by the conditions and situation of the area to be planted. Usually there are no more than five or six conditions that are of vital importance, plus perhaps one or two desirable ones, such as fragrance or autumn colour.

Since all plants of each height group are placed together, there is no need to look beyond the height group of your choice in order to find a plant to fit in with the other requirements.

By the nature of things, among the necessarily limited number of plants mentioned, there are bound to be occasions when it will not be possible to find a plant that will suit *all* your requirements and you may have to delete one or two of the least important ones. With certain plants, for example, height can be reduced by pruning, trimming or training and where this is possible, a higher height group might be chosen in the selection process.

Having found a plant name that seems to satisfy all your requirements, just turn to the page in the second part of the book (shown in the extreme right-hand column) for an illustration (most but not all plants are illustrated) as well as more information about the plant.

Using the charts

The charts are divided into two sections: Shrubs and Trees, which includes climbers and conifers (pages 12–47), and Herbaceous and Rock Plants (pages 48–57). Each section is subdivided into height categories. These are: Up to 60 cm (2 ft); 60 cm to 1.2 m (2 to 4 ft); 1.2 m to 2.5 m (4 ft to 8 ft); 2.5 m to 6 m (8 to 20 ft); over 6 m (20 ft).

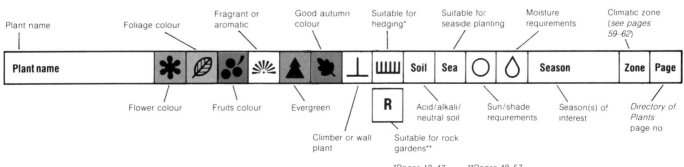

Plant Selection Charts

The charts are divided into two sections: Shrubs and Trees, which includes climbers and conifers (pages 12–47), and Herbaceous and Rock Plants (pages 48–57). Each section is sub-divided into height categories. These are: Up to 60 cm (2 ft); 60 cm to 1.2 m (2 to 4 ft); 1.2 m to 2.5 m (4 ft to 8 ft); 2.5 m to 6 m (8 to 20 ft); over 6 m (20 ft).

KEY TO THE SYMBOLS

✳	FLOWERS (including catkins)	🍒	FRUIT
✳	Flowers in shades of red	🍒	Berries, fruits, cones or seed heads in shades of red, orange or brown
✳	Flowers in shades of pink	🍒	Berries, fruits, cones or seed heads in shades of yellow or gold
✳	Flowers in shades of yellow, yellow/green, gold or orange	🍒	White or cream berries, fruits, cones or seed heads
✳	Flowers in shades of white or cream	🍒	Berries, fruits, cones or seed heads in shades of blue, purple or black
✳	Flowers in shades of blue or purple	🍒	Plant produces berries in various colours (sample shows red or yellow)
✳	Bi-colour flowers (sample shows pink/white)		No symbol indicates non-fruiting plant, or plant with non-decorative cones
	No symbol indicates insignificant flowers or non-flowering plant	Acid	Requires acid soil
🍃	FOLIAGE	Alkali	Requires alkaline soil
🍃	Silver or white foliage	T	Neutral soil or soil tolerant
🍃	Foliage in shades of red or purple-red	Sea	Suitable for seaside planting
🍃	Foliage in shades of yellow or gold	○	Full sun
🍃	Blue or glaucous foliage	●	Full shade
🍃	Foliage in shades of green	◑	Sun or light shade
🍃	Variegated foliage (sample shows green/white)	Ⓣ	Sun or shade tolerant
☀	Fragrant or aromatic flowers or foliage	◇	Dry conditions
▲	Evergreen	◆	Moist conditions
🍂	Good autumn colour	◐	Semi-moist conditions
⊥	Climber or wall plant or plant requiring the protection of a wall	Season	Season(s) of interest (No entry indicates plant has year-round interest)
⊔⊔⊔	Suitable for hedging	△5	Climatic zone (*see pages 59–62 for more detailed information.*)
R	Suitable for rock gardens	Page	Page reference to *Directory of Plants* for more details

A beautiful garden of mixed herbaceous perennials (Ablington Manor).

SHRUBS AND TREES

Plant name	❋	🍃	🍒	🔆	🌲	🍂	⊥	⊞	Soil	Sea	○	💧	Season	Zone	Page
Daboecia cantabrica 'Bicolor'	❋	🍃			🌲				Acid		◐	◗	Summer/Autumn	5	128
Fuchsia 'Golden Treasure'	❋	🍃	🍒						T	Sea	○	●	Summer/Autumn	7	144
Fuchsia 'Tom Thumb'	❋	🍃	🍒						Acid	Sea	◐	●	Summer/Autumn	6	145
Fuchsia magellanica 'Pumila'	❋	🍃	🍒						T	Sea	◐	●	Summer/Autumn	6	145
Coriaria japonica	❋	🍃	🍒			🍂			T		○	◗	Summer	9	118
Fuchsia 'Display'	❋	🍃	🍒						T	Sea	◐	●	Summer/Autumn	7	144
Erica herbacea 'Vivellii'	❋	🍃			🌲				T		○	◗	Winter/Spring	5	137
Philesia magellanica	❋	🍃			🌲				Acid		◐	●	Summer/Autumn	9	190
Daboecia cantabrica 'Atropurpurea'	❋	🍃			🌲				Acid		◐	●	Summer/Autumn	5	128
Calluna vulgaris 'Allportii Praecox'	❋	🍃			🌲				Acid		○	◗	Summer	4	99
Erica cinerea 'Atrosanguinea Smith's Var.'	❋	🍃			🌲				Acid		○	◗	Summer	5	136
Mitraria coccinea	❋	🍃			🌲				T		◐	◗	Summer	9	182
Spiraea japonica 'Shirobana'	❋	🍃							T		◐	◗	Summer	5	221
Erica tetralix 'Pink Star'	❋	🍃			🌲				Acid		○	●	Summer/Autumn	5	137
Calluna vulgaris 'Silver Queen'	❋	🍃			🌲				Acid		○	◗	Summer	4	99
Erica cinerea 'Golden Drop'	❋	🍃			🌲				Acid		○	◗	Summer	5	136
Erica herbacea 'Aurea'	❋	🍃			🌲				T		○	◗	Winter/Spring	5	137
Calluna vulgaris 'Orange Queen'	❋	🍃			🌲				Acid		○	◗	Summer	4	99
Spiraea japonica 'Golden Princess'	❋	🍃							T		◐	◗	Summer	5	221
Daphne retusa	❋	🍃	🍒	🔆	🌲				Alkali		◐	◗	Spring	4	129
Fuchsia 'Alice Hoffman'	❋	🍃	🍒						T	Sea	◐	●	Summer	6	144
Erica × darleyensis 'Darley Dale'	❋	🍃			🌲				T		○	◗	Winter/Spring	5	136
Erica herbacea 'King George'	❋	🍃			🌲				T		○	◗	Winter/Spring	5	137
Erica herbacea 'Loughrigg'	❋	🍃			🌲				T		○	◗	Winter/Spring	5	137
Erica herbacea 'Atrorubra'	❋	🍃			🌲				T		○	◗	Spring	5	137
Daphne cneorum	❋	🍃		🔆	🌲				T		◐	◗	Spring	5	129
Andromeda polifolia 'Compacta'	❋	🍃			🌲	🍂			Acid		◐	●	Spring	3	83

SHRUBS AND TREES

Plant name	✳	🌿	🍒	☀	🌲	🍂	⊥	⊔⊔⊔	Soil	Sea	◐	💧	Season	Zone	Page
Spiraea japonica 'Alpina'	✳	🌿							T		◐	💧	Summer	4	221
Calluna vulgaris 'H.E. Beale'	✳	🌿			🌲				Acid		○	💧	Summer	4	99
Calluna vulgaris 'Elsie Purnell'	✳	🌿			🌲				Acid		○	💧	Summer	4	99
Calluna vulgaris 'County Wicklow'	✳	🌿			🌲				Acid		○	💧	Summer	4	99
Calluna vulgaris 'Peter Sparkes'	✳	🌿			🌲				Acid		○	💧	Summer	4	99
Erica vagans 'St Keverne'	✳	🌿			🌲				Acid		○	💧	Summer	5	137
Erica vagans 'Mrs D.F. Maxwell'	✳	🌿			🌲				Acid		○	💧	Summer	5	137
Erica cinerea 'Pink Ice'	✳	🌿			🌲				Acid		○	💧	Summer	5	136
Erica cinerea 'C.D. Eason'	✳	🌿			🌲				Acid		○	💧	Summer	5	136
Santolina chamaecyparissus	✳	🌿		☀	🌲				T		○	💧	Summer	6	215
Helichrysum serotinum	✳	🌿			🌲				T		○	💧	Summer	7	155
Hypericum × moseranum 'Tricolor'	✳	🌿							Alkali		◐	💧	Summer/Autumn	8	160
Berberis thunbergii 'Atropurpurea Nana'	✳	🌿	🍒					⊔⊔⊔	T		◐	💧	Spring	5	95
Berberis thunbergii 'Aurea'	✳	🌿	🍒						T		○	💧	Spring	7	95
Berberis candidula	✳	🌿	🍒		🌲				T		◐	💧	Spring	5	94
Berberis × stenophylla 'Corallina Compacta'	✳	🌿	🍒		🌲				T		◐	💧	Spring	7	95
Cytisus ardoinii	✳	🌿							Acid		○	💧	Spring	5	127
Cytisus × beanii	✳	🌿							T		○	💧	Spring	6	127
Cytisus × kewensis	✳	🌿							T		○	💧	Spring	6	127
Potentilla arbuscula	✳	🌿							T		○	💧	Spring	5	198
Potentilla arbuscula 'Beesii'	✳	🌿							T		○	💧	Summer/Autumn	6	198
Potentilla 'Tangerine'	✳	🌿							T		○	💧	Summer/Autumn	6	199

Key (see also p 9 and p 11)		✳	Flower colour	🌿	Foliage colour	🍒	Berries/fruits/cones/seed heads colour
☀	Fragrant or aromatic	🌲	Evergreen	🍂	Good autumn colour	⊥	Climber or wall plant
⊔⊔⊔	Suitable for hedging	Soil	Acid/alkali/tolerant	Sea	Suitable for maritime or seaside conditions	○	Sun/shade requirements
💧	Moisture requirements	Season	Season(s) of interest	Zone	Climatic zone (see pages 59–62)	Page	Page reference to Directory of Plants

SHRUBS AND TREES: up to 60 cm (2 ft)

Plant name	✱	❦	⁂	☼	▲	✿	⊥	⊞	Soil	Sea	○	◊	Season	Zone	Page
Hypericum calycinum	✱	❦			▲				T		Ⓣ	○	Summer	5	160
Genista tinctoria 'Royal Gold'	✱	❦							T		○	○	Summer	6	147
Calceolaria integrifolia	✱	❦			▲				T		○	◑	Summer	9	98
Pachysandra terminalis 'Variegata'	✱	❦			▲				T		◑	●	Spring	5	186
Calluna vulgaris 'Gold Haze'	✱	❦			▲				Acid		◑	◑	Summer	4	99
Hebe ochracea	✱	❦			▲				T	Sea	○	◑	Summer	5	153
Hebe albicans	✱	❦			▲				T	Sea	○	◑	Summer	5	151
Hebe pinguifolia 'Pagei'	✱	❦			▲				T	Sea	○	◑	Summer	5	153
Cotoneaster dammeri	✱	❦	⁂		▲				T		Ⓣ	◑	Spring	4	123
Gaultheria procumbens	✱	❦	⁂		▲				Acid		◑	●	Summer	4	146
Vaccinium vitis-idaea	✱	❦	⁂		▲				Acid		◑	●	Summer	3	230
Cotoneaster microphyllus	✱	❦	⁂		▲				T		◑	◑	Summer	5	124
Cornus canadensis	✱	❦	⁂						Acid		◑	◑	Summer	5	119
Sarcococca humilis	✱	❦	⁂	☼	▲				Alkali		●	○	Winter	5	215
Erica herbacea 'Springwood White'	✱	❦			▲				T		○	◑	Winter / Spring	5	137
Erica × darleyensis 'Silberschmelze'	✱	❦			▲				T		○	◑	Winter / Spring	5	136
Cassiope 'Edinburgh'	✱	❦			▲				Acid		◑	●	Spring	6	103
Pachysandra procumbens	✱	❦			▲				T		◑	●	Spring	4	186
Pachysandra terminalis	✱	❦			▲				T		◑	●	Spring	4	186
Chamaedaphne calyculata 'Nana'	✱	❦			▲				Acid		◑	◑	Spring	6	110
Potentilla davurica 'Abbotswood'	✱	❦							T		○	◑	Summer/Autumn	6	198
Potentilla davurica 'Manchu'	✱	❦							T		○	◑	Summer/Autumn	6	198
Daboecia cantabrica 'Alba'	✱	❦			▲				Acid		◑	◑	Summer/Autumn	5	128
Erica tetralix 'Alba Mollis'	✱	❦			▲				Acid		○	●	Summer	5	137
× *Halimiocistus* 'Ingwersenii'	✱	❦			▲				T	Sea	○	○	Summer	7	150
Calluna vulgaris 'Alba Plena'	✱	❦			▲				Acid		○	◑	Summer	4	99
Hebe buchananii	✱	❦			▲				T	Sea	○	◑	Summer	6	152

SHRUBS AND TREES: up to 60 cm (2 ft)

Plant name	Flower colour ✳	Foliage colour 🍃	Berries/fruits 🍒	Fragrant/aromatic 🔆	Evergreen 🔺	Good autumn colour 🍂	Climber ⊥	Hedging ⊍	Soil	Sea	Sun ○	Moisture 💧	Season	Zone	Page
Hebe macrantha	✳	🍃			🔺				T	Sea	○	half	Summer	7	152
Erica vagans 'Lyonesse'	✳	🍃			🔺				Acid		○	half	Summer	5	137
Leiophyllum buxifolium	✳	🍃			🔺				Acid		half	full	Summer	5	171
Lavandula angustifolia 'Hidcote'	✳	🍃		🔆	🔺			⊍	T	Sea	○	mid	Summer	5	170
Lavandula stoechas	✳	🍃		🔆	🔺			⊍	T	Sea	○	mid	Summer	5	170
Calluna vulgaris 'Multicolor'	✳	🍃			🔺	🍂			Acid		○	half	Summer	4	99
Calluna vulgaris 'Robert Chapman'	✳	🍃			🔺	🍂			Acid		○	half	Summer	4	99
Calluna vulgaris 'Sister Anne'	✳	🍃			🔺				Acid		○	half	Summer	4	99
Hebe pimeleoides 'Glaucocaerulea'	✳	🍃			🔺				T	Sea	○	mid	Summer	5	153
Vinca major	✳	🍃			🔺				T		half	mid	Spring/Summer	4	233
Vinca minor	✳	🍃			🔺				T		half	mid	Spring/Summer	4	233
Rosmarinus lavandulaceus	✳	🍃		🔆	🔺				T		○	mid	Spring/Summer	7	212
Ceratostigma plumbaginoides	✳	🍃				🍂			T		○	full	Summer/Autumn	8	106
Lavandula angustifolia 'Munstead'	✳	🍃		🔆	🔺			⊍	T	Sea	half	mid	Summer	5	170
Calluna vulgaris 'Hammondii Rubrifolia'	✳	🍃			🔺				Acid		half	mid	Summer	4	99
Hebe 'Carl Teschner'	✳	🍃			🔺				T	Sea	○	half	Summer	6	152
Erica cinerea 'Purple Beauty'	✳	🍃			🔺				Acid		○	mid	Summer	5	136
Taxus baccata 'Repens Aurea'		🍃			🔺				Alkali		half	full		6	226
Calluna vulgaris 'Golden Feather'		🍃			🔺	🍂			Acid		○	full		4	99
Juniperus horizontalis 'Bar Harbor'		🍃		🔆	🔺				Alkali		half	mid		4	166
Juniperus horizontalis 'Glauca'		🍃		🔆	🔺				Alkali		half	mid		4	166
Juniperus horizontalis 'Montana'		🍃		🔆	🔺				Alkali		○	mid		4	166

SHRUBS AND TREES

Key (see also p 9 and p 11)	✳ Flower colour	🍃 Foliage colour	🍒 Berries/fruits/cones/seed heads colour
🔆 Fragrant or aromatic	🔺 Evergreen	🍂 Good autumn colour	⊥ Climber or wall plant
⊍ Suitable for hedging	Soil — Acid/alkali/tolerant	Sea — Suitable for maritime or seaside conditions	○ Sun/shade requirements
💧 Moisture requirements	Season — Season(s) of interest	Zone — Climatic zone (see pages 59–62)	Page — Page reference to Directory of Plants

SHRUBS AND TREES: up to 60 cm (2 ft)

Plant name	❋	🍃	🍒	🌿	▲	🍁	⊥	�	Soil	Sea	○	◊	Season	Zone	Page
Picea mariana 'Nana'		🍃			▲				T		○	●		2	192
Taxus baccata 'Repandans'		🍃	🍒		▲				Alkali		Ⓣ	◊		6	226
Juniperus conferta		🍃		🌿	▲				Alkali		◑	◐		5	166
Juniperus communis 'Repanda'		🍃		🌿	▲				Alkali		○	◊		4	166
Juniperus horizontalis 'Plumosa'		🍃		🌿	▲				Alkali		○	◊		4	166
Juniperus horizontalis 'Douglasii'		🍃		🌿	▲				Alkali		◑	●		4	166
Buxus sempervirens 'Suffruticosa'		🍃		🌿	▲			ⱴ	T		Ⓣ	●		5	98
Picea abies 'Gregoryana' *Picea abies* 'Nidiformis'		🍃			▲				T		◑	●		4	192
Arundinaria pumila		🍃			▲				T		○	◊		5	88
Chamaecyparis obtusa 'Nana'		🍃			▲				T		◑	◊		5	109
Juniperus sabina 'Tamariscifolia'		🍃		🌿	▲				Alkali		◑	◐		5	167
Juniperus recurva 'Embley Park'		🍃		🌿	▲				Alkali		◑	◊		4	167
Juniperus procumbens 'Nana'		🍃		🌿	▲				Alkali		◑	◊		5	167

SHRUBS AND TREES: 60 cm – 1.2 m (2 ft – 4 ft)

Plant name	❋	🍃	🍒	🌿	▲	🍁	⊥	ⱴ	Soil	Sea	○	◊	Season	Zone	Page
Fuchsia 'Madame Cornelissen'	❋	🍃							T	Sea	◑	●	Summer/Autumn	6	144
Fuchsia magellanica 'Variegata'	❋	🍃							T	Sea	◑	●	Summer/Autumn	7	145
Chamaecyparis laws. 'Pygmaea Argentea'	❋	🍃			▲				T		◑	◊	Spring	6	108
Rosa gallica var. *officinalis*	❋	🍃	🍒	🌿					T		○	◊	Summer	5	210
Rosa gallica 'Versicolor'	❋	🍃	🍒	🌿				ⱴ	T		○	●	Summer	5	210
Azalea 'Mother's Day'	❋	🍃			▲				Acid		◑	●	Spring	5	93
Azalea 'John Cairns'	❋	🍃			▲				Acid		◑	●	Spring	5	93
Azalea 'Hinodegiri'	❋	🍃			▲				Acid		◑	◊	Spring	5	93
Azalea 'Addy Wery'	❋	🍃			▲				Acid		◑	●	Spring	5	92
Cytisus scoparius 'Lena'	❋	🍃							T	Sea	○	◊	Spring / Summer	5	128
Prunus tenella 'Firehill'	❋	🍃							Alkali		◑	◐	Spring	5	202
Phygelius capensis	❋	🍃			▲		⊥		T		○	◊	Summer/Autumn	8	191
Potentilla fruticosa 'Red Ace'	❋	🍃							T		○	◐	Summer/Autumn	6	198

Plant name	✳	🍃	🫐	🎐	🔺	🍂	⊥	⊔⊔⊔	Soil	Sea	◐	💧	Season	Zone	Page
Kalmia angustifolia 'Rubra'	✳	🍃			🔺				Acid		◐	●	Summer	3	168
Lavandula angustifolia 'Loddon Pink'	✳	🍃		🎐	🔺			⊔⊔⊔	T	Sea	○	◊	Summer	5	170
Spiraea × bumalda 'Goldflame'	✳	🍃							T		○	◊	Summer	5	221
Rhododendron yakushimanum	✳	🍃			🔺				Acid		◐	●	Spring/Summer	5	206
Azalea 'Blaauw's Pink'	✳	🍃			🔺				Acid		◐	●	Spring	5	92
Azalea 'Hinomayo'	✳	🍃			🔺				Acid		◐	●	Spring	5	93
Azalea 'Johann Strauss'	✳	🍃			🔺				Acid		◐	●	Spring	5	93
Erica erigena 'Brightness'	✳	🍃			🔺				T		○	◊	Spring	5	137
Potentilla fruticosa 'Princess'	✳	🍃							T		○	◊	Summer/Autumn	6	198
Potentilla fruticosa 'Royal Flush'	✳	🍃							T		○	◊	Summer/Autumn	6	198
Spiraea × bumalda	✳	🍃							T		◐	◊	Summer	4	221
Cistus 'Silver Pink'	✳	🍃			🔺				T	Sea	○	◊	Summer	8	112
Salix lanata	✳	🍃							T		○	●	Spring	5	214
Artemisia arborescens	✳	🍃							T		◐	◊	Summer	8	87
Senecio 'Sunshine'	✳	🍃			🔺				T	Sea	◐	◊	Summer	5	218
Ruta graveolens	✳	🍃		🎐					T		○	◊	Spring	8	212
Berberis wilsoniae	✳	🍃	🫐			🍂		⊔⊔⊔	T		○	◊	Spring/Autumn	5	96
Berberis × rubrostilla	✳	🍃	🫐			🍂			T		◐	◊	Spring	5	94
Lonicera microphylla	✳	🍃	🫐						T		◐	◊	Spring	5	175
Hypericum × inodorum 'Elstead'	✳	🍃	🫐		🔺				T		○	◊	Summer/Autumn	5	160
Berberis verruculosa	✳	🍃	🫐		🔺				T		◐	◊	Spring	5	96
Lonicera pileata	✳	🍃	🫐		🔺				T		Ⓣ	◊	Spring	5	176

Key (see also p 9 and p 11)

✳ Flower colour — 🍃 Foliage colour — 🫐 Berries/fruits/cones/seed heads colour — 🎐 Fragrant or aromatic — 🔺 Evergreen — 🍂 Good autumn colour — ⊥ Climber or wall plant — ⊔⊔⊔ Suitable for hedging — Soil Acid/alkali/tolerant — Sea Suitable for maritime or seaside conditions — ○ Sun/shade requirements — 💧 Moisture requirements — Season Season(s) of interest — Zone Climatic zone (see pages 59–62) — Page Page reference to Directory of Plants

17

SHRUBS AND TREES

Plant name	✳	🍃	🫐	☀	🌲	🍂	⊥	⫿⫿	Soil	Sea	○	💧	Season	Zone	Page
Genista lydia	✳	🍃							T		○	💧	Spring / Summer	7	147
Potentilla fruticosa 'Goldfinger'	✳	🍃							T		○	💧	Summer/Autumn	6	198
Phlomis fruticosa	✳	🍃			🌲				T	Sea	○	💧	Summer	7	190
Halimium lasianthum	✳	🍃			🌲				T	Sea	○	💧	Summer	7	150
Artemisia abrotanum	✳	🍃		☀					T		○	💧	Summer	8	86
Cytisus decumbens	✳	🍃							T		○	💧	Summer	5	127
Coronilla emerus var. emeroides	✳	🍃							T		◐	💧	Summer	7	121
Salix 'Fuiji-Koriangi'	✳	🍃							T		◐	💧	Spring	4	213
Olearia mollis	✳	🍃			🌲				Alkali	Sea	○	💧	Summer	9	184
Convolvulus cneorum	✳	🍃			🌲				T		○	💧	Summer	9	118
Cotoneaster horizontalis 'Variegatus'	✳	🍃	🫐						T		◐	💧	Summer	5	124
Yucca filamentosa 'Variegata'	✳	🍃			🌲				T		◐	💧	Summer	8	235
Euonymus fortunei 'Silver Queen'	✳	🍃			🌲		⊥		T		◐	💧	Summer	5	141
Euonymus fortunei 'Emerald 'n' Gold'	✳	🍃			🌲				T		◐	💧	Summer	5	140
Pernettya mucronata	✳	🍃	🫐		🌲				Acid		○	💧	Summer/Autumn	5	188
Prunus laurocerasus 'Otto Luyken'	✳	🍃	🫐		🌲				T		Ⓣ	💧	Spring	6	200
Prunus laurocerasus 'Zabeliana'	✳	🍃	🫐		🌲				T		Ⓣ	💧	Spring	5	200
Skimmia reevesiana	✳	🍃	🫐	☀	🌲				Acid	Sea	◐	💧	Spring	5	219
Gaulnettya × wisleyensis 'Wisley Pearl'	✳	🍃	🫐		🌲				Acid		◐	💧	Summer	4	146
Cotoneaster horizontalis	✳	🍃	🫐			🍂	⊥		T		Ⓣ	💧	Summer	4	123
Cotoneaster conspicuus 'Decorus'	✳	🍃	🫐		🌲				T		◐	💧	Summer	4	123
Danae racemosa	✳	🍃	🫐		🌲				T		◐	💧	Summer	6	128
Viburnum davidii	✳	🍃	🫐		🌲				T		◐	💧	Summer	7	231
Sarcococca confusa	✳	🍃	🫐	☀	🌲				Alkali		◐	💧	Winter	5	215
Sarcococca hookerana var. digyna	✳	🍃	🫐	☀	🌲				Alkali		◐	💧	Winter	5	215
Azalea 'Palestrina'	✳	🍃			🌲				Acid		◐	💧	Spring	5	93

SHRUBS AND TREES: 60 cm – 1.2 m (2 ft – 4 ft)

Symbol columns left to right: ✳ Flower colour · 🍃 Foliage colour · 🍒 Berries/fruits/cones · ☀ Fragrant/aromatic · 🌲 Evergreen · 🍂 Good autumn colour · ⊥ Climber/wall plant · ⫿ Suitable for hedging

Plant name	✳	🍃	🍒	☀	🌲	🍂	⊥	⫿	Soil	Sea	○ Sun	💧 Moist.	Season	Zone	Page
Prunus tenella 'Alba'	✳	🍃							Alkali		◐	half	Spring	5	202
Skimmia japonica 'Rubella'	✳	🍃		☀	🌲				T		◐	half	Spring	5	219
Fothergilla gardenii	✳	🍃		☀		🍂			Acid		◐	half	Spring	5	143
Ledum palustre	✳	🍃			🌲				Acid		◐	half	Spring	5	170
Yucca filamentosa	✳	🍃			🌲				T	Sea	○	half	Summer	8	235
Spiraea nipponica var. *tosaensis*	✳	🍃							T		◐	half	Summer	4	221
Deutzia × *rosea* 'Campanulata'	✳	🍃							T		◐	half	Summer	4	131
Philadelphus 'Manteau d'Hermine'	✳	🍃		☀					Alkali		◐	half	Summer	5	189
Philadelphus 'Sybille'	✳	🍃		☀					Alkali		◐	half	Summer	5	190
Itea virginica	✳	🍃		☀					Acid		◐	half	Summer	5	163
Ozothamnus ledifolius	✳	🍃		☀	🌲				T		○	half	Summer	8	185
Cistus × *corbariensis*	✳	🍃			🌲				T	Sea	○	half	Summer	8	112
Abeliophyllum distichum	✳	🍃		☀					T		○	half	Winter	7	74
Lavandula angustifolia	✳	🍃		☀	🌲			⫿	T	Sea	○	outline	Summer	5	170
Lavandula angustifolia 'Vera'	✳	🍃		☀	🌲			⫿	T	Sea	○	outline	Summer	5	170
Perovskia atriplicifolia 'Blue Spire'	✳	🍃							Alkali	Sea	○	outline	Summer/Autumn	7	188
Hebe hulkeana	✳	🍃			🌲		⊥		Alkali	Sea	◐	half	Spring/Summer	9	152
Azalea 'Blue Danube'	✳	🍃			🌲				Acid		◐	filled	Spring	5	92
Cytisus purpureus	✳	🍃							T	Sea	○	outline	Spring	5	128
Hebe 'Autumn Glory'	✳	🍃			🌲				T	Sea	○	half	Summer/Autumn	7	151
Ceratostigma willmottianum	✳	🍃				🍂			T		○	outline	Summer/Autumn	8	106
Hydrangea serrata 'Blue Bird'	✳	🍃							T	Sea	◐	filled	Summer/Autumn	5	159

Key *(see also p 9 and p 11)*

✳	Flower colour
🍃	Foliage colour
🍒	Berries/fruits/cones/seed heads colour
☀	Fragrant or aromatic
🌲	Evergreen
🍂	Good autumn colour
⊥	Climber or wall plant
⫿	Suitable for hedging
Soil	Acid/alkali/tolerant
Sea	Suitable for maritime or seaside conditions
○	Sun/shade requirements
💧	Moisture requirements
Season	Season(s) of interest
Zone	Climatic zone *(see pages 59–62)*
Page	Page reference to *Directory of Plants*

SHRUBS AND TREES

Plant name	✻	🍃	🍒	🎇	🌲	🍂	⊥	⊞	Soil	Sea	◐	💧	Season	Zone	Page
Hydrangea serrata 'Grayswood'	✻	🍃							T		◐	●	Summer	5	159
Hebe × franciscana 'Blue Gem'	✻	🍃			🌲			⊞	T	Sea	◐	◓	Summer	6	152
Ceanothus thyrsiflorus var. repens	✻	🍃			🌲				T		○	◓	Summer	7	104
Caryopteris × clandonensis	✻	🍃							Alkali		○	◓	Autumn	5	103
Arundinaria variegata		🍃			🌲				T		○	●		5	88
Chamaecyparis laws. 'Nana Albospica'		🍃			🌲				T		◐	◓		5	108
Cryptomeria japonica 'Globosa'		🍃			🌲				Acid		◐	●		7	125
Cryptomeria japonica 'Vilmoriniana'		🍃			🌲				Acid		◐	●		5	125
Juniperus communis 'Depressa Aurea'		🍃		🎇	🌲				Alkali		◐	◓		4	165
Juniperus × davurica 'Expansa Aureospicata'		🍃		🎇	🌲				Alkali		○	◓		5	166
Chamaecyparis lawsoniana 'Minima Aurea'		🍃			🌲				T		◐	◓		6	108
Chamaecyparis obtusa 'Nana Lutea'		🍃			🌲				T		○	◓		5	109
Chamaecyparis pisifera 'Plumosa Aurea Nana'		🍃			🌲				Acid		◐	◓		6	110
Chamaecyparis pisifera 'Plumosa Rogersii'		🍃			🌲				Acid		◐	◓		6	110
Juniperus communis 'Compressa'		🍃		🎇	🌲				Alkali		◐	◓		4	165
Picea pungens 'Globosa'		🍃			🌲				Acid		◐	●		2	192
Picea pungens 'Procumbens'		🍃			🌲				Acid		◐	●		2	192
Chamaecyparis pisifera 'Boulevard'		🍃			🌲				Acid		◐	◓		5	109
Chamaecyparis lawsoniana 'Gimbornii'		🍃			🌲				T		◐	◓		5	108
Juniperus squamata 'Blue Star'		🍃		🎇	🌲				Alkali		◐	◓		5	167
Taxus cuspidata 'Densa'		🍃			🌲				Alkali		◐	◓		4	226
Thuja occidentalis 'Danica'		🍃			🌲				Alkali		◐	◓		4	227
Abies balsamea 'Hudsonia'		🍃	🍒		🌲				Acid		◐	●		3	75
Juniperus sargentii		🍃	🍒	🎇	🌲				Alkali		◐	◓		5	167
Aronia melanocarpa		🍃	🍒			🍂			T		◐	◓	Spring/Autumn	4	86
Buxus microphylla		🍃		🎇	🌲			⊞	T		Ⓣ	◓		5	98
Picea abies 'Clanbrassiliana'		🍃			🌲				T		◐	●		4	192

SHRUBS AND TREES: 60 cm – 1.2 m (2 ft – 4 ft)

Plant name	✳	🍃	🫐	☀	🌲	🍂	⊥	⊞	Soil	Sea	○	💧	Season	Zone	Page
Chamaecyparis laws. 'Minima Glauca'		🍃			🌲				T		◑	💧		6	108
Chamaecyparis lawsoniana 'Nana'		🍃			🌲				T		◑	💧		6	108
Chamaecyparis obtusa 'Nana Gracilis'		🍃			🌲				T		◑	💧		5	109
Cryptomeria japonica 'Lobbii Nana'		🍃			🌲	🍂			T		◑	💧		5	125
Cryptomeria japonica 'Pygmaea'		🍃			🌲	🍂			T		○	💧		5	125
Chamaecyparis obtusa 'Pygmaea'		🍃			🌲				T		◑	💧		5	109
Podocarpus nivalis		🍃			🌲				T		◑	💧		6	197
Chamaecyparis pisifera 'Pygmaea'		🍃			🌲				Acid		◑	💧		5	110

SHRUBS AND TREES: 1.2 m – 2.5 m (4 ft – 8 ft)

Plant name	✳	🍃	🫐	☀	🌲	🍂	⊥	⊞	Soil	Sea	○	💧	Season	Zone	Page
Cytisus scoparius 'Andreanus'	✳	🍃							T	Sea	○	💧	Spring	5	128
Cytisus scoparius 'Firefly'	✳	🍃							T	Sea	○	💧	Spring	5	128
Cytisus scoparius 'Goldfinch'	✳	🍃							T	Sea	○	💧	Spring	5	128
Rosa foetida 'Bicolor'	✳	🍃							T		○	💧	Summer	5	210
Fuchsia 'Mrs Popple'	✳	🍃	🫐						T	Sea	◑	💧	Summer/Autumn	6	145
Fuchsia magellanica var. *gracilis*	✳	🍃	🫐						T	Sea	◑	💧	Summer/Autumn	6	144
Fuchsia magellanica 'Riccartonii'	✳	🍃	🫐					⊞	T	Sea	◑	💧	Summer/Autumn	6	145
Buddleia davidii 'Harlequin'	✳	🍃		☀					Alkali		○	💧	Summer	5	97
Cytisus scoparius 'Burkwoodii'	✳	🍃							T	Sea	○	💧	Spring	5	128
Daphne mezereum	✳	🍃	🫐	☀					Alkali		◑	💧	Winter/Spring	4	129
Rosa rugosa 'Roseraie de l'Hay'	✳	🍃	🫐					⊞	T	Sea	○	💧	Summer/Autumn	5	211

Key *(see also p 9 and p 11)*	✳ Flower colour	🍃 Foliage colour	🫐 Berries/fruits/cones/seed heads colour
☀ Fragrant or aromatic	🌲 Evergreen	🍂 Good autumn colour	⊥ Climber or wall plant
⊞ Suitable for hedging	**Soil** Acid/alkali/tolerant	**Sea** Suitable for maritime or seaside conditions	○ Sun/shade requirements
💧 Moisture requirements	**Season** Season(s) of interest	**Zone** Climatic zone *(see pages 59–62)*	**Page** Page reference to *Directory of Plants*

SHRUBS AND TREES

Plant name	❋	🍃	🍒	☀	▲	🍂	⊥	⊞	Soil	Sea	○	💧	Season	Zone	Page
Rosa moyesii 'Geranium'	❋	🍃	🍒						T		○	💧	Summer	5	211
Rosa chinensis 'Mutabilis'	❋	🍃	🍒	☀					T		○	💧	Summer	5	210
Punica granatum 'Flore Pleno'	❋	🍃	🍒				⊥		T		○	💧	Summer	8	203
Chaenomeles japonica	❋	🍃	🍒				⊥		T		Ⓣ	💧	Spring	4	107
Chaenomeles × speciosa 'Simonii'	❋	🍃	🍒				⊥		T		Ⓣ	💧	Spring	4	107
Chaenomeles × superba 'Crimson and Gold'	❋	🍃	🍒				⊥		T		Ⓣ	💧	Spring	4	107
Ribes sanguineum 'King Edward VII'	❋	🍃	🍒					⊞	T		Ⓣ	💧	Spring	5	207
Hibiscus syriacus 'Woodbridge'	❋	🍃							T		○	💧	Summer/Autumn	5	156
Weigela 'Bristol Ruby'	❋	🍃							T		◑	💧	Spring/Autumn	4	234
Rhododendron cinnabarinum	❋	🍃			▲				Acid		◑	💧	Spring/Summer	5	205
Azalea 'Balzac'	❋	🍃		☀		🍂			Acid		◑	💧	Spring/Autumn	5	91
Azalea 'Dracula' *Azalea* 'Gibraltar'	❋	🍃				🍂			Acid		◑	💧	Spring/Autumn	5	92
Rosa 'Climbing Etoile de Hollande'	❋	🍃		☀			⊥		T		○	💧	Summer/Autumn	5	209
Escallonia 'Crimson Spire'	❋	🍃			▲			⊞	T	Sea	○	💧	Summer/Autumn	5	139
Escallonia 'C.F. Ball'	❋	🍃		☀	▲			⊞	T	Sea	○	💧	Summer/Autumn	5	139
Kalmia latifolia 'Ostbo Red'	❋	🍃			▲				Acid		◑	💧	Summer	4	168
Callistemon citrinus 'Splendens'	❋	🍃			▲				T		○	💧	Summer	8	98
Hebe speciosa 'Simon Deleaux'	❋	🍃			▲				T	Sea	○	💧	Summer	8	153
Hebe speciosa 'Purple Queen'	❋	🍃			▲				T	Sea	○	💧	Summer	8	153
Hydrangea macrophylla 'Mariesii'	❋	🍃							T	Sea	◑	💧	Summer	5	158
Weigela florida 'Variegata'	❋	🍃							T		◑	💧	Spring/Summer	4	234
Daphne odora 'Aureomarginata'	❋	🍃		☀	▲				T		◑	💧	Winter/Spring	6	129
Weigela florida 'Foliis Purpureis'	❋	🍃							T		◑	💧	Spring/Summer	5	234
Ribes sanguineum 'Brocklebankii'	❋	🍃	🍒						T		◑	💧	Spring	5	207
Camellia × williamsii 'Golden Spangles'	❋	🍃			▲				Acid		◑	💧	Winter/Spring	7	101
Abelia × grandiflora 'Francis Mason'	❋	🍃		☀	▲				T		○	💧	Summer/Autumn	7	74
Rosa rubrifolia	❋	🍃	🍒						T	Sea	○	💧	Summer	5	211

Plant name	✳ Flower	Foliage	Berries	Fragrant	Evergreen	Autumn	Climber	Hedging	Soil	Sea	Sun/shade	Moisture	Season	Zone	Page
Rosa rugosa 'Frau Dagmar Hastrup'	✳	●	●	✷				⊔⊔⊔	T	Sea	○	◐	Summer	5	211
Symphoricarpos × doorenbosii 'Magic Berry'	✳	●	●					⊔⊔⊔	T		Ⓣ	◐	Summer/Autumn	3	223
Rosa centifolia	✳	●	●	✷					T		○	◐	Summer	5	210
Lycium barbarum	✳	●	●						T	Sea	◑	◐	Summer	6	177
Chaenomeles × speciosa 'Rosea Plena'	✳	●	●				⊥		T		Ⓣ	◐	Spring	4	107
Chaenomeles × superba 'Pink Lady'	✳	●	●				⊥		T		Ⓣ	◐	Spring	4	107
Symphoricarpos rivularis	✳	●	●					⊔⊔⊔	T		Ⓣ	◐	Summer	3	224
Vaccinium corymbosum	✳	●	●			🍂			Acid		○	●	Spring/Summer	3	230
Syringa microphylla 'Superba'	✳	●		✷					Alkali		◑	◐	Spring/Summer/Autumn	4	224
Daphne × burkwoodii 'Somerset'	✳	●		✷	▲				T		◑	◐	Spring/Summer	4	129
Clematis macropetala 'Markham's Pink'	✳	●					⊥		Alkali		◑	◐	Spring/Summer	5	115
Camellia japonica 'Elegans'	✳	●			▲				Acid		◑	●	Spring/Winter	7	100
Camellia × williamsii 'Donation'	✳	●			▲				Acid		◑	●	Spring/Winter	7	101
Rhododendron 'Temple Belle'	✳	●			▲				Acid		◑	●	Spring/Winter	5	205
Rhododendron williamsianum	✳	●			▲				Acid		◑	●	Spring	5	206
Azalea 'Comte de Gomer'	✳	●				🍂			Acid		◑	●	Spring	5	92
Prunus glandulosa 'Sinensis'	✳	●							Alkali		◑	◐	Spring	4	200
Magnolia stellata 'Rubra'	✳	●		✷					Acid		◑	◐	Spring	5	180
Hydrangea serrata 'Preziosa'	✳	●							T		◑	●	Summer/Autumn	5	159
Indigofera gerardiana	✳	●					⊥		T		○	○	Summer/Autumn	4	161
Escallonia 'Apple Blossom'	✳	●		✷	▲			⊔⊔⊔	T	Sea	○	◐	Summer/Autumn	5	139
Escallonia 'Donard Radiance'	✳	●			▲			⊔⊔⊔	T	Sea	○	◐	Summer/Autumn	5	139

Key (see also p 9 and p 11)	✳ Flower colour		Foliage colour		Berries/fruits/cones/seed heads colour
✷ Fragrant or aromatic	▲ Evergreen		🍂 Good autumn colour		⊥ Climber or wall plant
⊔⊔⊔ Suitable for hedging	Soil Acid/alkali/tolerant		Sea Suitable for maritime or seaside conditions		○ Sun/shade requirements
◐ Moisture requirements	Season Season(s) of interest		Zone Climatic zone (see pages 59–62)		Page Page reference to Directory of Plants

SHRUBS AND TREES

SHRUBS AND TREES

Plant name	✳	🍃	🍒	🌿	🌲	🍂	⊥	⊔⊔⊔	Soil	Sea	○	💧	Season	Zone	Page
Abelia × grandiflora	✳	🍃		🌿	🌲				T		○	💧	Summer/Autumn	7	74
Kalmia latifolia	✳	🍃			🌲				Acid		◑	●	Summer/Autumn	3	168
Hydrangea macrophylla	✳	🍃							T	Sea	◑	●	Summer	5	158
Kolkwitzia amabilis	✳	🍃							T		○	💧	Summer	4	169
Clerodendrum-bungei	✳	🍃		🌿			⊥		T		○	💧	Summer	6	117
Deutzia 'Mont Rose'	✳	🍃							T		◑	💧	Summer	4	130
Spiraea × billardii 'Triumphans'	✳	🍃							T		◑	💧	Summer	4	221
Clematis 'Hagley Hybrid'	✳	🍃					⊥		Alkali		◑	💧	Summer	5	116
Syringa velutina	✳	🍃		🌿					Alkali		◑	💧	Summer	4	224
Menziesia ciliicalyx	✳	🍃							Acid		◑	💧	Summer	8	182
Lonicera syringantha	✳	🍃		🌿					T		Ⓣ	💧	Summer	4	176
Cistus × purpureus	✳	🍃			🌲				T	Sea	○	💧	Summer	8	112
Hebe speciosa 'Gauntlettii'	✳	🍃			🌲				T	Sea	◑	💧	Summer	8	153
Hebe 'Great Orme'	✳	🍃			🌲				Alkali	Sea	◑	💧	Summer	7	152
Abelia floribunda	✳	🍃			🌲		⊥		T		○	💧	Summer	9	74
Raphiolepis × delacourii	✳	🍃			🌲		⊥		T		○	💧	Summer	△	204
Lavatera olbia 'Rosea'	✳	🍃							T	Sea	○	💧	Summer	5	170
Lespedeza thunbergii	✳	🍃							T		○	💧	Autumn	5	171
Kerria japonica 'Variegata'	✳	🍃					⊥		T		Ⓣ	💧	Spring	4	168
Berberis thunbergii 'Red Chief'	✳	🍃	🍒						T		◑	💧	Spring	5	95
Berberis thunbergii 'Rose Glow'	✳	🍃	🍒						T		◑	💧	Spring	5	95
Berberis thunbergii 'Helmond Pillar'	✳	🍃	🍒					⊔⊔⊔	T		◑	💧	Spring	5	95
Berberis aggregata 'Barbarossa'	✳	🍃	🍒			🍂			T		◑	💧	Spring	5	94
Chaenomeles × superba 'Boule de Feu'	✳	🍃	🍒				⊥		T		Ⓣ	💧	Spring	4	107
Mahonia aquifolium	✳	🍃	🍒		🌲	🍂			Alkali		Ⓣ	💧	Spring	5	180
Berberis sargentiana	✳	🍃	🍒		🌲			⊔⊔⊔	T		◑	💧	Spring	5	94
Berberis gagnepainii 'Lancifolia'	✳	🍃	🍒		🌲			⊔⊔⊔	T	Sea	◑	💧	Spring	5	94

Plant name	❋	⬗	⚬	⛭	▲	❧	⊥	⊞	Soil	Sea	◐	◊	Season	Zone	Page
Petteria ramentacea	❋	⬗		⛭					T		◐	◊	Spring/Summer	5	189
Salix moupinensis	❋	⬗							T		◐	◊	Spring	5	214
Azalea 'Annabelle'	❋	⬗				❧			Acid		◐	◊	Spring/Summer	5	91
Azalea 'Hollandia'	❋	⬗				❧			Acid		◐	◊	Spring/Summer	5	92
Azalea 'Orange Truffles'	❋	⬗				❧			Acid		◐	◊	Spring/Summer	5	92
Cytisus scoparius 'Golden Sunlight'	❋	⬗							T	Sea	○	◊	Spring/Summer	5	128
Chamaecyparis nootkatensis 'Compacta'	❋	⬗			▲				T		◐	◊	Spring	4	109
Stachyurus praecox	❋	⬗							T		◐	◊	Spring	5	222
Forsythia 'Lynwood'	❋	⬗						⊞	T		◐	◊	Spring	4	143
Forsythia 'Beatrix Farrand'	❋	⬗							T		◐	◊	Spring	4	143
Corylopsis pauciflora	❋	⬗		⛭					Acid		◐	◊	Spring	5	121
Cytisus × praecox	❋	⬗							T	Sea	○	◊	Spring	5	127
Cytisus × praecox 'Allgold'	❋	⬗							T	Sea	○	◊	Spring	5	127
Colutea arborescens	❋	⬗	⚬						T		◐	◊	Summer	5	118
Hypericum 'Hidcote'	❋	⬗			▲				T		◐	◊	Summer/Autumn	5	160
Euonymus alatus	❋	⬗				❧			Alkali		◐	◊	Summer	5	140
Jasminum humile 'Revolutum'	❋	⬗		⛭	▲		⊥		T		○	◊	Summer	8	164
Cytisus nigricans	❋	⬗							T	Sea	○	◊	Summer	5	127
Lomatia tinctoria	❋	⬗			▲				T		◐	◊	Summer	7	173
Mahonia bealei	❋	⬗		⛭	▲				T		◐	◊	Winter	6	180
Mahonia 'Charity'	❋	⬗		⛭	▲				T		◐	◊	Winter	7	181
Mahonia japonica	❋	⬗		⛭	▲				T		◐	◊	Winter	7	181

Key (see also p 9 and p 11)	❋	Flower colour	⬗	Foliage colour	⚬	Berries/fruits/cones/seed heads colour
⛭	Fragrant or aromatic	▲	Evergreen	❧	Good autumn colour	⊥	Climber or wall plant
⊞	Suitable for hedging	**Soil**	Acid/alkali/tolerant	**Sea**	Suitable for maritime or seaside conditions	○	Sun/shade requirements
◊	Moisture requirements	**Season**	Season(s) of interest	**Zone**	Climatic zone (see pages 59–62)	**Page**	Page reference to Directory of Plants

SHRUBS AND TREES: 1.2 m – 2.5 m (4 ft – 8 ft)

Plant name	❋	🍃	🍒	🔆	🌲	🍂	⊥	⊔⊔⊔	Soil	Sea	◐	💧	Season	Zone	Page
Lonicera × purpusii 'Winter Beauty'	✓	✓		✓	✓				T		◐	✓	Winter	5	176
Hamamelis mollis	✓	✓		✓		✓			Acid		◐	✓	Winter	5	151
Fuchsia 'Chillerton Beauty'	✓	✓	✓	✓					T	Sea	◐	✓	Summer/Autumn	5	144
Lonicera fragrantissima	✓	✓	✓	✓					T		◐	✓	Winter/Spring	6	174
Stranvaesia davidiana 'Palette'	✓	✓	✓		✓	✓			T		◐	✓	Summer	6	223
Photinia glabra 'Variegata'	✓	✓			✓				Alkali		◐	✓	Spring	8	191
Cornus alba 'Elegantissima'	✓	✓				✓			T		◐	●	Spring	2	119
Pieris japonica 'Variegata'	✓	✓		✓	✓				Acid		◐	●	Spring	7	193
Osmanthus heterophyllus 'Variegatus'	✓	✓		✓	✓			✓	T		○	✓	Autumn	8	185
Olearia × scilloniensis	✓	✓			✓				T	Sea	○	✓	Summer	9	184
Leptospermum cunninghamii	✓	✓			✓		⊥		Acid	Sea	○	✓	Summer	9	171
Leucothoe fontanesiana 'Rainbow'	✓	✓			✓				Acid		Ⓣ	✓	Summer	6	171
Prunus × cistena	✓	✓	✓					✓	Alkali		◐	✓	Spring	3	200
Choisya ternata 'Sundance'	✓	✓		✓	✓				T	Sea	◐	✓	Summer/Autumn	7	111
Philadelphus coronarius 'Aureus'	✓	✓		✓					Alkali		◐	◌	Summer	7	189
Cornus alba 'Spaethii'	✓	✓				✓			T		◐	●	Spring	2	119
Erica arborea 'Gold Tips'	✓	✓		✓	✓				Acid		○	✓	Spring	7	136
Elaeagnus × ebbingei 'Gilt Edge'	✓	✓		✓	✓				T		◐	✓	Autumn	5	134
Skimmia japonica 'Foremanii'	✓	✓	✓	✓	✓				T	Sea	◐	✓	Spring	5	218
Prunus pumila 'Depressa'	✓	✓	✓			✓			Alkali		◐	✓	Spring	5	201
Rosa rugosa 'Blanc Double de Coubert'	✓	✓	✓	✓		✓		✓	T	Sea	○	✓	Summer	5	211
Nandina domestica	✓	✓	✓		✓	✓			T		○	✓	Summer	8	183
Leycesteria formosa	✓	✓	✓						T	Sea	◐	✓	Summer/Winter	7	172
Cotoneaster simonsii	✓	✓	✓		✓			✓	T	Sea	◐	✓	Summer	5	124
Chaenomeles × speciosa 'Nivalis'	✓	✓	✓				⊥		T		Ⓣ	✓	Spring	4	107
Osmanthus delavayi	✓	✓		✓	✓				T		◐	✓	Spring	7	185
Weigela 'Mont Blanc'	✓	✓							T		◐	✓	Spring/Summer/Autumn	5	234

SHRUBS AND TREES: 1.2 m – 2.5 m (4 ft – 8 ft)

Plant name	✳	🍃	🍒	🔆	🌲	🍂	⊥	⦙⦙⦙	Soil	Sea	◐	💧	Season	Zone	Page
Salix hastata 'Wehrhahnii'	✳	🍃							T		◐	💧	Spring	4	213
Viburnum carlesii	✳	🍃	🍒	🔆					T		◐	💧	Spring	5	231
Viburnum × juddii	✳	🍃		🔆		🍂			T		◐	💧	Spring	5	232
Viburnum × carlcephalum	✳	🍃		🔆		🍂			T		◐	💧	Spring	5	231
Viburnum × burkwoodii	✳	🍃		🔆	🌲				T		◐	💧	Spring	5	231
Rhododendron 'Unique'	✳	🍃			🌲				Acid		◐	◑	Spring	5	205
Pieris japonica	✳	🍃		🔆	🌲				Acid		◐	💧	Spring	5	193
Pieris 'Brouwer's Beauty'	✳	🍃			🌲		⊥		Acid		◐	💧	Spring	5	193
Pieris floribunda	✳	🍃			🌲				Acid		◐	💧	Spring	5	193
Azalea 'Raphael de Smet'	✳	🍃				🍂			Acid		◐	💧	Spring	5	92
Spiraea × arguta	✳	🍃							T		○	◑	Spring	4	220
Prunus glandulosa 'Albiplena'	✳	🍃							Alkali		◐	💧	Spring	4	200
Spiraea thunbergii	✳	🍃							T		◐	💧	Spring	4	222
Skimmia japonica 'Fragrans'	✳	🍃		🔆	🌲				T	Sea	◐	◑	Spring	5	218
Spiraea prunifolia 'Plena'	✳	🍃				🍂			T		◐	◑	Spring	4	221
× Osmarea 'Burkwoodii'	✳	🍃		🔆	🌲			⦙⦙⦙	Alkali		◐	💧	Spring	6	185
Fothergilla major	✳	🍃		🔆		🍂			Acid		◐	◑	Spring	5	143
Magnolia stellata	✳	🍃		🔆					Acid		◐	◑	Spring	5	180
Enkianthus perulatus	✳	🍃				🍂			Acid		◐	◑	Spring	6	135
Erica arborea 'Alpina'	✳	🍃		🔆	🌲				Acid		○	◑	Spring	7	136
Cytisus × praecox 'Albus'	✳	🍃							T	Sea	○	◑	Spring	5	127
Hibiscus syriacus 'Hamabo' *Hibiscus syriacus* 'W.R. Smith'	✳	🍃							T		○	◑	Summer/Autumn	5	156

Key *(see also p 9 and p11)*	✳	Flower colour	🍃	Foliage colour	🍒	Berries/fruits/cones/seed heads colour
🔆 Fragrant or aromatic	🌲	Evergreen	🍂	Good autumn colour	⊥	Climber or wall plant
⦙⦙⦙ Suitable for hedging	**Soil**	Acid/alkali/tolerant	**Sea**	Suitable for maritime or seaside conditions	○	Sun/shade requirements
💧 Moisture requirements	**Season**	Season(s) of interest	**Zone**	Climatic zone *(see pages 59–62)*	**Page**	Page reference to *Directory of Plants*

SHRUBS AND TREES: 1.2 m – 2.5 m (4 ft – 8 ft)

Plant name	✱	❦	●●	≋	▲	✿	⊥	ШШШ	Soil	Sea	○	◈	Season	Zone	Page
Clethra alnifolia	✱	❦		≋		✿			Acid	Sea	○	◆	Summer/Autumn	3	117
Escallonia 'Donard White'	✱	❦		≋	▲			ШШШ	T	Sea	○	◈	Summer/Autumn	3	139
Hydrangea arborescens 'Grandiflora'	✱	❦							T		◑	◆	Summer	5	157
Paeonia suffruticosa	✱	❦							T		◑	◆	Summer	6	187
Hydrangea quercifolia	✱	❦				✿			T		◑	◆	Summer	7	159
Hydrangea macrophylla 'Veitchii'	✱	❦							Alkali	Sea	◑	◆	Summer	5	158
Cornus stolonifera 'Flaviramea'	✱	❦				✿			T		◑	◆	Summer	2	120
Lyonia ligustrina	✱	❦							Acid		◑	◆	Summer	4	177
Deutzia × *magnifica*	✱	❦							T		◑	◈	Summer	4	130
Deutzia vilmoriniae	✱	❦							T		◑	◈	Summer	4	131
Spiraea × *vanhouttei*	✱	❦							T		○	◈	Summer	4	220
Philadelphus × *lemoinei*	✱	❦		≋					Alkali		◑	◈	Summer	5	189
Philadelphus 'Belle Etoile'	✱	❦		≋					Alkali		◑	◈	Summer	5	189
Olearia × *haastii*	✱	❦			▲			ШШШ	T	Sea	◑	◈	Summer	7	184
Stephanandra incisa	✱	❦				✿			T		◑	◈	Summer/Autumn	7	222
Stephanandra tanakae	✱	❦				✿			T		◑	◈	Summer/Autumn	5	222
Hebe salicifolia	✱	❦			▲				Alkali	Sea	○	◈	Summer	7	153
Hebe brachysiphon	✱	❦			▲			ШШШ	Alkali	Sea	◑	◈	Summer	5	151
Cistus × *aguilari* 'Maculatus'	✱	❦			▲				T	Sea	○	◈	Summer	8	112
Lomatia myricoides	✱	❦		≋	▲				T		◑	◈	Summer	7	173
Viburnum farreri	✱	❦		≋					T		◑	◆	Winter	6	232
Callicarpa bodinieri var. *giraldii*	✱	❦	●●			✿			T		◑	◈	Summer	6	98
Clematis macropetala	✱	❦					⊥		Alkali		◑	◈	Spring/Summer	5	115
Rosmarinus officinalis 'Fastigiatus'	✱	❦		≋	▲			ШШШ	T	Sea	○	◈	Spring/Summer	7	212
Rosmarinus officinalis	✱	❦		≋	▲			ШШШ	T	Sea	○	◈	Spring/Summer	7	212
Ceanothus 'Southmead'	✱	❦			▲		⊥		T		○	◈	Spring	7	104
Hydrangea villosa	✱	❦							T		◑	◆	Summer/Autumn	4	159

SHRUBS AND TREES: 1.2 m – 2.5 m (4 ft – 8 ft)

Plant name	✳	🌿	🍒	☀	🌲	🍂	⊥	⊞	Soil	Sea	○	💧	Season	Zone	Page
Ceanothus 'A.T. Johnson'	✳	🌿			🌲		⊥		T		○	💧	Summer/Autumn	7	104
Ceanothus 'Burkwoodii'	✳	🌿			🌲		⊥		T		○	💧	Summer/Autumn	7	104
Hibiscus syriacus 'Blue Bird'	✳	🌿							T		○	💧	Summer/Autumn	5	156
Hydrangea aspera	✳	🌿							T		◑	💧	Summer	7	157
Hydrangea macrophylla 'Blue Wave'	✳	🌿							Acid	Sea	◑	💧	Summer	5	158
Ceanothus 'Gloire de Versailles'	✳	🌿		☀			⊥		T		○	💧	Summer	9	104
Ceanothus 'Topaz'	✳	🌿					⊥		T		○	💧	Summer	7	104
Olearia stellulata 'Master Michael'	✳	🌿			🌲				T	Sea	○	💧	Summer	9	184
Hebe speciosa 'Veitchii'	✳	🌿			🌲				T	Sea	○	💧	Summer	8	153
Hebe 'Midsummer Beauty'	✳	🌿			🌲				Alkali	Sea	○	💧	Summer	7	152
Hebe × andersonii	✳	🌿			🌲				T	Sea	○	💧	Summer	7	151
Ceanothus 'Autumnal Blue'	✳	🌿			🌲		⊥		T		○	💧	Autumn	7	104
Griselinia littoralis 'Bantry Bay'		🌿			🌲			⊞	Alkali	Sea	○	💧		8	149
Chamaecyparis pisifera 'Squarrosa Sulphurea'		🌿			🌲				Acid		◑	💧		5	110
Buxus sempervirens 'Aureo-variegata'		🌿		☀	🌲			⊞	T		Ⓣ	💧		5	98
Buxus sempervirens 'Elegantissima'		🌿		☀	🌲			⊞	T		Ⓣ	💧		5	98
Lonicera nitida 'Baggesen's Gold'		🌿			🌲			⊞	T		○	💧		4	175
Thuja occidentalis 'Rheingold'		🌿			🌲				T		○	💧		4	227
Thuja orientalis 'Aurea Nana'		🌿	🍒		🌲				T		○	💧		5	228
Taxus baccata 'Semperaurea'		🌿			🌲				Alkali		◑	💧		6	226
Juniperus chinensis 'Kuriwao Gold'		🌿		☀	🌲				T		◑	💧		5	165
Juniperus × media 'Old Gold'		🌿		☀	🌲				Alkali		○	💧		5	166

SHRUBS AND TREES

Key (see also p 9 and p 11)	✳	Flower colour	🌿	Foliage colour	🍒	Berries/fruits/cones/seed heads colour
☀	Fragrant or aromatic	🌲	Evergreen	🍂	Good autumn colour	⊥	Climber or wall plant
⊞	Suitable for hedging	Soil	Acid/alkali/tolerant	Sea	Suitable for maritime or seaside conditions	○	Sun/shade requirements
💧	Moisture requirements	Season	Season(s) of interest	Zone	Climatic zone (see pages 59–62)	Page	Page reference to Directory of Plants

SHRUBS AND TREES: 1.2 m – 2.5 m (4 ft – 8 ft)

Plant name	✻	🍃	⬤	🔆	🌲	🍂	⊥	⊔⊔⊔	Soil	Sea	○	💧	Season	Zone	Page
Thuja plicata 'Rogersii'		🍃		fan	🌲				T		○	◖		5	228
Juniperus × media 'Pfitzerana Aurea'		🍃		fan	🌲				Alkali		○	◖		5	166
Abies lasiocarpa 'Compacta'		🍃	⬤		🌲				Acid		◐	●		5	75
Abies pinsapo 'Glauca'		🍃	⬤		🌲				T		◐	●		6	75
Juniperus virginiana 'Grey Owl'		🍃		fan	🌲				T		◐	◖		4	167
Pinus strobus 'Nana'		🍃	⬤		🌲				Acid		○	●		3	196
Juniperus sabina 'Blue Danube'		🍃		fan	🌲				Alkali		◐	◖		5	167
Pinus mugo 'Gnom'		🍃	⬤		🌲				Alkali	Sea	○	◖		2	194
Pinus pumila		🍃	⬤		🌲				Acid		○	●		3	195
Salix caprea 'Pendula'		🍃							Alkali		○	●	Spring	4	213
Picea glauca var. *albertiana* 'Conica'		🍃			🌲				Acid		◐	●		4	192
× *Fatshedera lizei*		🍃			🌲		⊥		T	Sea	◐	◌		6	142
Cephalotaxus harringtonia var. *drupacea*		🍃	⬤		🌲				Alkali		◐	◖		5	106
Tsuga canadensis 'Bennett'		🍃			🌲				Alkali		◐	◖		4	229
Juniperus chinensis 'Japonica'		🍃		fan	🌲				T		◐	◖		4	165
Chamaecyparis pisifera 'Filifera Nana'		🍃			🌲				Acid		◐	◖		5	109
Juniperus × media 'Hetzii'		🍃		fan	🌲				Alkali		◐	◖		4	166
Tsuga canadensis 'Pendula'		🍃			🌲				Alkali		◐	◖		5	229
Cedrus libani 'Nana'		🍃			🌲				T		○	◖		6	105
Pinus sylvestris 'Beuvronensis'		🍃			🌲				T		○	◖		3	196
Pinus nigra 'Pygmaea'		🍃			🌲	🍂			Alkali	Sea	○	◖		4	195
Pinus mugo var. *pumilio*		🍃			🌲				Alkali	Sea	○	◖		2	195
Pinus nigra 'Hornbrookiana'		🍃			🌲				Alkali	Sea	○	◖		4	195
Chamaecyparis thyoides 'Ericoides'		🍃			🌲				Acid		○	◖		5	110
Pinus densiflora 'Umbraculifera'		🍃			🌲				Acid		○	◖		4	194
Chamaecyparis lawsoniana 'Tamariscifolia'		🍃			🌲				T		◐	◖		5	108
Lonicera nitida		🍃			🌲			⊔⊔⊔	T		Ⓣ	◖		4	175

Plant name	✳	🍃	🍒	☀	🌲	🍂	⊥	IIIII	Soil	Sea	◐	💧	Season	Zone	Page

SHRUBS AND TREES: 2.5 m – 6 m (8 ft – 20 ft)

Plant name	✳	🍃	🍒	☀	🌲	🍂	⊥	IIIII	Soil	Sea	◐	💧	Season	Zone	Page
Lonicera periclymenum 'Belgica'	✳	🍃	🍒	☀			⊥		T		◐	💧	Spring/Summer	5	176
Lonicera japonica var. repens	✳	🍃		☀	🌲		⊥		T		◐	💧	Summer/Autumn	5	175
Lonicera × heckrottii	✳	🍃		☀			⊥		T		◐	💧	Summer	5	174
Pittosporum tenuifolium 'Purpureum'	✳	🍃		☀	🌲			IIIII	Alkali		◐	💧	Spring	7	196
Pittosporum tenuifolium 'Garnettii'	✳	🍃		☀	🌲			IIIII	Alkali		◐	💧	Spring	7	196
Pittosporum tenuifolium 'Irene Paterson'	✳	🍃		☀	🌲			IIIII	Alkali		◐	💧	Spring	8	196
Pittosporum tenuifolium 'Abbotsbury Gold'	✳	🍃		☀	🌲			IIIII	Alkali		◐	💧	Spring	7	196
Magnolia 'Susan'	✳	🍃		☀					T		◐	💧	Spring	5	179
Leptospermum scoparium 'Burgundy Queen'	✳	🍃			🌲		⊥		Acid	Sea	○	💧	Summer	9	171
Leptospermum scoparium 'Nichollsii'	✳	🍃			🌲		⊥		Acid	Sea	○	💧	Summer	9	171
Leptospermum scoparium 'Red Damask'	✳	🍃			🌲		⊥		Acid	Sea	○	💧	Summer	9	171
Ribes speciosum	✳	🍃	🍒		🌲		⊥		T		○	💧	Spring/Summer	5	207
Rosa 'Altissimo'	✳	🍃		☀			⊥		T		○	💧	Summer	5	209
Magnolia × soulangiana 'Rustica Rubra'	✳	🍃							Acid		◐	💧	Spring/Summer	5	179
Magnolia 'Jane'	✳	🍃		☀					T		◐	💧	Spring/Summer	5	179
Syringa vulgaris 'Charles Joly'	✳	🍃		☀					Alkali		◐	💧	Spring/Summer	3	225
Syringa vulgaris 'Souvenir de Louis Späth'	✳	🍃		☀					Alkali		◐	💧	Spring/Summer	3	225
Magnolia liliiflora 'Nigra'	✳	🍃							Acid		◐	💧	Spring/Summer	5	179
Camellia japonica 'Adolphe Audusson'	✳	🍃			🌲				Acid		◐	💧	Spring	7	100
Camellia japonica 'Donckelarii'	✳	🍃			🌲				Acid		◐	💧	Spring	7	100
Camellia japonica 'Mathotiana'	✳	🍃			🌲				Acid		◐	💧	Spring	7	100

SHRUBS AND TREES

Key (see also p 9 and p 11)			
✳ Flower colour		🍃 Foliage colour	🍒 Berries/fruits/cones/seed heads colour
☀ Fragrant or aromatic	🌲 Evergreen	🍂 Good autumn colour	⊥ Climber or wall plant
IIIII Suitable for hedging	Soil Acid/alkali/tolerant	Sea Suitable for maritime or seaside conditions	○ Sun/shade requirements
💧 Moisture requirements	Season Season(s) of interest	Zone Climatic zone (see pages 59–62)	Page Page reference to Directory of Plants

31

SHRUBS AND TREES

Plant name	❋	🍃	🫐	☼	▲	🍁	⊥	⊞	Soil	Sea	◐	💧	Season	Zone	Page
Crinodendron hookeranum	❋	🍃			▲		⊥		Acid		◐	●	Spring	8	125
Akebia quinata	❋	🍃	🫐	☼			⊥		T		Ⓣ	💧	Spring	4	81
Pittosporum tenuifolium	❋	🍃		☼	▲			⊞	Alkali		◐	💧	Spring	7	196
Embothrium coccineum	❋	🍃			▲				Acid		◐	💧	Spring	8	134
Rosa 'Sympathie' / Rosa 'Crimson Showers'	❋	🍃		☼			⊥		T		◐	💧	Summer/Autumn	5	208 / 209
Rosa 'Parkdirektor Riggers'	❋	🍃					⊥		T		○	💧	Summer/Autumn	5	208
Corylus maxima 'Purpurea'	❋	🍃	🫐				⊥		T		○	💧	Spring/Winter	5	122
Eccremocarpus scaber	❋	🍃			▲		⊥		T		○	💧	Summer/Autumn	9	133
Lapageria rosea	❋	🍃			▲		⊥		Acid		◐	💧	Summer/Autumn	8	169
Rosa 'Climbing Ena Harkness'	❋	🍃		☼			⊥		T		○	💧	Summer	5	208
Lonicera × brownii 'Fuchsioides'	❋	🍃		☼			⊥		T		◐	💧	Summer	5	174
Clematis 'Ernest Markham'	❋	🍃					⊥		Alkali		◐	💧	Summer	5	116
Calycanthus occidentalis	❋	🍃		☼					T		○	💧	Summer	4	99
Buddleia davidii 'Royal Red'	❋	🍃		☼					Alkali		○	💧	Summer	5	97
Desfontainea spinosa	❋	🍃			▲				T		◐	💧	Summer	8	130
Berberidopsis corallina	❋	🍃			▲		⊥		Acid		●	💧	Summer	4	93
Ribes sanguineum 'Pulborough Scarlet'	❋	🍃	🫐	☼					T		Ⓣ	💧	Spring	5	207
Magnolia × soulangiana	❋	🍃							Acid		◐	💧	Spring	5	179
Jasminum polyanthum	❋	🍃		☼			⊥		T		○	💧	Spring/Summer	9	164
Magnolia × loebneri 'Leonard Messel'	❋	🍃		☼					T		◐	💧	Spring/Summer	5	179
Prunus cerasifera 'Pissardii'	❋	🍃							T		◐	💧	Spring	3	200
Cotinus coggygria 'Royal Purple'	❋	🍃				🍁			T		○	💧	Summer	4	123
Lonicera tatarica	❋	🍃	🫐						T		Ⓣ	💧	Summer	4	176
Lonicera korolkowii	❋	🍃	🫐						T		Ⓣ	💧	Summer	5	175
Malus floribunda	❋	🍃	🫐						T		◐	💧	Spring	4	181
Rhododendron 'Pink Pearl'	❋	🍃			▲				T		◐	●	Spring/Summer	5	175
Clematis 'Nelly Moser'	❋	🍃					⊥		T		◐	💧	Spring/Summer	5	116

32

Plant name	✳	🍃	🫐	🎆	🌲	🍂	⊥	⊞	Soil	Sea	◐	💧	Season	Zone	Page
Syringa × *josiflexa* 'Bellicent'	✳	🍃		🎆					Alkali		◐	◐	Spring/Summer	3	224
Camellia 'Leonard Messel'	✳	🍃			🌲				Acid		◐	●	Spring	7	100
Camellia japonica 'Lady Clare'	✳	🍃			🌲				Acid		◐	●	Spring	7	100
Cornus florida var. *rubra*	✳	🍃	🫐			🍂			T		◐	●	Spring	4	120
Rhododendron rubiginosum	✳	🍃			🌲				Acid		◐	●	Spring	5	206
Prunus 'Amanogawa'	✳	🍃		🎆					Alkali		○	💧	Spring	5	200
Prunus triloba	✳	🍃							Alkali	Sea	◐	💧	Spring	5	202
Tamarix tetrandra	✳	🍃						⊞	T	Sea	○	💧	Spring	5	225
Prunus persica 'Clara Meyer'	✳	🍃							Alkali		○	💧	Spring	3	201
Rosa 'Aloha' *Rosa* 'Compassion'	✳	🍃		🎆			⊥		T		○	💧	Summer/Autumn	5	209
Rosa 'New Dawn'	✳	🍃		🎆			⊥		T		○	💧	Summer/Autumn	5	209
Rosa 'Pink Perpétue'	✳	🍃		🎆			⊥		T		○	💧	Summer/Autumn	5	209
Rosa 'Zéphirine Drouhin'	✳	🍃		🎆			⊥		T		○	💧	Summer/Autumn	5	209
Clematis 'Barbara Dibley'	✳	🍃					⊥		Alkali		◐	💧	Summer	5	116
Jasminum × *stephanense*	✳	🍃		🎆			⊥		T		○	💧	Summer	5	164
Buddleia davidii 'Pink Pearl'	✳	🍃		🎆					Alkali		○	💧	Summer	5	97
Cotinus coggygria	✳	🍃				🍂			T		○	💧	Summer	4	122
Cotinus obovatus	✳	🍃				🍂			T		○	💧	Summer	5	123
Tamarix pentandra	✳	🍃						⊞	T	Sea	○	💧	Summer	4	225
Abelia schumannii	✳	🍃							T		○	💧	Summer	9	74
Viburnum × *bodnantense*	✳	🍃		🎆					T		◐	●	Winter	5	231
Sambucus nigra 'Pulverulenta'	✳	🍃	🫐	🎆					T		◐	💧	Summer	5	214

Key *(see also p 9 and p 11)*	✳		Flower colour	🍃		Foliage colour	🫐		Berries/fruits/cones/seed heads colour
🎆		Fragrant or aromatic	🌲		Evergreen	🍂		Good autumn colour	⊥		Climber or wall plant
⊞		Suitable for hedging	**Soil**		Acid/alkali/tolerant	**Sea**		Suitable for maritime or seaside conditions	○		Sun/shade requirements
💧		Moisture requirements	**Season**		Season(s) of interest	**Zone**		Climatic zone *(see pages 59–62)*	**Page**		Page reference to *Directory of Plants*

SHRUBS AND TREES

SHRUBS AND TREES

Plant name	❋	🍃	🍇	🌿	▲	🍂	⊥	⊔⊔⊔	Soil	Sea	○	💧	Season	Zone	Page
Cytisus battandieri	❋	🍃		🌿			⊥		T	Sea	○	◐	Summer	7	127
Hippophae rhamnoides	❋	🍃	🍇					⊔⊔⊔	T	Sea	◑	◐	Spring	3	156
Sambucus racemosa 'Plumosa Aurea'	❋	🍃	🍇						T		◑	●	Spring	5	215
Coronilla emerus var. *emeroides*	❋	🍃		🌿	▲				T		◑	◐	Summer	7	121
Cornus mas	❋	🍃	🍇			🍂			T		◑	●	Spring/Winter	4	120
Berberis × stenophylla	❋	🍃	🍇		▲			⊔⊔⊔	T		◑	◐	Spring	5	94
Berberis linearifolia 'Orange King'	❋	🍃	🍇		▲			⊔⊔⊔	T		◑	◐	Spring	6	94
Berberis darwinii	❋	🍃	🍇		▲			⊔⊔⊔	T		◑	◐	Spring	5	94
Lonicera involucrata	❋	🍃	🍇						T	Sea	Ⓣ	◐	Summer	5	174
Decaisnea fargesii	❋	🍃	🍇						T		◑	◐	Summer	5	129
Rhododendron wardii	❋	🍃			▲				Acid		◑	●	Spring/Summer	5	206
Syringa vulgaris 'Primrose'	❋	🍃		🌿					Alkali		◑	◐	Spring/Summer	3	225
Rosa banksiae 'Lutea'	❋	🍃		🌿	▲		⊥		T		○	◐	Spring/Summer	5	210
Jasminum nudiflorum	❋	🍃					⊥		T		Ⓣ	◐	Spring/Winter	5	164
Corylus avellana 'Contorta'	❋	🍃							T		◑	◐	Spring/Winter	4	122
Corylus avellana 'Pendula'	❋	🍃	🍇						T		◑	◐	Spring/Winter	4	122
Salix matsudana 'Tortuosa'	❋	🍃							T		◑	●	Spring	4	214
Salix sachalinensis 'Sekka'	❋	🍃							T		◑	●	Spring	4	214
Laburnum anagyroides	❋	🍃		🌿					T		○	◐	Spring	5	169
Betula pendula 'Youngii'	❋	🍃							Acid		◑	◐	Spring	2	96
Forsythia suspensa 'Nymans'	❋	🍃					⊥		T		◑	◐	Spring	4	143
Azara lanceolata	❋	🍃		🌿	▲		⊥		T		◑	◐	Spring	7	93
Kerria japonica 'Pleniflora'	❋	🍃							T		Ⓣ	◐	Spring	4	168
Enkianthus campanulatus	❋	🍃				🍂			Acid		◑	◐	Spring	4	135
Laurus nobilis	❋	🍃		🌿	▲			⊔⊔⊔	Alkali		○	◐	Spring	5	170
Jasminum mesnyi	❋	🍃					⊥		T		◑	◐	Spring	8	163
Rosa 'Golden Showers'	❋	🍃		🌿			⊥		T		Ⓣ	◐	Summer/Autumn	5	209

SHRUBS AND TREES: 2.5 m – 6 m (8 ft – 20 ft)

Plant name	✳	🍃	●●	☀	🌲	🍂	⊥	⊞	Soil	Sea	○	💧	Season	Zone	Page
Rosa 'Maigold'	✳	🍃		☀			⊥		T		Ⓣ	◖	Summer/Autumn	5	209
Rosa 'Climbing Lady Hillingdon'	✳	🍃		☀			⊥		T		◐	◖	Summer/Autumn	7	209
Clematis orientalis	✳	🍃	●●	☀			⊥		Alkali		◐	◖	Summer/Autumn	5	115
Clematis tangutica	✳	🍃	●●				⊥		Alkali		◐	◖	Summer/Autumn	5	116
Rosa 'Schoolgirl'	✳	🍃		☀			⊥		T		○	◖	Summer/Autumn	5	209
Fremontodendron californicum	✳	🍃			🌲		⊥		Alkali		○	◖	Summer/Autumn	8	143
Genista aetnensis	✳	🍃							T		○	◖	Summer	6	146
Rosa 'Emily Gray'	✳	🍃		☀			⊥		Acid		○	◖	Summer	5	209
Aristolochia macrophylla	✳	🍃					⊥		T		◐	◖	Summer	4	86
Spartium junceum	✳	🍃		☀	🌲				T	Sea	○	◖	Summer	7	220
Pittosporum tobira	✳	🍃		☀	🌲		⊥		Alkali		○	◖	Summer	8	197
Chimonanthus praecox	✳	🍃		☀			⊥		Alkali		○	◗	Winter	5	110
Clematis cirrhosa var. balearica	✳	🍃			🌲		⊥		Alkali		○	◖	Winter	7	114
Prunus lusitanica 'Variegata'	✳	🍃	●●	☀	🌲			⊞	Alkali		◐	◖	Summer	6	201
Actinidia kolomikta	✳	🍃	●●	☀					Acid		○	◖	Summer	4	80
Ligustrum lucidum 'Tricolor'	✳	🍃			🌲				T		◐	◖	Summer	6	172
Myrtus communis 'Variegata'	✳	🍃	●●	☀	🌲		⊥		T	Sea	○	◖	Summer Autumn	9	183
Cornus alternifolia 'Argentea'	✳	🍃							T		◐	◗	Spring	5	119
Pyrus salicifolia 'Pendula'	✳	🍃					⊥		T		○	◖	Spring	5	204
Pieris forrestii 'Wakehurst'	✳	🍃			🌲				Acid		◐	◗	Spring	5	193
Photinia × fraseri 'Red Robin'	✳	🍃			🌲				Alkali		◐	◖	Spring	8	191
Aucuba japonica 'Variegata'	✳	🍃	●●		🌲			⊞	Alkali	Sea	○	◗	Spring	7	91

Key (see also p 9 and p 11)	✳ Flower colour	🍃 Foliage colour	●● Berries/fruits/cones/seed heads colour
☀ Fragrant or aromatic	🌲 Evergreen	🍂 Good autumn colour	⊥ Climber or wall plant
⊞ Suitable for hedging	**Soil** Acid/alkali/tolerant	**Sea** Suitable for maritime or seaside conditions	○ Sun/shade requirements
💧 Moisture requirements	**Season** Season(s) of interest	**Zone** Climatic zone (see pages 59–62)	**Page** Page reference to Directory of Plants

SHRUBS AND TREES: 2.5 m – 6 m (8 ft – 20 ft)

Plant name	✱	🍃	⁂	✺	▲	🍂	⊥	ШШШ	Soil	Sea	○	💧	Season	Zone	Page
Ligustrum lucidum 'Excelsum Superbum'	✱	🍃			▲				T		◑	◐	Summer	6	172
Myrtus apiculata 'Glenleam Gold'	✱	🍃	⁂	✺	▲				T		○	◐	Autumn	9	182
Euonymus japonicus 'Ovatus Aureus'	✱	🍃			▲			ШШШ	T	Sea	○	◐	Summer	5	141
Elaeagnus × ebbingei 'Limelight'	✱	🍃		✺	▲				T		◑	◐	Autumn	5	134
Elaeagnus pungens 'Dicksonii'	✱	🍃		✺	▲				T		◑	◐	Autumn	5	134
Elaeagnus pungens 'Maculata'	✱	🍃		✺	▲				T		◑	◐	Autumn	5	134
Prunus laurocerasus 'Rotundifolia'	✱	🍃	⁂		▲			ШШШ	T		Ⓣ	◐	Spring	6	200
Prunus lusitanica	✱	🍃	⁂	✺	▲			ШШШ	Alkali		Ⓣ	◐	Summer	5	201
Rosa omeiensis var. *pteracantha*	✱	🍃	⁂						T		○	◐	Spring/Summer	5	211
Viburnum opulus	✱	🍃	⁂			🍂			T		◑	●	Spring/Summer	3	232
Viburnum rhytidophyllum	✱	🍃	⁂		▲				T		◑	●	Spring/Autumn	7	232
Prunus padus 'Watereri'	✱	🍃	⁂	✺					Alkali		○	◐	Spring	4	201
Euonymus europaeus 'Red Cascade'	✱	🍃	⁂			🍂			Alkali		◑	◐	Spring/Autumn	5	140
Stranvaesia davidiana	✱	🍃	⁂		▲	🍂			T		◑	◐	Summer	5	223
Pyracantha 'Orange Glow'	✱	🍃	⁂		▲		⊥	ШШШ	T		◑	◐	Summer/Winter	5	203
Pyracantha coccinea 'Lalandei'	✱	🍃	⁂		▲		⊥	ШШШ	T		◑	◐	Summer/Winter	5	203
Pyracantha atalantioides	✱	🍃	⁂		▲		⊥	ШШШ	T		◑	◐	Summer/Winter	5	203
Magnolia sieboldii	✱	🍃	⁂	✺					Acid		◑	◐	Summer	5	179
Cotoneaster salicifolius	✱	🍃	⁂		▲				T	Sea	◑	◐	Summer	6	124
Rosa filipes 'Kiftsgate'	✱	🍃	⁂	✺	▲				T		○	◐	Summer	5	210
Lonicera maackii	✱	🍃	⁂	✺					T		◑	◐	Summer	4	175
Rhus typhina	✱	🍃	⁂			🍂			T		○	◐	Summer/Autumn	3	207
Malus × robusta 'Yellow Siberian'	✱	🍃	⁂						T		◑	◐	Spring	4	181
Stranvaesia davidiana 'Fructuluteo'	✱	🍃	⁂		▲	🍂			T		◑	◐	Summer	5	223
Cotoneaster 'Rothschildianus'	✱	🍃	⁂		▲				T	Sea	◑	◐	Summer	6	124
Pyracantha rogersiana 'Flava'	✱	🍃	⁂		▲				T		◑	◐	Summer/Winter	5	203
Cornus amomum	✱	🍃	⁂		▲			ШШШ			○	●	Autumn/Winter	5	119

SHRUBS AND TREES: 2.5 m – 6 m (8 ft – 20 ft)

Plant name	Flower colour	Foliage colour	Berries/fruits/cones/seed heads	Fragrant/aromatic	Evergreen	Good autumn colour	Climber or wall plant	Suitable for hedging	Soil	Sea	Sun/shade	Moisture	Season	Zone	Page
Amelanchier lamarckii	✳	▨	◓			🍂			T		◐	◐	Spring	4	82
Clerodendrum trichotomum	✳	▨	◓	✺					T		○	◐	Summer/Autumn	5	117
Cornus controversa	✳	▨	◓			🍂			T		◐	●	Summer	5	120
Ligustrum ovalifolium	✳	▨	◓	✺	▲			⊞	T		Ⓣ	◐	Summer	5	172
Myrtus apiculata	✳	▨	◓	✺	▲		⊥		T		○	◐	Autumn	9	182
Myrtus communis	✳	▨	◓	✺	▲		⊥		T		○	◐	Summer	8	183
Garrya elliptica	✳	▨	◓		▲		⊥		T	Sea	◐	◐	Winter	5	146
Viburnum plicatum·plicatum	✳	▨							T		◐	●	Spring/Summer	4	232
Viburnum opulus 'Sterile'	✳	▨				🍂			T		◐	●	Spring/Summer	3	232
Rhododendron 'Sappho'	✳	▨			▲				Acid		◐	●	Spring/Summer	5	205
Magnolia × loebneri 'Merrill'	✳	▨		✺					T		◐	◐	Spring/Summer	5	179
Syringa vulgaris 'Madame Lemoine'	✳	▨		✺					Alkali		◐	◐	Spring/Summer	3	225
Parrotiopsis jacquemontiana	✳	▨				🍂			T		◐	◐	Spring/Summer	7	187
Magnolia × soulangiana 'Lennei'	✳	▨					⊥		Acid		◐	◐	Spring/Summer	5	179
Clematis 'Duchess of Edinburgh'	✳	▨		✺			⊥		Alkali		◐	◐	Spring/Summer	5	116
Viburnum tinus	✳	▨			▲			⊞	T	Sea	◐	●	Winter/Spring	7	233
Camellia 'Cornish Snow'	✳	▨			▲				Acid		◐	●	Spring	7	100
Camellia japonica 'Contessa Lavinia Maggi'	✳	▨			▲				Acid		◐	●	Spring	7	100
Camellia japonica 'Devonia'	✳	▨			▲				Acid		◐	●	Spring	7	100
Camellia japonica 'Mathotiana Alba'	✳	▨			▲				Acid		◐	●	Spring	7	100
Cornus alba	✳	▨				🍂			T		◐	●	Summer/Winter	2	119
Cornus nuttallii	✳	▨	◓			🍂			Acid		◐	●	Spring/Autumn	6	120

Key (see also p 9 and p 11)	✳ Flower colour	▨ Foliage colour	◓ Berries/fruits/cones/seed heads colour
✺ Fragrant or aromatic	▲ Evergreen	🍂 Good autumn colour	⊥ Climber or wall plant
⊞ Suitable for hedging	**Soil** Acid/alkali/tolerant	**Sea** Suitable for maritime or seaside conditions	○ Sun/shade requirements
◐ Moisture requirements	**Season** Season(s) of interest	**Zone** Climatic zone (see pages 59–62)	**Page** Page reference to Directory of Plants

Plant name	❋	🍃	🍒	☀	🌲	🍂	⊥	▥	Soil	Sea	◐	💧	Season	Zone	Page
Pieris 'Forest Flame'	❋	🍃			🌲				Acid		◐	💧	Spring	5	193
Rubus tridel	❋	🍃							T		◐	💧	Spring	5	212
Magnolia denudata	❋	🍃		☀					Acid		◐	💧	Spring	5	178
Magnolia × highdownensis	❋	🍃		☀					Alkali		◐	💧	Spring	5	178
Drimys winteri	❋	🍃		☀	🌲		⊥		T		◐	💧	Spring	8	133
Halesia carolina	❋	🍃	🍒						Acid		◐	💧	Spring	5	150
Clematis armandii	❋	🍃		☀	🌲		⊥		Alkali		○	💧	Spring	8	114
Exochorda × macrantha 'The Bride'	❋	🍃							Acid		○	💧	Spring	5	142
Pileostegia viburnoides	❋	🍃			🌲		⊥		T		Ⓣ	💧	Summer/Autumn	5	194
Clematis flammula	❋	🍃		☀			⊥		Alkali		◐	💧	Summer/Autumn	5	114
Rosa 'Climbing Iceberg'	❋	🍃					⊥		T		○	💧	Summer/Autumn	5	209
Rosa 'White Cockade'	❋	🍃		☀			⊥		T		○	💧	Summer/Autumn	5	209
Rosa 'Swan Lake'	❋	🍃					⊥		T		○	💧	Summer/Autumn	5	209
Escallonia 'Donard Seedling'	❋	🍃		☀	🌲			▥	T	Sea	○	💧	Summer/Autumn	5	139
Choisya ternata	❋	🍃		☀	🌲		⊥		T	Sea	◐	💧	Summer/Autumn	7	111
Eucryphia glutinosa	❋	🍃				🍂			Acid		◐	💧	Summer	6	140
Eucryphia × nymansensis 'Nymansay'	❋	🍃			🌲				Acid		◐	💧	Summer	6	140
Hydrangea paniculata 'Grandiflora'	❋	🍃							T		◐	💧	Summer	5	159
Chionanthus virginicus	❋	🍃		☀			⊥		T		○	💧	Summer	4	111
Cornus kousa	❋	🍃	🍒						T		◐	💧	Summer	5	120
Deutzia scabra 'Macrocephala'	❋	🍃							T		◐	💧	Summer	4	131
Sorbaria aitchisonii	❋	🍃							T		◐	💧	Summer	5	220
Euonymus japonicus	❋	🍃			🌲			▥	T	Sea	Ⓣ	💧	Summer	5	141
Oxydendrum arboreum	❋	🍃				🍂			Acid		Ⓣ	💧	Summer	5	185
Itea ilicifolia	❋	🍃		☀	🌲				Acid		◐	💧	Summer	5	163
Olearia ilicifolia	❋	🍃		☀	🌲			▥	T	Sea	◐	💧	Summer	8	184
Trachelospermum asiaticum	❋	🍃		☀	🌲		⊥		Acid		○	💧	Summer	7	229

Plant name	✲	🍃	🫐	🎇	🌲	🍂	⊥	𝗺	Soil	Sea	◯	💧	Season	Zone	Page
Trachelospermum jasminoides	✲	🍃		🎇	🌲		⊥		Acid		◯	💧	Summer	7	229
Hoheria glabrata	✲	🍃		🎇			⊥		T		◑	💧	Summer	6	156
Hoheria sexstylosa	✲	🍃			🌲		⊥		T		◑	💧	Summer	8	157
Philadelphus 'Virginal'	✲	🍃		🎇					Alkali		◑	💧	Summer	5	190
Olearia macrodonta	✲	🍃			🌲			𝗺	T	Sea	◑	💧	Summer	7	184
Stuartia malacodendron	✲	🍃				🍂			Acid		◑	💧	Summer	6	223
Clematis florida 'Sieboldii'	✲	🍃					⊥		Alkali		◯	💧	Summer	5	114
Carpenteria californica	✲	🍃		🎇	🌲		⊥		T		◯	💧	Summer	9	103
Buddleia davidii 'White Bouquet'	✲	🍃		🎇					Alkali		◯	💧	Summer	5	97
Clethra barbinervis	✲	🍃		🎇		🍂			Acid	Sea	◯	💧	Summer	5	117
Leptospermum scoparium 'Album Flore Pleno'	✲	🍃			🌲		⊥		Acid	Sea	◯	💧	Summer	9	171
Cordyline australis	✲	🍃		🎇	🌲				T	Sea	◯	💧	Summer	8	118
Fatsia japonica	✲	🍃			🌲				T		Ⓣ	💧	Autumn	7	142
Elaeagnus × ebbingei	✲	🍃	🫐	🎇	🌲			𝗺	T	Sea	◑	💧	Autumn	5	134
Clematis cirrhosa	✲	🍃	🫐		🌲		⊥		Alkali		◯	💧	Winter/Spring	7	114
Buddleia 'Lochinch'	✲	🍃		🎇					T		◯	💧	Summer	5	98
Rhododendron 'Purple Splendour'	✲	🍃			🌲				Acid		◑	💧	Spring/Summer	5	205
Syringa vulgaris 'Katherine Havemeyer'	✲	🍃		🎇					Alkali		◑	💧	Spring/Summer	3	225
Abutilon vitifolium	✲	🍃					⊥		T		◯	💧	Spring/Summer	8	76
Wisteria floribunda	✲	🍃		🎇			⊥		T		◯	💧	Spring/Summer	4	235
Wisteria floribunda 'Macrobotrys'	✲	🍃		🎇			⊥		T		◯	💧	Spring/Summer	4	235
Clematis 'Mrs Cholmondeley'	✲	🍃					⊥		Alkali		◑	💧	Spring/Summer	5	116

Key (see also p 9 and p 11)	✲	Flower colour	🍃	Foliage colour	🫐	Berries/fruits/cones/seed heads colour
🎇 Fragrant or aromatic	🌲	Evergreen	🍂	Good autumn colour	⊥	Climber or wall plant
𝗺 Suitable for hedging	Soil	Acid/alkali/tolerant	Sea	Suitable for maritime or seaside conditions	◯	Sun/shade requirements
💧 Moisture requirements	Season	Season(s) of interest	Zone	Climatic zone (see pages 59–62)	Page	Page reference to Directory of Plants

SHRUBS AND TREES

Plant name	✳	🍃	🫐	🎆	🌲	🍂	⊥	⫿⫿	Soil	Sea	◐	💧	Season	Zone	Page
Clematis 'Vyvyan Pennell'	✳	🍃					⊥		Alkali		◐	💧	Spring/Summer	5	116
Rhododendron augustinii	✳	🍃			🌲				Acid		◐	💧	Spring	5	205
Ceanothus 'Delight'	✳	🍃			🌲		⊥		T		○	💧	Spring/Summer	7	104
Ceanothus impressus	✳	🍃			🌲		⊥		T		○	💧	Spring	7	104
Solanum crispum 'Glasnevin'	✳	🍃			🌲		⊥		Alkali		◐	💧	Summer/Autumn	8	219
Clematis × jackmanii	✳	🍃					⊥		Alkali		◐	💧	Summer/Autumn	5	115
Clematis 'Jackmanii Superba'	✳	🍃					⊥		Alkali		◐	💧	Summer/Autumn	5	116
Clematis 'The President'	✳	🍃					⊥		Alkali		◐	💧	Summer/Autumn	5	116
Clematis viticella 'Abundance'	✳	🍃					⊥		Alkali		◐	💧	Summer/Autumn	5	116
Clematis 'William Kennett'	✳	🍃					⊥		Alkali		◐	💧	Summer	5	116
Lippia citriodora	✳	🍃		🎆			⊥		T		○	💧	Summer	8	173
Buddleia alternifolia	✳	🍃		🎆					T		○	💧	Summer	5	97
Buddleia davidii 'Black Knight'	✳	🍃		🎆					T		○	💧	Summer	5	97
Buddleia davidii 'Empire Blue'	✳	🍃		🎆					T		○	💧	Summer	5	97
Buddleia davidii 'Ile de France'	✳	🍃		🎆					T		○	💧	Summer	5	97
Disanthus cercidifolius	✳	🍃				🍂			Acid		◐	💧	Autumn	7	132
Chamaecyparis laws. 'Ellwood's White'		🍃			🌲				T		◐	💧		6	108
Chamaecyparis lawsoniana 'Albovariegata'		🍃			🌲			⫿⫿	T		◐	💧		6	108
Hedera canariensis 'Gloire de Marengo'		🍃			🌲		⊥		T		◐	💧		5	154
Ilex aquifolium 'Argenteo-marginata'		🍃	🫐		🌲			⫿⫿	T	Sea	◐	💧	Spring/Winter	5	161
Ilex aquifolium 'Silver Queen'		🍃			🌲			⫿⫿	T	Sea	◐	💧		5	161
Cryptomeria japonica 'Elegans'		🍃			🌲	🍂			Acid		◐	💧	Spring	5	125
Hedera helix 'Chicago'		🍃			🌲		⊥		T		◐	💧		5	154
Acer palmatum 'Atropurpureum'		🍃							T		◐	💧	Summer	5	77
Acer palmatum 'Dissectum Atropurpureum'		🍃							Acid		◐	💧	Summer	5	77
Vitis vinifera 'Purpurea'		🍃	🫐			🍂	⊥		T		◐	💧		6	234
Ligustrum ovalifolium 'Aureum'		🍃	🫐	🎆	🌲			⫿⫿	T		◐	💧	Summer	5	173

SHRUBS AND TREES: 2.5 m – 6 m (8 ft – 20 ft)

Plant name	Flower colour	Foliage colour	Berries/fruits/cones/seed heads colour	Fragrant or aromatic	Evergreen	Good autumn colour	Climber or wall plant	Suitable for hedging	Soil	Sea	Sun/shade	Moisture	Season	Zone	Page
Ilex × altaclarensis 'Golden King'		✓	✓		✓			✓	T	Sea	◑	◐	Winter	6	160
Thuja plicata 'Aureovariegata'		✓	✓	✓	✓			✓	T		○	◐		5	228
Calocedrus decurrens 'Aureovariegata'		✓			✓				T		○	◐		5	99
Taxus baccata 'Fastigiata Aurea'		✓	✓		✓				Alkali		◑	○		6	226
Chamaecyparis laws. 'Ellwood's Gold'		✓			✓				T		◑	◐		6	108
Juniperus chinensis 'Aurea'		✓		✓	✓				T		◑	◐		5	165
Juniperus chinensis 'Kaizuka Aurea'		✓		✓	✓				T		◑	◐		4	165
× *Cupressocyparis leylandii* 'Castlewellan'		✓			✓			✓	T	Sea	◑	◐		5	126
Chamaecyparis pisifera 'Filifera Aurea'		✓			✓				Acid		◑	◐		5	109
Chamaecyparis pisifera 'Plumosa Aurea'		✓			✓				Acid		◑	◐		5	109
Juniperus × media 'Plumosa Aurea'		✓		✓	✓				Alkali		◑	◐		5	166
Cedrus atlantica 'Aurea'		✓			✓				T		○	◐		7	105
Cedrus deodara 'Aurea'		✓			✓				T		○	◐		6	105
Chamaecyparis nootkatensis 'Lutea'		✓			✓				T		○	◐		4	109
Cupressus macrocarpa 'Goldcrest'		✓		✓	✓				T		○	◐		7	126
Pinus contorta		✓	✓		✓			✓	Acid	Sea	○	◐		7	194
Thuja orientalis 'Conspicua'		✓	✓	✓	✓				T		○	◐		5	228
Thuja occidentalis 'Lutea Nana'		✓		✓	✓				T		○	◐		5	227
Chamaecyparis lawsoniana 'Lanei'		✓			✓				T		◑	◐		6	108
Chamaecyparis lawsoniana 'Spek'		✓			✓				T		◑	◐		6	108
Juniperus communis 'Hibernica'		✓		✓	✓				Alkali		◑	◐		4	166
Juniperus virginiana 'Burkii'		✓		✓	✓				Alkali		◑	◐		4	167

Key (*see also p 9 and p 11*)	
✱	Flower colour
(leaf)	Foliage colour
(berries)	Berries/fruits/cones/seed heads colour
(fan)	Fragrant or aromatic
▲	Evergreen
(autumn leaf)	Good autumn colour
⊥	Climber or wall plant
ШШ	Suitable for hedging
Soil	Acid/alkali/tolerant
Sea	Suitable for maritime or seaside conditions
○	Sun/shade requirements
(drop)	Moisture requirements
Season	Season(s) of interest
Zone	Climatic zone (*see pages 59–62*)
Page	Page reference to *Directory of Plants*

SHRUBS AND TREES

Plant name	✳	🍃	🍒	🌿fan	▲	🍁	⊥	〣	Soil	Sea	○	💧	Season	Zone	Page
Juniperus virginiana 'Skyrocket'		●		fan	▲				Alkali		◑	◐		5	167
Juniperus squamata 'Meyeri'		●		fan	▲				Alkali		◑	◐		5	167
Juniperus virginiana 'Blue Heaven'		●		fan	▲				Alkali		◑	◐		4	167
Juniperus chinensis 'Pyramidalis'		●		fan	▲				T		◑	◐		5	165
Picea pungens 'Hoopsii'		●			▲				Acid		◑	●		2	192
Chamaecyparis laws. 'Chilworth Silver'		●			▲				T		◑	●		6	108
Picea abies 'Acrocona'		●	●		▲				T		◑	●		4	192
Pseudotsuga menziesii 'Fletcheri'		●	●	fan	▲				Acid		○	●		5	202
Taxus baccata 'Fastigiata'		●	●		▲				Alkali		◑	○		6	225
Vitis 'Brandt'		●	●			🍁	⊥		T		◑	◐		6	234
Abies koreana		●	●		▲				Acid		◑	●		5	75
Ilex aquifolium		●	●		▲			〣	T	Sea	◑	◐	Winter	5	161
Ilex aquifolium 'Bacciflava'		●	●		▲			〣	T	Sea	◑	◐	Autumn/Winter	5	161
Ilex aquifolium 'Pyramidalis'		●	●		▲			〣	T	Sea	◑	◐	Winter	5	161
Ilex aquifolium 'J.C. van Tol'		●	●		▲			〣	T	Sea	◑	◐	Winter	5	161
Thuja occidentalis 'Holmstrup'		●		fan	▲				T		◑	◐		4	227
Thuja occidentalis 'Smaragd'		●		fan	▲			〣	T		◑	◐		4	227
Acer griseum		●				🍁			T		◑	●	Autumn/Winter	5	77
Acer japonicum		●				🍁			Acid		◑	●	Spring/Autumn	5	77
Acer palmatum 'Dissectum Viridis'		●				🍁			Acid		◑	◐	Summer/Autumn	5	77
Acer palmatum 'Heptalobum Osakazuki'		●				🍁			Acid		◑	◐	Summer/Autumn	5	77
Nyssa sinensis		●				🍁			Acid		○	●		6	183
Arundinaria japonica		●			▲				T		○	●		5	87
Griselinia littoralis		●							Alkali	Sea	Ⓣ	◐		6	149
Chamaecyparis lawsoniana 'Ellwoodii'		●							T		◑	◐		5	108
Chamaecyparis laws. 'Ellwood's Pillar'		●			▲				T		◑	◐		5	108
Juniperus chinensis 'Kaizuka'		●		fan	▲				T		◑	◐		4	165

SHRUBS AND TREES: 2.5 m – 6 m (8 ft – 20 ft)

Plant name	✳	🍂	🍒	☀	🌲	🍁	⊥	▥	Soil	Sea	○	◌	Season	Zone	Page
Chamaecyparis thyoides 'Andelyensis'		🍂			🌲				Acid		◐	●		5	110
Juniperus × media 'Blaauw'		🍂		☀	🌲				Alkali		◐	◖		4	166
Calocedrus decurrens		🍂		☀	🌲				T		◐	◌		5	99
Pinus sylvestris 'Watereri'		🍂			🌲				T		○	◌		3	196
Pinus aristata		🍂			🌲				Acid		○	◌		5	194

SHRUBS AND TREES: over 6 m (20 ft)

Plant name	✳	🍂	🍒	☀	🌲	🍁	⊥	▥	Soil	Sea	○	◌	Season	Zone	Page
Lonicera sempervirens	✳	🍂			🌲		⊥		T		○	◖	Summer	5	176
Crataegus oxyacantha 'Coccinea Plena'	✳	🍂			🌲				T	Sea	◐	◌	Spring	4	125
Campsis radicans	✳	🍂					⊥		T		○	◌	Summer/Autumn	8	103
Campsis × tagliabuana 'Madame Galen'	✳	🍂					⊥		T		○	◌	Summer/Autumn	8	103
Clematis montana 'Tetrarose'	✳	🍂					⊥		Alkali		◐	◌	Spring	5	115
Clematis montana var. *rubens*	✳	🍂					⊥		Alkali		◐	◌	Spring	5	115
Prunus sargentii	✳	🍂							Alkali		○	◌	Spring	5	201
Prunus 'Accolade'	✳	🍂							Alkali		○	◌	Spring	5	199
Rosa 'Albertine'	✳	🍂		☀			⊥		T		Ⓣ	◌	Summer	5	209
Solanum jasminoides 'Album'	✳	🍂			🌲		⊥		Alkali		◐	◌	Summer/Autumn	8	219
Acer platanoides 'Drummondii'	✳	🍂							Alkali		◐	●	Spring	5	78
Acer platanoides 'Crimson King'	✳	🍂							Alkali		◐	◌	Spring	5	78
Salix alba 'Chermesina'	✳	🍂							T		◐	●	Spring	2	213
Salix × chrysocoma	✳	🍂							T		◐	●	Spring	2	213
Rhododendron falconeri	✳	🍂		☀	🌲				Acid		◐	●	Spring	5	205

Key (see also p 9 and p 11)	✳	Flower colour	🍂	Foliage colour	🍒	Berries/fruits/cones/seed heads colour
☀	Fragrant or aromatic	🌲	Evergreen	🍁	Good autumn colour	⊥ Climber or wall plant
▥	Suitable for hedging	Soil	Acid/alkali/tolerant	Sea	Suitable for maritime or seaside conditions	○ Sun/shade requirements
◌	Moisture requirements	Season	Season(s) of interest	Zone	Climatic zone (*see pages 59–62*)	Page Page reference to *Directory of Plants*

SHRUBS AND TREES: over 6 m (20 ft)

Plant name	✽	🍃	🍒	☀	🌲	🍂	⊥	⪢	Soil	Sea	○	💧	Season	Zone	Page
Laburnum × watereri 'Vossii'	✽	🍃		☀					T		○	◒	Spring	5	169
Betula pendula	✽	🍃							T		◑	💧	Spring	2	97
Acacia dealbata	✽	🍃		☀	🌲				Acid		Ⓣ	💧	Spring	9	76
Lonicera japonica 'Halliana'	✽	🍃		☀	🌲		⊥		T		◑	💧	Summer/Autumn	5	175
Rosa 'Mermaid'	✽	🍃			🌲		⊥		T		◑	💧	Summer/Autumn	5	209
Quercus ilex	✽	🍃	🍒		🌲			⪢	T	Sea	○	💧	Summer	7	204
Lonicera × americana	✽	🍃		☀			⊥		T		◑	💧	Summer	5	174
Passiflora caerulea	✽	🍃	🍒		🌲		⊥		T		◑	💧	Summer/Autumn	8	188
Sorbus aria 'Lutescens'	✽	🍃	🍒						Alkali	Sea	◑	💧	Spring/Summer	2	220
Cornus controversa 'Variegata'	✽	🍃	🍒						T		◑	●	Summer	5	120
Lonicera japonica 'Aureoreticulata'	✽	🍃		☀	🌲		⊥		T		○	💧	Summer/Autumn	7	174
Malus 'John Downie'	✽	🍃	🍒	☀					T		◑	💧	Spring	4	181
Sorbus aucuparia	✽	🍃	🍒			🍂			Acid		◑	💧	Spring/Autumn	2	220
Sorbus hupehensis	✽	🍃	🍒			🍂			T		◑	💧	Summer/Autumn	4	220
Rhododendron sinogrande	✽	🍃			🌲				Acid		◑	●	Spring	6	206
Clematis montana	✽	🍃					⊥		Alkali		◑	💧	Spring	5	115
Prunus × yedoensis	✽	🍃		☀					Alkali		○	💧	Spring	5	202
Polygonum baldschuanicum	✽	🍃					⊥		T		◑	●	Summer/Autumn	5	197
Jasminum officinale	✽	🍃		☀			⊥		T		○	💧	Summer/Autumn	6	164
Eucalyptus niphophila	✽	🍃		☀	🌲				Acid		○	●	Summer	6	139
Hydrangea petiolaris	✽	🍃					⊥		T		Ⓣ	●	Summer	4	159
Magnolia grandiflora	✽	🍃		☀	🌲		⊥		Acid		◑	●	Summer	7	178
Rosa 'Albéric Barbier'	✽	🍃		☀	🌲		⊥		T		○	💧	Summer	5	209
Prunus subhirtella 'Autumnalis'	✽	🍃							Alkali		○	💧	Autumn/Winter	3	201
Wisteria sinensis	✽	🍃		☀			⊥		T		○	●	Spring/Summer	5	235
Paulownia tomentosa	✽	🍃		☀					T		○	●	Spring	6	188
Parthenocissus henryana		🍃	🍒			🍂	⊥		T		◑	💧		6	187

Plant name	✳ Flower	🍃 Foliage	◕ Berries	☀ Fragrant	▲ Evergreen	🍂 Autumn	⊥ Climber	⊞ Hedging	Soil	Sea	◐ Sun/shade	◓ Moisture	Season	Zone	Page
Hedera helix 'Glacier'		🍃			▲		⊥		T		◐	◓		5	154
Acer negundo 'Variegatum'		🍃							T		◐	◓	Spring/Summer	5	77
Chamaecyparis laws. 'Columnaris Aurea'		🍃			▲				T		◐	◓		6	108
Chamaecyparis lawsoniana 'Lutea'		🍃			▲				T		◐	◓		6	108
Chamaecyparis lawsoniana 'Maas'		🍃			▲				T		◐	◓		5	108
Chamaecyparis lawsoniana 'Stewartii'		🍃			▲				T		◐	◓		6	108
Chamaecyparis laws. 'Winston Churchill'		🍃			▲				T		◐	◓		6	108
Robinia pseudoacacia 'Frisia'		🍃		☀					T		○	◓	Summer	3	207
Gleditsia triacanthos 'Sunburst'		🍃	◕						T		Ⓣ	◓		3	149
Chamaecyparis obtusa 'Crippsii'		🍃			▲				T		◐	◓		5	109
Chamaecyparis lawsoniana 'Erecta Aurea'		🍃			▲				T		◐	◓		6	108
Chamaecyparis lawsoniana 'Westermannii'		🍃			▲				T		◐	◓		5	108
Hedera colchica 'Dentata Variegata'		🍃			▲		⊥		T		◐	◓		5	154
Hedera colchica 'Paddy's Pride'		🍃			▲		⊥		T		◐	◓		5	154
Hedera helix 'Goldheart'		🍃			▲		⊥		T		Ⓣ	◓		5	154
Chamaecyparis lawsoniana 'Allumii'		🍃			▲				T		◐	◓		5	108
Chamaecyparis lawsoniana 'Blue Nantais'		🍃			▲				T		◐	◓		5	108
Chamaecyparis laws. 'Columnaris Glauca'		🍃			▲				T		◐	◓		6	108
Chamaecyparis lawsoniana 'Pembury Blue'		🍃			▲				T		◐	◓		6	108
Abies procera 'Glauca'		🍃	◕		▲				Acid		◐	◆		2	75
Picea pungens var. *glauca*		🍃			▲				Acid		◐	◆		2	192
Picea pungens 'Koster'		🍃			▲				Acid		◐	◆		2	192

Key (see also p 9 and p 11)	✳ Flower colour	🍃 Foliage colour	◕ Berries/fruits/cones/seed heads colour
☀ Fragrant or aromatic	▲ Evergreen	🍂 Good autumn colour	⊥ Climber or wall plant
⊞ Suitable for hedging	**Soil** Acid/alkali/tolerant	**Sea** Suitable for maritime or seaside conditions	○ Sun/shade requirements
◓ Moisture requirements	**Season** Season(s) of interest	**Zone** Climatic zone (see pages 59–62)	**Page** Page reference to Directory of Plants

SHRUBS AND TREES

Plant name	❋	🍃	🍇	✳	🌲	🍁	⊥	▥	Soil	Sea	○	💧	Season	Zone	Page
Pinus parviflora		🍃	🍇		🌲				Acid		○	●		5	195
Cupressus glabra 'Conica'		🍃		✳	🌲				T		◐	◐		7	126
Cedrus atlantica var. glauca		🍃	🍇		🌲				T	Sea	○	◐		6	105
Cedrus atlantica 'Glauca Pendula'		🍃	🍇		🌲				T	Sea	○	◐		6	105
Abies lasiocarpa 'Arizonica'		🍃	🍇		🌲				Acid		◐	●		5	75
Pseudotsuga menziesii		🍃	🍇	✳	🌲			▥	Acid		○	●		5	202
Taxus baccata		🍃	🍇		🌲			▥	Alkali		Ⓣ	◐		6	225
Pinus sylvestris		🍃	🍇		🌲				T		○	◐		3	196
Pinus pinea		🍃	🍇		🌲				T	Sea	◐	◐		8	195
Pinus nigra		🍃	🍇		🌲				Alkali	Sea	○	◐		4	195
Taxodium distichum		🍃	🍇			🍁			T		◐	●		4	225
Pinus leucodermis		🍃	🍇		🌲				Alkali		○	○		5	194
Parthenocissus quinquefolia		🍃	🍇			🍁	⊥		T		Ⓣ	◐	Autumn	5	187
Parthenocissus tricuspidata 'Veitchii'		🍃	🍇			🍁	⊥		T		Ⓣ	◐	Autumn	5	187
Vitis coignetiae		🍃	🍇			🍁	⊥		T		◐	●	Autumn	5	234
Picea abies		🍃			🌲				Acid		◐	●		4	192
Thuja plicata		🍃		✳	🌲			▥	T		◐	●		5	228
Chamaecyparis lawsoniana 'Fletcheri'		🍃			🌲				T		◐	◐		5	108
Chamaecyparis lawsoniana 'Green Pillar'		🍃			🌲				T		◐	◐	Spring	5	108
Chamaecyparis lawsoniana 'Pottenii'		🍃			🌲				T		◐	◐	Spring	6	108
Chamaecyparis lawsoniana 'Wisselii'		🍃			🌲				T		◐	◐		5	108
Chamaecyparis nootkatensis 'Pendula'		🍃	🍇		🌲				T		◐	◐		4	109
Metasequoia glyptostroboides		🍃	🍇			🍁			T		○	●	Spring/Autumn	5	182
Larix decidua		🍃	🍇			🍁			T		○	●	Spring/Autumn	2	169
Buxus sempervirens		🍃		✳	🌲			▥	T		Ⓣ	◐		5	98
Celastrus orbiculatus		🍃	🍇			🍁	⊥		T		◐	◐	Autumn	3	105
Sequoiadendron giganteum		🍃			🌲				T		○	●		6	218

Plant name	✱	🍃	🍒	☀	🌲	🍂	⊥	⊥⊥⊥	Soil	Sea	◯	💧	Season	Zone	Page
Quercus coccinea		🍃	🍒			🍂			T		◯	●	Autumn	4	204
Nyssa sylvatica		🍃				🍂			Acid		◯	●	Autumn	6	183
Populus nigra 'Italica'		🍃							T	Sea	◯	◐		2	197
Chamaecyparis lawsoniana 'Erecta Viridis'		🍃			🌲				T		◑	◐		6	108
× Cupressocyparis leylandii		🍃			🌲			⊥⊥⊥	T	Sea	◑	◐		5	126
Cupressus macrocarpa		🍃	🍒	☀	🌲			⊥⊥⊥	T	Sea	◑	◐		6	126
Tsuga canadensis		🍃	🍒		🌲				Alkali		◑	◐		4	229
Chamaecyparis lawsoniana		🍃			🌲			⊥⊥⊥	T		◑	◐		5	107
Araucaria araucana		🍃	🍒		🌲				T		◯	◐		6	85
Cedrus deodara		🍃	🍒		🌲				T		◯	◐		6	105
Cedrus libani		🍃	🍒		🌲				T		◯	◐		6	105
Cupressus sempervirens 'Stricta'		🍃		☀	🌲				T		◯	◊		8	126
Pinus cembra		🍃			🌲				Acid		◯	◐		4	194
Ginkgo biloba		🍃				🍂			T		◯	◐	Autumn	4	149

SHRUBS AND TREES

Key *(see also p 9 and p 11)*	✱	Flower colour	🍃	Foliage colour	🍒	Berries/fruits/cones/seed heads colour
☀	Fragrant or aromatic	🌲	Evergreen	🍂	Good autumn colour	⊥	Climber or wall plant
⊥⊥⊥	Suitable for hedging	**Soil**	Acid/alkali/tolerant	**Sea**	Suitable for maritime or seaside conditions	◯	Sun/shade requirements
💧	Moisture requirements	**Season**	Season(s) of interest	**Zone**	Climatic zone (*see pages 59–62*)	**Page**	Page reference to *Directory of Plants*

47

HERBACEOUS AND ROCK PLANTS

Plant name	❋	leaf	berries	fan	▲	❦	⊥	R	Soil	Sea	○	◊	Season	Zone	Page
Antennaria dioica var. rubra	❋	leaf			▲			R	Acid		○	◊	Spring/Summer	7	84
Bergenia 'Ballawley'	❋	leaf			▲	❦			Alkali		◐	◆	Spring	4	96
Epimedium × rubrum	❋	leaf			▲	❦		T			●	◊	Spring	7	135
Aubrieta deltoidea	❋	leaf			▲			R	Alkali		○	◑	Spring	4	90
Primula × pruhoniciana 'Wanda'	❋	leaf						R	Acid		◐	●	Winter/Spring	4	199
Sedum spurium 'Schorbusser Blut'	❋	leaf			▲			R	T	Sea	○	◊	Summer/Autumn	3	217
Sedum cauticola	❋	leaf						R	T	Sea	◐	◊	Summer/Autumn	3	216
Echinacea purpurea	❋	leaf							T		◐	◆	Summer/Autumn	4	133
Polygonum affine 'Darjeeling Red'	❋	leaf				❦			T		◐	◆	Summer/Autumn	4	197
Potentilla atrosanguinea 'Gibson's Scarlet'	❋	leaf							T		○	◆	Summer	4	198
Dianthus deltoides 'Brilliant'	❋	leaf						R	T		◐	◆	Summer	5	131
Aster novi-belgii 'Jenny'	❋	leaf							T		◐	●	Autumn	4	89
Sedum spectabile	❋	leaf			▲				Alkali	Sea	◐	◊	Summer/Autumn	3	217
Potentilla nitida 'Rubra'	❋	leaf							T		○	◆	Summer	4	199
Dianthus alpinus	❋	leaf			▲			R	Alkali	Sea	○	◆	Spring/Summer	4	131
Dianthus × allwoodii	❋	leaf			▲				Alkali	Sea	○	◆	Summer/Autumn	5	132
Dianthus Old fashioned pinks	❋	leaf							T	Sea	○	◆	Summer/Autumn	5	132
Bergenia × schmidtii	❋	leaf			▲				Alkali		◐	●	Spring/Summer	4	96
Androsace sarmentosa var. chumbyi	❋	leaf						R	Alkali		○	◊	Spring/Summer	7	83
Geranium endressii	❋	leaf							T		◐	◆	Spring/Summer	4	148
Armeria maritima	❋	leaf			▲			R	T	Sea	○	◆	Spring/Summer	6	86
Arabis aubrietioides	❋	leaf			▲			R	T		◐	◆	Spring/Summer	4	85
Phlox amoena	❋	leaf						R	T		○	◆	Spring/Summer	5	190
Incarvillea delavayi	❋	leaf							T		○	◆	Spring/Summer	5	161
Saxifraga umbrosa var. primuloides	❋	leaf			▲			R	T		◐	◆	Spring/Summer	5	216
Helleborus orientalis	❋	leaf			▲				T		◐	●	Winter/Spring	5	156
Bergenia cordifolia	❋	leaf			▲	❦			Alkali		◐	●	Spring	2	96

HERBACEOUS AND ROCK PLANTS: up to 60 cm (2 ft)

Plant name	✳	🍃	⚫	🔅	🌲	🍂	⊥	R	Soil	Sea	◐	💧	Season	Zone	Page
Aethionema 'Warley Rose'	✳	🍃						R	T		◐	💧	Spring	5	80
Aubrieta deltoidea	✳	🍃			🌲			R	Alkali		◐	💧	Spring	4	90
Saxifraga moschata 'Atropurpurea'	✳	🍃			🌲			R	T		◐	💧	Spring	5	216
Anemone × hybrida 'Bressingham Glow'	✳	🍃							T		◐	💧	Summer/Autumn	5	83
Geranium 'Ballerina'	✳	🍃						R	T		◐	💧	Summer/Autumn	5	147
Geranium sanguineum 'Lancastriense'	✳	🍃							T		◐	💧	Summer/Autumn	4	148
Astrantia major	✳	🍃							T		◐	💧	Summer	4	90
Gypsophila repens 'Fratensis'	✳	🍃						R	Alkali	Sea	○	💧	Summer	4	150
Gypsophila repens 'Rosea'	✳	🍃						R	Alkali	Sea	○	💧	Summer	5	150
Sempervivum montanum	✳	🍃			🌲			R	T	Sea	○	💧	Summer	5	217
Erigeron mucronatus	✳	🍃						R	T		○	💧	Summer	5	138
Geranium dalmaticum	✳	🍃				🍂		R	T		◐	💧	Summer	4	148
Thymus serpyllum	✳	🍃		🔅	🌲			R	T		○	💧	Summer	5	228
Sempervivum arachnoideum	✳	🍃			🌲			R	T	Sea	○	💧	Summer	3	217
Crepis incana	✳	🍃						R	T		○	💧	Summer	5	125
Aster novi-belgii 'Little Pink Baby'	✳	🍃							T		◐	💧	Autumn	4	89
Alyssum montanum	✳	🍃		🔅	🌲			R	Alkali		○	💧	Spring/Summer	4	81
Alyssum saxatile	✳	🍃			🌲			R	Alkali		○	💧	Spring/Summer	4	82
Raoulia australis	✳	🍃			🌲			R	T		◐	💧	Spring	7	204
Sedum spathulifolium 'Cappa Blanca'	✳	🍃			🌲			R	T	Sea	○	💧	Summer/Autumn	3	217
Anthemis sancti-johannis	✳	🍃		🔅					Alkali		○	💧	Summer	6	84
Achillea taygetea 'Moonshine'	✳	🍃							T		○	💧	Summer	5	79

Key *(see also p 9 and p 11)*			
✳ Flower colour	🍃 Foliage colour		⚫ Berries/fruits/cones/seed heads colour
🔅 Fragrant or aromatic	🌲 Evergreen	🍂 Good autumn colour	⊥ Climber or wall plant
R Suitable for rock gardens	**Soil** Acid/alkali/tolerant	**Sea** Suitable for maritime or seaside conditions	○ Sun/shade requirements
💧 Moisture requirements	**Season** Season(s) of interest	**Zone** Climatic zone *(see pages 59–62)*	**Page** Page reference to *Directory of Plants*

HERBACEOUS AND ROCK PLANTS

Plant name	✹	🍃	🫐	𖤍	▲	🍂	⊥	R	Soil	Sea	○	💧	Season	Zone	Page
Sedum spathulifolium 'Purpureum'	✹	🍃			▲			R	T	Sea	○	◐	Summer/Autumn	3	217
Paeonia mlokosewitschii	✹	🍃	🫐			🍂			T		◐	◐	Spring/Autumn	5	186
Geum chiloense 'Lady Stratheden'	✹	🍃							T		◐	◐	Spring/Summer	6	148
Doronicum caucasicum	✹	🍃							T		◐	●	Spring	5	132
Trollius europaeus 'Superbus'	✹	🍃							T		◐	●	Spring/Summer	3	229
Tellima grandiflora	✹	🍃			▲				T		◐	◐	Spring/Summer	4	227
Caltha palustris 'Flore Plena'	✹	🍃							Acid		◐	●	Spring	4	99
Adonis vernalis	✹	🍃							T		◐	●	Spring	7	80
Iris pumila	✹	🍃						R	Alkali		◐	●	Spring	4	162
Helleborus corsicus	✹	🍃			▲				T		◐	●	Spring	6	155
Euphorbia epithymoides	✹	🍃			▲				T		◐	◐	Spring	4	141
Saxifraga 'Elizabethae'	✹	🍃			▲				T		◐	◐	Spring	5	216
Coreopsis grandiflora	✹	🍃							Alkali		○	●	Summer/Autumn	3	118
Coreopsis verticillata	✹	🍃							Alkali		○	◐	Summer/Autumn	3	118
Inula hookeri	✹	🍃							T		○	◐	Summer/Autumn	5	161
Alchemilla mollis	✹	🍃							T		◐	●	Summer	3	81
Aster linosyris	✹	🍃							T		◐	●	Summer	5	89
Oenothera missouriensis	✹	🍃							T		○	◐	Summer	4	183
Rudbeckia fulgida 'Deamii'	✹	🍃							T		◐	◐	Summer	3	212
Helianthemum nummularium	✹	🍃			▲				Alkali		○	●	Summer	5	155
Achillea tomentosa	✹	🍃							T		○	◇	Summer/Autumn	5	79
Cerastium biebersteinii	✹	🍃			▲				T		○	◇	Spring/Summer	4	106
Androsace villosa var. arachnoidea	✹	🍃							Alkali		○	◇	Spring/Summer	6	83
Arabis ferdinandi-coburgii 'Variegata'	✹	🍃			▲				T		○	◐	Spring/Summer	4	85
Actaea alba	✹	🍃	🫐					R	T		◐	●	Spring/Summer	5	80
Anaphalis margaritacea	✹	🍃			▲				Alkali		◐	●	Summer	5	82
Dryas octopetala	✹	🍃			▲			R	Alkali		○	◐	Spring/Summer	5	133

HERBACEOUS AND ROCK PLANTS: up to 60 cm (2 ft)

Plant name	✳ Flower colour	⬭ Foliage colour	Berries/fruits/cones/seed heads	☀ Fragrant/aromatic	▲ Evergreen	❧ Good autumn colour	⊥ Climber/wall	R	Soil	Sea	◯ Sun/shade	◊ Moisture	Season	Zone	Page
Arenaria balearica	✳	⬭			▲				T		●	◊	Spring/Summer	△5	86
Arenaria montana	✳	⬭			▲				T		Ⓣ	◊	Spring/Summer	△5	86
Arabis albida	✳	⬭			▲				T		◐	◊	Spring/Summer	△4	85
Arabis albida 'Flore Pleno'	✳	⬭			▲				T		◐	◊	Spring/Summer	△4	85
Silene alpestris	✳	⬭			▲				T		◐	◊	Spring/Summer	△5	218
Helleborus niger	✳	⬭			▲				T		●	◆	Spring/Winter	△4	156
Iris pumila	✳	⬭							Alkali		◐	◆	Spring	△4	162
Epimedium youngianum 'Niveum'	✳	⬭			▲	❧			T		◐	◊	Spring	△7	135
Anacyclus depressus	✳	⬭							T		◯	◊	Summer	△5	82
Leontopodium alpinum	✳	⬭							T		◯	◊	Summer	△3	171
Aster novi-belgii 'Snowsprite'	✳	⬭							T		◐	◆	Autumn	△4	89
Saxifraga fortunei	✳	⬭			▲				T		◐	◊	Autumn	△5	216
Aubrieta deltoidea 'Variegata'	✳	⬭			▲				Alkali		◯	◊	Spring/	△4	91
Hosta undulata 'Medio-variegata'	✳	⬭							T		◐	◆	Summer	△4	157
Hosta fortunei 'Albopicta'	✳	⬭							T		◐	◆	Summer	△4	157
Ajuga reptans 'Multicolor'	✳	⬭			▲				T		◐	◆	Spring/Summer	△6	81
Ajuga reptans 'Burgundy Glow'	✳	⬭			▲				T		●	◆	Spring/Summer	△6	81
Stachys lanata	✳	⬭			▲				T		◐	◊	Summer	△4	222
Festuca cinerea	✳	⬭			▲				T		◯	◊	Summer	△4	142
Hosta sieboldiana	✳	⬭							T		●	◆	Summer	△4	157
Nepeta × *faassenii*	✳	⬭							T		◯	◊	Spring–Autumn	△4	183
Veronica incana	✳	⬭							T		◐	◊	Summer	△5	230

Key (see also p 9 and p 11)	✳ Flower colour	⬭ Foliage colour	Berries/fruits/cones/seed heads colour
☀ Fragrant or aromatic	▲ Evergreen	❧ Good autumn colour	⊥ Climber or wall plant
R Suitable for rock gardens	Soil Acid/alkali/tolerant	Sea Suitable for maritime or seaside conditions	◯ Sun/shade requirements
◊ Moisture requirements	Season Season(s) of interest	Zone Climatic zone (see pages 59–62)	Page Page reference to Directory of Plants

HERBACEOUS AND ROCK PLANTS: up to 60 cm (2 ft)

Plant name	✳	🍃	🍒	🔅	▲	🍂	⊥	R	Soil	Sea	○	◊	Season	Zone	Page
Aquilegia alpina	✳	🍃						R	T		◑	●	Spring/Summer	4	84
Centaurea montana	✳	🍃							T		◑	◐	Spring/Summer	3	106
Ajuga pyramidalis	✳	🍃			▲				T		◑	●	Spring/Summer	6	80
Polemonium caeruleum	✳	🍃							T		◑	◐	Spring/Summer	4	197
Phlox douglasii	✳	🍃						R			◑	◐	Spring/Summer	5	191
Helleborus foetidus	✳	🍃			▲				T		●	●	Spring/Winter	4	155
Iris unguicularis	✳	🍃		🔅	▲				Alkali		○	◇	Winter/Spring	5	163
Primula denticulata	✳	🍃						R	T		◑	●	Spring	3	199
Iris pumila	✳	🍃						R	Alkali		◑	●	Spring	4	162
Gentiana acaulis	✳	🍃						R	Alkali		◑	◐	Spring	5	147
Aubrieta deltoidea	✳	🍃			▲			R	Alkali		○	◇	Spring	4	90
Catananche caerulea 'Major'	✳	🍃							T		○	◇	Summer/Autumn	6	103
Clematis integrifolia 'Hendersonii'	✳	🍃							Alkali		○	◐	Summer/Autumn	5	114
Campanula poscharskyana	✳	🍃						R	T		○	◐	Summer/Autumn	4	102
Stokesia laevis	✳	🍃							T		◑	◇	Summer/Autumn	5	222
Scabiosa caucasica	✳	🍃							Alkali		○	◐	Summer/Autumn	4	216
Iris laevigata	✳	🍃							T		◑	●	Summer	5	162
Eryngium maritimum	✳	🍃							Alkali	Sea	○	◇	Summer/Autumn	6	138
Aster alpinus	✳	🍃						R	T		○	◐	Summer	5	88
Erigeron × speciosum 'Dignity'	✳	🍃							T		○	◐	Summer	5	138
Linum narbonense	✳	🍃							T		○	◐	Summer	6	173
Astilbe chinensis var. pumila	✳	🍃							T		◑	◐	Summer	4	90
Campanula carpatica	✳	🍃						R	T		◑	◐	Summer	5	101
Campanula cochlearifolia Campanula garganica	✳	🍃						R	T		◑	◐	Summer	4	101
Campanula glomerata 'Superba'	✳	🍃							T		◑	◐	Summer	5	102
Campanula lactiflora 'Pouffe'	✳	🍃							T		◑	◐	Summer	6	102
Erigeron macranthus	✳	🍃							T		◑	◐	Summer	5	138

HERBACEOUS AND ROCK PLANTS: up to 60 cm (2 ft)

Plant name	✳	🍃	🍒	🔅	🌲	🍂	⊥	R	Soil	Sea	○	💧	Season	Zone	Page
Aster amellus	✳	🍃									◑	◓	Summer/Autumn	6	88
Veronica spicata	✳	🍃									◑	💧	Summer	4	230
Erinus alpinus 'Dr Hanelle'	✳	🍃			🌲			R			○	💧	Summer	6	138
Lithospermum diffusum 'Heavenly Blue'	✳	🍃			🌲			R	Acid		◑	◆	Summer	7	173
Aster novi-belgii 'Audrey'	✳	🍃									◑	◆	Autumn	4	89
Gentiana × macaulayi	✳	🍃						R	Acid		◑	💧	Autumn	5	147
Acaena microphylla		🍃	🍒					R			○	💧	Autumn	5	76

HERBACEOUS PLANTS: 60 cm – 1.2 m (2 ft – 4 ft)

Plant name	✳	🍃	🍒	🔅	🌲	🍂	⊥	R	Soil	Sea	○	💧	Season	Zone	Page
Gaillardia aristata	✳	🍃					T				◑	💧	Summer/Autumn	5	146
Euphorbia griffithii	✳	🍃					T				◑	💧	Spring/Summer	3	141
Papaver orientale	✳	🍃					T				○	💧	Spring/Summer	7	187
Liatris pycnostachya	✳	🍃					T				○	💧	Summer/Autumn	5	172
Lythrum salicaria 'Firecandle'	✳	🍃					T				◑	◆	Summer/Autumn	3	178
Monarda didyma	✳	🍃		🔅			T				◑	💧	Summer/Autumn	4	182
Kniphofia caulescens	✳	🍃					T			Sea	○	💧	Summer/Autumn	7	168
Kniphofia galpinii	✳	🍃					T			Sea	○	💧	Summer/Autumn	7	169
Astilbe × arendsii 'Fanal'	✳	🍃					T				◑	◆	Summer	4	90
Astilbe × arendsii 'Granat'	✳	🍃					T				◑	◆	Summer	4	90
Lychnis chalcedonica	✳	🍃					T				◑	◆	Summer	4	177
Hemerocallis hybrids	✳	🍃					T				◑	◆	Summer	4	156
Phlox paniculata	✳	🍃		🔅			T				◑	◆	Summer	4	191
Aquilegia 'McKana Hybrid'	✳	🍃					T				◑	💧	Summer	4	84

Key (see also p 9 and p 11)	✳	Flower colour	🍃	Foliage colour	🍒	Berries/fruits/cones/seed heads colour
🔅	Fragrant or aromatic	🌲	Evergreen	🍂	Good autumn colour	⊥ Climber or wall plant
R	Suitable for rock gardens	Soil	Acid/alkali/tolerant	Sea	Suitable for maritime or seaside conditions	○ Sun/shade requirements
💧	Moisture requirements	Season	Season(s) of interest	Zone	Climatic zone (see pages 59–62)	Page Page reference to Directory of Plants

HERBACEOUS PLANTS: 60 cm – 1.2 m (2 ft – 4 ft)

Plant name	✱	❦	⁂	☼	▲	❧	⊥	R	Soil	Sea	○	◊	Season	Zone	Page
Paeonia lactiflora	✱	❦		☼					T		◑	◑	Summer	3	186
Lupinus 'Russell Hybrids'	✱	❦							Acid		◑	◑	Summer	5	177
Iris, tall bearded	✱	❦							Alkali		○	◑	Summer	4	163
Aster novi-belgii 'Crimson Brocade'	✱	❦							T		◑	●	Autumn	4	89
Achillea millefolium 'Cerise Queen'	✱	❦							T		○	◑	Summer	5	78
Dicentra spectabilis	✱	❦							T		◑	◑	Spring/Summer	3	132
Centranthus ruber	✱	❦	⁂						Alkali		○	◑	Summer/Autumn	6	106
Chrysanthemum rubellum 'Clara Curtis'	✱	❦		☼					Alkali		○	◑	Summer/Autumn	7	112
Anemone × *hybrida* 'Queen Charlotte'	✱	❦							T		◑	◑	Summer/Autumn	5	84
Astilbe × *arendsii* 'Bressingham Pink'	✱	❦							T		◑	●	Summer	4	90
Hemerocallis hybrids	✱	❦							T		◑	●	Summer	4	156
Phlox paniculata	✱	❦		☼					T		◑	●	Summer	4	191
Filipendula hexapetala	✱	❦							T		◑	●	Summer	4	142
Campanula lactiflora 'Loddon Anna'	✱	❦							T		◑	◑	Summer	5	102
Aquilegia 'McKana Hybrid'	✱	❦							T		◑	◑	Summer	4	84
Sidalcea malvaeflora	✱	❦							T		◑	◑	Summer	4	218
Physostegia virginiana 'Vivid'	✱	❦							T		◑	◑	Summer	6	191
Paeonia lactiflora	✱	❦		☼					T		◑	◑	Summer	3	186
Lupinus 'Russell Hybrids'	✱	❦							Acid		◑	◑	Summer	5	177
Asclepias incarnata	✱	❦							Acid		○	◑	Summer	8	88
Delphinium 'Belladonna Hybrids'	✱	❦							T		○	◑	Summer/Autumn	5	130
Iris, tall-bearded	✱	❦							Alkali		○	◑	Summer	4	163
Aster novi-belgii 'Fellowship'	✱	❦							T		◑	●	Autumn	4	89
Iris foetidissima	✱	❦	⁂						T		◑	◑	Summer	5	162
Euphorbia wulfenii	✱	❦			▲				T		◑	◑	Spring/Summer	6	142
Doronicum plantagineum	✱	❦							T		◑	●	Spring/Summer	5	133
Helenium autumnale 'Wyndley'	✱	❦							T		◑	◑	Summer/Autumn	5	154

HERBACEOUS PLANTS: 60 cm – 1.2 m (2 ft – 4 ft)

Plant name	✳	🍃	🫐	☀	🌲	🍂	⊥	R	Soil	Sea	◯	💧	Season	Zone	Page
Solidago virgaurea	✳	🍃							T		◐	💧	Summer/Autumn	3	219
Hemerocallis hybrids	✳	🍃							T		◐	●	Summer	4	156
Heliopsis scabra	✳	🍃							T		◯	💧	Summer	5	155
Aquilegia 'McKana Hybrid'	✳	🍃							T		◐	💧	Summer	4	84
Alstroemeria aurantiaca 'Dover Orange'	✳	🍃							T		◐	💧	Summer	9	81
Lupinus 'Russell Hybrids'	✳	🍃							Acid		◐	💧	Summer	5	177
Achillea filipendulina 'Coronation Gold'	✳	🍃							T		◯	💧	Summer	5	78
Iris, tall-bearded	✳	🍃							Alkali		◯	💧	Summer	4	163
Acanthus spinosus	✳	🍃							T		◐	💧	Summer	7	76
Acanthus mollis var. *latifolius*	✳	🍃							T		◐	💧	Summer	6	76
Artemisia 'Silver Queen'	✳	🍃							T		◐	💧	Summer	5	87
Delphinium Belladonna Hybrid'	✳	🍃							T		◯	💧	Summer/Autumn	5	130
Anemone × *hybrida* 'Alba'	✳	🍃							T		◐	💧	Summer/Autumn	5	83
Astilbe × *arendsii* 'Deutschland'	✳	🍃							T		◐	●	Summer	4	90
Phlox paniculata	✳	🍃		☀					T		◐	●	Summer	4	191
Gypsophila paniculata	✳	🍃							Alkali	Sea	◯	💧	Summer	4	150
Campanula lactiflora 'Alba'	✳	🍃							T		ⓣ	💧	Summer	5	102
Aquilegia 'McKana Hybrid'	✳	🍃							T		◐	💧	Summer	4	84
Paeonia lactiflora	✳	🍃		☀					T		◐	💧	Summer	3	186
Lupinus 'Russell Hybrids'	✳	🍃							Acid		◐	💧	Summer	5	177
Achillea ptarmica 'The Pearl'	✳	🍃							T		◯	💧	Summer	3	78
Chrysanthemum maximum 'Wirral Supreme'	✳	🍃							Alkali		◯	💧	Summer	5	111

Key *(see also p 9 and p 11)*	✳	Flower colour	🍃	Foliage colour	🫐	Berries/fruits/cones/seed heads colour
☀	Fragrant or aromatic	🌲	Evergreen	🍂	Good autumn colour	⊥	Climber or wall plant
R	Suitable for rock gardens	**Soil**	Acid/alkali/tolerant	**Sea**	Suitable for maritime or seaside conditions	◯	Sun/shade requirements
💧	Moisture requirements	**Season**	Season(s) of interest	**Zone**	Climatic zone *(see pages 59–62)*	**Page**	Page reference to *Directory of Plants*

HERBACEOUS PLANTS: 60 cm – 1.2 m (2 ft – 4 ft)

Plant name	✳	🍃	🍒	🌾	🌲	🍂	⊥	R	Soil	Sea	○	💧	Season	Zone	Page
Iris, tall-bearded	✳	🍃							Alkali		○	◐	Summer	4	163
Aster novi-belgii 'Blandie'	✳	🍃							T		◐	●	Autumn	4	89
Cimicifuga foetida 'White Pearl'	✳	🍃							T		◐	●	Autumn	4	112
Aster ericoides	✳	🍃							T		◐	◔	Autumn	6	89
Thalictrum aquilegifolium	✳	🍃							T		◐	●	Spring/Summer	5	227
Iris pallida 'Variegata'	✳	🍃		🌾					Alkali		◐	◔	Spring/Summer	5	162
Meconopsis betonicifolia	✳	🍃							Acid		◐	●	Spring	5	181
Clematis heracleifolia	✳	🍃							Alkali		○	●	Summer/Autumn	5	114
Aster × frikartii	✳	🍃							Alkali		◐	●	Summer/Autumn	6	89
Aconitum × arendsii	✳	🍃							T		◐	●	Summer/Autumn	3	79
Aconitum fischeri	✳	🍃							T		◐	●	Summer/Autumn	3	79
Geranium pratense 'Johnson's Blue'	✳	🍃							T		◐	◔	Summer/Autumn	4	148
Agapanthus 'Headbourne Hybrid'	✳	🍃							T		○	●	Summer/Autumn	8	80
Delphinium 'Belladonna Hybrids'	✳	🍃							T		○	◔	Summer/Autumn	5	130
Echinops ritro	✳	🍃							Alkali		○	◔	Summer/Autumn	5	133
Phlox paniculata	✳	🍃		🌾					T		◐	●	Summer	4	191
Iris kaempferi	✳	🍃							Acid		◐	●	Summer	5	162
Iris sibirica	✳	🍃							Acid		◐	●	Summer	4	162
Hosta fortunei	✳	🍃							T		◐	●	Summer	4	157
Aconitum napellus 'Bressingham Spire'	✳	🍃							T		◐	●	Summer	3	79
Eryngium alpinum	✳	🍃							T	Sea	○	○	Summer	6	138
Anchusa azurea 'Loddon Royalist'	✳	🍃							T		○	◔	Summer	5	83
Aquilegia 'McKana Hybrid'	✳	🍃							T		◐	◔	Summer	4	84
Campanula persicifolia	✳	🍃			🌲				T		◐	◔	Summer	4	102
Lupinus 'Russell Hybrids'	✳	🍃							Acid		◐	◔	Summer	5	177
Iris, tall-bearded	✳	🍃							Alkali		○	◔	Summer	4	163
Aster novi-belgii 'Ada Ballard'	✳	🍃							T		◐	●	Autumn	4	89

HERBACEOUS PLANTS: 60 cm – 1.2 m (2 ft – 4 ft)

Plant name	✳	🌿	🫐	🎆	🌲	🍂	⊥	R	Soil	Sea	○	💧	Season	Zone	Page
Aster novi-belgii 'Chequers'	✳	🌿								T		◑	●	Autumn	△4	89
Aster novi-belgii 'Marie Ballard'	✳	🌿								T		◑	●	Autumn	△4	89

HERBACEOUS PLANTS: 1.2 m – 2.5 m (4 ft – 8 ft)

Plant name	✳	🌿	🫐	🎆	🌲	🍂	⊥	R	Soil	Sea	○	💧	Season	Zone	Page
Rheum palmatum	✳	🌿								T		○	●	Summer	△3	204
Aster novae-angliae 'September Ruby'	✳	🌿								T		◑	●	Autumn	△5	89
Eremurus elwesii	✳	🌿		🎆						Alkali		○	◐	Spring	△6	135
Delphinium 'Pacific Hybrids'	✳	🌿								T		○	●	Summer/Autumn	△5	130
Aster novae-angliae 'Harrington's Pink'	✳	🌿								T		◑	●	Autumn	△5	89
Helianthus decapetalus	✳	🌿								T		○	◐	Summer/Autumn	△5	155
Anthemis tinctoria 'Grallagh Gold'	✳	🌿								T		○	○	Summer	△6	84
Delphinium 'Pacific Hybrid'	✳	🌿								T		○	◐	Summer/Autumn	△5	130
Artemisia lactiflora	✳	🌿		🎆						Acid		◑	◐	Summer/Autumn	△4	87
Crambe cordifolia	✳	🌿								Alkali		○	◐	Summer	△7	125
Aruncus dioicus	✳	🌿								T		●	●	Summer	△3	87
Cortaderia selloana	✳	🌿			🌲					T		○	○	Autumn	△7	121
Thalictrum dipterocarpum	✳	🌿								T		◑	●	Summer	△5	227
Delphinium 'Pacific Hybrids'	✳	🌿								T		○	◐	Summer/Autumn	△5	130

Key *(see also p 9 and p 11)*	✳ Flower colour	🌿 Foliage colour	🫐 Berries/fruits/cones/seed heads colour
🎆 Fragrant or aromatic	🌲 Evergreen	🍂 Good autumn colour	⊥ Climber or wall plant
R Suitable for rock gardens	**Soil** Acid/alkali/tolerant	**Sea** Suitable for maritime or seaside conditions	○ Sun/shade requirements
💧 Moisture requirements	**Season** Season(s) of interest	**Zone** Climatic zone *(see pages 59–62)*	**Page** Page reference to *Directory of Plants*

Guidelines for Successful Growing

This book lists over 1,100 garden plants which are suitable for planting in most districts. It is impossible to be totally accurate in describing all the qualities of a plant as these vary according to the circumstances.

Climate

In the matter of hardiness, no one can be absolutely sure where a borderline should come, as winters can be unpredictable in their severity. A winter with severe frosts can prove to be less damaging than a slightly warmer one in which there is excessive near-freezing rain. A persistent freezing wind can lower the ambient·air temperature by several degrees through wind chill. A reasonable fall of snow can serve to protect completely some small plants, and the lower parts of larger ones, from the direct adverse effects of frosts and wind.

Probably the worst type of winter is one in which there is excessive dampness. This is particularly harmful to evergreens which have to maintain transpiration at all times. So while a climate might, in theory, suit a shrub in a matter of average winter temperature, it might not be ideal for average winter precipitation.

The rock plants, for instance, come from the high mountain regions of the world. There they have the winter protection of snow. In lowland gardens of Northern Europe and climatically similar areas of North America, the winters can be comparatively mild and wet at the time when alpine plants should be experiencing a cold, dry period of rest. While it is not possible to provide snow, the required dryness can be provided to some degree by planting on the raised areas of

Early summer in an English garden, with lilacs or syringas (Clare College, Cambridge).

the rock garden, and by incorporating grit into the compost and on the surface around the plants.

Wall protection is often advocated for garden plants which originate in climates warmer than those in which they are to be planted as this gives them some protection against damage from biting north or east winds, and to some extent from frosts.

The climatic conditions of the district in which the garden is situated must be a prime consideration when deciding what to plant, but even within the garden itself there will be some areas that will be warmer than others. While some may be exposed to the directions from which the coldest winds will come, others will be protected by shrubs, hedges or walls.

Zones

The Plant Hardiness Zone System used in this book is based on the system devised by *The United States Department of Agriculture* for use in southern Canada and the United States (excluding Alaska and the Hawaiian Islands).

An attempt has been made here to increase the scope of the system to include Australia, New Zealand, South Africa and Western Europe, including the United Kingdom and Eire.

As will be seen from the zone map of the USA, the USDA system divides North America into 10 climatic zones separated by average **minimum** winter temperatures, in stages of 10°F from −50°F and below at Zone 1, up to +40°F at Zone 10.

For the purpose of this book, a rough translation to Celsius has been made and both the Fahrenheit and the Celsius figures are shown in the key to the maps.

Every plant included in the charts has been given a zone number indicating

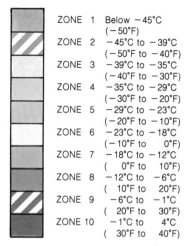

	ZONE 1	Below −45°C
		(−50°F)
	ZONE 2	−45°C to −39°C
		(−50°F to −40°F)
	ZONE 3	−39°C to −35°C
		(−40°F to −30°F)
	ZONE 4	−35°C to −29°C
		(−30°F to −20°F)
	ZONE 5	−29°C to −23°C
		(−20°F to −10°F)
	ZONE 6	−23°C to −18°C
		(−10°F to 0°F)
	ZONE 7	−18°C to −12°C
		(0°F to 10°F)
	ZONE 8	−12°C to −6°C
		(10°F to 20°F)
	ZONE 9	−6°C to −1°C
		(20°F to 30°F)
	ZONE 10	−1°C to 4°C
		(30°F to 40°F)

that it should withstand the **average *minimum* winter temperature of that zone** and **also those zones with higher numbers** and therefore higher minimum temperatures. For more detailed range of zones refer to the entry in the Plant Directory. It must, however, be realised that other factors, such as precipitation patterns and high maximum summer temperatures, may well make life insupportable for plants with low zone numbers.

No claim is made as to precise accuracy.

It is indeed difficult to contemplate a climatic zone system that can be 100% accurate, simply because the variations in annual temperatures and precipitation can be so considerable from one year to another. Working as one must from a basis of averages means that, in all probability, there will be few if any seasons in any area that fully correspond to the averages in any climatic consideration.

Within each zone there are bound to be local variations in climate due to a variety of circumstances. Low-lying areas can be frost pockets, while only a few metres higher up a hillside the growing season may be a good two weeks longer than in a garden near the top.

In temperate areas of low summer rainfall, while the climate may be suitable in every other way, unless there is sufficient mains or stored water for the garden, survival of plants may be uncertain unless chosen with care.

By observing what grows in other people's gardens, or in municipal parks nearby, it is possible to make a reasonable assessment of the planting possibilities for your own garden.

Every plant has a transpiration rate

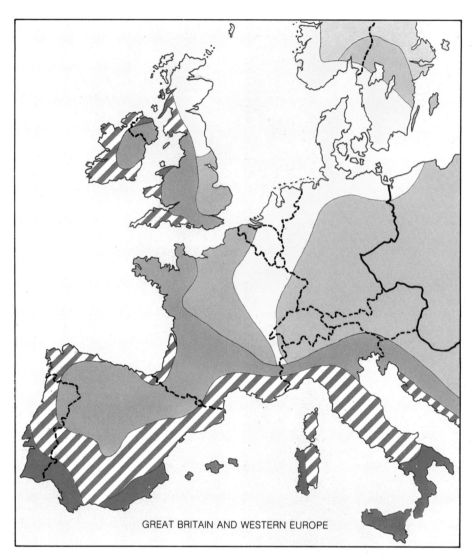

GREAT BRITAIN AND WESTERN EUROPE

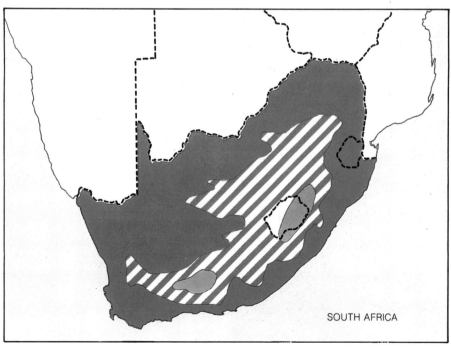

SOUTH AFRICA

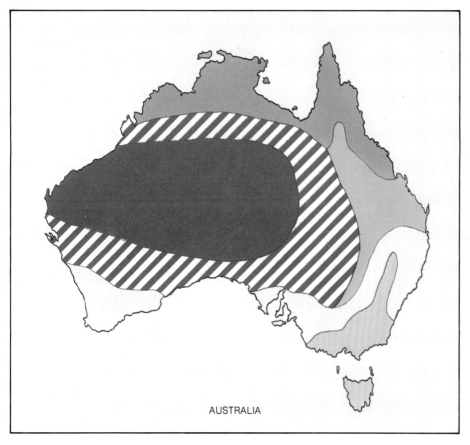

AUSTRALIA

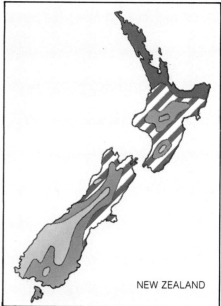

NEW ZEALAND

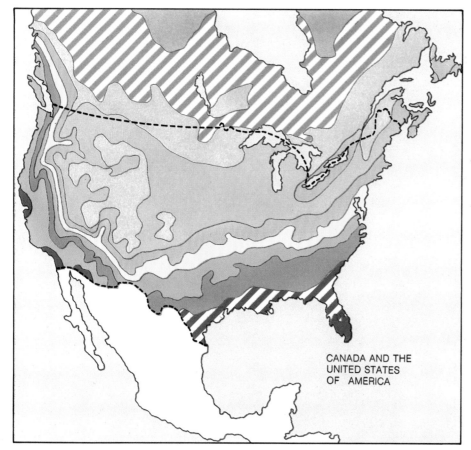

CANADA AND THE
UNITED STATES
OF AMERICA

(the amount of water loss through the leaves) suited to the climate of its natural habitat. Thus, plants indigenous to areas of high humidity are unsuited to areas of excessive dryness, even though temperatures may be suitable, because their roots would be unable to supply sufficient water to satisfy an increased rate of transpiration.

Equally, plants found in very dry areas and having a slower rate of transpiration are prone to rotting in wetter climates even though temperatures may be comparable.

Statistics showing levels of annual rainfall are of little use. It is the distribution of the total throughout the year that is of most significance. Two regions, while having roughly the same levels of annual precipitation, and even similar winter and summer temperatures, will not both be able to satisfy the requirements of a given plant if the total rainfall of one region is concentrated within a few months while the other has a more even distribution throughout the year.

In South Africa, for instance, there is a very marked difference in the levels of annual precipitation between the east and the west coasts. The east coast is swept by the warm Agulhas current which flows from north to south. This not only keeps the eastern coastal margin warm and frost free, but also ensures adequate levels of rainfall throughout the year well into the interior.

The current which flows up the west coast roughly from Cape Town northwards, known as the Benguela current, is considerably cooler, chilling the lower air which, interacting with hotter upper layers, establishes exceptionally stable conditions in which rainfall is rare.

In the Durban region on the east coast over 1,000 mm of rain falls over the year. At Port Nolloth on the west coast less than 60 mm falls, almost all of it in the winter. Temperatures here are in fact cooler throughout the year than those of Durban.

Soil

For those with a new garden or a well-established one my advice is to take the trouble to know your garden. Do not rush off to the nearest garden centre to purchase that special shrub you've always cherished. First ascertain whether your new garden is suitable for it. We all have our favourites and with care, forethought and preparation it is quite possible that we may be able to accommodate them.

There are a great number of garden plants to suit almost any situation, but it is vitally important to understand the characteristics of the situation before selecting the plants.

Soil types vary and you must get to know yours before designing the garden or selecting your plants. A really enthusiastic gardener may even look at the soil before buying the house.

The soil test kits obtainable at garden centres can be useful if used correctly and with necessary care.

The most important difference in soil types is between acid (lime-free) and alkaline (chalky or limy) – for this dictates many of the plants that can satisfactorily be grown.

For simplicity, soils are normally divided into three basic types: acid, neutral or normal and alkaline or chalk. The acid soils are usually peaty or black and sandy, though some clay soils may be acid.

Neutral soils have a reasonable level of humus and all necessary nutrients. They are generally quite workable in all but the most adverse weather conditions. They are also readily adaptable to the soil requirements of most hardy garden plants, merely by incorporating a mixture of well-rotted manure or garden compost suitable for their needs into the hole when planting.

Highly alkaline soils, in extreme cases can pose the greatest problems for, not only do you have to be selective in choice of plants, but also the soil may be difficult to penetrate with a spade or fork where a thin layer of chalky clay sits only 10 cm (4 in) or so thick on the underlying solid white chalk.

However, not all are as bad as that, and any soil can be termed alkaline, if its pH is over 7.00 (see page 64).

Aspect

Once the type of soil is known and understood, there are several other factors it is advisable to examine, such as, which areas lie wet in winter or are excessively dry in summer, are shaded by trees or houses and never actually see the sun, are exposed to winter winds, or are at the end of narrow passage-ways which will be extremely draughty.

Look out the windows, especially those most used, to see if any neighbouring houses overlook you, or if there are any unsightly views you may wish to screen.

Planning your garden

The best way to make a start is to draw up a plan or bird's eye view of the plot on squared paper using reasonably accurate paced-out measurements. Mark in steps and paths you wish to retain and walls, and the position of windows and doors of the dwelling.

It is better to design the layout of the garden as a single entity from the outset, even if you complete the construction of it over a period of years.

Then comes the fascinating job of filling in the details. Try to involve all the family. Future recriminations will be avoided and, if the garden is of sufficient size, most tastes and requirements can be catered for. Remember very young children, and even children as yet unborn, for it would not be advisable to incorporate a pond nor those shrubs with vicious spines or prickly leaves, or plants with poisonous berries or fruits. If you must have them, plant them where inquisitive toddlers are unable or unlikely to go. The Yucca with its needle-sharp tips to the rigid sword-like leaves could so easily damage eyes if a child should run or fall into it.

In a sitting-out area there are several considerations. Sunny, private positions are usually desired, which are sheltered from the wind and have a pleasant view. If you like to have meals outside, site it near the house.

What is the purpose of your lawn? Is it to be a play area or to become the perfect greensward?

For some smaller gardens paving would be more suitable than a lawn. Where lack of time or age are considerations to be taken into account an area of paving with borders round and gaps left at intervals for planting can be very attractive and trouble-free once laid.

Plants should be chosen according to soil and aspect. For instance, in a shady part of a garden with cool moist soil it is possible to grow a wide range of flowering and foliage plants such as ivies, hostas and ferns.

Be certain that you have chosen the paving you want, be it natural stone, crazy-paving or manufactured slabs, and that it is well laid. Once it is down it is costly to lift and replace.

Paving will also be needed for a patio area, although it will be used in association with a lawn and planted borders. If possible, it should be laid so that it's surface is fractionally lower than that of the lawn, to allow the mower to run over it, minimizing the need for hand-trimming the lawn edge.

Manures, compost and fertilizers

There is a certain amount of confusion as to the difference between fertilizers and manures.

Manures

Manures are *organic* and bulky. They include farmyard manure, stable manure, garden compost, sewage sludge and seaweed. These are all excellent means of supplying organic matter to the soil. If farmyard manure is fresh, and the straw has hardly started to decompose, it will be at its highest state of nutritional value, but it can prove fatal to plants if it is incorporated near their roots. It might also contain a fair amount of weed seeds.

The nitrogen level in organic manures is fairly rapidly diminished once it is spread, so, if it is to be dug in, it should be left in heaps and not spread over the ground until the work of digging can be done.

Well-rotted, or fully decomposed manures are of most use for they are practically odourless, and easy to handle and improve the structure of the soil, even though they have lost much of their nutritional value during the rotting process. However, this loss can be made up with concentrated artificial or organic fertilizers. Chicken manure from deep litter houses is the most concentrated, and care is needed not to over-use it as this again can damage plant roots.

Garden compost

Most garden owners have access to some of the following: fallen leaves, lawn mowings, soft clippings and vegetable refuse from the kitchen, all of which can be composted to make a valuable source of organic matter for the garden with

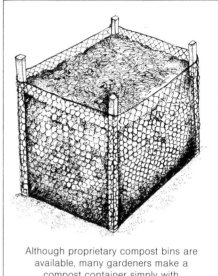

Although proprietary compost bins are available, many gardeners make a compost container simply with galvanized wire netting supported by stout wooden stakes.

very little effort and expense.

Larger and coarser refuse, such as woody prunings from shrubs and long herbaceous stems, if of sufficient quantity to be worth the expense, can be broken down with electric shredders that reduce them to a state suitable for incorporation into the compost heap. Hard twigs and long herbaceous stems must never be used in the compost heap unless chopped up finely as they will keep it too open, and prevent the breaking down process from taking place. At the other extreme, short lawn mowings will pack down too densely if used on their own. Air will be excluded, and the heap will not heat up sufficiently.

Consider the site of the compost heap. It is best to select a position that is accessible but hidden from view. Generally, an area of approximately 1–1.5 sq m (10–15 sq ft) seems about right. Too small and it will not heat up properly. Too large and air may not reach the centre, so again it will not heat properly. The width should be 90 cm (3 ft), though the length can be more.

Compost heaps are made on the surface, though any turf must always be removed first. They can be completely open-sided, or fenced-in with bricks, boards or corrugated iron, so long as holes are provided for the passage of air. Two heaps are even better, for one can then be rotting down while the other is being built up. Proprietary compost bins can also be obtained.

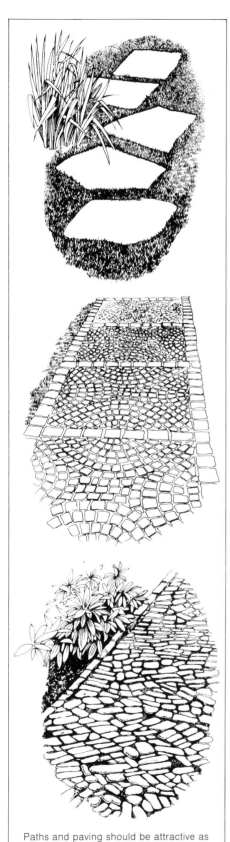

Paths and paving should be attractive as well as utility features. Stepping stones set in a lawn create an informal effect, as do old paviours and random stone.

The first layer of refuse, preferably of mixed materials, should be spread over the area, and firmed down to a thickness of 15 cm (6 in) or so, before covering the surface with a compost accelerator which will contain both nitrogen and lime. Then spread another 15 cm (6 in) layer of refuse topped with a sprinkling of accelerator, and so on up to a height of about 1.2 m (4 ft). Each layer should be well watered. As an alternative to a proprietary accelerator, one can alternate a dressing of sulphate of ammonia with a dressing of garden lime (calcium carbonate). When the heap is completed, leave it undisturbed until ready for use.

Fertilizers

The subject of fertilizers can be extremely complicated, but the amateur gardener has no need to know more than a few basic rules.

So long as there is no obvious imbalance in a garden soil, the general purpose or balanced compound fertilizers will do a good job if used correctly. Some of these are organic based, while others are inorganic (artificial). The latter are cheaper, but return no organic matter to the soil, and, while it is always good advice to incorporate some form of bulk humus when applying any fertilizer, it is essential when the fertilizers are inorganic.

If in doubt about the fertility of your soil, soil test kits can tell you the levels of nitrogen (N), phosphates (P) and potash (K), and also the pH – the acidity/alkalinity level. Use them with care following the instructions on the pack or they will be a waste of money, and totally misleading. If you apply fertilizer according to the results arrived at by use of a soil test kit, then you will use a mixture of straight fertilizers and not a ready-made compound fertilizer.

Nitrogen (N) is essential for growth and foliage colour. Any deficiency will show in stunted growth and yellowing of the leaves which will also be small. The most usually recommended source for amateurs is sulphate of ammonia.

Phosphorus (P) is needed for the encouragement of good root formation, and it also helps in the ripening of seed and fruit. Bonemeal is an organic source of supply, but only in acid soils. Superphosphate is the generally accepted source, and is suitable on all soil types.

Potash (K) stimulates healthy grown, and also encourages good flowering and fruiting. Wood or plant ash is a source of potassium, usually in the form of K_2O. Other elements include magnesium, iron, and phosphorus, and sometimes a little manganese. The form of potash most easily purchased by amateur gardeners is sulphate of potash.

Lime is not, strictly speaking, a plant food, but is essential to their well-being. Only when lime is present can plant foods in the soil be made available. Lime is lost from cultivated soils in various ways. Fertilizers or manures use up lime in the processes that make the food values available to plants. Rainfall 'leaches' out more and, in any case, lime tends to sink in the ground, eventually to below the area in which it is needed.

The soil test kits for lime will indicate the amount of lime necessary to achieve a pH level suitable for the plants or crops to be grown. Most soils benefit in terms of improved drainage, and general workability from applications of lime.

pH This is a measure of acidity and alkalinity. Soils with a pH of 7.0 are referred to as neutral soils. Those with a pH level of less than 7 are referred to as acid soils and, above that figure, as alkaline soils. pH4 is very acid, but pH5 is ideal for many plants, such as rhododendrons and camellias, which are calcifuges and cannot tolerate any lime in the soil.

Planting

The vast majority of plants, be they trees, shrubs or herbaceous perennials, are purchased container grown. Some types that form exceptions are the cheaper hedging plants which are not worth the expense of potting.

Container-grown plants

The benefits of the container-growing 'revolution' are considerable to both the purchaser and the vendor, for it allows plants to be sold and planted at any time of the year. So long as they are watered as necessary, they may be left unplanted for a reasonable time without worry. It has become possible to see a shrub or even a tree in full flower at the garden centre on a morning in spring or summer and to have it planted in your own garden the same afternoon.

There is an important difference to be found between 'container grown' and 'containerized' plants. The former are plants that have lived in pots since their early days, being potted on to selling size without root disturbance, while the latter are bare-rooted plants that are potted later in life.

Sometimes such plants are offered for sale before they have sufficiently re-established their roots. It should be possible to pick up a container-grown plant by the stem, using necessary care, of course. If the container and soil drop off, don't buy the plant.

Before planting a container-grown plant always prepare the planting hole properly. This should mean double-digging a hole of generous size, i.e. digging two spits (spade blades) deep, turning over the lower spit on its own level. If time does not permit, then the

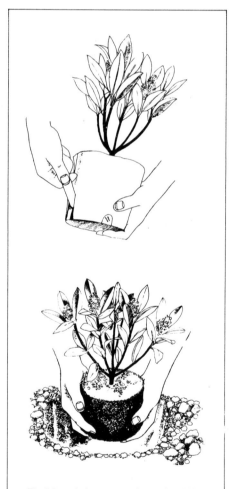

Flexible polythene containers should be slit and carefully peeled away before inserting plants in well-prepared planting holes which have been double-dug.

lower spit should at least be forked over to loosen it up. Then incorporate well-rotted manure or garden compost; fresh manures and composts which have not properly rotted should never be used. Position the plant in the hole and replace the soil, firming well as you go, so that the new soil level coincides with the soil level in the container.

Bare-rooted plants

The planting of bare-rooted shrubs and trees is best done in the autumn while the soil is still warm. If this is not possible, then there is no great harm done by planting at any time between autumn and early spring, as long as the soil is workable. If planting becomes impossible, and a bare-rooted shrub or tree is delivered, then its roots should be moistened and wrapped well in damp sacking or cloth, and the plant stored in a garage or shed until the ground becomes workable. This treatment will also apply if the ground becomes waterlogged after a prolonged period of heavy rains. Never wrap the roots in plastic as this does not 'breath' and roots can rot.

When a break in the weather permits, planting should be carried out as follows. Firstly, dig a hole larger than the area of root spread so that the roots can be spread out. The soil from the hole should be mixed well with peat and fertilizer, and, after forking over the bottom of the hole, some of the mixture should be placed in the centre to form a shallow mound so the roots sit naturally. Do not prepare the hole before the plant is available for planting, as both the hole and the soil removed from it may become too wet or too frozen for successful planting. There are many usable fertilizers available. My preference is for organic rather than chemical, and with a reasonably high potash element to encourage flowers and fruits.

Any damaged or over-long roots should be trimmed back with sharp secateurs. If, in the case of deciduous ornamental or fruit trees, there is a markedly greater spread of branches than of roots, cut back the branches to equal the root size. The cuts should be cleanly done with sharp secateurs immediately above a bud or pair of buds.

When planting a standard or a half-standard tree, hammer in a stake before the hole is filled in to avoid damaging the roots of the plant. When the stake is firmly in place, the tree can be attached with a tree tie, or, if the stem requires straightening or is of a weak or floppy nature, two tree ties might be needed, one at the top and the other about half way up. Nylon stockings make very effective tree ties. Once the tree is attached to the stake the mixture of soil, peat and fertilizer should be returned to the hole working it well round the roots. When the hole is filled, tread the soil down firmly. Firm planting is essential to the tree's future success, but should not be done when the ground is sticky or waterlogged when you should not be planting anyway.

Shrubs or trees with a close-knit mass of fibrous roots should be gently moved up and down several times once sufficient fine soil has been returned to the hole to cover the roots. This settles the soil down well among the fibrous roots. If a stake is needed, it should be hammered into position before the roots are covered, and the plant tied to it at the end of the planting operation.

General guidelines

After a period of exceptionally frosty weather go round and firm any plants lifted by the frost, especially the more shallow-rooted subjects.

Plant to the previous planting depth using the soil mark on the stem as your guide. Many ornamental trees, some shrubs and nearly all fruit trees, are propagated by grafting or budding onto a chosen rootstock, which will determine the growth habit of the plant. The planting depth should leave the union of stock and scion between 10–15 cm (4–6 in) above ground level. If they are planted above the union, or mulching raises the soil level above it, then either rooting of the scion will take place (which will defeat the object of the graft), or buried stems of lower branches may rot and the ultimate result will be the death of the plant.

One exception, where deep planting is desirable, is with clematis where it can prevent the loss of the plant through clematis wilt. This fungus disease can attack and kill all the above ground parts of a clematis with remarkable speed, but does not attack the roots or any of the stem below ground. Deeper planting makes it possible for the clematis to produce new growth from the buried lower stem.

Some heathers are tolerant of deepish

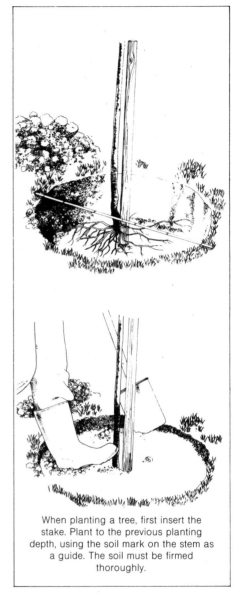

When planting a tree, first insert the stake. Plant to the previous planting depth, using the soil mark on the stem as a guide. The soil must be firmed thoroughly.

planting where it results in the production of roots. The new plants that result can later be lifted, separated and planted elsewhere.

Pruning

It is essential to use sharp cutting instruments for all pruning, cutting-back, trimming or clipping.

Tools and their use

It pays to buy the best quality tools you can afford. Cheap ones will almost certainly have cutting blades of inferior material. Considerable damage can be done by blunt cutting edges, and the work becomes much harder. All tools should be kept clean, well-oiled and rust-free so as to be ready to do the best job when required.

Never over-strain a tool by trying to make it do more than the tasks for which it is designed. This particularly applies to secateurs. It is tempting to save a journey back to the shed to collect a saw or the loppers in order to cut one thick branch when the secateurs have managed all others. So the secateurs are opened wide, and all the strength of both hands applied to wrench back and forth until the branch falls away with a bruised and jagged cut. These secateurs will probably never again be capable of a true, clean cut. Going up a scale, loppers can suffer the same way if used too roughly.

Pruning cuts

Where possible when using pruning saws or loppers, the outward end of the branch to be cut should be supported to avoid tearing of the bark at the cutting point just before the cut is completed.

All cuts should be cleaned up with a sharp pruning knife, and, where the branches cut are of suitable diameter, they should be painted over with a proprietary sealing compound, which will help to keep out damp and frost, and protect against harmful organisms.

Where possible, all cuts should be made at an angle to the horizontal, so as to form a water-shed so no water remains on bare wood to start up any rot.

Pruning cuts on shrubs and trees should always be just above a bud and sloping away from it, or, in the case where there is a pair of buds opposite each other, then the cut should slope sideways to avoid water shedding off into the buds. Cuts should never be made too close to the buds (the bud will be damaged), nor too far above as the resulting stump will almost certainly die back.

When to prune, what to prune

Many people are frightened of pruning their shrubs or trees, because they are afraid of damaging or even killing them. The fact is that pruning is essential for many plants in the garden. It keeps them within a certain area and it can help in the production of flowers and decorative foliage. In the case of the red- or yellow-stemmed dogwoods and some coloured-stemmed willows, hard pruning or cutting back of about one third of the stems every year keeps the wood young and at its most colourful.

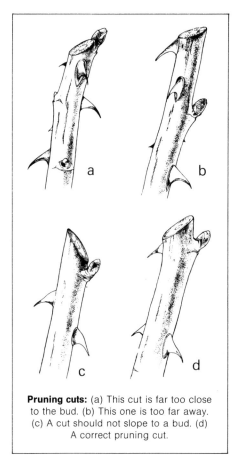

Pruning cuts: (a) This cut is far too close to the bud. (b) This one is too far away. (c) A cut should not slope to a bud. (d) A correct pruning cut.

The difference between pruning and cutting back is that whereas pruning is a surgical operation done with the intention of benefiting the plant, cutting-back is carried out to achieve a size or a shape that suits the gardener. Weak, dead or damaged stems should be pruned out, as should any over-abundance of twiggery. If this is done the chances of fungal and insect problems are likely to be considerably reduced, not only by the reduction of branches on which these problems can occur, but by increasing the circulation of air around those that remain.

The strict theory of pruning is fairly complicated, as it affects the length of a plant's life, season of flowering and whether, in fact, the plant will flower at all. For instance, pruning of spring- or early summer-flowering plants should be carried out immediately after flowering. If left to the autumn much, if not all, of the initiating flower buds will be destroyed. These may not be visible to the eye, but are nevertheless forming within the plant.

However, some plants definitely need pruning or cutting back. The butterfly bush (*Buddleia davidii*) is a good example

as it puts on so much growth each season, which is unattractive if left standing in the winter months. The long flowering stems of the previous summer may be cut back to just above a pair of buds near the base of the plant at any time during late autumn, winter or spring. The earlier the better if the unsightly branches are not to cause a blemish on the beauty of your winter garden, but any time during the dormant season will do. A later flowering season than normal can be manipulated simply by leaving the pruning until late spring, well after the plant has started into strong growth. This may be useful if the buddleia is required to blend with, say, Michaelmas daisies round its base.

Winter pruning may be done on any shrub that flowers on new growth in summer or autumn just so long as it is sufficiently hardy. With caryopteris, fuchsias and other plants where hardiness is in doubt, pruning is best left until the spring, judging each season as it comes. The old flower heads and branches give a measure of protection to new growth.

Other shrubs that are best tackled in the winter when the leaves are off and you can see what you are doing, are deutzias, philadelphus, weigelas, early-flowering spiraeas and the beauty bush (*Kolkwitzia amabilis*).

Wall shrubs

Choosing a shrub to train against a wall requires a fair amount of thought. Don't rush into purchasing any plant that takes your fancy. It is important to know something of the potential growth of the plant and, if hard pruning is going to be required to keep it within a restricted area, what damage is going to be done to its flowering potential. Pyracanthas, for instance, often surprise people by the amount of growth they can produce each season, and, if the longest flowering life span is to be achieved, there must be enough space to avoid the need for drastic cutting at least for some years.

An evergreen ceanothus also makes an excellent wall shrub. There are two important facts to remember regarding pruning. Never cut beyond the base of the previous season's growth as ceanothus, as well as a number of other plants, do not readily break from older wood. Always prune immediately after flowering, for if it is left until the autumn thousands of next season's potential flowers will be destroyed. There are no

Contrast in foliage colours from shrubs and conifers. (Garden designed by Kathleen Chattaway.)

berries to consider so there is no reason to delay the task.

Neglected plants

If you are faced with overgrown and tangled shrubs in a negelected garden there are two alternatives. Dig out the offending tangle and start again with new plants, or prune right back to the main stems, removing all but the best young shoots which emanate from a reasonably low level. This somewhat drastic treatment does not suit all shrubs. An overgrown Spanish broom (*Spartium junceum*) for instance could succumb to grey mould (*Botrytis*). It would be much simpler and better to replace with a young plant.

Hedges

The pruning of hedges is normally referred to as clipping or trimming with shears or an electric hedge trimmer.

While these are excellent tools for use on many, or perhaps even most, hedging plants, they are not the ideal tool for pruning larger leaved hedging plants, such as laurel or holly. These are better

pruned with sharp secateurs, as shears tend to damage a lot of leaves making the hedge unsightly.

There are rules that should be applied to the clipping of even the simplest of hedges. Some, such as beech and hornbeam, should not be cut at all for the first two years after planting, while most

Large-leaved hedging plants are best pruned with secateurs as shears tend to damage a lot of leaves.

other deciduous hedges are best cut back hard to about 30 cm (1 ft) in their first spring. Privets and *Lonicera nitida*, require the same treatment.

The Leyland cypress, × *Cupressocyparis leylandii*, or the golden 'Castlewellan', are among the best conifers for hedging. Growing at a rate of approximately 75 cm ($2\frac{1}{2}$ ft) per year they form an excellent thick, sound absorbing screen when stopped at not less than 1.8 m (6 ft).

Clipping should be done twice a year in spring and late summer. For the thickest and most beautiful screen, the ends of *all* branches should be tipped during the year after planting. This must include those growing lengthways as well as those growing out from the line of the hedge, and will have the effect of thickening the growth. It should be repeated until the individual plants have knitted together, after which the hedge is trimmed twice a year along its sides and top in the usual manner.

Hedges should be trained from an early age so that they are narrower at the top than at the base. The reverse must never be allowed to occur, or browning off of the bottom growth may be the result.

All hedges should be shaped so as to be rather narrower across at the top than at their base. The reverse must never be allowed to occur, or browning off of the bottom growths will probably result.

Topiary is a specialized form of hedging where specific shapes are the end result. Peacocks, globes, spirals, or even more ambitious projects can be brought to rewarding fruition by careful and patient clipping. The best subjects for this treatment are box and yew.

Propagation

There is a great deal of satisfaction to be had from raising your own plants, for it is both calming and an exciting challenge. You can also save yourself some money. Although not all plants are easy to propagate, most can be increased quite simply and quickly.

There are two main methods of increasing plants. The first is from seeds or, in the case of ferns, spores. The second is by vegetative means of which there are several methods.

Seed

This is, in theory, possible for all plants, but the resultant seedlings are not identically true to the form of either parent; each one has its own genetic character. This difference is minimal, and of no concern in the species, but is not acceptable for the perpetuation of cultivars or hybrids.

For the successful germination of seed and the raising of seedlings, there are three essential basic requirements – warmth, air and moisture. Failure to provide any one of these can result in failure, as can too much moisture or too high a temperature.

Care should be taken in the selection of seed compost. John Innes composts are still popular and reputable brands bearing the John Innes symbol of approval may be used with great success. There are also many peat-based or soil-less composts which are also very good. These universal or seed and potting composts are suitable for most purposes, pricking-out and potting-on, as well as seed sowing, whereas with the John Innes there are four separate strengths for different uses, including sowing seed. The main disadvantage with the peat-based compost is that if allowed to get too dry it becomes difficult to re-wet.

Seed of plants from cold or temperate climates can be sown outdoors in prepared seedbeds. Some hardcoated seed require a period of freezing to break their dormancy, and such conditions are provided by sowing outdoors in autumn. Soaking for two or three days in warm water will help to soften hard seed covers. Seeds of plants from warmer climates must be sown in warmth. The seed compost should be about 15–20°C (60–68°F) and this is best provided by thermostatically controlled electric soil-heating cables set at about 27°C (80°F).

Seeds should always be sown in previously moistened compost. Sow thinly, as overcrowding will result in spindly weak seedlings. As a general rule, seeds should be covered to approximately twice their own depth with moist compost, although the finest seed is best left uncovered.

Seed sown in trays of seed compost should be stood on a bench or in a propagator if heat is required. Cover the trays with a sheet of glass and some sheets of newspaper, or something similar until germination. The glass avoids moisture loss, and the paper keeps seed in the dark and slows down evaporation. The paper must be removed at the first sign of·

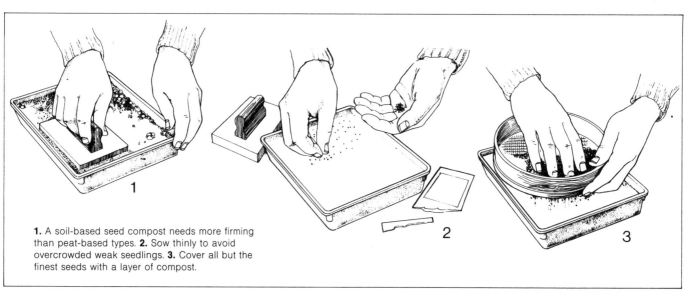

1. A soil-based seed compost needs more firming than peat-based types. 2. Sow thinly to avoid overcrowded weak seedlings. 3. Cover all but the finest seeds with a layer of compost.

germination. The glass should be slightly raised at one side on germination and taken off completely after a few days. When the seedlings are large enough to handle they can be pricked out into small individual pots.

Vegetative propagation

The most commonly used method of vegetative propagation is by means of cuttings. This entails the removal from the plant of sections of stems or roots, or in some cases leaves or buds. Eventually they will grow into a new plant identical in all respects to their parent.

Cuttings

Certain conditions apply to all kinds of cuttings. For successful rooting, there must be sufficient moisture, warmth, light and air. The rooting medium must, therefore, be moisture-retentive, and yet well enough drained to ensure the free passage of air. It must also be free of pests and diseases. John Innes seed compost is suitable. Other good rooting mediums consist of equal parts by volume of coarse (*not* builders') sand and peat, or peat and vermiculite.

If taken at the right time, cuttings will usually root fairly readily, but, for extra security, rooting hormones may be used. They are readily obtainable as a liquid dip, or as a powder from garden centres, and must be used in accordance with the manufacturers' instructions.

For the majority of hardy garden plants, cuttings of semi-ripe growth taken during summer can be induced to root in an unheated greenhouse or cold frame. Hardwood cuttings taken in the autumn need only a sheltered site in the open, but leaf or bud cuttings, and cuttings taken in the winter months from actively growing plants, require in addition the assistance of some artificially provided heat. A temperature of 13–18°C (55–64°F) is generally sufficient, though some subjects may require more. This can be provided in a frame or greenhouse by soil-warming cables or, for a few cuttings, by a small electric propagator. Whichever the case, a high humidity should be maintained using glass or plastic covers. This is necessary in order to provide the close moist conditions that will reduce transpiration (water loss through the leaves). It is also beneficial to spray the cuttings with tepid water occasionally.

Softwood cuttings These are taken from immature shoot tips, and on outdoor plants are best removed in early to mid-summer. Short, non-flowering sideshoots about 5–10 cm (2–4 in) long are best. They must be rooted under warm conditions in a frame or propagator. When the selected shoots have been severed from the plant, they should be cut cleanly with a sharp knife or razor blade just below a node. These, termed nodal cuttings, are generally considered to root most easily, but in some cases, such as clematis, it is preferable to cut between the nodes, that is inter-nodally.

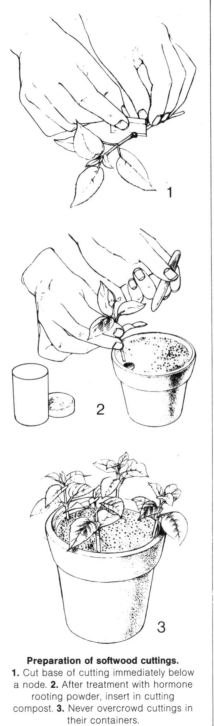

Preparation of softwood cuttings.
1. Cut base of cutting immediately below a node. **2.** After treatment with hormone rooting powder, insert in cutting compost. **3.** Never overcrowd cuttings in their containers.

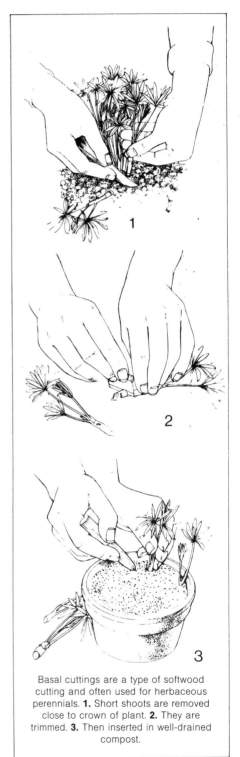

Basal cuttings are a type of softwood cutting and often used for herbaceous perennials. **1.** Short shoots are removed close to crown of plant. **2.** They are trimmed. **3.** Then inserted in well-drained compost.

Semi-ripe cuttings are longer than softwoods and often removed with a heel of older wood attached.

Semi-ripe cuttings These are taken from midsummer to early autumn and require no heat. But, while some might root successfully in the open, most need the protection of a cold frame or cloche. This is the method best suited for increasing deciduous and evergreen shrubs, and for many conifers.

Semi-ripe cuttings take longer to root than softwood ones, so, since they will use up more of their own food reserves, they should be about 10–15 cm (4–6 in) long. Leaves should be removed from the lower half which is to be inserted in the rooting medium, but left on the top half.

Hardwood cuttings These afford the easiest method of propagation for shrubs

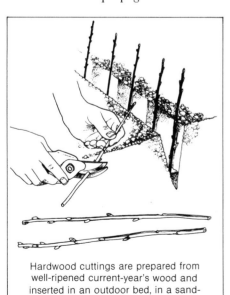

Hardwood cuttings are prepared from well-ripened current-year's wood and inserted in an outdoor bed, in a sand-lined slit trench. Firm them well in.

and trees. They are taken from mid-autumn through winter, and inserted in a sheltered bed outdoors. Rooting takes even more time than semi-ripe cuttings, and the cuttings should be 20–38 cm (8–15 in). In many cases they root more successfully if taken with a heel of older wood (a strip of the main stem that remains when a side shoot is pulled away). If the tip is soft and unripened it should be removed just above a bud using a sharp knife.

Propagation of conifers
Cuttings are the most commonly used method of propagating conifers, as cultivars do not come true from seed. Cuttings of most species are not difficult to strike, but it is difficult to get good results from cultivars of *Cedrus*, *Cupressus*, *Pinus* and *Pseudotsuga*. These must be increased either by seed or by grafting.

Hardwood cuttings The simplest method is to take these in late autumn. The length will vary from 10–25 cm (4–10 in) according to species. Cuttings should be of firm wood of the current season's growth, taken with a 'heel'.

Most conifers pose a problem to propagation by reason of their high resin content inhibiting rooting. For this reason, it is better to take cuttings from young established plants rather than old trees. Some of the resin that appears at the base of the cutting may be removed by immersing for a few minutes in luke-warm water, about 38°C (100°F).

Remove the lower leaves as you would for any evergreen plant and use a rooting hormone, either powder or liquid. The cuttings should then be inserted into a clay pot or seed tray containing equal parts by volume of peat and sharp sand, and well firmed in. Place in a light situation, but not in direct sunlight, in a cold frame or outside covered with a sheet of glass to reduce transpiration.

Some cuttings may have rooted by the following spring, while others may take as long as two years.

Semi-ripe cuttings These are taken in summer. Shoot tips of the current year's growth are taken 5–15 cm (2–6 in) long. Cut from just beneath a bud and remove the bottom leaves. After dipping in rooting hormone, liquid or powder, they should be inserted into a cutting medium consisting of a peat and sharp sand mix,

roughly equal parts by volume, or a peat and vermiculite mix.

Place cuttings in a greenhouse or cold frame and if possible supply some bottom heat by means of electric soil-warming cables laid in sand or use an electrically heated propagator. A temperature of 18°C (65°F) is sufficient, and this may well be equalled or exceeded by nature in a reasonable summer.

Conifer cuttings tend to dry out very quickly. Therefore cover the cuttings with the lid of the propagator, sheets of glass, clear polythene, or ideally, if intended production merits the expense, use a mist propagator. The latter will certainly lead to greater percentage success, and considerably quicker rooting.

Rooting should take place before winter sets in. As soon as a root system has formed pot up separately, protect from frost for the winter months, and then either plant out into a nursery bed or pot on into containers and place outside in late spring, to grow on to planting size.

Root cuttings
This method is used for propagating many herbaceous plants and some shrubs that have fleshy roots. They are taken during the dormant period in autumn or winter. If only a small quantity are needed they can, with care, be taken from

Thin root cuttings are best laid on the surface of compost in a seed tray, and then covered with a thin layer of compost. Insert thick cuttings vertically.

the plant *in situ*, but generally they are taken from lifted plants. While the thickness of root will vary from one plant type to another, cuttings of woody plants, and of thick fleshy-rooted shrubs should be about $\frac{1}{2}$–1 cm ($\frac{1}{4}$–$\frac{1}{2}$ in) in thickness, and 5–15 cm (2–6 in) in length. They are prepared by making a horizontal cut at the top and a diagonal one at the bottom. They are then inserted, sloping cut downwards, either in open ground or in pots or trays in a compost made up of equal parts by volume of peat, coarse sand and loam.

Some herbaceous perennials, for example border phlox, with thinner roots may also be increased readily by root cuttings. In these cases, cuttings about 8–10 cm (3–4 in) are taken and laid horizontally in trays of rooting medium and covered by 1 cm ($\frac{1}{2}$ in) of sand.

Layering

This is a method whereby a stem, while remaining attached to a plant, is encouraged to produce roots. It has several advantages, not least of which is that it more-or-less looks after itself until rooted, being supplied with nutrients and water from the parent plant. Also, as a layered shoot is usually considerably larger than a cutting, a larger plant is achieved in a shorter time. However, these advantages only really apply where very few new plants are required, as the actual time needed for individual preparation is much greater than for cuttings.

This is the best and simplest method for all rhododendron cultivars, including the azaleas. Dig out a shallow hole and fill it with a mixture of peat, sand and leafmould. Choose a young, low-growing branch. It should be fastened to a short stake with raffia or twine and pegged down where it passes through the trench. If the stem is split lengthwise where it is buried, rooting will be hastened. Never allow the rooting area to become too dry.

Stooling

This is another method of branch rooting similar to layering. The shrub to be increased is cut down to just above ground level, and covered with humus-rich soil, so only the tips show. The shoots eventually produce roots, and later they can be separated from the parent and planted in their new situation. It is a popular method of increasing heathers, pinks and border carnations.

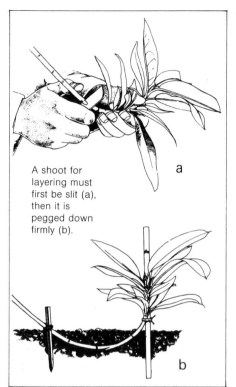

A shoot for layering must first be slit (a), then it is pegged down firmly (b).

Division

This is a much used method for increasing herbaceous perennials. It entails lifting a clump of plants with care and separating out individual or small groups of growing points, each with a root or two attached. Division can be carried out anytime between late autumn and the onset of spring. The lifted clumps can either be teased apart by hand or cut into small pieces with a knife or spade. The old central portion should be discarded and the outer parts planted out in their growing positions.

Grafting

This last method is one not normally of interest to the amateur gardener. A portion of the plant to be increased is grafted on to a suitable rootstock, and this method is used by commercial nurserymen in a variety of ways, from the **budding** of roses to the grafting of fruit and ornamental trees. It is a complex subject and beyond the scope of this book.

Plants can be divided by pulling them apart (a) or by cutting them (b).

Divisions must have plenty of roots (c) and should be replanted immediately (d) and well firmed in (e).

Directory of Plants

In this section the plants are listed under their full botanical names. Then follows the name of the family to which the plant belongs. If the plant has one, the common or colloquial name follows. The zone numbers come next, together with an indication of the type of plant (in other words, shrub; herbaceous perennial, conifer, etc.).

It is important that both sections of the book are used together. Consult either the plant selection charts first, or this plant directory, but always use the two together to enable you to choose quickly exactly the right plant for a specific situation or a set of requirements.

Those who are not familiar with many garden plants will find the illustrations invaluable as an aid to plant selection. Most, but not all, of the hundreds of plants described here are illustrated.

The descriptions of the plants are necessarily brief due to the very large number of plants included in this book, but nevertheless they give all the information that is needed.

Heights of plants are given in every instance, in both metric and imperial. There are descriptions of flowers, and in every instance flowering time is stated. As appropriate there are descriptions of berries, cones and fruits.

Foliage details for every plant include colour and shape, and whether it is evergreen (holds its leaves all the year round) or deciduous (loses them in the autumn). Autumn leaf colour is described where appropriate.

The best position for each plant is recommended – for instance, sun, shade, shelter and so on. Included are soil requirements, and you will see that many plants tolerate a wide range of soils.

The habit of the plant follows. This refers mainly to the shape of the plant.

The method (or methods) of propagation is given for each plant, together with the best time of the year. Pruning details, too, are given, if applicable. Remember that more detail on soils, propagation, pruning, planting and so on can be found in the 'Guidelines for Successful Growing'.

Further useful tips and hints are given under most entries, such as suggested uses of plants, and suggestions for plant associations. Plus any further noteworthy characteristics or habits.

A traditional herbaceous border in mid-summer, featuring delphiniums.

Abelia floribunda
Caprifoliaceae
ZONES 9–10   SHRUB
Height: 1.8–2.5 m (6–8 ft), **Flowers:** bright carmine-red, late spring – mid-summer, **Foliage:** mid-green, evergreen, **Position:** wall shelter even in mild areas, **Soil:** suits most soil, **Habit:** rounded, bushy, **Propagation:** cuttings in mid-summer from current season's growth.
□ A very bright and attractive, free-flowering shrub if you have a cosy enough position against a south-facing wall. Cut out very old stems after flowering.

Abelia × *grandiflora*
Caprifoliaceae
ZONES 7–10   SHRUB
Height: 1.8–2.5 m (6–8 ft), **Flowers:** pinkish white, slightly scented, mid-summer – mid-autumn, **Foliage:** bright green, semi-evergreen, **Position:** sunny, protect from cold winds, **Soil:** suits most soils, **Habit:** rounded, bushy, **Propagation:** cuttings in mid-summer from current season's wood.
□ Looks well in association with golden foliage shrubs and, for flower contrast, with *Ceratostigma willmottianum* or *Caryopteris* × *clandonensis*. Cut out very old stems after flowering.

Right: *Abelia floribunda*

Abelia × *grandiflora* 'Francis Mason'
Caprifoliaceae
ZONES 7–10   SHRUB
Height: 1.8–2.5 m (6–8 ft), **Flowers:** pinkish white, slightly scented, mid-summer – mid-autumn, **Foliage:** variegated with light golden green, semi-evergreen, **Position:** sunny, protect from cold winds, **Soil:** most soils, **Habit:** rounded, bushy, **Propagation:** cuttings in mid-summer from the current season's wood.
□ Well partnered by red-purple-leaved shrubs or foliage of *Berberis darwinii*. Cut out old stems after flowering.

Abelia schumannii
Caprifoliaceae
ZONES 8–10   SHRUB
Height: 3 m (10 ft), **Flowers:** pink, early summer – early autumn, **Foliage:** dark green, deciduous, **Position:** sunny, sheltered from cold winds, **Soil:** most soils, **Habit:** bushy, **Propagation:** cuttings in mid-summer from previous season's wood.
□ Somewhat delicate and tips may be damaged by frosts, but the shrub is not generally killed. Cut out very old stems in late winter.

Abeliophyllum distichum
Oleaceae
ZONES 7–10   SHRUB
Height: 1 m (3 ft), **Flowers:** white, tinted with pink, fragrant, late winter – early spring, **Foliage:** green, deciduous, **Position:** sunny, better with wall protection in cold districts, **Soil:** any reasonable, well drained soil, **Habit:** elegant growth, erect shoots, slow grower, **Propagation:** cuttings or layering.
□ Prune back fairly hard after flowering. Looks good planted with garrya.

Top left: *Abies balsamea* 'Hudsonia'
Top right: *Abies pinsapo* 'Glauca'
Below: *Abies lasiocarpa* 'Compacta'

Abies balsamea 'Hudsonia'
Pinaceae Silver Fir
ZONES 3–9   CONIFER
Height: 30 cm (1 ft), **Spread:** 45 cm (1½ ft) after 10 years. Eventually attains 90 cm (3 ft) in height, **Flowers:** and cones: of no particular decorative merit, **Foliage:** shiny green with two greyish-white bands underneath, evergreen, **Position:** sun or partial shade avoiding exposed situations, **Soil:** a slightly acid soil preferred, moist, but well-drained, **Habit:** a flattish topped, spreading bush, **Propagation:** by grafting in spring.
☐ Useful for rock or heather garden.

Abies koreana
Pinaceae Silver fir, Korean fir
ZONES 5–9   CONIFER
Height: 1.8 m (6 ft) after 10 years, eventually attains 15 m (50 ft), **Cones:** bright purple/blue, produced at an early age, **Foliage:** shiny green above, whitish below, evergreen, **Position:** sun or partial shade, **Soil:** a deep, slightly acid soil preferred, moist but well-drained, **Habit:** conical, **Propagation:** seed sown in spring.
☐ Makes a good lawn specimen in large gardens.

Abies lasiocarpa 'Arizonica'
Pinaceae Cork fir
ZONES 5–9   CONIFER
Height: 4 m (13 ft) after 10 years, eventual height 15 m (50 ft), **Flowers:** purple or violet-blue, spring, not significant, followed by purple cones, **Foliage:** silver-grey, evergreen, **Position:** sun or partial shade, **Soil:** a deep, moist but well-drained, slightly acid soil preferred, **Habit:** conical, **Propagation:** by seed sown in spring.
☐ Maintain a single dominant leading shoot. Lawn specimen for large garden.

Abies lasiocarpa 'Compacta'
Pinaceae Silver fox
ZONES 5–9   CONIFER
Height: 60 cm (2 ft) after 10 years, eventually attains 2.4 m (8 ft), **Cones:** purple when young, cylindrical, **Foliage:** blue-grey, very attractive in spring and early summer, evergreen, **Position:** sun or partial shade, **Soil:** a well-drained but moist slightly acid soil preferred, **Habit:** dense compact and irregularly conical, **Propagation:** by grafting in spring.
☐ Useful conifer for heather gardens.

Abies pinsapo 'Glauca'
Pinaceae Spanish fir
ZONES 6–9   CONIFER
Height: 1.8–2.5 m (6–8 ft) after 10 years. Eventually attains 24 m (80 ft), **Cones:** cylindrical, **Foliage:** distictive blue-grey, radially arranged, evergreen, **Position:** sun or partial shade, **Soil:** a deep, moist but well-drained, slightly acid soil preferred, but also lime tolerant, **Habit:** pyramidal, **Propagation:** by grafting in spring.
☐ Ensure a single dominant leading shoot. Often used as a lawn specimen in large gardens.

Abies procera 'Glauca'
(**syn. *A. nobilis***)
Pinaceae Noble fir
ZONES 6–9   CONIFER
Height: 2.5–3 m (8–10 ft) after 10 years. Eventually attains 24 m (80 ft), **Cones:** brown, upright and cylindrical, large, **Foliage:** blue-grey, evergreen, **Position:** sun or partial shade, **Soil:** a deep, moist but well-drained, slightly acid soil preferred, **Habit:** slender and conical, **Propagation:** best raised by grafting in spring.
☐ This Abies is ultimately rather too large for most gardens.

Abutilon vitifolium
Malvaceae
Zones 8–9   Shrub
Height: 2.5 m (8–12 ft), **Flowers:** pinkish mauve, early summer – early autumn, **Foliage:** mid-green covered with short white hairs, semi-evergreen, **Position:** sunny, with wall protection, **Soil:** any reasonably well-drained soil, **Habit:** bushy in mild climates, elsewhere less branched, **Propagation:** seed sown in spring.
☐ Somewhat delicate and will only reach full height in warm, sheltered positions. In other areas may be short lived.

Acacia dealbata
Leguminosae   Silver wattle, mimosa
Zones 9–10   Tree
Height: 4.5–7.5 m (15–25 ft), **Flowers:** yellow, fragrant, borne in long sprays, mid – late spring, **Foliage:** greyish, feathery or fernlike, evergreen, **Position:** sunny and sheltered, suitable for warmer districts only, **Soil:** preferably slightly acid, **Habit:** quick-growing, spreading tree, **Propagation:** seeds sown in mid-spring in seed compost at 16°C (61°F).
☐ If plant becomes too tall, cut it back when flowering is over.

Acaena microphylla
Rosaceae   New Zealand burr
Zones 5–10   Rock plant
Height: 2–5 cm (1–2 in), **Flowers:** insignificant, but followed by attractive crimson burrs or seed heads, **Foliage:** bronze-green, ferny, deciduous, **Position:** full sun, **Soil:** well-drained, **Habit:** ground cover spreading to 60 cm (2 ft), excellent for planting in paving, **Propagation:** seeds sown early autumn – early spring, or by dividing and replanting early autumn – early spring.

Acanthus mollis var. *latifolius*
Acanthaceae   Bear's breeches
Zones 6–10   Herbaceous perennial
Height: 1 m (3 ft), **Flowers:** white and purple on 45 cm (18 in) long stems, summer, **Foliage:** mid green, glossy, large and spectacular, deciduous, **Position:** sun or partial shade, **Soil:** well-drained, **Habit:** striking perennial, upright flower spikes and ornamental foliage, a good companion for purple-foliage shrubs or shrub roses, **Propagation:** root cuttings in winter; seeds sown in light compost in spring; or by division in spring or autumn.

Acanthus spinosus
Acanthaceae   Bear's breeches
Zones 7–10   Herbaceous perennial
Height: 90–120 cm (3–4 ft), **Flowers:** white and purple, carried on 45 cm (18 in) spikes, summer, **Foliage:** spiny, deeply cut, dark green, deciduous, **Position:** sun or partial shade, **Soil:** any reasonably well-drained soil, **Habit:** striking perennial with upright flower spikes and ornamental foliage, excellent companion for shrubs, **Propagation:** root cuttings in winter; seeds sown in light compost in spring; or by division in spring or autumn.

Left: Handsome spikes of *Acanthus spinosus*

Acer griseum
Aceraceae   Paperbark maple
ZONES 5–9   TREE
Height: about 6 m (20 ft), **Flowers:** insignificant, **Foliage:** green, trifoliate, brilliant scarlet and crimson colour in autumn, deciduous, **Position:** sun or partial shade, sheltered, **Soil:** well-drained but moisture-retentive, **Habit:** upright branched tree, narrowish domed head, **Propagation:** seeds sown in mid-autumn in a garden frame, or, where possible, by layering in autumn.
☐ Very attractive russet-coloured peeling bark gives interest throughout the year, especially in winter. Underplant with winter-flowering heathers.

Acer japonicum
Aceraceae   Downy Japanese maple
ZONES 5–9   TREE
Height: 4.5–6 m (15–20 ft), **Flowers:** insignificant, **Foliage:** pale green, lobed, colour brilliant crimson in autumn, deciduous, **Position:** sun or dappled shade, sheltered, **Soil:** cool, moist, well drained, neutral or slightly acid, **Habit:** slow growing tree, bushy habit, **Propagation:** seed sown in mid-autumn in a garden frame.
☐ An excellent companion plant is pampas grass (cortaderia).

Acer negundo 'Variegatum'
Aceraceae   Variegated box elder
ZONES 5–8   TREE
Height: about 6 m (20 ft), **Flowers:** insignificant, **Foliage:** white and green variegated pinnate leaves, deciduous, **Position:** sun or partial shade, **Soil:** well-drained but moisture-retentive, **Habit:** spreading, rounded head, **Propagation:** grafting.
☐ Popular specimen tree, ideal for town gardens.

Acer palmatum 'Atropurpureum'
Aceraceae   Japanese maple
ZONES 5–9   SHRUB
Height: 6 m (20 ft), **Flowers:** yellow, insignificant, early summer, **Foliage:** reddish bronze, deciduous, **Position:** sun or dappled shade, protect from wind, **Soil:** humus rich, reasonably lime tolerant, **Habit:** upright rounded , ultimately tree-like, growth is slow, **Propagation:** layering or grafting.
☐ This beautiful shrub will grow in partial shade, but its colour will be enhanced in full sun provided shelter against wind is given. Try an underplanting of hostas for contrast in foliage shape and colour.

Acer palmatum 'Dissectum Atropurpureum'
Aceraceae   Japanese maple
ZONES 5–9   SHRUB
Height: 3 m (10 ft), **Flowers:** yellow, insignificant, early summer, **Foliage:** reddish bronze, finely cut, deciduous, **Position:** sun or partial shade, protect from wind, **Soil:** humus-rich, neutral or slightly acid, **Habit:** low spreading bush, **Propagation:** layering or grafting.
☐ Associates well with evergreen azaleas and golden callunas. *Choisya ternata* 'Sundance' will make a lovely partner.

Acer palmatum 'Dissectum Viridis'
Aceraceae   Japanese maple
ZONES 5–9   SHRUB
Height: 3 m (10 ft), **Flowers:** yellow, not significant, early summer, **Foliage:** bright green turning yellow and orange in autumn, deciduous, **Position:** sun or partial shade, protect from wind, **Soil:** humus-rich, neutral or slightly acid, **Habit:** low spreading bush, **Propagation:** layering or grafting.
☐ Good companion for evergreen azaleas.

Top left: *Acer griseum* **Top right:** *Acer palmatum* 'Dissectum Atropurpureum'
Above: *Acer japonicum*

Acer palmatum 'Heptalobum Osakazuki'
Aceraceae   Japanese maple
ZONES 5–9   SHRUB
Height: 6 m (20 ft), **Flowers:** yellow, insignificant, early summer, **Foliage:** medium green, magnificent autumn colour, deciduous, **Position:** sun or partial shade, protect from wind, **Soil:** humus-rich, neutral or slightly acid, **Habit:** upright rounded, shrub or small tree, **Propagation:** layering.
☐ The leaves of the Heptalobum group of Japanese maples are larger than those of the species and usually seven-lobed.
☐ Try pampas grass (cortaderia) as a companion for this maple.

Acer platanoides 'Crimson King'
Aceraceae   Purple-leafed Norway maple
ZONES 5–9   TREE
Height: 9–12 m (30–40 ft), **Flowers:** yellow, small but attractive, spring, **Foliage:** intense purple – crimson, deciduous, **Position:** sun or partial shade, tolerant of atmospheric pollution, **Soil:** moist, tolerates chalk soils, **Habit:** broad headed, **Propagation:** grafting or layering.
☐ Looks well with golden-foliage shrubs or *Robinia pseudoacacia* 'Frisia' as a partner.

Acer platanoides 'Drummondii'
Aceraceae   Variegated form of Norway maple
ZONES 5–9   TREE
Height: 9–12 m (30–40 ft), **Flowers:** yellow, inconspicuous, spring, **Foliage:** green with a neat white edge, true maple-leaf shape, deciduous, **Position:** sun or partial shade; tolerant of atmospheric pollution, **Soil:** moist, tolerates chalk soils, **Habit:** broad headed tree, **Propagation:** by grafting or layering.
☐ Useful for lighting up a dark backdrop.

Right: Useful for lighting up a dark backdrop, *Acer platanoides* 'Drummondii'

Achillea filipendulina 'Coronation Gold'
Compositae   Yarrow
ZONES 5–10   HERBACEOUS PERENNIAL
Height: 90–120 cm (3–4 ft), **Flowers:** yellow in flat heads, summer, **Foliage:** medium green, deciduous, **Position:** full sun, **Soil:** any soil which is well-drained, **Habit:** hardy and upright perennial, flowers dry well for indoor decoration, **Propagation:** by dividing and replanting in autumn or spring.
☐ Good companion for delphiniums.

Achillea millefolium 'Cerise Queen'
Compositae   Milfoil
ZONES 5–10   HERBACEOUS PERENNIAL
Height: 60–75 cm (2–2½ ft), **Flowers:** bright red, early – mid-summer, **Foliage:** dark green, deciduous, **Position:** full sun, **Soil:** suits most well-drained soils, **Habit:** hardy and upright perennial, **Propagation:** by dividing and replanting in autumn or spring.
☐ Looks good with silver-foliage perennials.

Achillea ptarmica 'The Pearl'
Compositae   Sneezewort
ZONES 3–10   HERBACEOUS PERENNIAL
Height: 60–75 cm (2–2½ ft), **Flowers:** white, double, in loose clusters, mid-summer – early autumn, **Foliage:** long, medium green notched, deciduous, **Position:** sun, **Soil:** any soil which is well-drained, **Habit:** perennial with upright stems, informal flowers, **Propagation:** by division and replanting in autumn or spring.
☐ Good companion for strong-coloured perennials.

Achillea taygetea 'Moonshine'
Compositae Yarrow
ZONES 5–10   HERBACEOUS PERENNIAL
Height: 60 cm (2 ft), **Flowers:** light yellow, carried in flat heads, early summer – early autumn, **Foliage:** attractively cut, silvery, deciduous, **Position:** full sun, **Soil:** any soil which is well-drained, **Habit:** stiff-stemmed, upright perennial, **Propagation:** by division and replanting in autumn or spring.
☐ Useful cut flower. Delphiniums make good companions.

Achillea tomentosa
Compositae 'Alpine yarrow'
ZONES 5–9   ROCK PLANT
Height: 15 cm (6 in), **Flowers:** yellow, in flat heads, mid-summer – early autumn, **Foliage:** greyish, finely divided, deciduous, **Position:** full sun, **Soil:** poor, well-drained, **Habit:** forms a prostrate mat spreading to 30 cm (1 ft); **Propagation:** divide clumps in spring.
☐ Grown on rock garden, in paving or at edge of border.

Aconitum × arendsii
Ranunculaceae Monkshood
ZONES 3–9   HERBACEOUS PERENNIAL
Height: 1.2 m (4 ft), **Flowers:** brilliant blue, hooded, in loose spikes, late summer – mid-autumn, **Foliage:** mid green, deeply cut, deciduous, **Position:** partial shade, ideal for planting under trees, **Soil:** humus-rich, moisture-retentive, **Habit:** strong growing perennial, sturdy and upright, needs no support, **Propagation:** divide clumps in autumn or spring.
☐ Every part of this plant is poisonous.

Aconitum fischeri
Ranunculaceae Monkshood
ZONES 3–9   HERBACEOUS PERENNIAL
Height: 1 m (3 ft), **Flowers:** deep-blue, hooded, in racemes, late summer – early autumn, **Foliage:** deep green, shiny, deep cut, deciduous, **Position:** partial shade, ideal for planting under trees, **Soil:** humus-rich, moisture-retentive, **Habit:** strong-growing perennial, sturdy and upright, needs no support, **Propagation:** divide clumps in autumn or spring.
☐ Every part of this plant is poisonous.

Aconitum napellus 'Bressingham Spire'
Ranunculaceae Monkshood
ZONES 3–9   HERBACEOUS PERENNIAL
Height: 1 m (3 ft), **Flowers:** deep-blue, in bold spikes, mid – late summer, **Foliage:** deep green, ferny, deciduous, **Position:** partial shade, ideal for planting under trees, **Soil:** any humus-rich, moisture-retentive soil, **Habit:** strong-growing perennial, sturdy and upright, needs no support, **Propagation:** divide clumps in autumn or spring.
☐ Every part of this plant is poisonous.

Left: *Aconitum napellus* 'Bressingham Spire'

Actaea alba
(syn. *A. pachypoda*)
Ranunculaceae Baneberry
ZONES 5–9   ROCK PLANT
Height: 45 cm (18 in), **Flowers:** white, in loose spikes, late spring – early summer, followed by white berries on red stalks, **Foliage:** golden green, deciduous, **Position:** partial or full shade, **Soil:** humus-rich, **Habit:** bushy, needs no support, **Propagation:** by seeds sown in spring; or by division in autumn or spring.
□ Very attractive foliage plant for the rock garden. Good for cutting.

Actinidia kolomikta
Actinidiaceae Kolomikta vine
ZONES 4–10   CLIMBER
Height: 2.5–4 m (8–13 ft), **Flowers:** white, rounded, slightly fragrant, yellow fruits (on female plants), **Foliage:** deep green, marked with white and pink at tip end, deciduous, **Position:** south-facing wall, full sun, **Soil:** well-drained, humus-rich and lime-free, **Habit:** hardy twining climber, **Propagation:** by seed sown in garden frame in autumn; or by cuttings of half-ripe shoots in sand and peat mix in a garden frame in summer.
□ Thin out old stems in late winter.

Adonis vernalis
Ranunculaceae
ZONES 7–9   ROCK PLANT
Height: 15–30 cm (6–12 in), **Flowers:** yellow, mid – late spring, **Foliage:** green ferny, deciduous, **Position:** sun or partial shade, **Soil:** well-drained, moisture-retentive, plenty of humus, **Habit:** rounded and bushy perennial, disappears below ground by mid-summer, **Propagation:** sow seed in early – late summer in seed compost in a garden frame, or by division in early – mid-autumn.
□ Looks attractive when planted with purple aubrieta.

Aethionema 'Warley Rose'
Cruciferae
ZONES 5–9   ROCK PLANT
Height: 10–15 cm (4–6 in), **Flowers:** deep pink, in fat spikes, mid – late spring, **Foliage:** long, thin, greyish, **Position:** sunny, **Soil:** well-drained, **Habit:** forms a dense carpet, **Propagation:** by cuttings of non-flowering growths taken in early – mid-summer.
□ Good for ground cover. Also grow on rock garden or in paving.

Agapanthus 'Headbourne Hybrids'
Liliaceae African lily
ZONES 8–10   HERBACEOUS PERENNIAL
Height: 60–75 cm (2–2½ ft), **Flowers:** blue, in roughly spherical umbels, mid-summer – early autumn, **Foliage:** green, strap-like, generally deciduous outdoors, **Position:** full sun and shelter, not suitable for cold districts, **Soil:** rich, well-drained, moisture-retentive, **Habit:** perennial with upright flower stems, thick, brittle roots, **Propagation:** dividing in mid-spring.
□ Agapanthus are excellent perennials for growing with shrubs. They are also suitable for ornamental containers.

Ajuga pyramidalis
Labiatae Bugle
ZONES 6–10   HERBACEOUS PERENNIAL
Height: 25 cm (10 in), **Flowers:** blue, in short spikes, mid-spring – early summer, **Foliage:** green, generally evergreen, **Position:** sun or partial shade, **Soil:** any moist soil in reasonable condition, **Habit:** perennial, excellent low-growing ground cover, **Propagation:** divide clumps in autumn or spring.
□ A good companion plant is *Lysimachia nummularia* 'Aurea' with golden foliage.

***Ajuga reptans* 'Burgundy Glow'**
Labiatae Bugle
ZONES 6–10   ROCK PLANT
Height: 10 cm (4 in), **Flowers:** pale blue,
in short spikes, late spring – early summer,
Foliage: shades of red, generally ever-
green, **Position:** sun or partial shade,
Soil: any moist soil in reasonable condi-
tion, **Habit:** prostrate and spreading,
Propagation: divide clumps in autumn
or spring.
☐ Good ground cover for a shrub border.

***Ajuga reptans* 'Multicolor'
(syn. 'Rainbow')**
Labiatae Bugle
ZONES 6–10   ROCK PLANT
Height: 10 cm (4 in), **Flowers:** blue, late
spring – early summer, **Foliage:** pink,
yellow and bronzy leaves, evergreen, **Position:** sun or partial shade, **Soil:** moist
soil in reasonable condition, **Habit:** prostrate and spreading; **Propagation:** divide
clumps in autumn or spring.
☐ Good ground cover for a shrub border.

Akebia quinata
Lardizabalaceae
ZONES 4–10   CLIMBER
Height: about 6 m (20 ft), **Flowers:**
scented, reddish purple, mid-spring,
flowers followed by 8 cm (3 in) long purplish fruits, **Foliage:** mid green, comprising five oblong leaflets, semi-evergreen,
Position: sun or shade, **Soil:** suits most
soils, **Habit:** vigorous, hardy, twining,
Propagation: by layering or by cuttings.
☐ Useful climber for growing through old
trees or large shrubs.

Alchemilla mollis
Rosaceae Lady's mantle
ZONES 3–9   HERBACEOUS PERENNIAL
Height: 30–45 cm (1–1½ ft), **Flowers:**
greeny yellow, early – late summer, **Foliage:** pale green, palmate, **Position:** sun
or partial shade, **Soil:** moisture-retentive
yet well-drained, **Habit:** spreading self-
seeding ground cover perennial, **Propagation:** by seeds which readily germinate,
producing masses of self-sown seedlings.
☐ Good for flower arrangements. Excellent for cottage gardens and for ground
cover in shrub borders.

***Alstroemeria aurantiaca* 'Dover
Orange'**
Alstroemeriaceae Peruvian lily
ZONES 9–10   HERBACEOUS PERENNIAL
Height: 1 m (3 ft), **Flowers:** reddish-
orange, lily-like, early summer – early
autumn, **Foliage:** green, grassy, deciduous, **Position:** sun or partial shade, **Soil:**
humus-rich, well-drained, **Habit:** somewhat invasive perennial, excellent cut
flower, **Propagation:** by careful division
of clumps in early or mid-spring; try not to
disturb the roots too much.
☐ Good companions are silver-foliage
perennials like artemisias.

Alyssum montanum
Cruciferae Madwort
ZONES 4–9   ROCK PLANT
Height: 8–10 cm (3–4 in), **Flowers:** yellow, fragrant, late spring – early summer,
Foliage: greyish-green, evergreen, **Position:** plenty of sun needed, **Soil:** well-
drained, preferably alkaline, **Habit:** low
growing, spreading to 30 cm (1 ft), **Propagation:** by seeds sown in early spring and
stood in a garden frame; or by cuttings in
early summer.
☐ Cut back after flowering to keep compact. A good companion for aubrieta.

Alyssum saxatile
Cruciferae   Gold dust
ZONES 4–9   ROCK PLANT
Height: 23–30 cm (9–12 in), **Flowers:**
bright yellow, prolifically mid-spring –
early summer, **Foliage:** greyish – good
background for the flowers, evergreen,
Position: best in full sun, **Soil:** well-
drained, preferably alkaline, **Habit:** compact, free flowering perennial, spreading
to 45 cm (1½ ft), **Propagation:** by seeds
sown in early spring and stood in a garden
frame; or by cuttings in early summer
inserted in mix of peat and sand in a
garden frame.
☐ Cut back after flowering to keep bushy
and promote long life. Associates well with
aubrieta and arabis.

Right: Yellow *Alyssum saxatile* and purple
Aubrieta deltoidia growing over a drystone
wall

Amelanchier lamarckii
Rosaceae   Snowy mespilus, June berry
ZONES 4–9   SHRUB
Height: 5 m (16 ft), **Flowers:** white in
pendulous clusters; mid-spring, **Foliage:**
opening bronze, turning green with glorious autumn tints, deciduous, **Position:**
sun or partial shade, **Soil:** fertile, moisture-retentive, **Habit:** slender upright,
suckering, **Propagation:** seeds, layering
or by separating rooted suckers.
☐ Outstanding at all seasons. Even the
winter twigs are attractive, while the
flowers in spring and autumn foliage colours are truly magnificent. Black edible
fruits are produced.

Anacyclus depressus
Compositae   Mount Atlas daisy
ZONES 5–9   ROCK PLANT
Height: 5 cm (2 in), **Flowers:** pure white,
yellow centred daisies, reddish in bud,
early – late summer, **Foliage:** greyish-
green, ferny, **Position:** full sun essential,
Soil: light, gritty and well drained, **Habit:**
forms a colourful prostrate carpet spreading to about 30 cm (1 ft), **Propagation:**
by seeds sown under glass in autumn; or by
cuttings of non-flowering growth under
glass in spring.
☐ Suitable for rock garden, scree bed or for
gaps in paving.

Anaphalis margaritacea
Compositae   Pearl everlasting
ZONES 5–9   HERBACEOUS PERENNIAL
Height: 30–45 cm (1–1½ ft), **Flowers:**
white in flat heads, late summer, **Foliage:**
greyish-green, evergreen, **Position:** sun or
partial shade, **Soil:** well drained, **Habit:**
erect clump-forming perennial, good cut
flower, **Propagation:** cuttings placed in a
garden frame in spring, or by division in
autumn or spring.
☐ Flowers can be dried, and hold their
colour and texture. Excellent for grouping
with brightly coloured perennials.

Anchusa azurea 'Loddon Royalist' (Syn. *A. italica*)

Boraginaceae Alkanet, bugloss
ZONES 5–10   HERBACEOUS PERENNIAL
Height: 1 m (3 ft), **Flowers:** vivid blue, in large panicles, early – late summer, **Foliage:** medium-green, lanceolate, covered in prickly hairs, deciduous, **Position:** full sun, **Soil:** suits most well-drained soils, **Habit:** clump forming perennial, straggly, branching flower stems, needs support, **Propagation:** division in spring, or by root cuttings in winter.
☐ Dead-head faded flower stems. Plant with oriental poppies or achilleas.

Andromeda polifolia 'Compacta'

Ericaceae Bog rosemary
ZONES 3–9   SHRUB
Height: 30 m (1 ft), **Flowers:** pink, pitcher shaped; late spring – mid-summer, **Foliage:** grey-green, evergreen; autumn tints, **Position:** sun or partial shade, **Soil:** humus-rich, moist, acid, **Habit:** ground covering, **Propagation:** by seed, cuttings, division, or layering in spring.
☐ Associates well with callunas and ericas and *Gaultheria procumbens* among other dwarf Ericaceous shrubs.

Androsace sarmentosa var. *chumbyi*

Primulaceae Rock jasmine
ZONES 7–10   ROCK PLANT
Height: 10 cm (4 in), **Flowers:** pink, mid-spring – early summer, **Foliage:** green, neat rosettes, **Position:** full sun and shelter, **Soil:** well-drained, gritty, ideally alkaline, **Habit:** low and spreading to about 60 cm (2 ft), **Propagation:** by cuttings of rosettes or basal shoots in a garden frame during early summer.
☐ For the rock or scree garden; also ideal for paving and dry-stone walls.

Androsace villosa var. *arachnoidea*

Primulaceae Rock jasmine
ZONES 6–10   ROCK PLANT
Height: 5–8 cm (2–3 in), **Flowers:** white, primrose-like; late spring – early summer, **Foliage:** grey-green, very hairy, **Position:** full sun and shelter, **Soil:** well-drained, gritty, ideally alkaline, **Habit:** very compact perennial, spreading to 30 cm (1 ft), **Propagation:** by cuttings of rosettes or basal shoots in a garden frame during early summer.
☐ For the rock or scree garden; also ideal for paving or dry-stone walls.

Anemone × hybrida 'Alba' (syn. *A. japonica* 'Alba')

Ranunculaceae Windflower
ZONES 5–9   HERBACEOUS PERENNIAL
Height: 75–90 cm (2½–3 ft), **Flowers:** white, single, late summer – mid autumn, **Foliage:** mid green; deciduous, **Position:** sunny or semi-shaded spot, **Soil:** any type, well-drained, **Habit:** free-flowering perennial when it is fully established, **Propagation:** by root cuttings taken late autumn – mid-winter in sand and peat mix in a garden frame; or by dividing.
☐ Cut stems down to ground level after flowering. A useful cut flower and associates well with autumn-colouring shrubs.

Anemone × hybrida 'Bressingham Glow' (syn. *A. japonica*)

Ranunculaceae Windflower
ZONES 5–9   HERBACEOUS PERENNIAL
Height: 45–60 cm (1½–2 ft), **Flowers:** pink, semi-double, late summer – mid-autumn, **Foliage:** mid-green, deciduous, **Position:** sunny or semi-shaded spot, **Soil:** any type, well-drained, **Habit:** free-flowering perennial when it is fully established, **Propagation:** root cuttings late autumn – mid-winter; or by dividing.
☐ A useful cut flower and associates well with autumn-colouring shrubs.

Anemone x *hybrida* 'Queen Charlotte' (**syn. *A. japonica***)

Ranunculaceae   Windflower

ZONES 5–9   HERBACEOUS PERENNIAL

Height: 75 cm–1 m (2½–3 ft), **Flowers:** pink, single, **Foliage:** mid green, deciduous, **Position:** sunny or semi-shaded spot, **Soil:** any type, well-drained, **Habit:** free-flowering perennial when it is fully established, **Propagation:** by root cuttings taken late autumn – mid-winter; or by dividing.

☐ Useful cut flower and associates well with autumn-colouring shrubs.

Antennaria dioica var. *rubra*

Compositae

ZONES 7–10   ROCK PLANT

Height: 10 cm (4 in), **Flowers:** deep pinky-red in clusters, late spring – early summer, **Foliage:** greyish-green, evergreen, **Position:** full sun, **Soil:** normal, well-drained with added grit, preferably acid, **Habit:** slow-spreading mat, **Propagation:** by division in spring.

☐ For rock garden, scree bed or gaps in paving.

Anthemis sancti-johannis

Compositae

ZONES 6–10   HERBACEOUS PERENNIAL

Height: 45 cm (1½ ft), **Flowers:** brilliant orange daisies, early – late summer, **Foliage:** hairy and greyish, fragrant, deciduous, **Position:** full sun, **Soil:** well-drained, **Habit:** clumpy and compact, **Propagation:** by seeds sown in late winter in gentle heat, or in mid-spring outdoors; or by cuttings taken in summer and inserted in sand and peat mix in a garden frame; division in autumn or early spring.

☐ A good companion for grey-foliage perennials.

Anthemis tinctoria 'Grallagh Gold'

Compositae   Ox-eye chamomile

ZONES 6–10   HERBACEOUS PERENNIAL

Height: 75 cm (2½ ft), **Flowers:** deep yellow, early – late summer, **Foliage:** medium green, attractively lobed, deciduous, **Position:** full sun, **Soil:** well-drained, **Habit:** tall and erect, **Propagation:** by division in autumn or spring; or by cuttings in summer inserted in sand and peat mix in a garden frame.

Aquilegia alpina

Ranunculaceae   Columbine

ZONES 4–9   ROCK PLANT

Height: 30 cm (1 ft), **Flowers:** dark blue, spurred, late spring – early summer, **Foliage:** greyish-green, ferny, deciduous, **Position:** sun or partial shade, **Soil:** moist, well drained with added leafmould, **Habit:** graceful, but short lived, **Propagathon:** by seeds sown when ripe mid – late summer, or by division mid-autumn – early spring.

☐ Dead-head after flowering. Excellent for the rock garden or scree bed.

Aquilegia 'McKana Hybrids'

Ranunculaceae   Columbine

ZONES 4–9   HERBACEOUS PERENNIALS

Height: 60–90 cm (2–3 ft), **Flowers:** red, pink, white with yellow or white corolla; or yellow, or blue with white corolla; summer, **Foliage:** light green, prettily fern-like, compound, deciduous, **Position:** sun or partial shade, **Soil:** any well-drained humus-rich soil, **Habit:** elegant, short-lived, **Propagation:** by division of clumps in autumn or spring.

☐ When flowering is over, cut down the stems. Lovely cut flowers. Ideal for cottage gardens and for growing with border irises.

Arabis albida
(syn. *A. caucasica*)
Cruciferae   Wall or rock cress
Zones 4–9   Rock plant
Height: 23 cm (9 in), **Flowers:** white, single, late winter – early summer, **Foliage:** greyish-green, farinose, evergreen, **Position:** sun or partial shade, **Soil:** suits most well-drained soils, **Habit:** carpeting, can spread extensively if not cut back annually, **Propagation:** by dividing clumps in autumn; by cuttings in a garden frame in mid-summer; or by seed sown under glass in spring or summer.
□ Cut back stems after flowering. Grow on steep bank as ground cover, or in a dry-stone wall. Good companion plants include the spring flowering aubrieta and yellow alyssum.

Arabis albida 'Flore Pleno'
Cruciferae   Wall or rock cress
Zones 4–9   Rock plant
Height: 15 cm (6 in), **Flowers:** white, double, late winter – early summer, **Foliage:** greyish-green, farinose, evergreen, **Position:** sun or partial shade, **Soil:** suits most well-drained soils, **Habit:** more compact than the species, **Propagation:** by dividing clumps in autumn; or cuttings in a garden frame in mid-summer.
□ Trim back stems after flowering.

Above: The wall or rock cress, *Arabis albida*, is ideal for drystone walls and for growing on steep banks

Arabis aubrietioides
Cruciferae   Wall or rock cress
Zones 4–9   Rock plant
Height: 15 cm (6 in), **Flowers:** rose-pink, single; spring – early summer, **Foliage:** greyish-green, evergreen, **Position:** sun or partial shade, **Soil:** any well-drained soil, **Habit:** compact, **Propagation:** by dividing clumps in autumn; or by cuttings in a garden frame in mid-summer.
□ Trim back stems after flowering. Useful for rock garden, paving and dry-stone walls.

Arabis ferdinandi-coburgii
'Variegata'
Cruciferae   Wall or rock cress
Zones 4–9   Rock plant
Height: 10 cm (4 in), **Flowers:** white, single, spring – early summer, **Foliage:** green with attractive white edges, evergreen, **Position:** sunny, **Soil:** any well-drained soil, **Habit:** very neat and compact, spreading to 30 cm (1 ft), **Propagation:** by dividing clumps in autumn; or by cuttings in a garden frame in mid-summer.

Araucaria araucana
(syn. *A. imbricata*)
Araucariaceae   Monkey puzzle
Zones 6–10   Conifer
Height: about 1.5 m (5 ft) after 10 years, ultimately 30 m (100 ft), **Flowers and cones:** insignificant, **Foliage:** deep green, leathery and overlapping, sharply pointed; evergreen, **Position:** open and sunny, **Soil:** any moist, but well-drained soil, **Habit:** when mature it is dome shaped, **Propagation:** best raised from seed in garden frame. Or tip cuttings in mid-summer in sand and peat.
□ Only recommended for large gardens.

Arenaria balearica

Caryophyllaceae Sandwort
ZONES 5–10   ROCK PLANT
Height: 2 cm (1 in), **Flowers:** starry white flowers in early spring – mid-summer, **Foliage:** medium-green, very small, evergreen, **Position:** shade; best on north side of rock garden, **Soil:** suits most well-drained soils, **Habit:** carpet forming, spreading to 45 cm (1½ ft), **Propagation:** by division in autumn or spring.
□ Also useful for planting in paving, choosing a shady spot.

Arenaria montana

Caryophyllaceae Sandwort
ZONES 5–9   ROCK PLANT
Height: 15 cm (6 in), **Flowers:** bright white, late spring – early summer, **Foliage:** deepish green, evergreen, **Position:** sun or semi-shade, **Soil:** well-drained, **Habit:** forms a dense carpet, spreading to 30 cm (1 ft), **Propagation:** by division in autumn or spring; or by cuttings of basal shoots taken early – late summer, inserted in sand and peat mix in a garden frame.

Aristolochia macrophylla

Aristolochiaceae Dutchman's pipe
ZONES 4–10   CLIMBER
Height: up to 6 m (20 ft), **Flowers:** yellow and brown, pipe-shaped, often hidden by leaves, early summer, **Foliage:** green, large, up to 30 cm (1 ft) long, deciduous, **Position:** full sun or semi-shade, **Soil:** well drained and rich, **Habit:** a vigorous twiner, **Propagation:** by summer cuttings in a propagator, or by layering.
□ Useful for covering unsightly walls or old tree stumps.

Armeria maritima

Plumbaginaceae Common thrift, Lady's pin cushion
ZONES 6–10   ROCK PLANT
Height: 20 cm (8 in), **Flowers:** globular pink flower heads produced late spring – mid-summer, **Foliage:** green, grass like, evergreen, **Position:** sunny position, **Soil:** well-drained, **Habit:** forms a dense mound of foliage, **Propagation:** by divison in early – mid-spring; or by seed sown in early – mid-spring in a garden frame.
□ Useful for rock gardens and paving. Thrives by the sea.

Aronia melanocarpa

Rosaceae Black chokeberry
ZONES 4–9   SHRUB
Height: 1 m (3 ft), **Flowers:** white, late spring – early summer, **Foliage:** green, colouring brown-red in autumn, deciduous, **Position:** sun or partial shade, **Soil:** deep, well-drained, **Habit:** bushy, **Propagation:** seed, cuttings or division in autumn.
□ Glossy black berries create additional interest. Pruning is unnecessary.

Artemisia abrotanum

Compositae Southernwood, old man, lad's love
ZONES 8–10   SHRUB
Height: 1 m (3 ft), **Flowers:** yellow, mid-summer – early autumn, **Foliage:** greyish below, sweetly fragrant, feathery, deciduous, **Position:** sun, **Soil:** not too rich, **Habit:** erect, bushy, **Propagation:** cuttings in mid-summer, division in mid-autumn.
□ Shoots damaged by frost, or any over-long straggly growths, can be cut back early in the spring. Good shrub for cottage garden. Ideally grown with old roses.

Artemisia arborescens
Compositae
ZONES 8–10   SHRUB
Height: 1 m (3 ft), **Flowers:** yellow, early
– mid-summer, **Foliage:** silver and feathery, deciduous semi-evergreen, **Position:**
sun, **Soil:** tolerates most soils, **Habit:**
round and bushy, **Propagation:** cuttings
in mid-summer, division in mid-autumn.
☐This shrub may be semi-evergreen in
mild winters but could be killed by severe
weather in cold parts of the country.
Lovely plant for cottage garden, especially
when grown with old roses.

Artemisia lactiflora
Compositae   White mugwort
ZONES 4–10   HERBACEOUS PERENNIAL
Height: 1.2–1.5 m (4–5 ft). **Flowers:**
creamy white, tiny, held in long plumes,
fragrant, late summer – early autumn,
Foliage: dark green, feathery, deciduous,
Position: sun or semi-shade, **Soil:** well-
drained, acid soil ideal, **Habit:** robust
perennial, **Propagation:** by dividing
clumps mid-autumn – early spring; by
cuttings taken in summer and inserted in a
garden frame; or by seeds sown outdoors in
spring.
☐Good for cottage gardens, in association
with old roses.

Right: *Artemisia lactiflora*

Artemisia 'Silver Queen'
Compositae
ZONES 5–10   HERBACEOUS PERENNIAL
Height: 75 cm (2½ ft), **Flowers:** white,
early – late summer, **Foliage:** silvery,
finely cut, deciduous, **Position:** sun or
semi-shade, **Soil:** tolerates most soils,
Habit: loosely upright perennial, **Propagation:** by dividing clumps mid-autumn –
early spring; or take cuttings in summer
and insert in a garden frame.
☐Attractive foliage plant, useful for
flower arranging. Good for cottage gardens, especially in association with old
roses.

Aruncus dioicus
(**syn.** *A. sylvester*)
Rosaceae   Goat's beard
ZONES 3–9   HERBACEOUS PERENNIAL
Height: 1.2–1.8 m (4–6 ft), **Flowers:**
feathery heads of creamy white blooms,
early summer, **Foliage:** pale green,
formed of several leaflets; deciduous, **Position:** prefers dappled shade, **Soil:** moisture-retentive, **Habit:** vigorous and erect
perennial, **Propagation:** by seeds sown in
spring, or by division in autumn or spring.
☐Most purchased plants are male with
better flowers than female. Associates well
with many ornamental shrubs.

Arundinaria japonica
Gramineae   Bamboo
ZONES 5–10   SHRUB
Height: 3–5 m (10–16 ft), **Flowers:** insignificant, rarely produced, **Foliage:** deep
green, shiny, more blue-green underneath, evergreen, **Position:** sunny, sheltered, **Soil:** suits most moisture-retentive
soils, **Habit:** tall, upright and invasive,
Propagation: division in spring.
☐Imparts a sub-tropical touch to a planting scheme.

Arundinaria pumila
Gramineae Bamboo
ZONES 5–10   SHRUB
Height: 30–60 cm (1–2 ft), **Flowers:** rarely produced and detrimental to the health of the plant when they do occur, **Foliage:** green, pointed, lanceolate, on purple stems, evergreen, **Position:** sunny, sheltered, **Soil:** suits most moisture-retentive soils, **Habit:** a dwarf bamboo, spreads readily, **Propagation:** divide and replant in spring.
□ Good ground cover for shrub borders and sheltered banks.

Arundinaria variegata
Gramineae Bamboo
ZONES 5–10   SHRUB
Height: 60 cm–1.2 m (2–4 ft), **Flowers:** insignificant, **Foliage:** green, striped white, evergreen, on deep green stems, **Position:** sunny, sheltered, **Soil:** suits most moisture-retentive soils, **Habit:** makes a dense thicket of canes, compact, **Propagation:** divide in spring.
□ Imparts a sub-tropical touch to a planting scheme.

Asclepias incarnata
Asclepiadaceae Swamp milkweed
ZONES 8–10   HERBACEOUS PERENNIAL
Height: 60 cm–1.2 m (2–4 ft), **Flowers:** palest pink, in umbels, mid – late summer, **Foliage:** long, medium green, deciduous, **Position:** sunny spot, sheltered from wind, **Soil:** moist, lime-free, humus-rich with added peat or leafmould, **Habit:** vigorous perennial, erect stems, some support advisable, **Propagation:** by division in autumn or spring; or by seeds sown in spring in a warm propagator.
□ A useful plant for the woodland garden or shrub border.

Aster alpinus
Compositae
ZONES 5–9   ROCK PLANT
Height: 15 cm (6 in), **Flowers:** violet, yellow-eyed daisies, mid-summer, **Foliage:** greyish green, deciduous, **Position:** full sun, **Soil:** any reasonably good soil, **Habit:** carpeting, **Propagation:** by seed sown outdoors or under glass in spring; or by division in autumn or spring.
□ Forms in various other colours are available too. Useful for front of border, rock garden or for gaps in paving.

Aster amellus
Compositae
ZONES 6–9   HERBACEOUS PERENNIAL
Height: 45–60 cm (1½–2 ft), **Flowers:** blue or pink shades, late summer – early autumn, **Foliage:** greyish green, deciduous, **Position:** sunny and open, partial shade, **Soil:** any reasonably good soil, **Habit:** clump-forming, erect perennial, **Propagation:** by division of clumps in autumn or spring.
□ Associates well with shrubs noted for autumn colour. Good for cutting.

Left: *Aster alpinus*, useful for the front of a border, rock garden or gaps in paving

Top left: *Aster linosyris*
Top right: *Aster novi-belgii* cultivar
Below: *Aster novae-angliae* 'Harrington's Pink'

Aster ericoides

Compositae Michaelmas daisy
ZONES 6–9   HERBACEOUS PERENNIAL
Height: 60 cm–1 m (2–3 ft), **Flowers:** white, flushed with pink, small but numerous, early – mid-autumn, **Foliage:** medium green, **Position:** sun or partial shade, **Soil:** any reasonably good soil, **Habit:** perennial with slender erect stems, **Propagation:** by seed sown outdoors or under glass in spring; or by division of clumps in autumn or spring.
☐ Flowers are good for cutting.

Aster × frikartii

Compositae Michaelmas daisy
ZONES 6–9   HERBACEOUS PERENNIAL
Height: 75 cm–1 m (2½–3 ft), **Flowers:** lavender-blue daisies, late summer – mid-autumn, **Foliage:** deep green, deciduous, **Position:** sun or partial shade, **Soil:** moist, but well drained and fertile chalk soil, **Habit:** erect stemed clump-forming perennial, **Propagation:** by division of clumps in autumn or spring.
☐ Excellent cut flower. Looks superb with shrubs grown for autumn leaf colour.

Aster linosyris

Compositae Goldilocks
ZONES 5–9   HERBACEOUS PERENNIAL
Height: 60 cm (2 ft), **Flowers:** yellow, late summer – early autumn, **Foliage:** matt green, lanceolate, deciduous, **Position:** sunny and open, partial shade, **Soil:** moist but well drained and fertile, **Habit:** upright perennial, **Propagation:** by seed sown outdoors or under glass in spring; or by division in autumn or spring.
☐ Excellent cut flower.

Aster novae-angliae

Compositae Michaelmas daisy
ZONES 5–9   HERBACEOUS PERENNIAL
Height: 1.2–1.5 m (4–5 ft), **Flowers:** early – mid-autumn, **Foliage:** matt green, lanceolate, deciduous, **Position:** sunny and open, partial shade, **Soil:** moist but well drained and fertile, **Habit:** upright perennial, needs some support, **Propagation:** by division in autumn or spring.
☐ Good for cutting. Cut back to ground level after flowering.
    'Harrington's Pink' is a beautiful shade of pink, 'September Ruby' is rich crimson. Grow with autumn-colouring shrubs.

Aster novi-belgii

Compositae Michaelmas daisy
ZONES 4–9   HERBACEOUS PERENNIAL
Height: 90 cm–1.2 m (3–4 ft), **Flowers:** shades of blue and mauve, double or single, early – mid-autumn, **Foliage:** mid-green, glossy, narrow and pointed, deciduous, **Position:** sunny and open, partial shade, **Soil:** moist but well drained and fertile, **Habit:** erect, excellent cut flower, **Propagation:** by division of clumps mid-autumn – early spring.
☐ Cut back to ground level after flowering. There are many excellent cultivars including '*Ada Ballard*', mauve-blue, double; '*Blandie*', white, double; '*Chequers*', deep purple-violet, single; '*Crimson Brocade*', red, double; '*Fellowship*', pink, semi-double; '*Marie Ballard*', light blue, double.

Aster novi-belgii

Compositae Dwarf Michaelmas daisy
ZONES 4–9   HERBACEOUS PERENNIAL
Height: 30–45 cm (12–18 in), **Flowers:** white and shades of blue and pink, single or double; early – mid-autumn, **Foliage:** mid-green, narrow and pointed, deciduous, **Position:** sunny and open, partial shade, **Soil:** moist but well drained and fertile, **Habit:** compact and bushy, **Propagation:** by division of clumps mid-autumn – early spring.
☐ Cut back stems to ground level after flowering. '*Audrey*', light blue, semi-double; '*Jenny*', red, double; '*Little Pink Baby*', pink single; '*Snowsprite*', white.

Astilbe × arendsii

Saxifragaceae False goat's beard
ZONES 4–9   HERBACEOUS PERENNIAL
Height: 60 cm–1 m (2–3 ft), **Flowers:** shades of pink, red and white, in pyramidal plumes, early – late summer, **Foliage:** mid green, deeply divided, coppery tinted when young, deciduous, **Position:** sun or partial shade, excellent for pond-side planting, **Soil:** must be moist, mulch with peat or leafmould in mid-spring, **Habit:** graceful clump-forming perennial, **Propagation:** divide clumps in early – mid-spring.
□ Cut to ground level in mid-autumn. Grow with other moisture loving plants like bog primulas and hostas.
   '*Bressingham Pink*' is pure pink; '*Deutschland*' is white; '*Fanal*' is deep red; '*Granat*' is deep crimson-pink.

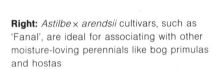

Right: *Astilbe × arendsii* cultivars, such as 'Fanal', are ideal for associating with other moisture-loving perennials like bog primulas and hostas

Astilbe chinensis var. pumila

Saxifragaceae False goat's beard
ZONES 4–9   ROCK PLANT
Height: 23 cm (9 in), **Flowers:** reddish-purple, in dense erect plumes, summer, **Foliage:** mid green, fern-like, deciduous, **Position:** sun or partial shade, **Soil:** suits most moist soils, **Habit:** dwarf, compact and clump-forming perennial, **Propagation:** divide clumps in early – mid-spring.
□ Suitable for a rock garden.

Astrantia major

Umbelliferae Masterwort
ZONES 4–9   HERBACEOUS PERENNIAL
Height: 60 cm (2 ft), **Flowers:** green and pink, star-shaped, early – mid-summer, **Foliage:** medium green, formed of three leaflets, deciduous, **Position:** partial shade, or sun provided soil stays moist, **Soil:** moisture-retentive, **Habit:** clump-forming perennial, flowerheads raised above the foliage, **Propagation:** divide clumps mid-autumn – early spring; or by seed sown in early autumn and germinated in a garden frame.
□ Cut down the stems in late summer.

Aubrieta deltoidea

Cruciferae Aubrieta, rock cress
ZONES 4–9   ROCK PLANT
Height: 15 cm (6 in), **Flowers:** purple, pink, red, or blue, early – late spring, **Foliage:** green or greyish green, evergreen, **Position:** sun, on rock garden, wall or bank, **Soil:** neutral or alkaline, **Habit:** trailing perennial, **Propagation:** by cuttings in sandy soil in a propagator during summer, or by division in spring.
□ Seeds of cultivars will not come true. Cut back after flowering. Grow with yellow alyssum and white arabis.

AZALEAS

In the strict botanical sense azaleas are included in the genus rhododendron. But I am keeping them separate in this book since most gardeners think of them as a separate group of shrubs.

Unfortunately, none of them tolerate any lime in the soil (or water), but where the garden soil does not suit them they can be grown in tubs filled with an ericaceous compost. They thrive in sheltered, semi-shaded situations.

The selection of azaleas here includes deciduous and evergreen kinds, belonging to different hybrid groups.

For more details on propagation see page 71.

Azaleas associate well with candelabra primulas, hostas and lilies.

The hybrid groups are:

Deciduous
  Ghent hybrids
  Knaphill hybrids
  Mollis azaleas
  Occidentale hybrids
  Rustica hybrids

Evergreen
  Gable hybrids
  Glenn Dale hybrids
  Indica hybrids
  Kaempferi hybrids
  Kurume hybrids
  Oldhamii hybrids
  Vuyk hybrids
Propagation: see page 71.

Azalea 'Annabelle'
Ericaceae Knaphill hybrid
ZONES 5–9   SHRUB
Height: 1.2–1.8 m (4–6 ft), **Flowers:** orange and yellow in bud opening to yellow, suffused with orange-rose, late spring – early summer, **Foliage:** green; good autumn colour, deciduous, **Position:** semi-shade, protect from winds, **Soil:** humus rich, acid, **Habit:** upright, bushy, **Propagation:** by layering, at any time of year.

Azalea 'Balzac'
Ericaceae Knaphill hybrid
ZONES 5–9   SHRUB
Height: 1.2–1.8 m (4–6 ft), **Flowers:** deep orange-red and orange, fragrant, late spring – early summer, **Foliage:** green, good autumn colour, deciduous, **Position:** semi-shade, protect from winds, **Soil:** humus-rich, acid, **Habit:** upright, bushy, **Propagation:** by layering at any time of year.

Aubrieta deltoidea 'Variegata'
Cruciferae Variegated aubrieta
ZONES 4–9   ROCK PLANT
Height: 10 cm (4 in), **Flowers:** purple, early – late spring, **Foliage:** green with prominent white margins, evergreen, **Position:** sun, on rock garden, wall or in paving, **Soil:** neutral or alkaline, **Habit:** more compact than the species, **Propagation:** by cuttings in sandy soil in a propagator during summer, or by division in spring.
□Combines well with yellow alyssum.

Below: *Azalea* 'Blue Danube'

Aucuba japonica 'Variegata'
Cornaceae Spotted laurel, Gold Dust Plant
ZONES 7–10   SHRUB
Height: 3m (10 ft), **Flowers:** greenish white, **Foliage:** green, speckled yellow, evergreen, **Position:** sun or shade, **Soil:** soil-tolerant, **Habit:** dense rounded bush, **Propagation:** by cuttings 10–15 cm (4–6 in) long in late summer – early autumn.
□This shrub will grow in any situation, but will hold its variegation best in an open position. It tolerates industrial pollution and thrives near the sea.

Above: *Azalea* 'Mother's Day'
Right: *Azalea* 'Gibraltar'
Below right: *Azalea* 'John Cairns'

Azalea 'Compte de Gomer'
Ericaceae Mollis azalea
ZONES 5–9   SHRUB
Height: 1.2–1.8 m (4–6 ft), **Flowers:** pink and orange, late spring, **Foliage:** green, good autumn colour, deciduous, **Position:** semi-shade, protect from winds, **Soil:** humus-rich, acid, **Habit:** upright, bushy, **Propagation:** by layering at any time of year.

Azalea 'Dracula'
Ericaceae Knaphill hybrid
ZONES 5–9   SHRUB
Height: 1.2–1.8 m (4–6 ft), **Flowers:** very dark red buds, opening to crimson-red, frilled edges, late spring – early summer, **Foliage:** opens bronzy, turning green, later good autumn colour, deciduous, **Position:** semi-shade, protect from winds, **Soil:** humus-rich, acid, **Habit:** upright, bushy, **Propagation:** by layering at any time of year.

Azalea 'Gibraltar'
Ericaceae Knaphill hybrid
ZONES 5–9   SHRUB
Height: 1.2–1.8 m (4–6 ft), **Flowers:** large orange-red, buds deep orange-crimson, late spring – early summer, **Foliage:** green, good autumn colour, deciduous, **Position:** semi-shade, protect from winds, **Soil:** humus-rich, acid, **Habit:** upright, bushy, **Propagation:** by layering at any time of year.

Azalea 'Hollandia'
Ericaceae Ghent hybrid
ZONES 5–9   SHRUB
Height: 1.5–2.5 m (5–8 ft), **Flowers:** yellow and orange, early summer, **Foliage:** green, deciduous, **Position:** semi-shade, protect from winds, **Soil:** humus-rich, acid, **Habit:** upright, bushy, **Propagation:** by layering at any time of year.

Azalea 'Orange Truffles'
Ericaceae Knaphill hybrid
ZONES 5–9   SHRUB
Height: 1.2–1.8 m (4–6 ft), **Flowers:** apricot with petals yellow inside flushed red outside, wavy margins, double, late spring – early summer, **Foliage:** young leaves coppery red, turning green, good autumn colour, deciduous, **Position:** semi-shade, protect from winds, **Soil:** humus-rich, acid, **Habit:** upright, bushy, **Propagation:** by layering at any time of year.

Azalea 'Raphael de Smet'
Ericaceae Ghent hybrid
ZONES 5–9   SHRUB
Height: 1.5–1.8 m (5–8 ft), **Flowers:** white, flushed pink, double, early summer, **Foliage:** green, good autumn colour, deciduous, **Position:** semi-shade, protect from winds, **Soil:** humus-rich, acid, **Habit:** upright, bushy, **Propagation:** by layering at any time of year.

Azalea 'Addy Wery'
Ericaceae Kurume hybrid
ZONES 5–9   SHRUB
Height: 60 cm–1.2 m (2–4 ft), **Flowers:** orange-scarlet, late spring, **Foliage:** green, evergreen, **Position:** semi-shade, **Soil:** humus-rich, acid, **Habit:** compact, bushy, **Propagation:** by cuttings taken from young growths from mid – late summer.

Azalea 'Blaauw's Pink'
Ericaceae Kurume hybrid
ZONES 5–9   SHRUB
Height: 60 cm–1.2 m (2–4 ft), **Flowers:** warm-pink, spring, **Foliage:** green, evergreen, **Position:** semi-shade, **Soil:** humus-rich, acid, **Habit:** compact, bushy, **Propagation:** by cuttings which are taken from young growths in mid – late summer.

Azalea 'Blue Danube'
Ericaceae Vuyk hybrid
ZONES 5–9   SHRUB
Height: 1.2 m (4 ft), **Flowers:** a most striking violet-blue, large, late spring, **Foliage:** green, evergreen, **Position:** semi-shade, **Soil:** humus-rich, acid, **Habit:** compact, bushy, **Propagation:** by cuttings taken from young growths, mid – late summer.

Right: *Azalea* 'Palestrina'

Azalea 'Hinodegiri'
Ericaceae Kurume hybrid
ZONES 5–9   SHRUB
Height: 60 cm–1.2 m (2–4 ft), **Flowers:** crimson-red, late spring, **Foliage:** green, evergreen, **Position:** semi-shade, **Soil:** humus rich, acid, **Habit:** compact, bushy, **Propagation:** by cuttings which are taken from young growths in mid – late summer.

Azalea 'Hinomayo'
Ericaceae Kurume hybrid
ZONES 5–9   SHRUB
Height: up to 1.5 m (5 ft), **Flowers:** soft pink, late spring, **Foliage:** green, evergreen, **Position:** semi-shade, **Soil:** humus-rich, acid, **Habit:** compact, bushy, **Propagation:** by cuttings taken from young growths, mid – late summer.

Azalea 'Johann Strauss'
Ericaceae Vuyk hybrid
ZONES 5–9   SHRUB
Height: 60 cm–1.2 m (2–4 ft), **Flowers:** warm pink with deeper markings, large, late spring, **Foliage:** green, evergreen, **Position:** semi-shade, **Soil:** humus-rich, acid, **Habit:** compact, bushy, **Propagation:** by cuttings taken from young growths, mid – late summer.

Azalea 'John Cairns'
Ericaceae Kaempferi hybrid
ZONES 5–9   SHRUB
Height: 1–1.2 m (3–4 ft), **Flowers:** deep reddish orange, late spring, **Foliage:** green, evergreen, **Position:** sun or partial shade, protect from cold winds, **Soil:** humus-rich, acid, **Habit:** compact, bushy, **Propagation:** by cuttings taken from young growths, mid – late summer.

Azalea 'Mother's Day'
Ericaceae Kurume × Indica hybrid
ZONES 5–9   SHRUB
Height: up to 1 m (3 ft), **Flowers:** rose-red, late spring, **Foliage:** green, evergreen, **Position:** sun or partial shade, protect from cold winds, **Soil:** humus-rich, acid, **Habit:** compact, bushy, **Propagation:** by cuttings taken from young growths, mid – late summer.

Azalea 'Palestrina'
Ericaceae Vuyk hybrid
ZONES 5–9   SHRUB
Height: 60 cm (2 ft), **Flowers:** white, spring, **Foliage:** green, evergreen, **Position:** sun or partial shade, protect from cold winds, **Soil:** humus-rich, acid, **Habit:** dwarf, compact and spreading, **Propagation:** by cuttings taken from young growths, mid – late summer.

Azara lanceolata
Flacourtiaceae
ZONES 7–10   SHRUB
Height: 6 m (20 ft), **Flowers:** showy yellow, fragrant, mid – late spring, **Foliage:** green, evergreen, **Position:** sun or partial shade, **Soil:** tolerates most soils, **Habit:** forms a round shrub in open ground or train against a wall, **Propagation:** cuttings in summer rooted in propagator. □ A very good shrub for south- or west-facing walls. Tolerates clipping which can be done after flowering.

Berberidopsis corallina
Flacourtiaceae Coral plant
ZONES 4–9   CLIMBER
Height: 4.5–6 m (15–20 ft), **Flowers:** dark crimson on pendulous stalks in late summer, **Foliage:** dark green above, glaucous beneath, almost holly-like, evergreen, **Position:** shady and sheltered, **Soil:** open or sandy loam, preferably neutral or acid, **Habit:** climber, requires support, **Propagation:** sow seed in sandy compost in spring and germinate in propagator; insert cuttings in similar compost and temperature, or increase by layering. □ Ivies make good companions.

Above: *Berberis darwinii*
Right: *Berberis × stenophylla*

Berberis aggregata 'Barbarossa'
Berberidaceae Barberry
ZONES 5–9 SHRUB
Height: 2.5 m (8 ft), **Flowers:** pale yellow, mid-summer, **Foliage:** green, turning brilliant orange and red in autumn, **Position:** best in sun but tolerates partial shade, **Soil:** tolerates most soils, **Habit:** bushy, rounded, easily kept to shape by pruning, **Propagation:** cuttings in autumn.
□ Produces heavy crops of red berries, plus excellent autumn foliage colour. Try associating it with Michalmas daisies – a stunning combination.

Berberis candidula
Berberidaceae Barberry
ZONES 5–9 SHRUB
Height: 60 cm (2 ft), **Flowers:** yellow, late spring – early summer; followed by black berries, **Foliage:** shiny deep green, evergreen, **Position:** sun or partial shade, **Soil:** soil-tolerant, **Habit:** compact and rounded, **Propagation:** seed or cuttings.
□ A useful species for the larger rock garden; or for planting at the front of a border.

Berberis darwinii
Berberidaceae Barberry
ZONES 5–9 SHRUB
Height: 3 m (10 ft), **Flowers:** deep yellow, or orange-yellow, followed by blue-black berries; late spring, **Foliage:** dark-green, shiny, like miniature holly leaves, evergreen, **Position:** sun or partial shade, **Soil:** tolerates most soils, **Habit:** bushy, **Propagation:** seed or cuttings.
□ This is one of the most popular barberries, excellent as a free-standing shrub or as a hedge which should be lightly trimmed back after flowering. Good for seaside planting.

Berberis gagnepainii 'Lancifolia'
Berberidaceae Barberry
ZONES 5–9 SHRUB
Height: 1.8 m (6 ft), **Flowers:** yellow, followed by blue-black berries; late spring, **Foliage:** dark green, evergreen, **Position:** sun or partial shade, **Soil:** soil-tolerant, **Habit:** forms a dense, upright bush, **Propagation:** seeds, cuttings or layering.
□ A robust shrub making an excellent hedge in most situations, including seaside.

Berberis linearifolia 'Orange King'
Berberidaceae Barberry
ZONES 6–9 SHRUB
Height: 3 m (10 ft), **Flowers:** deep orange, mid-spring, followed by blue-black berries, **Foliage:** shiny green, evergreen, **Position:** sun or partial shade, **Soil:** tolerates most soils, **Habit:** erect, slow growing, **Propagation:** cuttings.
□ A beautiful shrub. The flowers are more showy than those of any other berberis. Can be grown as an informal hedge.

Berberis × rubrostilla
Berberidaceae Barberry
ZONES 5–9 SHRUB
Height: 1 m (3 ft), **Flowers:** yellow, late spring, **Foliage:** greyish green, deciduous, bright red tints in autumn, **Position:** best in sun, tolerates partial shade, **Soil:** tolerates most soils, **Habit:** compact, **Propagation:** seed or cuttings.
□ Profusion of bright red oval berries greatly enhance the beauty of the autumn foliage. Specially good in association with *Ceratostigma willmottianum*.

Berberis sargentiana
Berberidaceae Barberry
ZONES 5–9 SHRUB
Height: 1.8 m (6 ft), **Flowers:** yellow, spring, **Foliage:** dark green, evergreen, **Position:** sun or partial shade, **Soil:** tolerates most soils, **Habit:** forms a thicket of erect stems, **Propagation:** seed or cuttings.
□ This berberis is armed with the longest spines in the entire genus. Black fruits in autumn.

Berberis × stenophylla
Berberidaceae Barberry
ZONES 5–10 SHRUB
Height: 3 m (10 ft), **Flowers:** yellow, mid-spring, followed by round purple-blue berries; **Foliage:** dark-green, ever-green, **Position:** sun or partial shade, **Soil:** tolerates most soils, **Habit:** forms a dense thicket of arching branches, **Propagation:** cuttings.
□ Can be grown as a hedge when it should be lightly trimmed back after flowering, or used as a specimen plant.

Top: *Berberis thunbergii* 'Rose Glow'
Above: *Berberis × stenophylla* 'Corallina Compacta'
Right: *Berberis thunbergii* 'Aurea'

Berberis × stenophylla 'Corallina Compacta'

Berberidaceae Barberry

ZONES 7–10   SHRUB

Height: 30–45 cm (1–1½ ft), **Flowers:** open yellow from red buds, **Foliage:** dark green, evergreen, **Position:** sun or partial shade, **Soil:** tolerates most soils, **Habit:** bun shaped, compact, **Propagation:** cuttings.

□ A useful pretty little dwarf shrub suitable for a rock garden.

Berberis thunbergii 'Atropurpurea Nana'

Berberidaceae Barberry

ZONES 5–9   SHRUB

Height: 30–45 cm (1–1½ ft), **Flowers:** yellow, spring, followed by red berries, **Foliage:** reddish purple in sunny positions, deciduous, **Position:** sun or partial shade, **Soil:** tolerates most soils, **Habit:** dwarf, compact, **Propagation:** cuttings.

□ This pleasing little shrub makes an excellent low hedge which should be trimmed in late summer. It produces the best-coloured deep reddish purple foliage when planted in full sun. Also makes an excellent plant for the larger rock garden.

Berberis thunbergii 'Aurea'

Berberidaceae Barberry

ZONES 7–9   SHRUB

Height: 45–60 cm (1½–2 ft), **Flowers:** yellow, spring, **Foliage:** yellow, but eventually turns light green, deciduous, **Position:** sun, **Soil:** tolerates most soils, **Habit:** dwarf, compact, **Propagation:** cuttings.

□ This dwarf shrub is grown primarily for its golden foliage. Scarlet berries follow on from the flowers. An excellent companion for purple-leaved barberries.

Berberis thunbergii 'Helmond Pillar'

Berberidaceae Barberry

ZONES 5–9   SHRUB

Height: 1.5 m (5 ft), **Flowers:** yellow, late spring, **Foliage:** deep red, deciduous, **Position:** sun or partial shade, **Soil:** tolerates most soils, **Habit:** fastigiate, **Propagation:** cuttings.

□ Excellent for low hedges. Foliage colour is richest in full sun. Red berries follow on from the flowers.

Berberis thunbergii 'Red Chief'

Berberidaceae Barberry

ZONES 5–9   SHRUB

Height: 1.8 m (6 ft), **Flowers:** yellow, late spring, followed by red berries, **Foliage:** shiny deep crimson, deciduous, **Position:** sun or partial shade, **Soil:** tolerates most soils, **Habit:** densely branching, **Propagation:** cuttings.

□ Good to associate with golden foliage. Best foliage colour in full sun.

Berberis thunbergii 'Rose Glow'

Berberidaceae Barberry

ZONES 5–9   SHRUB

Height: 1–1.5 m (3–5 ft), **Flowers:** yellow, late spring, followed by red berries, **Foliage:** purple when young, later splashed with silvery-pink, turning purplish-red before falling, **Position:** sun or partial shade, **Soil:** tolerates most soils, **Habit:** densely branching, **Propagation:** seed or cuttings.

□ Associates well with *Spiraea japonica* 'Goldflame' and should also complement *Choisya ternata* 'Sundance'. Best foliage colour in full sun.

Berberis verruculosa
Berberidaceae Barberry
ZONES 5–9 SHRUB
Height: about 1.2 (4 ft), **Flowers:** yellow, late spring – early summer, **Foliage:** dark green, holly-like, evergreen, **Position:** sun or partial shade, **Soil:** tolerates most soils, **Habit:** compact and spiky, **Propagation:** seed or cuttings.
☐ The yellow flowers are followed in autumn by blue-black berries.

Berberis wilsoniae
Berberidaceae Barberry
ZONES 5–9 SHRUB
Height: 1–1.5 m (3–5 ft), **Flowers:** yellow, mid-summer, **Foliage:** green, deciduous, excellent autumn colour, **Position:** sun for best autumn colour, **Soil:** tolerates most soils, **Habit:** low spreading, **Propagation:** seed or cuttings.
☐ A profusion of pinkish-red berries is produced which complements the colourful autumn foliage. This species can be used for ground cover or as an informal hedge.

Bergenia 'Ballawley'
Saxifragaceae Elephant's ears, megasea
ZONES 4–9 HERBACEOUS PERENNIAL
Height: 30–60 cm (18–24 in), **Flowers:** pinkish-red, in loose heads raised above foliage, mid – late spring, **Foliage:** green, tinged red, turning brighter red in autumn, evergreen, **Position:** sun or partial shade, **Soil:** any moist garden soil, tolerates lime, **Habit:** large evergreen leaves, spreading, **Propagation:** by division in autumn or spring.
☐ Overcrowded plants should be divided. Bergenia make good ground cover.

Bergenia cordifolia
Saxifragaceae Elephant's ears, megasea
ZONES 2–9 HERBACEOUS PERENNIAL
Height: 30 cm (1 ft), **Flowers:** mauve-pink, in loose heads raised above foliage, early – mid-spring, **Foliage:** green, glossy and leathery, evergreen, often reddish in the autumn, **Position:** sun or partial shade, **Soil:** any moist garden soil, tolerates lime, **Habit:** large evergreen leaves, spreading, **Propagation:** by division in autumn or spring.
☐ Good for ground cover.

Bergenia × schmidtii
Saxifragaceae Elephant's ears, megasea
ZONES 4–9 HERBACEOUS PERENNIAL
Height: 37 cm (15 in), **Flowers:** rose-pink, late spring – early summer, **Foliage:** green, glossy and leathery, evergreen, **Position:** sun or partial shade, **Soil:** suits moist soils and tolerates chalk, **Habit:** large leaves, spreading, **Propagation:** by division in autumn or spring.
☐ Good ground cover.

Betula pendula 'Youngii'
Betulaceae Young's weeping birch
ZONES 2–9 TREE
Height: 5–7.5 m (16–25 ft), **Flowers:** pale yellow catkins, spring, **Foliage:** mid-green, rhomboidal shaped leaves, deciduous, **Position:** sun or partial shade, **Soil:** any type, but best on slightly acid or neutral soils, **Habit:** ultimately a small pendulous mushroom-shaped tree, **Propagation:** by grafting on to young stock of *B. pendula*.
☐ Perfect small specimen tree for a lawn.

Betula pendula
(syn. *B. verrucosa*)

Betulaceae   Silver birch

ZONES 2–9   TREE

Height: 9–15 m (30–50 ft), **Flowers:** pale yellow catkins, spring, **Foliage:** mid green, almost diamond shaped, deciduous, **Position:** sunny and open or partial shade, **Soil:** any soil, acid or alkaline, but grows larger on slightly acid soils, **Habit:** elegant and dainty with silver bark, light canopy, **Propagation:** by seeds sown on the surface and gently pressed into sandy compost or a good seed compost in a garden frame. The numerous cultivars are grafted on to young stock of the type plant.
□ An excellent small tree for creating light woodland conditions, for rhododendrons, azaleas, camellias, etc.

Right: The spring catkins of the silver birch, *Betula pendula*

Buddleia alternifolia

Loganiaceae

ZONES 5–10   SHRUB

Height: 4–6 m (13–20 ft), **Flowers:** mauve-blue, fragrant, summer, **Foliage:** green leaves arranged alternately, deciduous, **Position:** sun, **Soil:** light loamy soil, **Habit:** makes a graceful arching specimen, **Propagation:** by 12–15 cm (5–6 in) long cuttings of partially-ripe side shoots taken with a heel in mid – late summer.
□ Extremely beautiful in full flower, this shrub can be trained as a standard, making an excellent specimen plant in a lawn.

Buddleia davidii

Loganiaceae   Butterfly bush

ZONES 5–10   SHRUB

Height: up to 3 m (10 ft), **Flowers:** vary in colour according to cultivar, often fragrant, held in long panicles, mid-summer early autumn, **Foliage:** narrow green leaves up to 30 cm (1 ft) long, white and downy beneath, deciduous, **Position:** sun, **Soil:** light loamy soil, tolerates lime, **Habit:** spreads widely, of open growth, **Propagation:** hardwood cuttings, 23–30 cm (10–12 in) long, taken in mid-autumn and inserted in the garden.
□ *B. davidii* cultivars and varieties are best pruned hard back in early spring to keep a shrub of manageable size. As common

Left: *Buddleia davidii* 'Black Knight'
Above: *Buddleia davidii* 'White Bouquet'

name suggests, these plants attract butterflies.

Recommended cultivars of *Buddleia davidii*

'*Black Knight*' – violet-blue flowers.
'*Empire Blue*' – blue, each with an orange centre.
'*Harlequin*' – reddish purple flowers; only grows to 1.8 m (6 ft) white-variegated foliage.
'*Ile de France*' – violet-blue flowers.
'*Pink Pearl*' – pink flowers.
'*Royal Red*' – large reddish-purple blooms.
'*White Bouquet*' – white flowers.

Buddleia 'Lochinch'
Loganiaceae
ZONES 5–10   SHRUB
Height: 1.5–3 m (5–10 ft), **Flowers:** pale violet-blue each with orange centre, held in erect spikes, fragrant, mid-summer – early autumn, **Foliage:** covered in white hairs when young, later green above and white below, deciduous, **Position:** sun, **Soil:** light loamy soil, **Habit:** makes a compact bushy specimen, **Propagation:** hardwood cuttings as for *B. davidii*.
☐ Probably a hybrid between *B. davidii* and *B. fallowiana*.

Buxus microphylla
Buxaceae   Small-leaved box
ZONES 5–10   SHRUB
Height: 1–1.2 m (3–4 ft), **Flowers:** greeny yellow, scented, mid-spring, insignificant, **Foliage:** green, evergreen, **Position:** sun or shade, **Soil:** tolerates most soils, **Habit:** slow-growing, compact, **Propagation:** by cuttings 5–8 cm (2–3 in) long, taken in late summer – early autumn.
☐ Clip plants in spring and late summer. Useful for the front of a shrub border and for containers.

Buxus sempervirens
Buxaceae   Common box
ZONES 5–10   SHRUB
Height: up to 2.4 m (8 ft), more if left unclipped, **Flowers:** greeny yellow, scented, mid-spring, insignificant, **Foliage:** green, 'Elegantissima' and 'Aureo-Variegata' have foliage variegated with cream, all are evergreen, **Position:** sun or shade, **Soil:** tolerates most soils, **Habit:** dense foliage, growth slow, **Propagation:** by cuttings 5–8 cm (2–3 in) long taken in late summer – early autumn.
☐ Trim in spring and late summer. An ideal shrub for topiary, low hedges and edgings. 'Suffruticosa' is edging box.

Calceolaria integrifolia
Scrophulariaceae
ZONES 9–10   SHRUB
Height: 60 cm (2 ft), **Flowers:** bright yellow, mid-summer – early autumn, **Foliage:** green, generally evergreen, **Position:** sun and maximum shelter, **Soil:** tolerates most soils, **Habit:** dense, erect growth, **Propagation:** seed or cuttings.
☐ This half-hardy sub-shrub is not suitable for overwintering outside in cold districts. But it is a delightfully colourful plant for a long period. Cut back by half in mid-spring.
  Its main use is for summer bedding.

Callicarpa bodinieri var. *giraldii*
Verbenaceae
ZONES 6–10   SHRUB
Height: 1.8 m (6 ft), **Flowers:** violet, mid – late summer, **Foliage:** matt green, deciduous, colours yellow and red in autumn, **Position:** full sun or partial shade, **Soil:** suits most soils, **Habit:** upright, **Propagation:** cuttings early – mid-summer.
☐ The flowers are followed by showy violet-blue berries. Best to grow two or three plants together as then more berries are produced.

Callistemon citrinus 'Splendens'
Myrtaceae   Bottle brush
ZONES 8–10   SHRUB
Height: 1.5–1.8 m (5–6 ft), **Flowers:** bright red stamens, mid-summer – early autumn, **Foliage:** green, evergreen, **Position:** sun, **Soil:** suits most soils, **Habit:** loose, arching, **Propagation:** seed or cuttings.
☐ This magnificent shrub thrives in mild and protected places such as against a south- or south-west facing wall, but is not hardy enough for colder areas.

Calluna vulgaris

Ericaceae Ling, heather

ZONES 4–8 SHRUB

Height: 15–80 cm (6–33 in), **Flowers:** white, shades of pink, mauve and purple, late summer – early autumn, **Foliage:** green, gold or orange, evergreen, **Position:** best in full sun, tolerates some shade, **Soil:** light, lime-free with added peat, **Habit:;** dwarf, compact and bushy suitable for ground cover, **Propagation:** heeled cuttings summer/autumn.

□Trouble-free plants; lightly clip off straggly growth and dead flowers. Associates well with other members of the Ericaceae and small conifers.

Recommended cultivars of *C. vulgaris*

'Alba Plena' – double white flowers; 45 cm (18 in) high; compact.

'Alportii Praecox' – crimson; 45 cm (18 in) high; compact.

'County Wicklow' – double pale pink flowers; 23 cm (10 in) high; spreading.

'Elsie Purnell' – double silvery pink flowers, darker in bud; 60–80 cm (2–2¾ ft); upright.

'Golden Feather' – golden foliage turns a soft orange in autumn; 45 cm (18 in) high; mauve flowers of little value; compact.

'Gold Haze' – white flowers; brilliant yellow foliage; 60 cm (2 ft) high; compact.

'Hammondii Rubrifolia' – purple flowers; young foliage bright red turning green with age; 45 cm (1½ ft) high; compact.

'H.E. Beale' – double rose-pink flowers; dark green foliage; 60 cm (2 ft) high; compact.

'Multicolor' ('Prairie Fire') – purple flowers; foliage in shades of yellow, orange and red throughout the year, especially bright in winter; 15 cm (6 in) high; the best prostrate cultivar.

'Orange Queen' – pink flowers; young foliage golden, becoming orange; 60 cm (2 ft) high; compact.

'Peter Sparkes' – double deep pink flowers;

Above left: Winter foliage of *Calluna vulgaris* cultivars 'Gold Haze' and 'Robert Chapman'
Above right: *Calluna vulgaris* 'Alba Plena'

45 cm (18 in) high; compact.

'Robert Chapman' – purple flowers; golden summer foliage turns flame-red in winter; 45 cm (18 in) high; compact.

'Silver Queen' – mauve-pink flowers; woolly, silver foliage; 45 cm (1½ ft) high; upright.

'Sister Anne' ('Hirsuta Compressa') – purple flowers; downy greyish-green foliage; 15 cm (6 in); prostrate.

Calocedrus decurrens

Cupressaceae Incense cedar

ZONES 5–10 CONIFER

Height: up to 2.5 m (8 ft) after 10 years, ultimately 30 m (100 ft), **Flowers and cones:** of no particular merit, **Foliage:** rich-green all year round, aromatic, 'Aureovariegata' has irregularly occurring golden shoots, evergreen, **Position:** open and sunny, **Soil:** any normal well-drained garden soil, **Habit:** slow-growing, narrowly columnar, **Propagation:** best raised from seed; or cuttings.

□Makes a magnificent lawn specimen in the large garden.

Caltha palustris 'Flore Plena'

Ranunculaceae Marsh marigold, kingcup

ZONES 4–9 HERBACEOUS PERENNIAL

Height: 15 cm (6 in), **Flowers:** yellow, double, early – late spring, **Foliage:** dark green, shiny, deciduous, **Position:** sun or partial shade, **Soil:** moist, loamy, neutral or moderately acid; or in water 15 cm (6 in) or more deep, **Habit:** compact and spreading, **Propagation:** by division in late spring – early summer after flowering.

□Good marginal plant for ponds or for moist herbaceous borders.

Calycanthus occidentalis

Calycanthaceae Allspice

ZONES 4–9 SHRUB

Height: 4 m (13 ft), **Flowers:** purplish red, smells unpleasantly, early summer – early autumn, **Foliage:** dark green; deciduous, **Position:** full sun, **Soil:** suits most soils, but add some peat, **Habit:** loose and open, the wood is aromatic, **Propagation:** best by layers, as seed does not always ripen. Suckers sometimes make it possible to propagate by division.

□An unusual shrub normally grown in a shrub or mixed border: best suited to the larger garden.

CAMELLIAS

Camellias, so handsome in flower and foliage, deserve to be more popular than they are. Perhaps it is their exotic appearance that suggests they must be difficult to grow. In fact they are generally hardy and, given the right soil and situation, can be grown with success. They require a good, light but completely lime-free soil with plenty of added peat and leafmould. If your soil does not satisfy this requirement then camellias make ideal tub plants if an ericaceous compost is used to fill the container.

The best position for a camellia is one sheltered from cold winds and frosts and protected by other shrubs or a wall, preferably facing north or west. Although they will flower more freely in an open sunny situation the blooms will be damaged by early morning sun on frosted blossoms and by heavy rain.

Camellia 'Cornish Snow'
Theaceae Camellia
ZONES 7–10 SHRUB
Height: 2.5–3 m (8–10 ft), **Flowers:** profusion of small white flowers all along the stems, late winter – mid-spring, **Foliage:** dark green, shiny, evergreen, **Position:** sun or partial shade, protected from north and east winds, **Soil:** moisture-retentive, acid or neutral peaty soil, **Habit:** bushy, upright, **Propagation:** take cuttings of half-ripe side shoots, 8–10 cm (3–4 in) long early – late summer.
□ Camellias thrive in a sunny position but bear in mind when planting that their flowers should be protected from early morning sun or frost damage will occur.

Camellia japonica
Theaceae Common camellia
ZONES 7–10 SHRUB
Height: 3–4 m (10–13 ft) or more, **Flowers:** single, semi-double or double, white or shades of red or pink, late winter – late spring, **Foliage:** deep green, shiny, evergreen, **Position:** sun or partial leafy shade, **Soil:** moisture-retentive acid or neutral soil with added peat, **Habit:** varies according to cultivar but generally pleasing, **Propagation:** by leaf-bud cuttings or semi-ripe side shoots 8–10 cm (3–4 in) long in early – late summer.
□ Unfortunately, camellia blossoms are easily damaged by frost and rain.

Top left: *Camellia* 'Cornish Snow'
Top right: *Camellia japonica* 'Lady Clare'
Right: An example of a formal double flower of *Camellia japonica*

Recommended cultivars of
C. japonica
'*Adolphe Audusson*' – big, semi-double flowers, rich-red with attractive stamens; vigorous yet restrained.
'*Contessa Lavinia Maggi*' – medium, formal double flowers, white with red-cerise flecks; bushy and upright.
'*Devonia*' – medium-sized, single cup-shaped, white flowers; upright, vigorous.
'*Donckelarii*' – large, semi-double flowers, red, maybe speckled white; bushy habit, slow-growing.
'*Elegans*' ('Chandleri Elegans') – large, anemone form flowers, pink flecked with white; compact, excellent for tub planting.
'*Lady Clare*' – big, deep pink, semi-double flowers; strong, wide grower.
'*Mathotiana*' – large, crimson, formal double flowers; vigorous, compact and erect.
'*Mathotiana Alba*' – large, white, formal double flowers; vigorous, compact and erect.

Camellia 'Leonard Messel'
Theaceae
ZONES 7–10 SHRUB
Height: 4 m (13 ft) or more, **Flowers:** big, rich pink, semi-double, early – mid-spring, **Foliage:** deep green, leathery, net-veined, evergreen, **Position:** sun or leafy, partial shade, **Soil:** moisture-retentive acid or neutral peaty soil, **Habit:** vigorous and tall growing, **Propagation:** by cuttings of half-ripe side shoots, 8–10 cm (3–4 in) long taken early – late summer.
□ A very beautiful tall, hardy, evergreen shrub producing flowers up to 15 cm (6 in) in diameter.

Camellia × williamsii 'Donation'

Theaceae

ZONES 7–10   SHRUB

Height: 1.8–3 m (6–10 ft), **Flowers:** large, soft-pink, semi-double, late autumn – mid-spring, **Foliage:** dark green, glossy, evergreen, **Position:** sun or leafy, partial shade, **Soil:** moisture-retentive acid or neutral peaty soil, **Habit:** upright vigorous grower, **Propagation:** take cuttings of half-ripe side shoots 8–10 cm (3–4 in) long in early – late summer.

☐ Possibly the most beautiful camellia, and certainly among the most popular.

Camellia × williamsii 'Golden Spangles'

Theaceae

ZONES 7–10   SHRUB

Height: 1.8–3 m (6–10 ft), **Flowers:** small, bright-pink, single, late autumn – mid-spring, **Foliage:** dark green with a central golden blotch, **Position:** sun or leafy, partial shade, **Soil:** moisture-retentive acid or neutral peaty soil, **Habit:** erect, **Propagation:** take cuttings of half-ripe side shoots 8–10 cm (3–4 in) long in early – late summer.

Right: *Camellia × williamsii* 'Golden Spangles'

Campanula carpatica

Campanulaceae   Bellflower

ZONES 5–9   ROCK PLANT

Height: 23–30 cm (9–12 in), **Flowers:** shades of blue, but can be white, mid – late summer, **Foliage:** green, deciduous, **Position:** semi-shade or full sun, **Soil:** well-drained, fertile, **Habit:** forms a compact clump, **Propagation:** sow seeds in mid-autumn or early – mid-spring under glass; or by cuttings of young basal shoots taken in mid – late spring, inserted in sand and peat in a garden frame.

☐ Suitable for rock garden, front of border or paving.

Campanula cochlearifolia (syn. *C. pusilla*)

Campanulaceae   Bellflower

ZONES 4–9   ROCK PLANT

Height: 10–15 cm (4–6 in), **Flowers:** blue, bell-shaped on thin stems, mid-summer – early autumn, **Foliage:** medium green, rounded, deciduous, **Position:** full sun or semi-shade, **Soil:** well drained, fertile, **Habit:** a tufted plant, **Propagation:** by seed sown in sandy compost in a garden frame or greenhouse, or by division in autumn or spring.

☐ 'Alba' (above) is pure white. Suitable for rock garden, front of border or paving.

Campanula garganica

Campanulaceae   Bellflower

ZONES 4–9   ROCK PLANT

Height: 12–15 cm (5–6 in), **Flowers:** blue, starry, profuse, in 15 cm (6 in) long sprays, mid-summer – early autumn, **Foliage:** medium green, kidney-shaped, deciduous, **Position:** full sun or semi-shade, **Soil:** well-drained, fertile, **Habit:** this perennial forms a neatly rounded clump, **Propagation:** by seed sown in sandy compost in a garden frame or greenhouse; or by division in autumn or spring.

Above left: *Campanula lactiflora*
Above centre: *Campanula lactiflora* 'Alba'
Above right: *Campanula persicifolia*
Right: *Campanula poscharskyana*

Campanula glomerata 'Superba'
Campanulaceae Bellflower
ZONES 5–10   HERBACEOUS PERENNIAL
Height: 60 cm (2 ft), **Flowers:** bell-shaped, purple, carried on upright stems, late spring – mid-autumn, **Foliage:** medium green, deciduous, **Position:** full sun or semi-shade, **Soil:** well-drained, fertile, **Habit:** upright, clump-forming perennial, **Propagation:** divide roots in autumn or spring, or sow seed in autumn or spring.
☐An excellent border plant, associating well with yellow achilleas.

Campanula lactiflora
Campanulaceae Bellflower
ZONES 5–10   HERBACEOUS PERENNIAL
Height: 1.2 m (4 ft), **Flowers:** blue, early – mid-summer, **Foliage:** pale green, deciduous, **Position:** full sun or semi-shade, **Soil:** well-drained, fertile, **Habit:** tall and erect, clump-forming, needs some support, **Propagation:** by division in autumn or spring.
☐'Loddon Anna' is an excellent cultivar with pinky flowers. 'Alba' has white flowers. 'Brantwood' is a good violet-purple. This campanula looks lovely planted with yellow achilleas.

Campanula lactiflora 'Pouffe'
Campanulaceae Bellflower
ZONES 6–10   HERBACEOUS PERENNIAL
Height: 30 cm (1 ft), **Flowers:** violet-blue, early – late summer, **Foliage:** green, deciduous, **Position:** full sun or semi-shade, **Soil:** tolerates most soils, **Habit:** low-growing and compact, clump-forming perennial, **Propagation:** divide in autumn or spring.
☐Plant in groups for best effect. Suitable for the front of a border.

Campanula persicifolia
Campanulaceae Peach-leaved bellflower
ZONES 4–10   HERBACEOUS PERENNIAL
Height: 60 cm–1 m (2–3 ft), **Flowers:** blue shades (sometimes white), cup-shaped, early – late summer, **Foliage:** medium green, rosettes, evergreen, **Position:** full sun or semi-shade, **Soil:** humus-rich, **Habit:** rigid stems, **Propagation:** by seed sown in seed compost in a garden frame or greenhouse; or by division, autumn or spring. Not true to type from seed.
☐The most popular campanula for border planting.

Campanula poscharskyana
Campanulaceae Bellflower
ZONES 4–9   ROCK PLANT
Height: 25 cm (10 in), **Flowers:** blue, starry flowers in long sprays, early summer – late autumn, **Foliage:** medium green, rounded, deciduous, **Position:** full sun, **Soil:** tolerates most soils, **Habit:** spreading and excessively vigorous, **Propagation:** by seed sown in spring or autumn in seed compost in a garden frame or greenhouse; or by division in autumn or spring.
☐A good ground cover plant.

Campsis radicans

Bignoniaceae   Trumpet vine, trumpet creeper

ZONES 8–10   CLIMBER

Height: about 10 m (33 ft), **Flowers:** orange-scarlet, tubular, late summer and early autumn, **Foliage:** green, pinnate, formed of seven to nine leaflets, deciduous, **Position:** sheltered wall in full sun, **Soil:** any fertile soil, **Habit:** eventually climbing by aerial roots, but requires some tying initially, **Propagation:** cuttings, summer, in propagator; or layering.

□ *Campis grandiflora* has larger flowers but is not so hardy.

Campsis × tagliabuana 'Madame Galen'

Bignoniaceae   Trumpet vine, trumpet creeper

ZONES 8–10   CLIMBER

Height: about 8 m (26 ft), **Flowers:** reddish salmon, tubular, **Foliage:** green, pinnate, with seven to nine leaflets, deciduous, **Position:** sheltered wall in full sun, **Soil:** any fertile soil, **Habit:** eventually self-clinging, but initially requires training, **Propagation:** cuttings of ripening shoots, summer, in propagator; or layering.

□ Cut back last year's shoots in late winter.

Carpenteria californica

Philadelphaceae

ZONES 9–10   SHRUB

Height: 3 m (10 ft), **Flowers:** large shining white, fragrant, early – mid-summer, **Foliage:** green, evergreen, **Position:** plenty of sun, shield from cold winds, **Soil:** tolerates most soils, **Habit:** bushy, **Propagation:** seed sown in early – mid-spring.

□ Pruning is unnecessary but untidy growth can be cut back when flowering is over. Good wall plant.

Caryopteris × clandonensis

Verbenaceae

ZONES 5–10   SHRUB

Height: 1 to 1.2 m (3–4 ft), **Flowers:** blue, early – mid-autumn, **Foliage:** green, deciduous, **Position:** best in full sun, **Soil:** well-drained, including chalk, **Habit:** bushy, **Propagation:** cuttings in late summer.

□ Prune back in early spring. This delightful shrub is attractive to bees.

Good as ground cover around autumn-colouring shrubs.

Cassiope 'Edinburgh'

Ericaceae

ZONES 6–10   SHRUB

Height: 18 cm (8 in), **Flower:** white, bell-like, red edge, mid – late spring, **Foliage:** green, evergreen, **Position:** light shade, open as possible, as it is a plant native to moorland, **Soil:** moist, acid, peaty, **Habit:** dwarf plant with thin deep green stems, **Propagation:** layers or cuttings in late summer.

□ Generally trouble-free and needs no pruning. Ideal subject for a peat garden, with dwarf rhododendrons, etc.

Catananche caerulea 'Major'

Compositae   Cupid's dart

ZONES 6–10   HERBACEOUS PERENNIAL

Height: 60 cm (2 ft), **Flowers:** blue, daisy-like, early summer – early autumn, **Foliage:** green, deciduous, **Position:** sunny, **Soil:** tolerates almost any soil, even one that is sandy and dry, **Habit:** short-lived perennial, **Propagation:** by root cuttings in early spring inserted in seed compost in a garden frame. Seeds can be sown in mid – late spring but will not come true to type.

□ Suitable for the front of a border; good for cutting and drying.

Top: *Ceanothus* 'A.T. Johnson'
Above: *Ceanothus impressus*
Right: *Ceanothus thyrsiflorus* var. *repens*

Ceanothus 'A.T. Johnson'

Rhamnaceae Californian lilac
ZONES 7–10   SHRUB
Height: 1.8–3 m (6–10 ft), **Flowers:** blue, summer and early autumn, **Foliage:** green, evergreen, **Position:** open, sunny in mild areas, but wall protection elsewhere, **Soil:** light, in good condition, well drained, **Habit:** branching, **Propagation:** cuttings of ripening side shoots in mid – late summer.
☐ No regular pruning. Good companion plants on walls are climbing roses.

Other Ceanothus hybrids

All ceanothus make ideal wall shrubs with initial training.
EVERGREEN
'*Autumnal Blue*' – light blue flowers from late summer through autumn; branching. ZONES 7–10.
'*Burkwoodii*' – intense blue flowers mid – late summer and mid-autumn; branching. ZONES 7–10.
'*Delight*' – intense blue flowers from late spring to early summer; hardy and bushy, requiring no regular pruning. ZONES 7–10.
'*Southmead*' – intense blue flowers in late spring and early summer; small leaves, dense and bushy habit. ZONES 7–10.

DECIDUOUS
'*Gloire de Versailles*' – pale blue scented flowers, early summer to mid autumn; strong growing, open habit, cut back hard in mid-spring by reducing last year's growth to about 10 cm (4 in) above old wood. ZONES 5–10.
'*Topaz*' – bright blue flowers, early summer to mid autumn; rounded and bushy; prune as above. ZONES 7–10.

Ceanothus impressus

Rhamnaceae Californian lilac
ZONES 7–10   SHRUB
Height: 3 m (10 ft), **Flowers:** dark blue, prolific, mid – late spring, **Foliage:** small, dark green, shiny, evergreen, **Position:** sun, sheltered by a sunny wall, **Soil:** light and well drained, **Habit:** bushy, **Propagation:** by cuttings 10 cm (4 in) long of ripening side shoots, preferably with a heel, taken in mid-summer.
☐ No regular pruning needed. A good wall shrub. Climbing or rambler roses make attractive companions.

Ceanothus thyrsiflorus var. repens

Rhamnaceae Californian lilac
ZONES 7–10   SHRUB
Height: 1.2 m (4 ft), **Flowers:** small, pale blue, late spring – early summer, **Foliage:** deep green and glossy, evergreen, **Position:** sun, **Soil:** light, well drained, **Habit:** low, spreading, **Propagation:** by cuttings of ripening side shoots preferably with a heel, taken in mid-summer.
☐ No regular pruning is needed. Makes good ground cover for a largish area: can be used for clothing steep banks.

Cedrus atlantica 'Aurea'
Pinaceae Atlas cedar

ZONES 7–10   CONIFER

Height: about 2.5 m (8 ft) after 10 years, ultimately 5 m (16 ft), **Cones:** large brown, barrel-shaped on mature trees only, **Foliage:** rich yellow, evergreen, **Position:** sunny and open, **Soil:** well-drained, **Habit:** slow-growing and not very vigorous, initially conical, but flat topped with age, **Propagation:** by grafting.
□ An attractive specimen tree for a lawn. Looks good with 'blue' conifers.

Cedrus atlantica var. *glauca*
Pinaceae Atlas cedar

ZONES 6–10   CONIFER

Height: about 4 m (13 ft) after 10 years, ultimately 30 m (100 ft), **Cones:** large, bluish, barrel-shaped, on mature trees only, **Foliage:** bluish-green or grey-green, evergreen, **Position:** sunny and open, suitable for seaside planting, **Soil:** suits most well-drained soils, **Habit:** loosely conical, **Propagation:** seed: select the bluest seedlings. Also by grafting.
□ 'Glauca Pendula' is smaller with weeping branches down to ground. Makes a fine lawn specimen in large gardens.

Right: Cones of *Cedrus atlantica*

Cedrus deodara
Pinaceae Deodar

ZONES 6–10   CONIFER

Height: about 5 m (16 ft) after 10 years, ultimately 30 m (100 ft) or more, **Cones:** light brown, about 10 cm (4 in) long, on old trees only, **Foliage:** blue-green when young, changing to deep green, evergreen, **Position:** sunny and open, **Soil:** well-drained, **Habit:** drooping branches and wide spreading, **Propagation:** seed.
□ Unsuitable for the smaller garden. 'Aurea' only grows to half the height of the species and has golden foliage in spring, turning green by autumn.

Cedrus libani
Pinaceae Cedar of Lebanon

ZONES 6–10   CONIFER

Height: about 2.5 m (8 ft) after 10 years, ultimately 30 m (100 ft) or more, **Cones:** light brown, barrel-shaped, on old trees only, **Foliage:** bright or deep green, evergreen, **Position:** sunny and open, **Soil:** well-drained, **Habit:** slow-growing, young specimens cone-shaped, older ones flat-topped, **Propagation:** best raised from seeds.
□ Only suitable for very large gardens. 'Nana' is dwarf, forming a dense conical bush 1 m (3 ft) high, but eventually taller.

Celastrus orbiculatus
Celastraceae Bittersweet

ZONES 3–9   CLIMBER

Height: up to 12 m (40 ft), **Flowers:** insignificant, mid-summer, followed by very attractive, sparkling scarlet and gold fruits surrounded by yellow calyces, **Foliage:** green, turning yellow in autumn, deciduous, **Position:** sun or partial shade, **Soil:** suits most soils, **Habit:** shrubby twiner, **Propagation:** by layering of young shoots. Or by semi-ripe cuttings in summer, or hardwood cuttings in autumn.
□ Train to grow through the branches of a mature tree or to cover an old stump.

Centaurea montana

Compositae Perennial cornflower

ZONES 3–9   HERBACEOUS PERENNIAL

Height: 45–60 cm (1½–2 ft), **Flowers:** blue, freely produced, late spring – late summer, **Foliage:** green, with white hairs, lanceolate, deciduous, **Position:** sun or partial shade, **Soil:** rich, well-drained, **Habit:** floppy growth, clump-forming perennial, spreads rapidly in good conditions, **Propagation:** by division of clumps mid-autumn – early spring.

☐ Cut back stems after flowering to encourage possible further flowering in autumn.

A useful front-of-the-border plant.

Centranthus ruber

Valerianaceae Red valerian

ZONES 6–10   HERBACEOUS PERENNIAL

Height: 60 cm–1 m (2–3 ft), **Flowers:** deep pink, in clusters on upright stems, early summer – early autumn, **Foliage:** blue-green, oval, deciduous, **Position:** sunny, **Soil:** dry, poor and chalky are all acceptable, **Habit:** short-lived perennial, informal, self-seeding, **Propagation:** sow seeds in the open ground during spring.

☐ Dead stems should be cut down mid-autumn onwards. Ideal perennial for those difficult hot dry spots.

Cephalotaxus harringtonia var. drupacea

Taxaceae Cow's tail pine, Japanese plum yew

ZONES 5–9   CONIFER

Height: about 1 m (3 ft) after 10 years, ultimately 2.5 m (8 ft), **Flowers:** insignificant, but ovoid green fruits 2–3 cm (about 1 in) long are produced, **Foliage:** yew-like but longer and with two silvery bands beneath, evergreen, **Position:** very tolerant, grows well in shade, **Soil:** tolerates most soils, including chalk, **Habit:** similar to a large-leaved yew, dense and compact, **Propagation:** by seeds.

☐ Useful for shaded areas and chalk soils.

Cerastium biebersteinii

Caryophyllaceae Snow in summer

ZONES 4–10   ROCK PLANT

Height: 10–15 cm (4–6 in), **Flowers:** white in profusion, late spring – early summer, **Foliage:** silvery and woolly, evergreen, **Position:** sunny, **Soil:** well drained, **Habit:** very invasive, **Propagation:** by seeds sown in spring, or by division in early – mid-spring.

☐ Good for covering banks.

Ceratostigma plumbaginoides

Plumbaginaceae Hardy plumbago

ZONES 8–10   SHRUB

Height: 30 cm (1 ft), **Flowers:** blue, mid-summer – late autumn, **Foliage:** green, deciduous, colouring red in autumn, **Position:** preferably full sun, **Soil:** dry, well-drained, **Habit:** wider than high, spreading sub-shrub, **Propagation:** cuttings of ripening side shoots in mid-summer.

☐ Makes good ground cover among larger shrubs but not suitable for colder districts.

Ceratostigma willmottianum

Plumbaginaceaea Hardy plumbago

ZONES 8–10   SHRUB

Height: 1–1.2 m (3–4 ft), **Flowers:** blue, mid-summer – mid-autumn, **Foliage:** green, deciduous, red-tinted in autumn, **Position:** preferably full sun, **Soil:** dry, well drained, **Habit:** bushy sub-shrub, **Propagation:** cuttings of ripening side shoots in mid-summer.

☐ Suitable for sheltered shrubberies or herbaceous borders. Michaelmas daisies make good companion plants.

Chaenomeles japonica

Rosaceae Maule's quince, Japanese
  quince

ZONES 4–9   SHRUB

Height: 2.5 m (8 ft), **Flowers:** bright
orange-red, early – mid-spring, **Foliage:**
green, deciduous, **Position:** sun or shade,
Soil: tolerates most soils, **Habit:** wide
spreading, **Propagation:** heeled cuttings
of side shoots in mid – late summer.

☐ Edible fruits are produced that can be
used in preserves. Can be trained against a
wall, when plants should be pruned after
flowering by cutting back last year's
shoots.

Chaenomeles × speciosa

Rosaceae Japonica

ZONES 4–9   SHRUB

Height: 1.8 m (6 ft), **Flowers:** mostly
shades of red, late winter – mid-spring,
Foliage: green, deciduous, **Position:**
open, or trained against shady or sunny
walls, **Soil:** tolerates most soils, **Habit:**
much branched and spreading, **Propagation:** heeled cuttings of side shoots in mid –
late summer; or layer stems in early
autumn. Ripe seeds can be sown in early –
mid-autumn.

☐ 'Nivalis' has large white flowers, 'Rosea
Plena', double pink and 'Simonii', bright
red. Pruning as for *C. japonica*. Fragrant
yellow fruits produced in autumn. Ideal
for training against a wall.

Chaenomeles × superba

Rosaceae Ornamental quince

ZONES 4–9   SHRUB

Height: 1.8 m (6 ft), **Flowers:** mostly
shades of red and orange, late winter –
mid-spring, **Foliage:** green, deciduous,
Position: sun or shade, good for wall
training of any aspect, **Soil:** suits most
soils, **Habit:** wide spreading with dense
foliage, **Propagation:** heeled cuttings,
10 cm (4 in) long, of side shoots in mid –
late summer.

☐ Impressive golden apple-like fruits are
produced in late summer. These are edible
but not tasty unless used for jams or jellies.
'Boule de Feu' has orange flowers, 'Crimson and Gold' rich crimson with yellow
anthers, 'Pink Lady', pink. All are suitable
for training against a wall.

Chamaecyparis lawsoniana

Cupressaceae Lawson cypress

ZONES 5–9   CONIFER

Height: about 3 m (10 ft) after 10 years,
ultimately 30 m (100 ft), **Cones:** small and
scaly in profusion but not specially attractive, **Foliage:** mid to dark green, evergreen, **Position:** sun or partial shade,
Soil: tolerates most soils, **Habit:** cone
shaped, **Propagation:** by seeds or
cuttings taken with a heel (see p. 70).

☐ A good hedging plant. Never cut into
old wood when trimming. There are many
cultivars available and most are used as
specimen plants in lawns, or the dwarf
cultivars can be grown in heather beds or
on rock gardens.

Left: *Chamaecyparis lawsoniana* 'Lutea'
(back) and *C. l.* 'Blue Nantais' (front).

107

Recommended cultivars of *Chamaecyparis lawsoniana*

Heights given are approximate, after 10 to 15 year's growth. Many of the taller growing cultivars will eventually reach well over 6 m (20 ft).

'*Albovariegata*' – 1.2–4.5 m (4–15 ft); foliage tipped with creamy white; dense, rounded bush. ZONES 6–9.

'*Allumii*' – 1.8–4.5 m (6–15 ft); pinkish or red male strobili in spring; soft bluish-grey foliage; columnar. ZONES 5–9.

'*Blue Nantais*' – 1.5–2.2 m (5–7 ft); red male strobili in spring; blue-green foliage, bluish white beneath; broadly conical. ZONES 5–9.

'*Chilworth Silver*' – 1.2–3 m (4–10 ft); silvery blue young foliage; densely columnar. ZONES 6–9.

'*Columnaris Aurea*' – 1.5–2.2 m (5–7 ft); pinkish to red male strobili in spring; greeny yellow foliage, brighter in full sun; broadly columnar. ZONES 6–9.

'*Columnaris Glauca*' – 1.8–4.5 m (6–15 ft); pinkish to red male strobili in spring; blue-grey foliage; forms a narrow pointed tipped pillar. ZONES 6–9.

'*Ellwoodii*' – 1.5–3 m (5–10 ft); dark grey-green foliage, turning bluish in winter; dense feathery sprays form a slow-growing column. ZONES 5–9.

'*Ellwood's Gold*' – 1.2–4.5 m (4–15 ft); yellow-tinted foliage; ZONES 6–9.

'*Ellwood's Pillar*' – 1.5–4.5 m (5–15 ft); grey-green foliage, bluish in winter; slow-growing column. ZONES 5–9.

'*Ellwood's White*' – 1.5–4.5 m (5–15 ft); dark grey-green foliage, some white tipped; slow growing column. ZONES 6–9.

'*Erecta Aurea*' – 1.8–2.5 m (6–8 ft); golden green foliage, tends to scorch in hot sun; dense and very erect. ZONES 6–9.

'*Erecta Viridis*' – 1.8–2.5 m (6–8 ft); bright shiny dark green foliage; compact, dense, very erect and pointed; can suffer damage in snow. ZONES 6–9.

'*Filiformis Compacta*' – 60–75 cm (2–2½ ft); dark green foliage on drooping thread-like branchlets; rounded bush. ZONES 5–9.

'*Fletcheri*' – 1.8–2.5 m (6–8 ft); pinkish to red male strobili; greyish-green foliage; several main stems. ZONES 5–9.

'*Gimbornii*' – 30–75 cm (1–2½ ft); blue-green leaves; slow growing, dwarf rounded bush. ZONES 5–9.

'*Green Pillar*' – 1.5–4.5 m (5–15 ft); pinkish to red male strobili; bright green foliage; dense compact and very erect similar to '*Erecta Viridis*' but hardier. ZONES 5–9.

'*Lanei*' – 1.8–2.2 m (6–7 ft); golden-green foliage with bright gold tips; loosely conical. ZONES 6–9.

'*Lutea*' – 1.8–2.2 m (6–7 ft); pinkish to red male strobili; gold-tipped foliage, colours better in sunny position; broadly columnar. ZONES 6–9.

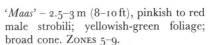

'*Maas*' – 2.5–3 m (8–10 ft), pinkish to red male strobili; yellowish-green foliage; broad cone. ZONES 5–9.

'*Minima Aurea*' – 25–75 cm (10–30 in); dense, brilliant yellow foliage; slow-growing, pyramid shape. Outstanding for a small garden, rock garden or heather bed. ZONES 6–9.

'*Minima Glauca*' – 30–75 cm (12–30 in); grey-green; slow grower; compact dome-shaped bush. ZONES 5–9.

'*Nana*' – 45–75 cm (1½–2½ ft); bright grey-green; broadly conical, similar to '*Minima Glauca*'. ZONES 5–9.

'*Nana Albospica*' – 45–75 cm (1½–2½ ft); green foliage with white tips gives an overall appearance of a cream coloured bush; broadly conical; protect from cold winds. ZONES 7–9.

'*Pembury Blue*' – 1.8–6 m (6–20 ft) pinkish to red male strobili; rich blue foliage; conical. ZONES 6–9.

'*Pottenii*' – 1.8–4.5 m (6–15 ft); pinkish to red male strobili; pale green, soft feathery foliage; protect from cold winter winds; very bushy. ZONES 6–9.

'*Pygmaea Argentea*' – 20–60 cm (8–24 in); pinkish red male strobili; blue-green leaves tipped white; slow growing, round and bushy. ZONES 6–9.

Top left: *Chamaecyparis lawsoniana* 'Minima Aurea'.
Top right: *C. l.* 'Lanei'. **Above left:** *C. l.* 'Pembury Blue'. **Above right:** *C. l.* 'Ellwoodii'

'*Spek*' – 1.8–2.5 m (6–8 ft); male strobili pinkish to red; foliage deeper blue than '*Pembury Blue*'; conical. ZONES 6–9.

'*Stewartii*' – 2.5–4 m (8–13 ft); pinkish to red male strobili; rich gold foliage turning yellowish-green in winter, best colour in a sunny position; conical, upright with narrow sprays. ZONES 6–9.

'*Tamariscifolia*' – 1–1.5 m (3–5 ft), pinkish to red male strobili; bright grey green foliage; spreading, semi-prostrate when young, mushroom-shaped when more mature. Slow growing. Associates well with golden-foliage conifers. ZONES 5–9

'*Westermanni*' – 2.5–3 m (8–10 ft); foliage light yellow held in pendulous sprays when young, turning green with age; loosely conical. ZONES 5–9.

'*Winston Churchill*' – 1.5–1.8 m (5–6 ft); pinkish to red male strobili; deep gold foliage throughout the year; broadly conical. ZONES 6–9.

'*Wisselii*' – 2.5–3 m (8–10 ft); profusion of red male strobili in spring; foliage blue-green; upright and distinctive. ZONES 5–9.

Chamaecyparis nootkatensis 'Compacta'

Cupressaceae   Nootka Cypress

ZONES 4–9   CONIFER

Height: 75 cm–1 m (2½–3 ft) after 10 years, ultimately 3 m (10 ft), **Flowers:** yellow male strobili in spring, **Foliage:** matt green, evergreen, **Position:** sun or partial shade, **Soil:** humus-rich, **Habit:** bushy, conical, **Propagation:** by cuttings (see p. 70).
□ Useful for the heather garden. 'Lutea' ('Aurea') is conical with golden yellow foliage. Best in full sun.

Chamaecyparis nootkatensis 'Pendula'

Cupressaceae   Nootka cypress

ZONES 4–9   CONIFER

Height: about 3 m (10 ft) after 10 years, ultimately 24 m (80 ft), **Flowers:** yellow male strobili in spring, dull blue cones, **Foliage:** matt green, rough feeling, evergreen, **Position:** sun or partial shade, **Soil:** humus-rich, **Habit:** pendulous, cone shaped, **Propagation:** by cuttings (see p. 70).
□ Train leading shoot vertically. Good as a lawn specimen.

Chamaecyparis obtusa 'Crippsii'

Cupressaceae

ZONES 5–9   CONIFER

Height: about 1.8 m (6 ft) after 10 years, ultimately 7.5 m (25 ft), **Flowers and cones:** insignificant, **Foliage:** deep yellow, evergreen, **Position:** sun or partial shade, best in an open, sunny position, **Soil:** suits most humus-rich soils, **Habit:** cone-shaped, growth slow, **Propagation:** by cuttings (see p. 70).
□ Occasional light pruning to maintain a thickness of growth.

Good as a lawn specimen, especially with 'blue' conifers.

Other recommended cultivars of *Chamaecyparis obtusa*   ZONES 5–9

'*Nana*' – about 23 cm (10 in) after 10 years; dark green foliage held in layers of concave, densly packed fans; small flat-topped bush.
'*Nana Gracilis*' – about 60 cm (2 ft) after 10 years; shiny deep green foliage; similar to but larger than 'Nana'.
'*Nana Lutea*' – about 30 cm (1 ft) after 10 years, can reach 75 cm (2½ ft) or more; leaves yellow and white; best in full sun; compact and bushy.
'*Pygmaea*' – about 23 cm (10 in) but can reach 75 cm (2½ ft) or more; leaves green, bronze-flushed in winter; slow growing, globular bush.

Chamaecyparis pisifera 'Boulevard'

Cupressaceae

ZONES 5–9   CONIFER

Height: about 1 m (3 ft) after 10 years, ultimately 2.5 m (8 ft), **Flowers and cones:** insignificant, **Foliage:** silver blue, evergreen, **Position:** sun or partial shade, best colour in partial shade, **Soil:** moisture-retentive but well-drained, preferably lime-free, **Habit:** dense and conical, **Propagation:** by cuttings (see p. 70).
□ Excellent conifer for heather gardens.

Other recommended cultivars of *Chaemaecyparis pisifera*
Sawara cypress
'*Filifera Aurea*' – 1.2–3 m (4–10 ft); bright yellow, cord-like foliage; slow growing, rounded bush. ZONES 5–9.
'*Filifera Nana*' – about 1.3 m (4½ ft) or more; green foliage on long cord-like branchlets; rounded bush. ZONES 5–9.
'*Plumosa Aurea*' – 1–3 m (3–10 ft) or more; soft feathery foliage, yellow in summer, but it becomes more green in winter; slow growing, broadly conical. ZONES 5–9.

Top left: *Chamaecyparis obtusa* 'Pygmaea'
Top right: *Chamaecyparis obtusa* 'Nana'
Left: *Chamaecyparis pisifera* 'Filifera Aurea'

'*Plumosa Aurea Nana*' – 45–75 cm (1½–2½ ft); similar to 'Plumosa Aurea' but slower growing and more compact. ZONES 6–9.
'*Plumosa Rogersii*' – 30–75 cm (1–2½ ft); rich yellow foliage in full sun, dulls in winter; rounded compact cone; protect from cold winds. ZONES 6–9.
'*Pygmaea*' – 30–75 cm (1–2½ ft); fine, dense green young foliage; slow-growing compact cone. ZONES 5–9.
'*Squarrosa Sulphurea*' – 1–1.5 m (3–5 ft); foliage sulphur-yellow in full sun, turns pale bluish green in winter; feathery appearance, broadly conical. ZONES 5–9.

Chamaecyparis thyoides
'Andelyensis'

Cupressaceae   White cypress
ZONES 5–9   CONIFER
Height: 75 cm–1 m (2½–3 ft) after 8 years, ultimately 5 m (16 ft), **Cones:** small with a bloom, **Foliage:** bluish green, bronze tinged in winter, evergreen, **Position:** sun or partial shade, **Soil:** best in moist, humus-rich, lime-free soils, **Habit:** slow-growing, pillar-shaped, **Propagation:** by cuttings (see p. 70).
☐ Useful for the heather garden.

Chamaecyparis thyoides
'Ericoides'

Cupressaceae   White cypress
ZONES 5–9   CONIFER
Height: about 60 cm (2 ft) after 10 years, ultimately 1.5 m (5 ft), **Flowers and cones:** insignificant, **Foliage:** dark bronze green in summer, purplish in winter, evergreen, soft feeling, **Position:** sun and shelter from winds and frosts, **Soil:** best on moist, humus-rich, lime-free soils, **Habit:** compact and conical, **Propagation:** by cuttings (see p. 70).
☐ Excellent conifer for heather gardens.

Chamaedaphne calyculata 'Nana'
Ericaceae   Leather leaf
ZONES 6–9   SHRUB
Height: 30 cm (1 ft), **Flowers:** white, pendulous, mid – late spring, **Foliage:** green, evergreen, **Position:** open, sunny, **Soil:** lime-free, humus-rich, **Habit:** small, dense, wiry shrub with horizontal branches, **Propagation:** by seed or cuttings.
☐ A good shrub to associate with heathers and Japanese azaleas, which like the same conditions. Not always easy to obtain.

Chimonanthus praecox
(**syn. C. fragrans**)

Calycanthaceae   Winter sweet
ZONES 5–9   SHRUB
Height: 3 m (10 ft), **Flowers:** pale yellow marked purple at centre, not showy but very fragrant, winter, **Foliage:** green, deciduous, **Position:** sunny and sheltered, **Soil:** deep, rich and well-drained, will succeed on chalk, **Habit:** bushy, of dense growth, **Propagation:** ripe seeds sown in early – mid-autumn; or layer stems in early autumn.
☐ Can be wall-trained. Prune wall-trained shrubs in early spring; cut flowered shoots to within 10 cm (4 in) of their base.

A lovely shrub to have near the house where its scent can be easily savoured. Plant winter heathers around it.

Left: *Chimonanthus praecox*

110

Chionanthus virginicus
Oleaceae Fringe tree
Zones 4–10   Shrub
Height: 5 m (16 ft) or more, **Flowers:** white, in profusion in early – mid-summer, slight scent, **Foliage:** green, deciduous, **Position:** full sun, preferably protected by south- or west-facing wall, **Soil:** fertile loamy soil, **Habit:** erect, **Propagation:** cuttings of firm young wood in late summer or autumn.
☐Unusual but easy subject for the shrub border.

Choisya ternata
Rutaceae Mexican orange blossom
Zones 7–9   Shrub
Height: 3 m (10 ft), **Flowers:** white, scented, mid-spring, then at intervals until late autumn, **Foliage:** green, shiny, ever-green, aromatic, **Position:** plants for sun, or semi-shade, **Soil:** well-drained, lime tolerant, **Habit:** forms a rounded bush, **Propagation:** cuttings of semi-ripe side shoots in late summer.
☐An excellent shrub for seaside gardens.
   In cold areas it is best grown against a warm south- or west-facing wall.

Choisya ternata 'Sundance'
Rutaceae
Zones 7–9   Shrub
Height: 1.2–1.5 m (4–5 ft), **Flowers:** white, scented, mid-spring, then at intervals 'till late autumn, **Foliage:** bright yellow young foliage, holding colour throughout the year, **Position:** sunny and sheltered, **Soil:** well-drained, lime-tolerant, **Habit:** forms a rounded bush, **Propagation:** cuttings of semi-ripe side shoots in late summer.
☐This recent development is a winner. Smaller growing than the species and complementary to most other shrubs.

Chrysanthemum maximum
   'Wirral Supreme'
Compositae Shasta daisy
Zones 5–10   Herbaceous perennial
Height: 1 m (3 ft); **Flowers:** white, double, early – late summer, **Foliage:** green, longish with toothed edges, deciduous, **Position:** sunny, **Soil:** good drainage, fairly rich, ideally alkaline, **Habit:** erect-stemmed perennial, **Propagation:** cuttings of basal shoots in early spring in a garden frame; or by division of clumps in early spring.
☐Good cut flower. Grow with spire-like perennials, such as delphiniums.

Left: *Chrysanthemum maximum* 'Wirral Supreme'

Chrysanthemum rubellum 'Clara Curtis'

Compositae

ZONES 7–10   HERBACEOUS PERENNIAL
Height: 45–75 cm (1½–2½ ft), **Flowers:** rose-pink daisies, fragrant, mid-summer – mid-autumn, **Foliage:** medium-green, **Position:** sunny, **Soil:** good drainage, fairly rich, ideally alkaline, **Habit:** bushy and free-flowering perennial, **Propagation:** basal cuttings in early spring in a garden frame; or division in spring.
☐Good cut flower.

Cimicifuga foetida 'White Pearl'

Ranunculaceae   Bugbane

ZONES 4–9   HERBACEOUS PERENNIAL
Height: 1.2 m (4 ft), **Flowers:** white racemes, early – mid-autumn, **Foliage:** green and deciduous, **Position:** preferably partial shade but tolerates sun, **Soil:** moist, humus-rich, **Habit:** a graceful perennial with erect flower stems, **Propagation:** by division of clumps mid-autumn – early spring.
☐Particularly recommended for the shrub border or woodland garden.

Cistus × *aguilari* 'Maculatus'

Cistaceae   Sun rose

ZONES 8–10   SHRUB
Height: 1.2–1.5 m (4–5 ft), **Flowers:** large white with deep purple basal blotches, early – mid-summer, **Foliage:** pale green, evergreen, **Position:** full sun essential, **Soil:** well-drained, poor, **Habit:** erect bush, **Propagation:** heeled cuttings 10 cm (4 in) long of semi-ripe side shoots in mid – late summer.
☐Good for mild coastal gardens.

Cistus × *corbariensis*

Cistaceae   Sun rose

ZONES 8–10   SHRUB
Height: 1–1.2 m (3–4 ft), **Flowers:** white, yellow at base, red buds, late spring – early summer, **Foliage:** matt green, evergreen, **Position:** full-sun essential, **Soil:** well drained, poor, **Habit:** forms a low bush, **Propagation:** cuttings of semi-ripe side shoots in mid – late summer.
☐Hardier than most sun roses, but like all of them is an ideal plant for hot, dry places, and for coastal gardens.

Cistus × *purpureus*

Cistaceae   Sun rose

ZONES 8–10   SHRUB
Height: 1.2–1.5 m (4–5 ft), **Flowers:** deep purplish pink with chocolate basal blotches, late spring – mid-summer, **Foliage:** greyish green, evergreen, **Position:** full sun essential, **Soil:** well-drained, poor, **Habit:** erect bush, **Propagation:** cuttings of semi-ripe side shoots in mid – late summer.
☐Ideal for hot dry places and coastal gardens.

Cistus 'Silver Pink'

Cistaceae   Sun rose

ZONES 8–10   SHRUB
Height: 1 m (3 ft), **Flowers:** pink with a prominent cluster of yellow stamens, early – mid-summer, **Foliage:** green above, grey below, evergreen, **Position:** full sun, **Soil:** well-drained, poor, **Habit:** compact and bushy, **Propagation:** cuttings of semi-ripe, side shoots in mid – late summer.
☐This hybrid has flowers borne on upright stems well clear of the leaves. Ideal for hot dry places and coastal gardens.

CLEMATIS

These cause confusion in the matter of pruning. This is because there are basically three groups of clematis, each requiring different treatment, according to their time and habit of flowering.

Group A These flower between late winter and spring. Flowers carried directly on the previous season's growth. In this group are included all the *C. montana* cultivars, *C. armandii* and *C. chrysocoma*. These need no regular pruning, but, where space is restricted, all flowering shoots may be removed immediately after flowering, and young shoots will break from lower down the stems. These may then be trained into position to flower the following year.

Group B Flowering in late spring and early summer and in most cases again in autumn. Flowers are produced on short growths from the previous season's wood. In this group are included many of the large-flowered cultivars such as 'Barbara Dibley', 'Nelly Moser', the improved sport, double-flowered 'Vyvyan Pennell' and 'Duchess of Edinburgh'.

In spring, as soon as the buds start to show, all weak and dead wood must be cut out, and strong shoots re-tied into flowering position. In order that bushy growth is established during the formative years, it pays in the long run to cut all growth right down to about 23 cm (9 in) from ground level in the second year after planting.

On a wall where space is restricted, the new strong young shoots may be shortened, but never by more than a third or many early flowers will be lost. If the clematis is growing through trees, then no great amount of pruning is necessary which is a blessing because it could be difficult. Occasional thinning out old and dead wood is all that is required.

Group C Flowering from mid-summer onwards. The flowers carried on terminal shoots or from leaf axils of the summer growth. In this group are included the popular Jackmanii hybrids, many species, and cultivars such as 'Ernest Markham' and 'Hagley Hybrid'.

This group of clematis may be pruned down to about 30 cm (1 ft) of the ground level in spring. On a wall, it is a good idea to train two shoots horizontally at about 30 cm (1 ft) high, one each side of the planting position, to form permanent wood from which flowering stems will grow vertically each year. Every spring thereafter, pruning consists of cutting back all the previous season's flowering stems to just above a pair of plump buds near their bases.

Clematis 'Duchess of Edinburgh'

Simple layering.
1. partially cut the stem to form a tongue. **2.** hold the tongue open with a stone or small piece of wood. **3.** peg down the wounded part of the stem so that it is in firm contact with the soil.

Clematis armandii

Ranunculaceae   Virgin's bower

ZONES 8–10   CLIMBER

Height: 5–6 m (16–20 ft), **Flowers:** cream-white, very fragrant, borne in clusters, mid – late spring, **Foliage:** deep green, comprising three shiny leathery deeply veined leaflets, evergreen, **Position:** full sun and shelter, shade its roots, **Soil:** must be fertile, cool, moist, alkaline or neutral, **Habit:** climbs and twines by means of its leaf stalks, but requires some training, **Propagation:** cuttings very difficult, so increase from seeds when available. These can be sown when ripe or in the spring.
☐ Prune as for group A (see p. 113).

Clematis cirrhosa

Ranunculaceae   Virgin's bower

ZONES 7–10   CLIMBER

Height: up to 3 m (10 ft), **Flowers:** cream-white, mid-winter – early spring, followed by fluffy seed heads, **Foliage:** green, variable, simple to compound, evergreen, **Position:** sunny and sheltered, shade its roots, **Soil:** cool, moist but well-drained, fertile, alkaline or neutral, **Habit:** climbs and twines but needs initial training, **Propagation:** by cuttings 10–12 cm (4–5 in) long of semi-ripe growth taken in summer and rooted in peat/sand mix in propagator; or by seeds sown in sandy compost in spring.
☐ Prune as for group A (see p. 113).

Clematis cirrhosa var. balearica

Ranunculaceae   Fern-leaved clematis

ZONES 7–10   CLIMBER

Height: up to 3.6–4.5 m (12–15 ft), **Flowers:** pale yellow flecked with reddish spots inside, throughout winter, **Foliage:** green, segmented, bronzy-tinted during winter, evergreen, **Position:** sun and shelter, **Soil:** cool, moist but well drained, fertile, alkaline or neutral, **Habit:** climbs and twines but needs initial training, **Propagation:** by cuttings, see *C. cirrhosa* above.
☐ Prune as for group A (see p. 113).

Clematis flammula

Ranunculaceae   Virgin's bower

ZONES 5–9   CLIMBER

Height: 3 m (10 ft), **Flowers:** scented, white, late summer – mid-autumn, followed by fluffy seed heads, **Foliage:** bright green, formed of three leaflets, deciduous, **Position:** sunny situation preferred, shade roots, **Soil:** cool, moist but well drained, fertile, alkaline or neutral, **Habit:** vigorous, producing a dense profusion of growth, **Propagation:** by cuttings or seed (see *C. cirrhosa* above).
☐ Can prune back last year's growth in spring to restrict size.

Clematis florida 'Sieboldii' (syn. *C. florida* 'Bicolor')

Ranunculaceae   Virgin's bower

ZONES 5–9   CLIMBER

Height: about 3 m (10 ft), **Flowers:** white with a central ring of purple petal-like stamens, early – mid-summer, **Foliage:** glossy green, compound, comprising nine leaflets, deciduous, **Position:** sunny situation preferred, shade roots, **Soil:** cool, moist but well drained, fertile, alkaline or neutral, **Habit:** self-supporting by its twining leaf stalks, **Propagation:** by cuttings. See *C. cirrhosa* above.
☐ Prune as for group A (see p. 113).

Clematis heracleifolia

Ranunculaceae   Herbaceous clematis

ZONES 5–9   HERBACEOUS PERENNIAL

Height: 1–1.2 m (3–4 ft), **Flowers:** light blue, curled back petals, late summer – early autumn, **Foliage:** dark green, trifoliate, deciduous, **Position:** sunny, **Soil:** any moist, but well drained neutral or alkaline soil, **Habit:** a sub-shrub, lax habit, **Propagation:** by basal cuttings in spring inserted in sand and peat in a garden frame.
☐ Suitable for herbaceous or mixed borders. Cut down stems to 15 cm (6 in) in autumn.

Top left: *Clematis armandii*
Top right: *Clematis cirrhosa* var. *balearica*
Above: *Clematis heracleifolia*

Clematis integrifolia 'Hendersonii'

Ranunculaceae   Herbaceous clematis

ZONES 5–9   HERBACEOUS PERENNIAL

Height: 60 cm (2 ft), **Flowers:** deep blue, 5 cm (2 in) across, early summer – early autumn, **Foliage:** mid-green, prominently veined, deciduous, **Position:** sunny, **Soil:** any alkaline or neutral garden soil, **Habit:** requires support with twiggy sticks, **Propagation:** by basal cuttings taken in mid – late spring and inserted in sandy peaty compost in a garden frame.
☐ Suitable for herbaceous or mixed borders. Cut down stems to ground level in autumn.

Clematis × jackmanii

Ranunculaceae   Virgin's bower

ZONES 5–9   CLIMBER

Height: up to 4 m (13 ft), **Flowers:** deep purple, mid-summer – mid-autumn, **Foliage:** green, pinnate and twining, deciduous, **Position:** sun preferred, though more tolerant of some shade than most, shade roots, **Soil:** cool, moist but well drained, fertile, alkaline or neutral, **Habit:** climbs by its twining leaf stalks, **Propagation:** by layering or taking cuttings. See *C. cirrhosa* p. 114.
□ Prune as for group C (see p. 113).

Clematis macropetala

Ranunculaceae

ZONES 5–9   CLIMBER

Height: up to 2.4 m (8 ft), **Flowers:** violet-blue with paler blue; hanging and bell-like; late spring – early summer onwards; fluffy seed heads, **Foliage:** green, attractively divided, deciduous, **Position:** sunny situation preferred, shade roots, **Soil:** cool, moist but well drained, fertile, alkaline or neutral, **Habit:** climbs by its twining leaf stalks, **Propagation:** by seed or cuttings. See *C. cirrhosa* p. 114.
□ 'Maidwell Hall' is a deeper blue cultivar. Prune as for group A (see p. 113).

Clematis macropetala
'Markham's Pink'

Ranunculaceae

ZONES 5–9   CLIMBER

Height: up to 2.4 m (8 ft), **Flowers:** attractive deep-pink, hanging and bell-like; late spring – early summer onwards; seedheads fluffy, **Foliage:** green, prettily divided, deciduous, **Position:** sunny situation preferred, shade roots, **Soil:** cool, moist but well drained, fertile, alkaline or neutral, **Habit:** climbs by its twining leaf stalks, **Propagation:** by layering or cuttings. See *C. cirrhosa* p. 114.
□ Prune as for group A (see p. 113).

Clematis montana

Ranunculaceae   Virgin's bower

ZONES 5–9   CLIMBER

Height: up to 9 m (30 ft), **Flowers:** white, profuse, late spring, **Foliage:** deep green, three leaflets, twining leaf stalks, deciduous, **Position:** sun or partial shade, shade roots, **Soil:** cool, moist but well drained, fertile, alkaline or neutral, **Habit:** vigorous, even rampant, climbs by twining leaf stalks, **Propagation:** by layers or cuttings. See *C. cirrhosa* p. 114.
□ Vigorous and curtain forming, suitable for covering pergolas or verandas. 'Tetrarose' has mauve-pink flowers.
Prune as for group A (see p. 113).

Clematis orientalis

Ranunculaceae   Virgin's bower

ZONES 5–9   CLIMBER

Height: 6 m (20 ft), **Flowers:** yellow, pendulous, fragrant; late summer – mid-autumn; fluffy silvery seedheads, very decorative, **Foliage:** pale green, feathery, deeply cut, deciduous, **Position:** sunny

Top left: *Clematis × jackmanii*
Above: *Clematis macropetala*

situation preferred, shade roots, **Soil:** cool, moist but well drained, fertile, alkaline or neutral, **Habit:** strong grower, fairly dense growth, **Propagation:** by cuttings. See *C. cirrhosa* p. 114.
□ Prune as for group C (see p. 113).

Clematis montana var. rubens

Ranunculaceae   Virgin's bower

ZONES 5–9   CLIMBER

Height: 9 m (30 ft), **Flowers:** light pink, profuse, late spring, **Foliage:** flushed with bronze, three leaflets, twining leaf stalks, deciduous, **Position:** sun or partial shade, shade roots, **Soil:** cool, moist but well drained, fertile, alkaline or neutral, **Habit:** vigorous, rampant, climbs by its twining leaf stalks, **Propagation:** by layers of cuttings. See *C. cirrhosa* p. 114.
□ Prune as for group A (see p. 113).

Clematis tangutica

Ranunculaceae Virgin's bower
ZONES 5–9   CLIMBER
Height: up to 6 m (20 ft), **Flowers:** yellow, lantern-shaped; late summer – mid-autumn; followed by fluffy seed heads, **Foliage:** greyish green, divided, deciduous, **Position:** prefers sunny situation, shade its roots, **Soil:** cool, moist but well drained, fertile, alkaline or neutral, **Habit:** strong grower, but slim in habit, **Propagation:** by cuttings. See *C. cirrhosa* p. 114.
☐ Best when left to run free, either up trees, on fences or over banks.
    Prune as for group C (see p. 113).

Clematis viticella 'Abundance'

Ranunculaceae Virgin's bower
ZONES 5–9   CLIMBER
Height: up to 3.5 m (12 ft), **Flowers:** soft purple, bell-shaped and hanging, mid-summer – early autumn, **Foliage:** deep green, several leaflets, deciduous, **Position:** sun and shelter, shade its roots, **Soil:** cool, moist but well drained, fertile, alkaline or neutral, **Habit:** has a slim habit of growth, **Propagation:** by cuttings. See *C. cirrhosa* p. 114.
    Prune as for group C (see p. 113).

Clematis 'Barbara Dibley' (large-flowered hybrid)

Ranunculaceae Virgin's bower
ZONES 5–9   CLIMBER
Height: up to 4 m (13 ft), **Flowers:** pink with darker bars, single, 15 cm (6 in) across; early summer – mid-autumn, **Foliage:** green, three leaflets, with twining leaf stalks, deciduous, **Position:** prefers sunny situation, **Soil:** cool, moist but well drained, fertile and alkaline, **Habit:** climbing by its twining leaf stalks, **Propagation:** by layers or cuttings. See *C. cirrhosa* p. 114.
☐ Prune as for group B (see p. 113). Many large-flowered hybrids will grow against east- or north-facing walls.

Other recommended large-flowered hybrids

ZONES 5–9
'Duchess of Edinburgh' – up to 4 m (13 ft); white, double, scented, late spring – early summer and late summer; prune as for group B (see p. 113).
'Ernest Markham' – up to 4 m (13 ft); single red, early summer-early autumn; cut back to 30 cm (12 in) from ground in late winter-early spring; prune as for group C (see p. 113).
'Hagley Hybrid' – up to 2.5 m (8 ft); single deep pink, early summer – early-autumn; cut back to 30 cm (1 ft) from ground in late winter – early spring; prune as for group C.
'Jackmanii Superba' – up to 3 m (10 ft); large rich purple; mid summer – mid autumn; cut back to 30 cm (12 in) from ground in late winter; prune as for group C.
'Mrs Cholmondeley' – up to 3 m (10 ft); large light blue, late spring – late summer; cut back to 30 cm (1 ft) from ground in late winter – early spring; prune as for group B.
'Nelly Moser' – up to 4 m (13 ft); pale pinky mauve with deeper bars, late spring – early summer and late summer – early autumn; trim back dead flower head immediately after flowering; prune as for group B.
'The President' – up to 4 m (13 ft); large single bluish-purple, early summer – early autumn; trim back old flowering growth immediatly after flowering; prune as for group B.
'Vyvyan Pennell' – up to 4 m (13 ft); double violet-blue, late spring – mid-summer; prune back old flowering shoots immediately after flowering; prune as for group B.
'William Kennett' – up to 4 m (13 ft); crinkle-edged medium-blue with dark stamens, early – late summer; trim back old flowering growth immediately after flowering; prune as for group B.

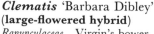

Top left: *Clematis tangutica*
Top right: *Clematis* 'Nelly Moser'
Left: *Clematis* 'William Kennett'

Clerodendrum bungei
Verbenaceae
ZONES 6–10   SHRUB
Height: 1.8–2.5 m (6–8 ft), **Flowers:**
starry, deep pink, scented, late summer –
early autumn, **Foliage:** large, rounded,
deep green, deciduous, **Position:** full sun,
sheltered from wind, **Soil:** rich, well
drained, **Habit:** upright thin stems, produces suckers, **Propagation:** remove
rooted suckers in early – mid-autumn or
early spring. Heeled cutting 12 cm (5 in)
long, of side shoots in late summer or early
autumn.
☐ It can be pruned almost to ground level
each spring. Can be grown against a warm
sunny wall.

Right: *Clerodendrum bungei*

Clerodendrum trichotomum
Verbenaceae
ZONES 5–10   SHRUB
Height: 5 m (16 ft), **Flowers:** white,
flushed pink, starry, fragrant, late summer, **Foliage:** medium green, deciduous,
unpleasant scent when crushed, **Position:**
full sun, sheltered from wind, **Soil:** rich,
well drained, **Habit:** large and bushy,
Propagation: cuttings as for *C. bungei*.
☐ The late flowers are followed by bright
blue berries surrounded by very attractive
red calyces. An outstanding large shrub for
late summer and autumn.

Clethra alnifolia
Clethraceae   Sweet pepper bush
ZONES 3–9   SHRUB
Height: 1.8 m (6 ft), **Flowers:** scented,
white, bell-shaped, late summer – mid-
autumn, **Foliage:** green, deciduous,
bright yellow in autumn, **Position:** open,
sunny, **Soil:** lime-free loam, moist, high in
humus, **Habit:** upright, bushy, **Propagation:** heeled cuttings of side shoots, 10 cm
(4 in) long, mid – late summer.
☐ Good for seaside planting.

Clethra barbinervis
Clethraceae
ZONES 5–9   SHRUB
Height: 4 m (13 ft), **Flowers:** white in
long racemes, fragrant, mid-summer –
early autumn, **Foliage:** green, deciduous,
turning red and yellow in autumn, **Position:** sunny and open, **Soil:** lime-free
loam, moist, high in humus, **Habit:** wide
spreading, **Propagation:** heeled cuttings
10 cm (4 in) long of side shoots, mid – late
summer.
☐ Remove some of the oldest stems each
winter. A good shrub for seaside planting.

Colutea arborescens
Leguminosae Bladder senna
ZONES 5–10   SHRUB
Height: 2.5 m (8 ft), **Flowers:** yellow,
similar to those of the pea, early summer –
early autumn, **Foliage:** ferny, pale green,
deciduous, **Position:** sun or partial shade,
suitable for hot, dry situations, **Soil:** tolerates most soils, **Habit:** bushy but airy
habit, **Propagation:** sow seeds outdoors
in early spring; or take heeled cuttings of
side shoots in early autumn.
☐ The main attraction of this shrub is its
8 cm (3 in) long inflated light green pods,
liberally tinted with red or bronzy-gold.
Last year's growth cut back in mid spring.

Convolvulus cneorum
Convolvulaceae
ZONES 9–10   SHRUB
Height: 1 m (3 ft) at most, **Flowers:**
creamy-white, buds pink, late spring –
early autumn, **Foliage:** long and narrow,
covered with shiny silver hairs; evergreen,
Position: sun and sheltered from wind,
Soil: tolerates most soils, **Habit:** low
bushy habit, **Propagation:** cuttings 8 cm
(3 in) long with a heel from basal or side
shoots, early – late summer.
☐ Not completely hardy but certainly
deserves a home with those who garden in
warmer areas. An attractive shrub for the
larger rock garden.

Cordyline australis
Agavaceae Cabbage tree
ZONES 8–10   SHRUB
Height: 4 m (13 ft) as a shrub, **Flowers:**
creamy white, scented, mid-summer, **Foliage:** greyish green, sword-like, evergreen, **Position:** full sun, mild districts
only, **Soil:** well-drained, moderately rich,
Habit: single erect trunk until flowering
age then erect branching, **Propagation:**
remove suckers in early – mid-spring, or
sow seeds in mid-spring.
☐ An exotic addition to the garden, can be
grown in a container. Thrives in seaside
gardens.

Coreopsis grandiflora
Compositae Tickseed
ZONES 3–9   HERBACEOUS PERENNIAL
Height: 45 cm (1½ft), **Flowers:** rich yellow, daisy-like on long slender stems, early
summer – mid-autumn, **Foliage:** green,
narrow, deciduous, **Position:** sunny and
open, **Soil:** moist but well drained,
alkaline, **Habit:** bushy and erect, can be
rather short-lived, **Propagation:** by division in autumn or spring; or by seed sown
outdoors or under glass in early spring.
☐ Taller cultivars include 'Badengold',
1 m (3 ft), 'Mayfield Giant', 75 cm (2½ft),
and 'Sunburst' 75 cm (2½ ft).

Coreopsis verticillata
Compositae Tickseed
ZONES 3–9   HERBACEOUS PERENNIAL
Height: 45–60 cm (1½–2 ft), **Flowers:** yellow, star-shaped, small but prolific, **Foliage:** green, divided into thin segments,
Position: sunny and open, **Soil:** alkaline
and not too heavy, **Habit:** upright, compact and bushy, **Propagation:** by division
in spring; by softwood cuttings taken in
mid – late summer; or by seed sown
outdoors or under glass in early spring.
☐ A good cultivar is 'Grandiflora'. Excellent for cutting.

Coriaria japonica
Coriariaceae
ZONES 9–10   SHRUB
Height: 60 cm (2 ft), **Flowers:** green at
first, becoming bright red then purplish
black, **Foliage:** green, ferny, deciduous,
Position: warm and sheltered, **Soil:** rich,
loamy soil, **Habit:** low-growing, renewing
itself by strong shoots from the base,
Propagation: this is not a long-lived
shrub, so should be renewed occasionally
from seeds or cuttings.
☐ Not suitable for cold districts. Red fruits
and autumn tints are additional bonuses.

Cornus alba
Cornaceae Red-stemmed dogwood
ZONES 2–9 SHRUB
Height: 3 m (10 ft), **Flowers:** small, yellowish, late spring – early summer, **Foliage:** green above, grey below, sometimes turning red in autumn, deciduous, **Position:** sun or partial shade, **Soil:** moist, **Habit:** upright and suckering, **Propagation:** 15 cm (6 in) hardwood cuttings in late autumn; or remove and replant suckers in late autumn.
☐ This shrub's main attraction is its thicket of bright red young shoots which come into their own in winter. To maintain these cut hard back in mid-spring. Cultivar 'Sibirica' has brilliant crimson shoots.

Cornus alba 'Elegantissima'
Cornaceae Dogwood, cornel
ZONES 2–9 SHRUB
Height: 1.8–2.5 m (6–8 ft), **Flowers:** small, yellowish, late spring – early summer, **Foliage:** white variegated, deciduous, **Position:** sun or partial shade, **Soil:** moist, **Habit:** suckering, forming a thicket of stems, brilliant red when young, **Propagation:** hardwood cuttings or replanting suckers removed with roots in late autumn.
☐ Young stems are brilliant red. Cut back in mid-spring to maintain stem colour.

Cornus alba 'Spaethii'
Cornaceae Dogwood, cornel
ZONES 2–9 SHRUB
Height: 1.8–2.5 m (6–8 ft), **Flowers:** small, yellowish, late spring – early summer, **Foliage:** variegated gold, very eye-catching, deciduous, **Position:** sun or partial shade, **Soil:** moist, **Habit:** suckering, forming a thicket of stems, brilliant red when young, **Propagation:** hardwood cuttings, or replanting rooted suckers removed in late autumn.
☐ Young stems brilliant red. Cut back in mid-spring to maintain stem colour.

Cornus alternifolia 'Argentea'
Cornaceae Dogwood, cornel
ZONES 5–9 SHRUB
Height: 2.5–3 m (8–10 ft), **Flowers:** white, late spring, **Foliage:** small, creamy-white edges, deciduous, **Position:** sun or partial shade, **Soil:** moist, **Habit:** horizontally spreading branches, **Propagation:** cuttings of firm shoots in summer.
☐ One of the best of all deciduous shrubs with variegated foliage. Particularly attractive with purple-leaved shrubs such as cotinus varieties.

Top: *Cornus canadensis*
Left: *Cornus alba*
Above: *Cornus alternifolia* 'Argentea'

Cornus amomum
Cornaceae Dogwood, cornel
ZONES 5–9 SHRUB
Height: 3 m (10 ft), **Flowers:** small, yellow-white, late spring – early summer, **Foliage:** dark green above, silky reddish down beneath, deciduous, **Position:** sunny, **Soil:** moist, **Habit:** more or less compact, **Propagation:** cuttings of firm shoots in summer.
☐ Thrives well in moist situations in all areas. Its distinctive features are its purple young stems and blue berries.

Cornus canadensis
Cornaceae Creeping dogwood
ZONES 5–9 SHRUB
Height: 10–20 cm (4–8 in), **Flowers:** white, early summer, **Foliage:** green, deciduous, **Position:** partial shade, **Soil:** peaty or rich in leafmould, slightly acid, **Habit:** low and creeping, **Propagation:** semi-ripe cuttings in mid – late summer.
☐ Edible red fruits are produced after the white flowers. An attractive groundcover plant for the shrub border or woodland garden.

Cornus controversa
Cornaceae Dogwood, cornel
ZONES 5–9 SHRUB
Height: 6 m (20 ft), **Flowers:** masses of white flowers in early – mid-summer followed by black fruits, **Foliage:** medium green, deciduous, some leaves may turn red in autumn, **Position:** sun or half shade, **Soil:** moist, humus-rich, **Habit:** branches form horizontal layers, **Propagation:** semi-ripe heel cuttings, in mid – late summer.
☐'Variegata' is an exquisite and most unusual shrub with silver variegated foliage. A fine feature plant.

Cornus florida var. rubra
Cornaceae Flowering dogwood
ZONES 4–9 SHRUB
Height: 5 m (16 ft), **Flowers:** insignificant, green, surrounded by four large deep pink bracts, late spring, **Foliage:** young leaves reddish, turning green, then autumn tinted, **Position:** sun or partial shade, **Soil:** humus-rich, moist, **Habit:** dense and bushy, **Propagation:** heeled semi-ripe cuttings, mid – late summer.
☐Round red fruits late summer and autumn.

Cornus kousa
Cornaceae Dogwood, cornel
ZONES 5–9 SHRUB
Height: 3 m (10 ft), **Flowers:** the white bracts are very showy, early summer, **Foliage:** medium to deep green, deciduous, **Position:** sun or partial shade, **Soil:** humus-rich, **Habit:** wide spreading, **Propagation:** heeled semi-ripe cuttings, mid – late summer.
☐Round red fruits in early autumn.

Cornus mas
Cornaceae Cornelian cherry
ZONES 4–9 SHRUB
Height: 4 m (13 ft), **Flowers:** yellow, on leafless stems in late winter – early spring, **Foliage:** green, deciduous, colouring well in autumn, **Position:** sun or partial shade, **Soil:** moist humus-rich, **Habit:** wide spreading, rather open, **Propagation:** seeds when ripe in late summer – early autumn; or by heeled, semi-ripe cuttings, 10 cm (4 in) long, in mid – late summer.
☐Red berries sometimes produced. Try an under planting of winter-flowering heathers.

Cornus nuttallii
Cornaceae Dogwood, cornel
ZONES 6–9 SHRUB
Height: 6 m (20 ft), **Flowers:** conspicuous white bracts, late spring, followed by red fruits, **Foliage:** green, deciduous, beautiful autumn colouring, **Position:** sun or partial shade, **Soil:** moist, humus-rich, not for chalk soils, **Habit:** upright and bushy, **Propagation:** seeds when ripe in late summer – early autumn; or by heeled semi-ripe cuttings 10 cm (4 in) long.
☐Not suitable for colder districts.

Cornus stolonifera 'Flaviramea'
Cornaceae Dogwood, cornel
ZONES 2–9 SHRUB
Height: 2.5 m (8 ft), **Flowers:** white, late spring – early summer, **Foliage:** green, deciduous, **Position:** sun or partial shade, **Soil:** moist, humus-rich, **Habit:** suckering, dense thickets of stems, **Propagation:** remove and replant rooted suckers in late autumn; or layer long shoots in early autumn and sever in the mid-autumn of following year; or hardwood cuttings late autumn.
☐Yellow winter bark associates well with the red stems of *C. alba*. Prune as for *C. alba*.

Top left: *Cornus florida* var. *rubra*
Top right: *Cornus kousa*
Right: *Cornus stolonifera* 'Flaviramea'

Coronilla emerus var. *emeroides*
Leguminosae
ZONES 6–10   SHRUB
Height: 1 m (3 ft), **Flowers:** pea-shaped, yellow, late spring – early summer, **Foliage:** green, ferny, deciduous, **Position:** sun or partial shade, warm and sheltered, **Soil:** fertile and well drained, **Habit:** dense and bushy, **Propagation:** cuttings in summer or nearly autumn or seeds sown in spring. Germination is improved if hot water, about 88°C (284°F) is poured over the seeds first.
☐ A useful shrub for underplanting trees and taller shrubs.

Coronilla glauca
Leguminosae
ZONES 7–10   SHRUB
Height: 3 m (10 ft), **Flowers:** pea-shaped, yellow, late spring – early summer, fragrant in daytime, **Foliage:** blue-green, pinnate, evergreen, **Position:** sun or partial shade, **Soil:** fertile, light and loamy, well drained, **Habit:** dense and bushy, rounded form, **Propagation:** cuttings in summer or early autumn.
☐ Best grown against a warm sheltered wall in most districts.

Right: *Coronilla glauca*

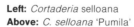

Cortaderia selloana
  (**syn. *C. argentea, Gynerium argenteum***)
Gramineae   Pampas grass
ZONES 7–10   HERBACEOUS PERENNIAL
Height: 1.8–3 m (6–10 ft), **Flowers:** silvery-white fluffy plumes, autumn, **Foliage:** green, narrow and arching, evergreen, **Position:** sunny and open, protected from wind, **Soil:** deep and well drained, rich, light and sandy, **Habit:** large perennial grass, **Propagation:** by seed sown in sandy compost in spring in a propagator; or by division in spring.

Left: *Cortaderia* selloana
Above: *C. selloana* 'Pumila'

☐ 'Pumila' is a dwarfer cultivar 1.2–1.5 m (4–5 ft) high. Plumes can be cut in autumn for house decoration.

A spectacular specimen plant, particularly set against a dark background.

Corylopsis pauciflora
Hamamelidaceae
ZONES 5–9   SHRUB
Height: 1.8 m (6 ft), **Flowers:** light yellow, early – mid-spring, highly fragrant, **Foliage:** green, deciduous, **Position:** full sun or semi-shade, sheltered, **Soil:** humus-rich, ideally acid, **Habit:** wide bushy shrub, **Propagation:** heeled cuttings of side shoots, in mid – late summer, or layer shoots in mid-autumn and sever from the parent plant a year or two later.

Corylus avellana 'Contorta'
Corylaceae   Corkscrew hazel
ZONES 4–9   SHRUB
Height: 3 m (10 ft), **Flowers:** yellow 'lamb's tail' catkins, late winter – early spring, **Foliage:** green, deciduous, yellow in autumn, **Position:** open, full sun, or partial shade, but sheltered from cold winds, **Soil:** well-drained, **Habit:** slow-growing, twisted branches, **Propagation:** by layers in summer or autumn and severed when rooted after one year, or by cuttings of ripe wood in mid – late summer.
☐ Though nuts are produced, the main interest is this shrub's twisted stems. An unusual specimen plant for a lawn, conspicuous in winter.

Corylus avellana 'Pendula'
Corylaceae   Weeping hazel
ZONES 4–9   SHRUB
Height: 5 m (16 ft), **Flowers:** pendulous yellow catkins, late winter – early spring, **Foliage:** green, deciduous, yellow in autumn, **Position:** open, full sun or partial shade, sheltered, **Soil:** well-drained, **Habit:** arching, weeping branches, **Propagation:** by layers or cuttings.
☐ Clusters each of four or five hazelnuts are produced and ripen in early – mid-autumn.

Corylus maxima 'Purpurea'
Corylaceae   Purple-leaf filbert
ZONES 5–9   SHRUB
Height: 4–5 m (13–16 ft), **Flowers:** long purplish catkins, late winter – early spring, **Foliage:** intense purple, deciduous, **Position:** sun or partial shade, **Soil:** well-drained, **Habit:** robust and bushy, **Propagation:** by layers and cuttings.
☐ Nuts, longer than the hazel's and sheathed in cup-like bracts, are produced singly or in pairs. This shrub with its deep purple foliage associates well with golden-foliage shrubs.

Cotinus coggygria
Anacardiaceae   Smoke tree
ZONES 4–9   SHRUB
Height: 3 m (10 ft), **Flowers:** buff-pink, fluffy-feathery, early – mid-summer, **Foliage:** green, smooth and rounded, deciduous, very good autumn colour, **Position:** sunny, **Soil:** well-drained, **Habit:** dense, bushy, wide-spreading shrub, **Propagation:** layer long shoots in early autumn, or take heeled cuttings, 10 to 12 cm (4–5 in) long, in late summer – early autumn.
☐ This shrub's flowers hang on, turning grey in late summer, creating a smoky effect which earns it its common name. One of the best shrubs for autumn foliage colour; good plant associations are pampas grass and Michaelmas daisies.

Left: *Cotinus coggygria*

Cotinus coggygria 'Royal Purple'
Anacardiaceae Smoke tree

ZONES 4–9　　　　　　　　SHRUB

Height: 3 m (10 ft), **Flowers:** buff-pink, fluffy-feathery flowers, early – mid-summer, **Foliage:** deep purple, turning reddish in autumn, deciduous, **Position:** sunny, **Soil:** well-drained, **Habit:** rounded, **Propagation:** layers or cuttings.

☐ Plant this shrub where the sun can shine through its foliage and you will see it light up as no other shrub can. Good companion plants are red or pink shrub roses.

Cotinus obovatus
Anacardiaceae

ZONES 4–9　　　　　　　　SHRUB

Height: 5 m (16 ft), **Flowers:** buff, fluffy-feathery, early – mid-summer, **Foliage:** green, deciduous, magnificent autumn colouring in shades of red, **Position:** sunny, **Soil:** well-drained, **Habit:** tree-like with red branches, **Propagation:** layers or cuttings.

☐ Deserves to be better known as it is one of the finest for autumn colour.

Right: *Cotinus obovatus*

Cotoneaster conspicuus 'Decorus'
Rosaceae

ZONES 4–9　　　　　　　　SHRUB

Height: up to 1 m (3 ft), **Flowers:** white, early summer, followed by numerous red berries, **Foliage:** small, dark green, evergreen, **Position:** sun or partial shade, **Soil:** tolerates most soils, **Habit:** low-growing, compact, **Propagation:** heeled cuttings 10 cm (4 in) long of ripening wood in mid – late summer, or layering in late autumn.

☐ This is very free-berrying. Useful for covering banks and areas between tall shrubs.

Cotoneaster dammeri
Rosaceae

ZONES 4–9　　　　　　　　SHRUB

Height: 20 cm (8 in), **Flowers:** white, late spring, **Foliage:** deep green, evergreen, **Position:** sun, partial or even full shade, **Soil:** tolerates most soils, **Habit:** quite prostrate with long spreading branches, **Propagation:** well adapted for layering in late autumn, usually rooting well within a year. Alternatively take cuttings of ripening wood, 10 cm (4 in) long, in mid – late summer.

☐ Useful for covering banks or as ground cover under trees. Coral-red berries.

Cotoneaster horizontalis
Rosaceae Herringbone cotoneaster

ZONES 4–9　　　　　　　　SHRUB

Height: roughly 1 m (3 ft), **Flowers:** white, late spring – early summer, **Foliage:** small deep green shiny leaves, with red autumn tints, deciduous, **Position:** sun, partial or full shade, **Soil:** tolerates most soils, **Habit:** branches of flat, herringbone pattern, **Propagation:** layering in late autumn or cuttings in mid – late summer.

☐ Red berries follow flowers. An invaluable shrub for north- or east-facing walls or for covering banks.

Above left: *Cotoneaster microphyllus*
Above centre: *Cotoneaster* 'Rothschildianus'
Above right: *Cotoneaster salicifolius*
Below right: *Cotoneaster salicifolius*

Cotoneaster horizontalis
'Variegatus'
Rosaceae
ZONES 5–9   SHRUB
Height: about 1 m (3 ft), **Flowers:** white, late spring – early summer, **Foliage:** cream variegated, flushed with red in autumn, deciduous, **Position:** sun or partial shade, **Soil:** tolerates most soils, **Habit:** densely spreading shrub with herringbone branch arrangement, **Propagation:** by layering in late autumn or cuttings in mid – late summer.
☐ Bright red berries follow flowers. Leaves colour in autumn. Ideal for planting against a wall.

Cotoneaster microphyllus
Rosaceae
ZONES 5–9   SHRUB
Height: 15 cm (6 in), **Flowers:** white, late spring – early summer, **Foliage:** small, deep green shiny leaves, evergreen, **Position:** sun or partial shade, **Soil:** suits most soils, **Habit:** very prostrate and spreading to 2.5 m (8 ft), **Propagation:** by layering in late autumn, or cuttings taken in mid-summer or mid-autumn.
☐ A very useful shrub for clothing banks, walls and manholes. The red berries are extra large.

Cotoneaster 'Rothschildianus'
Rosaceae
ZONES 6–9   SHRUB
Height: 1.8–3 m (6–10 ft), **Flowers:** white, late spring – early summer, followed by pale yellow berries, **Foliage:** medium green, semi-evergreen, **Position:** sun or partial shade, **Soil:** tolerates most soils, **Habit:** distinctive, spreading habit, **Propagation:** by layering in late autumn, or cuttings taken in mid – late summer.
☐ The cultivar 'Exburiensis' is similar in producing large clusters of yellow berries. Both excellent alongside autumn-foliage shrubs and tolerates the seaside.

Cotoneaster salicifolius
Rosaceae
ZONES 6–9   SHRUB
Height: 4.5 m (15 ft), **Flowers:** white, early summer, **Foliage:** dark-green, evergreen, **Position:** sun or partial shade, **Soil:** tolerates most soils, **Habit:** tall and graceful, **Propagation:** by layering in late autumn, or cuttings taken during mid – late summer.
☐ Bright red fruits. Suitable for a large shrub border. Grows well in seaside gardens.

Cotoneaster simonsii
Rosaceae
ZONES 5–9   SHRUB
Height: 1.8–2.5 m (6–8 ft), **Flowers:** white, early – mid-summer, **Foliage:** deep green, ovate, semi-evergreen, **Position:** sun or partial shade, **Soil:** tolerates most soils, **Habit:** upright growing, **Propagation:** by heeled cuttings 10 cm (4 in) long in mid – late summer.
☐ Makes an attractive hedge. Large crops of red-orange fruits and upright habit. Suitable for seaside gardens.

Crambe cordifolia
Cruciferae   Seakale

ZONES 7–9   HERBACEOUS PERENNIAL

Height: 1.2–1.5 m (4–5 ft), **Flowers:** white, in massive panicles, early – mid-summer, **Foliage:** greyish green, very large heart-shaped, deciduous, **Position:** sunny and open. **Soil:** alkaline, fertile, **Habit:** robust perennial with thick roots, needs considerable space, **Propagation:** by seed sown outdoors in spring, or by division in spring.

□ Ideal foliage plant for seaside gardens.

Crataegus oxyacantha 'Coccinea Plena'
(syn. 'Paul's Scarlet')
Rosaceae   Double scarlet hawthorn

ZONES 4–9   SHRUB

Height: 5–7.5 m (16–25 ft), **Flowers:** double scarlet, produced in profusion in late spring, followed in autumn by small red fruits, **Foliage:** mid green, deciduous, **Position:** full sun, open position but tolerates semi-shade, **Soil:** tolerates most soils, **Habit:** round headed, good for both town and seaside planting, **Propagation:** by grafting on to *C. monogyna* stocks in spring.

Crepis incana
Compositae   Hawksbeard

ZONES 5–9   ROCK PLANT

Height: 23–30 cm (9–12 in), **Flowers:** pale pink, mid – late summer, **Foliage:** greyish-green, ovate, deciduous, **Position:** sunny borders, banks or rock gardens, **Soil:** well-drained, **Habit:** forms a compact clump, **Propagation:** by seed sown in spring, or division in spring.

Crinodendron hookeranum
Elaeocarpaceae   Lantern tree

ZONES 8–10   SHRUB

Height: 3–5 m (10–16 ft), **Flowers:** deep red, lantern-shaped, pendulous, spring, **Foliage:** glossy green, evergreen, **Position:** semi-shade, sheltered from winds, **Soil:** acid, moisture retentive, fertile, **Habit:** densely branched, **Propagation:** heeled cuttings 10 cm (4 in) long of ripening shoots in mid – late summer.

□ A gem, but for mild districts only. Best grown against a warm sheltered wall.

Cryptomeria japonica 'Elegans'
Taxodiaceae   Japanese cedar

ZONES 5–9   CONIFER

Height: about 1.8 m (6 ft) after 10 years, ultimately 6 m (20 ft), **Flowers and cones:** strobili orange or reddish in early spring, roundish cones, not particularly noticeable, **Foliage:** rusty green in summer, copper coloured in winter, evergreen, **Position:** sun or partial shade, **Soil:** moisture retentive, acid or neutral, **Habit:** broadly conical or pyramidal, **Propagation:** by seed or cuttings (see p. 70).

□ Attractive fine-textured conifer. Good specimen tree for the larger lawn.

Above: *Cryptomeria japonica* 'Lobbii Nana'
Above right: *C. japonica* 'Vilmoriniana'

Other recommended cultivars of *Cryptomeria japonica*
ZONES 5–9

Heights given are after approximately 10 years growth. All are ideal for planting in heather beds or in rock gardens.

'*Globosa*' – 30–75 cm (1–2½ ft) high; foliage in summer yellow-green; reddish in winter; broad rounded bush.

'*Lobbii Nana*' ('Compacta') – 45–75 cm (1½–2½ ft) high; summer foliage pale green turning rusty; elegantly rounded bush.

'*Pygmaea*' – 30–75 cm (1–2½ ft) high; lime green foliage turning bronze in winter; slow-growing compact rounded bush.

'*Vilmoriniana*' (above) – 30–75 cm (1–2½ ft); summer foliage green-bronze turning reddish purple; forms packed ball.

x *Cupressocyparis leylandii*

Cupressaceae   Leyland cypress

ZONES 5–9   CONIFER

Height: about 10 m (33 ft) after 10 years if unrestricted, ultimate height 20 m (65 ft), **Cones:** round and brown, but of no decorative merit, **Foliage:** mid-green, evergreen, **Position:** sun or partial shade, suits maritime gardens, **Soil:** deep, well-drained, **Habit:** broad cone, very fast growing, **Propagation:** by cuttings (see p. 70).

□A specimen tree or excellent hedging plant. As a hedge plants should be spaced 1 m (3 ft) apart. It can be pruned hard.

'Castlewellan' has green-gold foliage, at its brightest in full sun. Makes a fine hedge.

Cupressus glabra 'Conica' (**syn. *C. arizonica* 'Conica'**)

Cupressaceae   Smooth Arizona cypress

ZONES 7–10   CONIFER

Height: about 4 m (13 ft) after 10 years, ultimately 15 m (50 ft), **Cones:** brown and rounded, noticeable but not of great decorative merit, **Foliage:** bluish-grey, aromatic, evergreen, **Position:** sun or partial shade, **Soil:** any type, well-drained, **Habit:** broadly cone or pyramid shaped, **Propagation:** by cuttings, as seed will not come true to type. (see p. 70).

Cupressus macrocarpa

Cupressaceae   Monterey cypress

ZONES 6–10   CONIFER

Height: about 6 m (20 ft) after 10 years, ultimately 20 m (65 ft), **Cones:** brown and rounded, numerous, **Foliage:** mid-green, becoming darker with age, aromatic, evergreen, **Position:** sun or part shade, excellent for seaside planting, **Soil:** any type, well drained, **Habit:** columnar with conical top when young, broadening with age, when lower growths tend to die off, **Propagation:** by seed (see p. 68).

□Now largely superseded by x *Cupressocyparis leylandii* which is faster growing, hardier and does not become bare at the bottom.

Good hedging conifer, or can be used as a specimen in a large lawn.

Cupressus macrocarpa 'Goldcrest'

Cupressaceae   Monterey cypress

ZONES 7–10   CONIFER

Height: 3 m (10 ft) after 10 years, ultimately 7.5 m (25 ft), **Flowers and cones:** insignificant, **Foliage:** brilliant yellow, very intense in winter, aromatic, evergreen, **Position:** open and sunny, protect from cold winds, **Soil:** any type, well-drained, **Habit:** neat, upright and conical, **Propagation:** by cuttings (see p. 70).

□Good companions are 'blue' or grey conifers of similar stature.

Cupressus sempervirens 'Stricta'

Cupressaceae   Italian cypress

ZONES 8–10   CONIFER

Height: about 3 m (10 ft) after 10 years, ultimately 20 m (65 ft), **Flowers and cones:** insignificant, **Foliage:** deep green, aromatic, evergreen, **Position:** sunny, shelter from cold winds, **Soil:** dry type, well-drained, **Habit:** very narrow column, **Propagation:** by cuttings (see p. 70).

□Excellent as a focal point in larger garden.

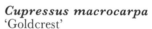

Left: *Cupressus macrocarpa* 'Goldcrest'

Right: *Cytisus* x *kewensis* (front) and
C. x *praecox*

Cytisus ardoinii
Leguminosae Broom
ZONES 5–10   SHRUB
Height: 20 cm (8 in), **Flowers:** yellow,
mid – late spring, **Foliage:** green, deciduous, **Position:** very sunny, **Soil:** does best
in neutral or slightly acid soils, **Habit:**
miniature, forms a carpet, **Propagation:**
seeds or heeled cuttings of sideshoots,
10 cm (4 in) long in late summer – early
autumn.
☐ Recommended for rock gardens and
ground cover (particularly on dry banks).

Cytisus battandieri
Leguminosae Algerian broom
ZONES 7–10   SHRUB
Height: 4 m (13 ft), **Flowers:** bright yellow, fruity scent, late spring – early summer, **Foliage:** silvery, deciduous,
Position: very sunny, **Soil:** best in neutral
or slightly acid soil, **Habit:** upright, **Propagation:** heeled cuttings of side shoots, in
late summer – early autumn.
☐ Very sheltered spot needed in cold areas
– excellent against a warm sunny wall
where it looks good with climbing roses of
all colours.

Cytisus × beanii
Leguminosae Broom
ZONES 6–10   SHRUB
Height: 60 cm (2 ft), **Flowers:** yellow,
late spring, **Foliage:** green, deciduous,
Position: sunny, **Soil:** best in neutral or
slightly acid soil, **Habit:** dwarf, compact,
Propagation: heeled cuttings of side
shoots in late summer.
☐ Suitable for the rock garden or planting
on dry sunny banks.

Cytisus decumbens
Leguminosae Broom
ZONES 5–10   SHRUB
Height: 1 m (3 ft), **Flowers:** yellow, late
spring – early summer, **Foliage:** green,
deciduous, **Position:** sunny, **Soil:** best in
neutral or slightly acid soil, **Habit:** a
prostrate shrub, wide spreading, **Propagation:** heeled cuttings 10 cm (4 in) long
of side shoots, taken in late summer – early
autumn.
☐ Makes good ground cover on a dry
sunny bank.

Cytisus × kewensis
Leguminosae Broom
ZONES 6–10   SHRUB
Height: 60 cm (2 ft), **Flowers:** creamy
yellow, late spring, **Foliage:** green, deciduous, **Position:** sunny, **Soil:** lime-tolerant, but best in neutral or slightly acid
soil, **Habit:** a low-growing shrub of pros-

trate habit, **Propagation:** seed or
cuttings.
☐ A very attractive little shrub, suitable
for the rock garden, dry bank or front of a
sunny border.

Cytisus nigricans
Leguminosae Broom
ZONES 5–10   SHRUB
Height: 1.5 m (5 ft), **Flowers:** yellow,
held in long sprays, early summer – early
autumn, **Foliage:** green, deciduous, **Position:** sunny, **Soil:** lime-tolerant, but best
in neutral or slightly acid soil, **Habit:**
erect, **Propagation:** seed or cuttings.
☐ A very useful shrub due to its exceptionally long flowering period.

Above left: *Cytisus battandieri*
Above: *Cytisus* × *beanii*

Cytisus × praecox
Leguminosae Warminster broom
ZONES 5–10   SHRUB
Height: 1.5 m (5 ft), **Flowers:** rich
cream, mid – late spring, **Foliage:** green,
insignificant, deciduous, **Position:** sunny,
Soil: tolerates most soils, even dry, poor
and stony, but not too acid or too limy,
Habit: erect and bushy, with arching
branches, **Propagation:** by cuttings taken in mid-summer.
☐ To stop this shrub becoming leggy, cut
back immediately after flowering, but not
into old, hard wood. 'Albus' has white
flowers, 'Allgold', bright yellow.

Cytisus purpureus
Leguminosae   Purple broom

ZONES 5–10   SHRUB

Height: 60 cm (2 ft) or a little more,
Flowers: purple, late spring – early summer, **Foliage:** deep-green, deciduous, **Position:** sunny, **Soil:** dry, normal garden
soil, even poor and stony, but not too acid
or alkaline, **Habit:** dwarf and compact,
Propagation: by cuttings taken in mid-
summer.
☐ A good little shrub for the front of a
sunny border or for the rock garden. Prune
young flowering stems after flowering.
Suitable for seaside gardens.

Cytisus scoparius 'Andreanus'
Leguminosae   Common broom

ZONES 5–10   SHRUB

Height: 2.5 m (8 ft), **Flowers:** yellow and
red, late spring – early summer, **Foliage:**
green, trifoliate, deciduous, **Position:**
sunny, **Soil:** tolerates most soils, even if
dry, poor or stony, but not too acid or too
limy, **Habit:** upright to arching branches,
Propagation: by cuttings taken in mid-
summer.
☐ Induce bushy growth by lightly cutting
back young stems immediately after
flowering. Good companion plants are
cistus. Suitable for seaside gardens.

Cytisus scoparius 'Burkwoodii'

Other recommended cultivars of *Cytisus scoparius*

ZONES 5–10

'Burkwoodii' – 1.8 m (6 ft); deep-red
flowers.
'Firefly' – 1.8 m (6 ft); yellow and deep red.
'Golden Sunlight' – 1.8 m (6 ft); bright gold-
en yellow flowers.
'Goldfinch' – 1.8 m (6 ft); purple, red and
yellow.
'Lena' – 1–1.5 m (3–5 ft); red and yellow
flowers; keep bushy and compact by
lightly cutting back flowering stems.

Daboecia cantabrica
'Atropurpurea'
Ericaceae   Connemara heath, St Dabeoc's
heath

ZONES 5–9   SHRUB

Height: up to 60 cm (2 ft), **Flowers:**
purple-pink, pitcher-shaped in long
racemes, early summer – late autumn,
Foliage: deep green, silvery underneath,
evergreen, **Position:** sun or partial shade,
Soil: lime-free, sandy peat or loam, **Habit:**
bushy and compact, **Propagation:** by
cuttings taken in mid – late summer, or by
layering shoots in autumn.

Above left: *Daboecia cantabrica*
Above: *Daboecia cantabrica* 'Alba'

☐ Clip over in spring with shears. 'Alba'
has white flowers, 'Bicolor' has purple-
pink and white flowers.
   Ideal subject for heather beds.

Danae racemosa
(syn. *Ruscus racemous*)
Ruscaceae   Alexandrian laurel

ZONES 6–10   SHRUB

Height: 1 m (3 ft), **Flowers:** greenish
white, summer, **Foliage:** glossy, bright
green leaf-like stems, evergreen, **Position:**
partial or full shade, **Soil:** most moist soils,
Habit: bamboo-like, **Propagation:** seeds
sown outdoors in early – mid-autumn, or
by division in spring.
☐ Orange-red fruits are sometimes produced after mild summers. Good for cutting for flower arranging. Useful shrub for
woodland conditions.

Daphne × burkwoodii 'Somerset'
Thymelaeaceae

ZONES 4–9   SHRUB

Height: 1.5 m (5 ft), **Flowers:** pale pink, in clusters, very fragrant, late spring – early summer, **Foliage:** green, evergreen, **Position:** sun or partial shade, **Soil:** well-drained, **Habit:** dense and rounded, **Propagation:** heeled cuttings, 5–10 cm (2–4 in) long, of side shoots in mid – late summer or early autumn.
□ No pruning is required. Should be in every shrub border.

Daphne cneorum
Thymelaeaceae   Garland flower

ZONES 5–9   SHRUB

Height: usually under 30 cm (1 ft), **Flowers:** fragrant, rich pink crowded in clusters, late spring, **Foliage:** green, evergreen, **Position:** sun or partial shade, **Soil:** well-drained, **Habit:** prostrate and spreading up to 1 m (3 ft), **Propagation:** by heeled cuttings, 4 or 5 cm (about 2 in) long, of side shoots mid-summer – early autumn.
□ No pruning is required. Often grown on large rock gardens.

Daphne mezereum
Thymelaeaceae   Mezereon

ZONES 4–9   SHRUB

Height: 1.5 m (5 ft), **Flowers:** purplish red, fragrant, covering previous season's growth, late winter – early spring, **Foliage:** green, deciduous, **Position:** sun or partial shade, **Soil:** thrives on chalk soils, **Habit:** upright, **Propagation:** by cuttings 10 cm (4 in) long mid-summer – early autumn.
□ The flowers are followed by poisonous red berries. For the shrub border or woodland garden.

Daphne odora 'Aureomarginata'
Thymelaeaceae

ZONES 4–9   SHRUB

Height: 1.5 m (5 ft), **Flowers:** pale purplish pink, fragrant, late winter and early spring, **Foliage:** green, edged with cream, evergreen, **Position:** sun or partial shade, **Soil:** normal garden soil, **Habit:** rounded bush, **Propagation:** cuttings of moderately ripened shoots in mid-summer, or by layering shoots in early autumn.
□ A good companion plant is *Cornus mas*.

Daphne retusa
Thymelaeaceae

ZONES 4–9   SHRUB

Height: up to 1 m (3 ft), **Flowers:** deep pinky purple, fragrant, late spring and early summer, **Foliage:** green, thick and leathery, evergreen, **Position:** sun or partial shade, **Soil:** tolerates soils containing chalk or lime, **Habit:** slow-growing rounded bush with stiff branches, **Propagation:** by cuttings of moderately ripened wood in mid-summer.
□ Red fruits (poisonous) sometimes follow the flowers.

Decaisnea fargesii
Lardizabalaceae

ZONES 5–9   SHRUB

Height: 3 m (10 ft), **Flowers:** greeny yellow, late spring – early summer, **Foliage:** green, pinnate, up to 1 m long, deciduous, **Position:** sun or partial shade, **Soil:** well-drained, **Habit:** broad with thick, erect stems, **Propagation:** by seed.
□ The flowers, in loose, drooping panicles 30–45 cm (1–1½ ft) long, are followed by cylindrical, dull blue fruits, about 8 cm (3 in) long.

129

Delphinium 'Belladonna Hybrids'
Ranunculaceae

ZONES 5–9   HERBACEOUS PERENNIAL

Height: 75 cm–1.2 m (2½–4 ft), **Flowers:** pink, white or shades of blue held in open spikes, early – mid-summer and mid-autumn, **Foliage:** green, deeply cut, deciduous, **Position:** sunny, sheltered from winds, **Soil:** any moisture-retentive but well drained soil, **Habit:** much branched, **Propagation:** by cuttings of basal shoots, or by division of roots in spring.

☐ Delphiniums need staking from early in the year. Grow achilleas with delphiniums for contrast in flower shape and colour.

Delphinium 'Pacific Hybrids'
Ranunculaceae

ZONES 5–9   HERBACEOUS PERENNIAL

Height: 1.35–1.8 m (4½–6 ft), **Flowers:** pink, blue, purple or white, large in long upright spikes, mid-summer – early autumn, **Foliage:** green, deeply cut, deciduous, **Position:** sunny and sheltered from winds, **Soil:** good, well drained and fertile, **Habit:** stately and erect, **Propagation:** by cuttings of basal shoots taken in mid-spring, by dividing clumps in early – mid-spring, or from seeds, which come reasonably true to colour.

Above: *Delphinium* 'Sir Galahad'

☐ Stake early in the year and tie in tall flower stems. 'Astolat' is probably the best-known pink hybrid, 'Sir Galahad' is a good white. Good companion plants are the flat-headed achilleas.

Desfontainia spinosa
Potaliaceae

ZONES 8–10   SHRUB

Height: 2.5–3 m (8–10 ft), **Flowers:** red and yellow, waxy, tubular, early – mid-summer, **Foliage:** deep green, like those of holly, evergreen, **Position:** prefers partial shade, sheltered, **Soil:** cool, deep, rich in peat, **Habit:** well-branched yet restrained habit, slow growing, **Propagation:** heeled cuttings, 10 cm (4 in) long, of side shoots in mid – late summer.

☐ Ideally grown against a wall.

Deutzia 'Mont Rose'
Philadelphaceae

ZONES 4–9   SHRUB

Height: 1.8–2.5 m (6–8 ft), **Flowers:** pink and purple, early summer, **Foliage:** green, deciduous, **Position:** sun or partial shade, **Soil:** tolerates most soils, **Habit:** stiffly upright and bushy, **Propagation:** by half-ripe cuttings of side shoots, 10 cm (4 in) long, in mid – late summer.

☐ Cut down to ground level the old flowered stems after flowering. This encourages new shoots.

Deutzia × *magnifica*
Philadelphaceae

ZONES 4–9   SHRUB

Height: 2.5 m (8 ft), **Flowers:** white, double, early summer, **Foliage:** greyish-green, rough, deciduous, **Position:** sun or partial shade, **Soil:** tolerates most soils, **Habit:** stiffly upright and bushy, **Propagation:** by half-ripe cuttings of side shoots, 10 cm (4 in) long, in mid – late summer.

☐ Prune as for 'Mont Rose'.

Deutzia × rosea 'Campanulata'
Philadelphaceae
ZONES 4–9   SHRUB
Height: 1 m (3 ft), **Flowers:** white with contrasting purple calyces, early – mid-summer, **Foliage:** green, deciduous, **Position:** sun or partial shade, **Soil:** tolerates most soils, **Habit:** upright and compact, **Propagation:** by half-ripe cutting of side shoots, 10 cm (4 in) long in mid to late summer after flowering.
☐One of the shorter growing deutzias, useful for this reason, as well as for its profusion of flowers. Prune as for 'Mont Rose'.

Deutzia scabra 'Macrocephala'
Philadelphaceae
ZONES 4–9   SHRUB
Height: 3 m (10 ft), **Flowers:** white, summer, **Foliage:** green, deciduous, **Position:** sun or partial shade, **Soil:** tolerates most soils, **Habit:** tall, erect branched, brown bark, which peels, **Propagation:** by half-ripe cuttings of side shoots, 10 cm (4 in) long in mid – late summer after flowering.
☐Prune as for 'Mont Rose'.

Right: *Deutzia × rosea* 'Campanulata'

Deutzia vilmoriniae
Philadelphaceae
ZONES 4–9   SHRUB
Height: 2.5 m (8 ft), **Flowers:** white, large, bell-shaped, early summer, **Foliage:** green, lance-shaped, grey beneath, deciduous, **Position:** sun or partial shade, **Soil:** tolerates most soils, **Habit:** rapid-growing, erect-branched, **Propagation:** by half-ripe cuttings of side shoots, 10 cm (4 in) long in mid – late summer.
☐Prune as for 'Mont Rose'.

Dianthus alpinus
Caryophyllaceae   Alpine pink
ZONES 4–9   ROCK PLANT
Height: 10 cm (4 in), **Flowers:** shades of pink, late spring – late summer, **Foliage:** mid to dark green, narrow, lanceolate, evergreen, **Position:** open, sunny rock gardens or banks, **Soil:** tolerates most soils, thrives on chalk or limestone, **Habit:** forms mats of green foliage, **Propagation:** by seed sown outdoors in a garden frame in spring, best selected forms from cuttings of firm young shoots in a frame in summer.
☐Alpine campanulas are good companions for pinks. Grows well by the sea.

Dianthus deltoides 'Brilliant'
Caryophyllaceae   Maiden pink
ZONES 5–10   ROCK PLANT
Height: 10 cm (4 in), **Flowers:** bright rose-red, early summer – early autumn, **Foliage:** darkish green, often tinged with purple, evergreen, **Position:** sun or partial shade, **Soil:** tolerates most soils, **Habit:** mat-forming, **Propagation:** by sown or self-sown seeds, seeds come fairly true unless from mixed plantings.
☐'Albus' has white flowers, 'Wisley Variety' is bright red.
Excellent plant for the rock garden or for planting in paving.

Dianthus × *allwoodii*
Caryophyllaceae Modern pink
ZONES 5–10 HERBACEOUS PERENNIAL
Height: 23–30 cm (9–12 in), **Flowers:** shades of pink, double, early – mid-summer and early – mid-autumn, **Foliage:** blue-grey, narrow, lanceolate, evergreen, **Position:** sunny, good for seaside gardens, **Soil:** well-drained, fertile and alkaline, **Habit:** clump-forming perennial with flowers held well above foliage, good cut flowers, **Propagation:** named hybrids are best increased from cuttings.
□ Good cut flowers. Excellent for edging a sunny border. Remove dead blooms.

Dianthus Old fashioned pinks
Caryophyllaceae
ZONES 5–10 HERBACEOUS PERENNIAL
Height: 23–30 cm (9–12 in), **Flowers:** shades of pink, bicolor or white, double or single, early summer and autumn, **Foliage:** blue-green, narrow, lanceolate, evergreen, **Position:** sunny, thrives in seaside gardens, **Soil:** well-drained, fertile and alkaline, **Habit:** a clump-forming perennial, **Propagation:** by cuttings in a garden frame in mid-summer.
□ These old favourites are still popular as border plants.

Right: *Dianthus* 'Mrs Sinkins'

Dicentra spectabilis
Fumariaceae Bleeding heart
ZONES 3–9 HERBACEOUS PERENNIAL
Height: 45–75 cm (1½–2½ ft), **Flowers:** rose-pink with white tips, gracefully dangling from arching stems, late spring – early summer, **Foliage:** blue-green, divided, deciduous, **Position:** best in partial shade, **Soil:** peaty but with good drainage, **Habit:** arching perennial, **Propagation:** by careful division of crowns in spring, by root cuttings inserted in sandy soil in spring or early summer.
□ Especially attractive when planted among spring-flowering shrubs.

Disanthus cercidifolius
Hamamelidaceae
ZONES 7–10 SHRUB
Height: 3 m (10 ft), **Flowers:** small, purplish, mid-autumn, **Foliage:** green, heart-shaped, excellent autumn colour, **Position:** partial shade, **Soil:** acid, moist, but well-drained, peaty, **Habit:** open-branched and twiggy, **Propagation:** by cuttings in mid – late summer.
□ This rather rare shrub has one outstanding feature – its foliage turns a wonderful mixture of reds suffused with orange in autumn.

Doronicum caucasicum
Compositae Leopard's bane
ZONES 5–9 HERBACEOUS PERENNIAL
Height: 30–45 cm (1–1½ ft), **Flowers:** bright yellow, single daisies, early – late spring, **Foliage:** green, deciduous, **Position:** sun or partial shade, **Soil:** any reasonably deep and moist soil, **Habit:** clump forming perennial, **Propagation:** by division in autumn or spring.
□ 'Spring Beauty' is an excellent double-flowered cultivar. A good companion plant is blue pulmonaria.

Doronicum plantagineum

Compositae Leopard's bane
ZONES 5–9   HERBACEOUS PERENNIAL
Height: 1 m (3 ft), **Flowers:** bright yellow, single, early – late spring into summer, **Foliage:** shiny dark green, deciduous, **Position:** sun or partial shade, **Soil:** any reasonably moist and deep soil, **Habit:** forms low clumps of foliage with flowers well above on long stems, **Propagation:** by dividing clumps in autumn or spring; or by seed sown in spring or by seed sown in spring or early summer.
□ 'Harpur Crewe' (syn. 'Excelsum') has larger flowers. Excellent for cutting.

Drimys winteri

Winteraceae Winter bark
ZONES 8–10   SHRUB
Height: 5 m (16 ft), **Flowers:** white, fragrant in loose clusters, mid – late spring, **Foliage:** large, green, greyish beneath, leathery, evergreen, **Position:** sun or partial shade, warm and sheltered, **Soil:** good loamy soil, **Habit:** neat and pleasing shrub or small tree, **Propagation:** by cuttings in summer or autumn, or by layering in spring.
□ Best grown against a wall.

Dryas octopetala

Rosaceae Mountain avens
ZONES 5–9   ROCK PLANT
Height: 10 cm (4 in), **Flowers:** white, with a golden centre, late spring – early summer, **Foliage:** medium to dark green, oak-like, evergreen, **Position:** full sun, **Soil:** well-drained, alkaline, **Habit:** evergreen, mat-forming, **Propagation:** heeled cuttings in late summer or early spring inserted in sand in a garden frame, or by seed sown in early – mid-autumn in a frame.
□ Suitable for ground cover and rock gardens.

Eccremocarpus scaber

Bignoniaceae Chilean glory vine
ZONES 9–10   CLIMBER
Height: 2.5–3 m (8–10 ft), **Flowers:** orange-red, tubular, early summer – mid-autumn, **Foliage:** pinnate, ending in a slender tendril, deep green, evergreen, **Position:** full sun, warmth and shelter, **Soil:** well drained, **Habit:** climbing by its leaf tendrils, some early support with twigs advisable, **Propagation:** by seed sown during late winter – early spring in seed compost in a heated propagator.
□ This plant is often killed back to the ground over winter.

Echinacea purpurea

Compositae Purple cone flower
ZONES 4–9   HERBACEOUS PERENNIAL
Height: 45–60 cm (1½–2 ft), **Flowers:** purplish red with orange peaked centres, mid-summer – early autumn, **Foliage:** longish, medium green, deciduous, **Position:** sunny, **Soil:** deep, rich and well drained, **Habit:** clump-forming perennial, **Propagation:** by dividing clumps in spring, or by seed sown in a cool greenhouse in spring.
□ Easy to grow but hungry. Cut off dead blooms regularly.

Echinops ritro

Compositae Globe thistle
ZONES 5–10   HERBACEOUS PERENNIAL
Height: 1–1.2 m (3–4 ft), **Flowers:** blue, almost spherical, mid-summer – early autumn, **Foliage:** grey-green, deeply lobed, long and thistle-like, deciduous, **Position:** best in full sun, **Soil:** well-drained, alkaline, **Habit:** upright clump-forming perennial, **Propagation:** by dividing clumps in autumn or spring, by root cuttings in winter, or by seeds sown outdoors in spring.
□ Attractive to bees, flowers can be dried for winter decoration.

Elaeagnus × *ebbingei*
Elaeagnaceae
ZONES 4–10   SHRUB
Height: 3 m (10 ft), **Flowers:** white, small but fragrant, followed by orange-red fruits, mid – late autumn, **Foliage:** dark green on top, silver below, evergreen; 'Limelight' has central gold variegation, **Position:** sun or partial shade, **Soil:** tolerates most soils, **Habit:** upright and bushy, **Propagation:** by cuttings 10 cm (4 in) long taken in late summer – early autumn.
☐ Excellent for screens, hedges and windbreaks, even by the sea. Shorten straggly shoots in late spring.

Elaeagnus × *ebbingei* 'Gilt Edge'
Elaeagnaceae
ZONES 5–10   SHRUB
Height: 2.5 m (8 ft), **Flowers:** white, small, fragrant, mid – late autumn, **Foliage:** leaves have broad gold margins, evergreen, **Position:** sun or partial shade, **Soil:** tolerates most soils, **Habit:** erect and bushy, less vigorous than type, **Propagation:** by cuttings, 10 cm (4 in) long taken in late summer – early autumn.
☐ A delightful foliage shrub to lighten up the garden, contrasting strikingly with dark green neighbours. 'Limelight' has a gold blotch in the centre of each leaf.

Right: *Elaeagnus × ebbingei* 'Gilt Edge'

Elaeagnus pungens 'Dicksonii' (syn. 'Aurea')
Elaeagnaceae
ZONES 5–9   SHRUB
Height: 4 m (13 ft), **Flowers:** white, small but fragrant, mid – late autumn, **Foliage:** two shades of green with variable yellow edge, evergreen, **Position:** sun or partial shade, **Soil:** tolerates most soils, **Habit:** dense and spreading, somewhat thorny, **Propagation:** by cuttings 10 cm (4 in) long taken in late summer – early autumn.
☐ A slow grower.

Elaeagnus pungens 'Maculata'
Elaeagnaceae
ZONES 5–9   SHRUB
Height: 4 m (13 ft), **Flowers:** white, small but fragrant, mid – late autumn, **Foliage:** leaves with central splash of yellow, evergreen, **Position:** sun or partial shade, **Soil:** tolerates most soils, **Habit:** dense and spreading, **Propagation:** by cuttings 10 cm (4 in) long taken in late summer – early autumn.
☐ Easy-care plant to brighten up the garden in winter.

Embothrium coccineum
Proteaceae   Chilean fire bush
ZONES 8–10   SHRUB
Height: 4–8 m (13–26 ft), **Flowers:** orange-scarlet, late spring – early summer, **Foliage:** dark, glossy green, somewhat leathery, evergreen, **Position:** sunny and sheltered, **Soil:** deep, moist but well-drained, lime-free loam, **Habit:** tall and erect, **Propagation:** sow seeds in early – mid-spring, or remove suckers.
☐ This magnificent shrub is, in Britain, unfortunately only suitable for warmer regions.

Enkianthus campanulatus
Ericaceae
ZONES 4–9 SHRUB
Height: 2.5–3 m (8–10 ft), **Flowers:** creamy, bell-shaped, late spring, **Foliage:** matt green, red autumn tints, deciduous, **Position:** sun or partial shade, sheltered, **Soil:** neutral or lime-free with plenty of peat or leafmould incorporated, **Habit:** upright, **Propagation:** heeled cuttings of side shoots, 7 or 8 cm (about 3 in) long taken in late summer – early autumn.
□No pruning required. Excellent woodland shrub: try an underplanting of hostas and primulas.

Enkianthus perulatus
Ericaceae
ZONES 6–9 SHRUB
Height: up to 1.8 m (6 ft), **Flowers:** white, spring, **Foliage:** green, clustered at ends of twigs, red autumn tints, deciduous, **Position:** sun or partial shade, **Soil:** neutral or lime-free with plenty of peat or leafmould incorporated, **Habit:** dense foliage, neat habit, growth very slow, **Propagation:** heeled cuttings of side shoots, 7 to 8 cm (about 3 in) long in late summer – early autumn.
□Excellent woodland shrub.

Right: *Enkianthus perulatus*

Epimedium × rubrum
Berberidaceae Barrenwort, bishop's hat
ZONES 7–9 HERBACEOUS PERENNIAL
Height: 30 cm (1 ft), **Flowers:** red, in loose sprays, late spring, **Foliage:** medium green, tinted with red when newly emerged, turning orange in autumn, evergreen, **Position:** shade or partial shade, **Soil:** tolerates any soil, suitable for dry shade, **Habit:** creeping by rhizomes, **Propagation:** by dividing rhizomes in autumn or after flowering.
□Flowers and foliage are both good for floral decoration. Excellent for ground cover in shrub borders.

Epimedium youngianum
'Niveum'
Berberidaceae Barrenwort, bishop's hat
ZONES 7–10 HERBACEOUS PERENNIAL
Height: 15–20 cm (6–8 in), **Flowers:** white, in loose sprays, mid – late spring, **Foliage:** medium green, red-tinted when newly emerged, orange-red in autumn, evergreen, **Position:** semi-shade, **Soil:** tolerates any soil, suitable for dry shade, **Habit:** creeping by rhizomes, **Propagation:** divide rhizomes in autumn or after flowering.
□Flowers and foliage both useful in floral decoration. Excellent for ground cover.

Eremurus elwesii
Liliaceae Foxtail lily
ZONES 6–10 HERBACEOUS PERENNIAL
Height: 2 m (6 ft), **Flowers:** pale pink, scented, 1–1.2 m (3–4 ft) long spikes, late spring, **Foliage:** pale green, lanceolate, deciduous, **Position:** full sun, **Soil:** deep, well-manured with good drainage, grows well in alkaline soils, **Habit:** very stately perennial, **Propagation:** by dividing clumps in autumn or spring.
□'Albus' is pure white. Good for cutting.

Above: *Erica arborea* 'Alpina'
Right: *Erica cinerea* 'Purple Beauty'
Below right: *Erica* × *darleyensis* 'Darley Dale'

ERICA
(Heaths and heathers)

All the heaths described here are evergreen and hardy and distinctive for their profusion of very small leaves, which can be mid green, dark green or gold. The plants range from tree-like *E. arborea* to mat-forming *E. herbacea*. The flowers vary from white through various shades of pink, red and purple. Different species and cultivars flowering at different times can be selected to cover every month of the year.

While tolerant of partial shade, they will flower better in sunny positions. Some, such as *E. herbacea* cultivars, tolerate lime in moderation, but always add peat when planting.

Apart from *E. arborea* and one or two other tall-growing kinds, heaths are best planted in groups of a size that is in scale with the area to be planted. They associate well with callunas (ling), dwarf rhododendrons, including azaleas and dwarf conifers.

Erica arborea 'Alpina'
Ericaceae   Tree heath
ZONES 7–9   SHRUB
Height: 1.5 m (5 ft) or more, **Flowers:** white, fragrant, early – mid-spring, **Foliage:** fresh green, evergreen, **Position:** full sun if possible, partial shade if necessary, **Soil:** peaty, acid soil is best but never pure peat, **Habit:** erect and bushy, **Propagation:** cuttings are most satisfactory, use sideshoots 4 or 5 cm (about 3 in) long, taken mid-summer – mid-autumn.

☐ In the cultivar 'Gold Tips' the young growths are golden.

Erica cinerea 'Atrosanguinea Smith's Variety'
Ericaceae   Bell heather
ZONES 5–9   SHRUB
Height: 15 cm (6 in), **Flowers:** bright scarlet, early summer – early autumn, **Foliage:** deep green, evergreen, **Position:** sunny and open, **Soil:** well-drained, acid, peaty soil, **Habit:** forms mats of wiry stems, **Propagation:** by cuttings 5 cm (about 2 in) long of ripening shoots with or without a heel, taken mid-summer – mid-autumn. Large plants can be propagated by layering.

Other recommended cultivars of *Erica cinerea*
'*C.D. Eason*' – deep rosy pink; 30 cm (1 ft) high; compact and bushy.
'*Golden Drop*' – purple-pink flowers of no great value; 30 cm (1 ft) high; coppery-orange foliage turning red in winter; dense and prostrate ground cover.
'*Pink Ice*' – pale pink; 20 cm (8 in) high; compact and bushy. An extremely attractive plant producing an abundance of flowers over a long season.
'*Purple Beauty*' – bright light purple flowers from early summer – mid-autumn; 30 cm (1 ft) high; compact and bushy.

Erica × *darleyensis* 'Darley Dale'
Ericaceae   Heath
ZONES 5–9   SHRUB
Height: 45–60 cm (1½–2 ft), **Flowers:** pale pink, early winter – late spring, **Foliage:** mid-green, evergreen, **Position:** sunny, **Soil:** well-drained peaty soil preferred, tolerates some lime, **Habit:** bushy, **Propagation:** by cuttings taken mid-summer – mid-autumn.

☐ Long flowering season, at its best in early and mid-spring. 'Silberschmelze' is a vigorous cultivar with white flowers in spring. Take cuttings in autumn or layer.

Left: *Erica vagans* 'Lyonesse'
Top: *Erica tetralix* 'Alba Mollis'
Above: *Erica herbacea* 'King George'

Erica erigena 'Brightness' (syn. *E. mediterranea, E. hibernica*)

Ericaceae Heath

ZONES 5–9   SHRUB

Height: up to 1.2 m (4 ft), **Flowers:** rosy pink, in profusion early – late spring, **Foliage:** coppery green, evergreen, **Position:** sunny, **Soil:** well-drained peaty soil preferred, tolerates some lime, **Habit:** upright and bushy, **Propagation:** by cuttings taken mid-summer – mid-autumn, or by layering.

Erica herbacea (syn. **E. carnea**)

Ericaceae Heath, heather

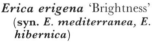

ZONES 5–9   SHRUB

Height: 20–23 cm (8–9 in), **Flowers:** white and shades of pink, red and purple-red, mid winter into spring, **Foliage:** shades of green or gold, evergreen, **Position:** sunny position prefered, **Soil:** tolerates some lime but prefers a well-drained peaty soil, **Habit:** dwarf, compact, some cultivars bushy, others spreading, **Propagation:** by cuttings 3–5 cm (about 3 in) long, of ripening shoots with or without a heel, taken mid-summer – mid-autumn. Large plants can be propagated by layering or stooling.

Recommended cultivars of *Erica herbacea* Zones 5–9.

'*Atrorubra*' – dark rose-pink, late winter – mid spring; mid-green foliage, eventually spreading.

'*Aurea*' – deep pink, lightening with age, mid winter – early spring; bright gold foliage; eventually spreading.

'*Loughrigg*' – pinkish-purple, mid winter – early spring; deep green; compact.

'*King George*' – bright rose-pink, early winter – early spring; mid green foliage, bushy.

'*Springwood White*' – white, long, mid winter – early spring; mid–green; low and spreading.

'*Vivellii*' – brilliant carmine, mid winter – early spring; dark green foliage with bronze tints in winter; bushy.

Erica tetralix 'Alba Mollis'

Ericaceae Cross-leaved heath

ZONES 5–9   SHRUB

Height: 20–23 cm (8–9 in), **Flowers:** white, early summer – mid-autumn, **Foliage:** dark grey-green, evergreen, **Position:** sunny, **Soil:** cool, moist, lime-free soil, **Habit:** erect, flowers point in all directions, **Propagation:** by cuttings 5 cm (about 2 in) long of ripening shoots with or without a heel, taken mid-summer – mid-autumn; large plants can be propagated by layering.

Erica tetralix 'Pink Star'

Ericaceae Cross-leaved heath

ZONES 5–9   SHRUB

Height: 15 cm (6 in), **Flowers:** bright pink star-like flowers, early summer – mid-autumn, **Foliage:** soft grey, **Position:** sun or partial shade, **Soil:** cool, moist, lime-free soil, **Habit:** compact and bushy, **Propagation:** by cuttings taken mid-summer – mid-autumn, or by layering.

Erica vagans 'Lyonesse'

Ericaceae Cornish heath

ZONES 5–9   SHRUB

Height: 45 cm (1½ ft), **Flowers:** ivory-white with golden brown anthers, late summer – early autumn, **Foliage:** green, evergreen, **Position:** sunny, **Soil:** acid or neutral, with added peat, **Habit:** tidy, compact habit, **Propagation:** by cuttings 5 cm (about 2 in) long of ripening shoots, with or without a heel, taken mid-summer – mid-autumn, or by layering.

□ 'Mrs D.F. Maxwell' has dark pink flowers, 'St Keverne' is rose-pink and lower growing than 'Lyonesse'.

Erigeron macranthus
Compositae Fleabane
ZONES 5–10   HERBACEOUS PERENNIAL
Height: 30 cm (12 in), **Flowers:** purple-blue, yellow centred daisies, mid – late summer, **Foliage:** mid green, deciduous, **Position:** sun, **Soil:** tolerates most well-drained soils, **Habit:** tight clumpy plant with upright flower stems, **Propagation:** by division in mid-autumn – early spring.
☐ Resembles a dwarf Michaelmas daisy, but earlier flowering. The flowers last well when cut.

Erigeron mucronatus
Compositae Fleabane
ZONES 5–10   ROCK PLANT
Height: 15–23 cm (6–9 in), **Flowers:** very pale pink turning deeper pink with age, early summer – early autumn, **Foliage:** green, small and lanceolate, deciduous, **Position:** full sun, **Soil:** light, well-drained, **Habit:** spreads by underground runners, to 60 cm (2 ft), **Propagation:** by seed sown outdoors in spring or early summer, or by division in autumn or spring.
☐ Good for cracks and crevices in walls and paving, also for rock gardens.

Erigeron × speciosum 'Dignity'
Compositae Fleabane
ZONES 5–10   HERBACEOUS PERENNIAL
Height: 45–60 cm (1½–2 ft), **Flowers:** lilac-blue daisies, early – late summer, **Foliage:** mid green, lanceolate, deciduous, **Position:** sunny, **Soil:** moist, but well-drained, **Habit:** clump forming perennial, **Propagation:** by dividing roots mid-autumn – early spring.
☐ Dead-head faded blooms to encourage later flowers. Cut back to the ground. Flowers excellent for cutting. Recommended for borders and island beds.

Other *E × speciosum* hybrids include 'Foerster's Liebling', pink, and 'Darkest of All', dark violet-blue.

Erinus alpinus
Scrophulariaceae Summer starwort
ZONES 6–9   ROCK PLANT
Height: 15 cm (6 in), **Flowers:** star-like, pink, **Foliage:** medium green, spoon-shaped, evergreen, **Position:** sunny, **Soil:** tolerates most well-drained soils, **Habit:** hardy and tufted, **Propagation:** by seeds sown where plants are to grow in spring; or by dividing plants in spring.
☐ Good for crevices in old walls or dryish rock gardens, 'Albus' has white flowers, 'Dr Hanelle' is carmine pink.

Eryngium alpinum
Umbelliferae Sea holly
ZONES 6–9   HERBACEOUS PERENNIAL
Height: 75 cm (2½ ft), **Flowers:** metallic blue, mid-summer – early autumn, **Foliage:** blue-green, deeply cut, deciduous, **Position:** sunny, good for seaside gardens, **Soil:** light, well drained, **Habit:** hardy clump-forming perennial, **Propagation:** by seeds sown in sandy soil in a garden frame in spring, root cuttings in winter, or divide in spring.
☐ Good for cutting and for drying.

Eryngium maritimum
Umbelliferae Sea holly
ZONES 6–10   HERBACEOUS PERENNIAL
Height: 30–45 cm (1–1½ ft), **Flowers:** steel blue, cone shaped, mid-summer – early autumn, **Foliage:** silver-green, thistle-like, deciduous, **Position:** sunny, good for seaside gardens, **Soil:** light sandy, well-drained, alkaline, **Habit:** well-branched clump-forming perennial, **Propagation:** by seeds sown in sandy soil in a garden frame in spring, root cuttings in winter, or by division in spring.

ESCALLONIA

With few exceptions, the 60 or so species of this useful genus are evergreen, as are all those described here. Most are slightly tender in exposed areas but grow well in mild climates, particularly by the sea, where they can be used for hedging. In colder districts they should be sheltered from cold winds. Their leaves are generally small, mid- to dark green and glossy. Their flowers range in colour from white through pink to red and are produced intermittently through the summer and autumn. Prune them immediately after a flowering period. All the cultivars mentioned are lime-tolerant and resist drought.

Escallonia hybrids
Escalloniaceae

ZONES 7–10   SHRUB

Height: 1.5–2.5 m (5–8 ft), **Flowers:** white and shades of pink and red, intermittently throughout summer and autumn, **Foliage:** generally small, green, shiny and sticky to touch, often aromatic, evergreen, **Position:** sunny, warm and sheltered, including by the sea, **Soil:** any well-drained soil, lime tolerant, **Habit:** vigorous and bushy, **Propagation:** heeled cuttings of ripening shoots 8–10 cm (3–4 in) long in late summer–early autumn. □ Good hedging plant, especially by the sea. Clip back lightly after flowering. Drought resistant.

Left: *Escallonia* 'Apple Blossom' **Centre:** *E.* 'Donard Radiance' **Right:** *E.* 'Donard Seedling'

Recommended hybrids of *Escallonia*

'*Apple Blossom*' – pink and white flowers; aromatic foliage, vigorous and bushy.
'*C.F. Ball*' – crimson flowers; aromatic foliage; vigorous and bushy.
'*Crimson Spire*' – crimson flowers; vigorous and upright.
'*Donard Radiance*' – bright rosy-red flowers; strong growing and compact.
'*Donard Seedling*' – white flowers from pink buds; vigorous and bushy.
'*Donard White*' – white flowers from pink buds; very free flowering; compact and rounded.

Eucalyptus niphophila
Myrtaceae   Snow gum

ZONES 6–9   TREE

Height: 6–7.5 m (20–25 ft), **Flowers:** white, in clusters in summer, **Foliage:** grey-green, large and leathery, aromatic, evergreen, **Position:** sunny, sheltered from wind, **Soil:** moist but well drained, reasonably fertile, acid or neutral, **Habit:** slow-growing to start with, but when established growth in height is rapid, **Propagation:** by seed in sandy soil in early spring in a heated propagator. □ Its bark is remarkable. On young trees it is bluish white, later becoming a delightful patchwork of cream, grey and white.

Left: *Eucalyptus niphophila*

Eucryphia glutinosa
Eucryphiaceae
ZONES 6–9   SHRUB
Height: 3 m ((10 ft) or more, **Flowers:** white, 6 cm (2½ in) across; mid – late summer, **Foliage:** dark green, pinnate, deciduous, beautiful autumn tints, **Position:** full sun or semi-shade, sheltered, **Soil:** moist loam, acid or neutral, **Habit:** tall upright open bush, slow growing, **Propagation:** heel cuttings 8–10 cm (3–4 in) long of side shoots, late summer – early autumn.
☐ With its large white flowers and glorious autumn colour, this is one of the most beautiful of shrubs. It can be used as a lawn specimen or grown in a shrub border.

Eucryphia × nymansensis
'Nymansay'
Eucryphiaceae
ZONES 6–9   SHRUB
Height: 4 m (13 ft) or more, **Flowers:** creamy white, late summer – early autumn, **Foliage:** shiny green, both single and pinnate leaves, evergreen, **Position:** full sun or semi-shade, sheltered, **Soil:** moist loam, acid or neutral, **Habit:** a fast grower, **Propagation:** by cuttings.
☐ Makes an impressive lawn specimen.

Right: *Eucryphia glutinosa*

Euonymus alatus
Celastraceae Winged spindle tree
ZONES 5–9   SHRUB
Height: 1.8–2.5 m (6–8 ft), **Flowers:** greeny yellow, late spring – early summer, **Foliage:** green, deciduous, magnificent autumn colour, **Position:** full sun or semi-shade, **Soil:** preferably chalky, **Habit:** fairly dense, **Propagation:** heeled cuttings of side shoots, 8–10 cm (3–4 in) long, late summer – early autumn.
☐ One of the best shrubs for autumn colour. Try Michaelmas daisies as companion plants.

Euonymus europaeus 'Red Cascade'
Celastraceae Spindle tree
ZONES 5–9   SHRUB
Height: 3 m (10 ft), **Flowers:** white, late spring, **Foliage:** green, deciduous, very attractive autumn tints, **Position:** full sun or semi shade, **Soil:** preferably chalky, **Habit:** vigorous, green stemmed, **Propagation:** heeled cuttings of side shoots, late summer–early autumn.
☐ This shrub is laden in autumn with rose-red lobed capsules containing poisonous orange seeds. Needs a background of dark evergreen foliage.

Euonymus fortunei 'Emerald 'N' Gold'
Celastraceae Evergreen spindle
ZONES 5–10   SHRUB
Height: 1 m (3 ft) but variable, **Flowers:** greeny white, insignificant, early summer, **Foliage:** emerald-green with a wide margin of gold, tinted red in winter, evergreen, **Position:** full sun or semi-shade, **Soil:** any well-drained soil, **Habit:** bushy and spreading, **Propagation:** heeled cuttings of side shoots, 8–10 cm (3–4 in) long, late summer – early autumn, or by division.
☐ An excellent shrub for ground cover.

Above: Variegated *Euonymus japonicus*
Right: *Euonymus japonicus* 'Ovatus Aureus'

Euonymus fortunei 'Silver Queen'

Celastraceae Evergreen spindle
ZONES 5–10   SHRUB
Height: 1 m (3 ft) but variable, up to 3 m (10 ft) against a wall, **Flowers:** greeny white, insignificant, early summer, **Foliage:** young leaves creamy yellow turning green, with broad white margin, evergreen, **Position:** full sun or semi-shade, **Soil:** any well-drained soil, **Habit:** compact or, in suitable places will climb, **Propagation:** heeled cuttings of side shoots 8–10 cm (3–4 in) long, late summer – early autumn, or by division.
□ Excellent wall plant.

Euonymus japonicus

Celastraceae Evergreen spindle
ZONES 5–10   SHRUB
Height: 5 m (16 ft), **Flowers:** greeny white, early – mid-summer, **Foliage:** oval, deep green, leathery and shiny, evergreen, **Position:** full sun or shade, **Soil:** tolerates most soils, **Habit:** erect and very dense, **Propagation:** heeled cuttings of side shoots, 8–10 cm (3–4 in) long, late summer – early autumn.
□ One of the best evergreens for seaside or town planting. Makes an excellent hedge.

Euonymus japonicus 'Ovatus Aureus'
(syn. 'Aureovariegatus')

Celastraceae Evergreen spindle
ZONES 5–9   SHRUB
Height: 3 m (10 ft), **Flowers:** greeny white, early – mid-summer, **Foliage:** green, edged and marked with creamy yellow, evergreen, **Position:** full sun or semi-shade, full sun for best colour, **Soil:** tolerates most soils, **Habit:** compact and bushy, but slow grower, **Propagation:** heeled cuttings of sideshoots, 8–10 cm (3–4 in) long, late summer – early autumn.
□ Most commonly used golden-variegated euonymus. Lightens up darkish places. Suitable for the seaside.

Euphorbia griffithii

Euphorbiaceae Spurge
ZONES 5–10   HERBACEOUS PERENNIAL
Height: 60–75 cm (2–2½ ft), **Flowers:** orange-red bracts surround insignificant flowers, late-spring – early summer, **Foliage:** medium green, with light pink central vein, deciduous, **Position:** sun or partial shade, **Soil:** tolerates most soils, **Habit:** forms a colourful clump, **Propagation:** by cuttings of basal shoots under glass in spring, or by division of clumps in autumn or spring.
□ A good cultivar is 'Fireglow'. Try planting it with silver-foliage shrubs.

Euphorbia epithymoides
(syn. *E. polychroma*)

Euphorbiaceae Spurge
ZONES 4–9   HERBACEOUS PERENNIAL
Height: 45 cm (1½ ft), **Flowers:** greeny-yellow bracts surround insignificant flowers, mid – late spring, **Foliage:** fresh green, evergreen, **Position:** sun or partial shade, **Soil:** suits most well-drained soils, **Habit:** neat and bushy, **Propagation:** by cuttings of basal shoots in a garden frame in spring, by division of clumps in autumn or spring, or seed early summer.
□ The pulmonarias make excellent companions, especially blue cultivars.

Euphorbia wulfenii

Euphorbiaceae Spurge

ZONES 6–9   HERBACEOUS PERENNIAL

Height: 1.2 m (4ft), **Flowers:** greeny yellow bracts surround insignificant flowers, late spring – mid-summer, **Foliage:** has a blue caste, lanceolate, evergreen, **Position:** sun or partial shade, **Soil:** suits most well-drained soils, **Habit:** bushy upright, **Propagation:** by basal cuttings under glass in spring, or divide clumps in autumn or spring.

□ Good for cutting. A distinctive plant, often used as a single specimen. Associates well with architecture and paving.

Exochorda × macrantha 'The Bride'

Rosaceae Pearl bush

ZONES 5–10   SHRUB

Height: 3 m (10 ft), **Flowers:** white, 5–6 cm across, smother the branches in late spring, **Foliage:** green, deciduous, **Position:** sunny, **Soil:** humus-rich and ideally acid or neutral, **Habit:** forms a compact mound of arching branches, **Propagation:** by cuttings taken mid – late summer.

□ Cut back shoots by two-thirds immediately after flowering. Remove weak branches.

× Fatshedera lizei

Araliaceae

ZONES 6–10   SHRUB

Height: 1.5–2.5 m (5–8 ft), **Flowers:** light greenish white, not particularly showy, mid–late autumn, **Foliage:** large, green, lobed and leathery, evergreen, **Position:** sun or shade, **Soil:** suits most soils, **Habit:** long flexible stems, easily trained, **Propagation:** by cuttings taken in summer and placed under glass.

□ A bigeneric hybrid of *Fatsia japonica* and *Hedera helix*. Tolerates shade, maritime conditions and atmospheric pollution. Can be used as ground cover or trained to walls and fences.

Fatsia japonica (syn. Aralia sieboldii)

Araliaceae Fatsia, castor oil plant

ZONES 7–10   SHRUB

Height: 2.5–4 m (8–13 ft), **Flowers:** white, in long panicles up to 45 cm (18 in), mid-autumn, **Foliage:** big palmate shining leaves, evergreen, **Position:** shade or full sun, sheltered, **Soil:** suits most soils in good condition, **Habit:** large upright shrub, **Propagation:** by cuttings taken from suckers, early – mid-spring, or sow seeds in mid-spring.

□ Grow against a warm wall in cold areas. Suitable for containers.

Festuca cinerea (syn. F. glauca)

Gramineae Blue fescue grass

ZONES 4–9   HERBACEOUS PERENNIAL

Height: 20–23 cm (8–9 in), **Flowers:** blue-purple spikes in summer, but not of great significance, **Foliage:** thin bluish grey, evergreen, **Position:** sunny, **Soil:** light sandy soil best, well-drained, **Habit:** tufty clumps, **Propagation:** divide in spring.

□ Most attractive ground cover, especially around purple-leaved shrubs.

Filipendula hexapetala

Rosaceae Dropwort

ZONES 4–9   HERBACEOUS PERENNIAL

Height: 75 cm (2½ ft), **Flowers:** very pale pink in large fluffy heads, early – mid-summer, **Foliage:** green, deeply cut, deciduous, **Position:** best in partial shade, **Soil:** suits most soils as long as moist, **Habit:** clump forming, **Propagation:** by division of clumps in autumn or spring.

□ Water well in dry weather. Cut down stems in autumn. 'Flore Pleno' has double-flowers, 'Rubra' is pink, growing to 1.8 m (6 ft). Looks good planted near a pool. The flowers can be cut.

Forsythia 'Beatrix Farrand'
Oleaceae Golden bells
ZONES 4–9 SHRUB
Height: 2.5 m (8 ft), **Flowers:** bright yellow, borne freely, early – mid-spring, **Foliage:** mid green, deciduous, **Position:** full sun or semi-shade, flowers more profuse in sun, **Soil:** suits most soils, **Habit:** erect and bushy, **Propagation:** by simple layering of shoots or by cuttings inserted outdoors in autumn.
☐ As soon as flowering is over prune back old branches and reduce in length the flowered shoots enough to maintain a tidy bush. 'Lynwood' has very large yellow flowers and is suitable for hedging.

Forsythia suspensa 'Nymans'
Oleaceae Golden Bells
ZONES 4–9 SHRUB
Height: 3 m (10 ft), or more against a wall, **Flowers:** pale-yellow, spring, **Foliage:** mid green, deciduous, **Position:** full sun or partial shade, flowers better in sun, **Soil:** suits most soils, **Habit:** pendulous branches, **Propagation:** by layering or cuttings.
☐ Good wall shrub, perhaps in association with chaenomeles. Prune back after flowering (the flowered shoots).

Right: *Forsythia* 'Beatrix Farrand'

Fothergilla gardenii
Hamamelidaceae
ZONES 5–9 SHRUB
Height: 1–1.2 m (3–4 ft), **Flowers:** upright clusters of white stamens, scented, mid – late spring, **Foliage:** green, large rounded leaves similar to those of hazel, spectacular autumn tints, **Position:** sun or partial shade, **Soil:** acid or neutral, will not tolerate lime, **Habit:** compact and bushy, **Propagation:** cuttings can be difficult, so layering stems in autumn is the most reliable method.
☐ Good companion for rhododendrons and azaleas.

Fothergilla major
Hamamelidaceae
ZONES 5–9 SHRUB
Height: 2–2.5 m (6–8 ft), **Flowers:** upright clusters of white stamens, scented, in late spring before foliage opens, **Foliage:** green large rounded, turning shades of gold and red in autumn, **Position:** sun or partial shade, **Soil:** acid or neutral, will not tolerate lime, **Habit:** slow-growing, bushy, **Propagation:** best by layering stems in autumn.
☐ Good companion for rhododendrons and azaleas.

Fremontodendron californicum (syn. *Fremontia californica*)
Sterculiaceae
ZONES 8–10 SHRUB
Height: 2.5–3.5 m (8–12 ft), **Flowers:** large bowl-shaped, deep yellow, late spring – mid-autumn, **Foliage:** matt green, palmate, semi-evergreen, **Position:** sunny and sheltered, only suitable for warm district, **Soil:** well-drained, light, excellent on chalk, **Habit:** upright, **Propagation:** sow seeds, early – mid-spring.
☐ No pruning is required apart from removing dead shoots in mid-spring. Good for training on sheltered, sunny walls.

Fuchsia 'Alice Hoffman'
Onagraceae   Hardy fuchsia
ZONES 6–9   SHRUB
Height: 45–60 cm (1½–2 ft), **Flowers:**
pink sepals and white corolla, double, mid-
summer onwards, **Foliage:** green, deciduous, **Position:** warm and sheltered, sunny
or partially shaded, **Soil:** moisture-retentive, well-fed soil, preferably neutral,
Habit: compact and bushy, hardy, **Propagation:** by cutting of young shoots taken
from spring until early autumn.
☐ Cut back all dead or damaged growth in
spring, to ground level if necessary. This
applies also to the following cultivars. All
hardy fuchsias are excellent for seaside and
cottage gardens, shrub borders and tubs.

Fuchsia 'Chillerton Beauty'
Onagraceae   Hardy fuchsia
ZONES 6–9   SHRUB
Height: 1–1.5 m (3–5 ft), **Flowers:** white
sepals with pink edges and violet corolla,
single, **Foliage:** green, deciduous, **Position:** sun or partial shade, **Soil:** moisture-
retentive, humus-rich, cool and deep,
preferably neutral, **Habit:** bushy and vigorous, masses of shoots, hardy, **Propagation:** by cuttings of young shoots taken
from spring to autumn.

Fuchsia 'Display'
Onagraceae   Fuchsia
ZONES 7–9   SHRUB
Height: 60 cm (2 ft), **Flowers:** sepals
rose-red, corolla single cerise, **Foliage:**
green, deciduous, **Position:** sun or partial
shade, **Soil:** humus-rich, fertile and moisture-retentive, preferably neutral, **Habit:**
compact and bushy, usually hardy in
warm districts, **Propagation:** by cuttings
of young shoots taken from spring to
autumn.
☐ Though not fully hardy, worth men-
tioning for its colour and bushy habit. Lift
and take indoors for winter in colder
districts.

Fuchsia 'Golden Treasure'
Onagraceae   Hardy fuchsia
ZONES 7–9   SHRUB
Height: 60 cm (2 ft), varies according to
climate, **Flowers:** sepals red, corolla rich
deep purple, single, mid-summer onwards, **Foliage:** bright gold, deciduous,
Position: sun or partial shade, brighter
foliage colour in sun, **Soil:** humus-rich,
fertile, moisture-retentive, preferably neutral, **Habit:** upright, compact and bushy,
Propagation: by cuttings of young shoots
taken from spring until autumn.

Above: A fuchsia garden featuring *F.
magellanica* 'Variegata' **Top:** *Fuchsia
magellanica* 'Pumila' **Above:** *Fuchsia* 'Display'

Fuchsia 'Madame Cornelissen'
Onagraceae   Hardy fuchsia
ZONES 6–9   SHRUB
Height: 1 m (3 ft), variable according to
climate, **Flowers:** sepals crimson, corolla
white veined cerise, mid-summer onwards, **Foliage:** green, deciduous, **Position:** sun or partial shade, **Soil:** humus-
rich, fertile and moist soil, preferably
neutral, **Habit:** upright, hardy, **Propagation:** by cuttings of young shoots taken
from spring until autumn.
☐ Good for training as a standard.

Fuchsia magellanica var. *gracilis*
Onagraceae   Hardy fuchsia
ZONES 6–9   SHRUB
Height: 1.8 m (6 ft), variable according to
climate, **Flowers:** sepals red, corolla deep
purple, single, long and thin, **Foliage:**
green, deciduous, **Position:** sun or partial
shade, **Soil:** humus-rich, fertile, moisture-
retentive soil, preferably neutral, **Habit:**
graceful arching branches, **Propagation:**
by cuttings of young shoots taken from
spring until autumn.

Fuchsia magellanica 'Pumila'

Onagraceae　Hardy fuchsia

ZONES 6–9　　　　　　　　SHRUB

Height: 15 cm (6 in), varies according to climate, **Flowers:** sepals red, corolla mauve, single, mid-summer onwards, **Foliage:** green, deciduous, **Position:** sun or partial shade, **Soil:** humus–rich, moisture-retentive, preferably neutral, **Habit:** very dwarf and compact, **Propagation:** by cuttings of young shoots taken from spring until autumn.

□ Ideal for rock gardens and window boxes, especially by the sea.

Fuchsia magellanica 'Riccartonii'

Onagraceae　Hardy fuchsia

ZONES 6–9　　　　　　　　SHRUB

Height: 1.8 m (6 ft), variable according to climate, **Flowers:** sepals red, corolla purple-blue, single, mid-summer onwards, **Foliage:** green, deciduous, **Position:** sun or partial shade, **Soil:** humus-rich, moisture-retentive, preferably neutral, **Habit:** robust-growing, upright, **Propagation:** by cuttings of young shoots taken from spring until autumn.

□ Deservedly one of the most popular for hedging, especially in seaside gardens.

Fuchsia magellanica 'Variegata'

Onagraceae　Hardy fuchsia

ZONES 7–9　　　　　　　　SHRUB

Height: 1.2 m (4 ft), variable according to climate, **Flowers:** sepals red, corolla purple, single, mid-summer onwards, **Foliage:** green, edged cream with a pink flush, deciduous, **Position:** sun or light shade, **Soil:** humus-rich, moisture-retentive, preferably neutral, **Habit:** bushy and graceful, **Propagation:** by cuttings of young shoots taken from spring until autumn.

□ Associates effectively with *Ceratostigma willmottianum* and *Caryopteris × clandonensis*. Suitable for seaside planting.

Fuchsia 'Mrs Popple'

Onagraceae　Hardy fuchsia

ZONES 6–9　　　　　　　　SHRUB

Height: up to 2.5 m (8 ft), varies according to climate, **Flowers:** sepals red, corolla deep purple, single, mid-summer onwards, **Foliage:** mid green, deciduous, **Position:** sun or partial shade, **Soil:** humus-rich, moisture-retentive, preferably neutral, **Habit:** vigorous and upright, **Propagation:** by cuttings of young shoots taken from spring until autumn.

□ The flowers are considerably larger than those of *F. magellanica*. Suitable for seaside planting.

Fuchsia 'Tom Thumb'

Onagraceae　Hardy fuchsia

ZONES 6–9　　　　　　　　SHRUB

Height: 45–60 cm (1½–2 ft), **Flowers:** sepals red, corolla mauve, single, mid-summer onwards, **Foliage:** green, deciduous, **Position:** sun or partial shade, **Soil:** humus-rich, moisture-retentive, preferably acid, **Habit:** bushy and compact, **Propagation:** by cuttings of young shoots taken from spring to autumn.

□ Flowers are small but produced in vast numbers. Suitable for seaside planting.

Top: *Fuchsia magellanica* 'Riccartonii'
Centre left: *Fuchsia magellanica* 'Variegata'
Centre right: *Fuchsia* 'Tom Thumb'
Left: *Fuchsia* 'Mrs Popple'

Gaillardia aristata
(syn. *G. grandiflora*)
Compositae   Blanket flower

ZONES 5–10   HERBACEOUS PERENNIAL
Height: 45–75 cm (1½–2½ ft), **Flowers:**
red or orange-red with yellow tips, daisy-
like, early summer – early autumn, **Foliage:** long and greyish green, deciduous,
Position: sun or partial shade, best in sun,
Soil: any well-drained reasonably light
soil, **Habit:** clump-forming, **Propagation:** by seeds sown under glass or outdoors in spring, or by division of clumps,
early spring.

Above: *Gaillardia aristata* 'Croftway Yellow'

☐Excellent named cultivars include 'Burgundy' (deep red), 'Croftway Yellow' (all
yellow) and 'Wirral Flame' (dark red with
yellow tips). All are first-class border
plants and the flowers are ideal for cutting.

Garrya elliptica
Garryaceae   Silk tassel bush
ZONES 5–9   SHRUB
Height: 2.5–4 m (8–13 ft), **Flowers:** long
pale greyish-green catkins (male) winter,
short catkins, purple fruits (female), separate bushes, the male catkins being much
longer and more showy, **Foliage:** thick,
oval, greyish-green, evergreen, **Position:**
grows well in sun or shade, but flowers
better in sun, **Soil:** well-drained, **Habit:**
bushy, slow to start, quick-growing once
established, **Propagation:** heeled cuttings, late summer – early autumn.
☐Splendid against a wall. Seaside shrub.

Gaulnettya × wisleyensis 'Wisley
Pearl'
(syn. × *Gaulthettya wisleyensis*)
Ericaceae
ZONES 4–9   SHRUB
Height: 1–1.2 m (3–4 ft), **Flowers:** white,
early summer, followed by blood-red fruits
in autumn, **Foliage:** 4 cm (almost 2 in)
long, dark-green, leathery, evergreen, **Position:** partial or full shade, **Soil:** moist,
lime-free, preferably peaty, **Habit:** dense
and bushy, **Propagation:** by cuttings 5–
8 cm (2–3 in) long of lateral shoots, preferably with a heel, mid – late summer.

Gaultheria procumbens
Ericaceae   Partridge berry
ZONES 4–9   SHRUB
Height: 15 cm (6 in), **Flowers:** white,
summer, followed by red cherry-sized berries, **Foliage:** dark green turning dark
purple in winter, evergreen, **Position:**
partial or full shade, **Soil:** humus-rich,
lime-free, **Habit:** prostrate, creeping, excellent ground cover, **Propagation:** by
seeds sown in peaty soil outdoors in
autumn, or by cuttings taken in summer or
autumn.

Genista aetnensis
Leguminosae   Mount Etna broom
ZONES 6–10   SHRUB
Height: 4 m (13 ft) or more, **Flowers:**
yellow, in profusion, mid – late summer,
Foliage: green, small, falling early, deciduous, **Position:** sun, **Soil:** suits most
normal well-drained soils, **Habit:** tall with
thin green branches, **Propagation:** by
heeled cuttings of side shoots, 8–10 cm (3–
4 in) long, in late summer, or from seed in
spring.

Genista lydia

Leguminosae Broom
ZONES 7–10   SHRUB

Height: up to 1 m (3 ft), **Flowers:** yellow, in profusion during late spring and early summer, **Foliage:** tiny, greyish-green, deciduous, **Position:** sunny, **Soil:** suits most normal well-drained soils, not too rich, **Habit:** wide-spreading and arching, **Propagation:** by heeled cuttings of side shoots in late summer, or from seed sown outdoors in a garden frame in early spring.
☐ Prune after flowering by shortening flowered stems, but do not cut into old wood.

Excellent ground-cover plant for hot dry banks. Suitable too for the larger rock garden.

Genista tinctoria 'Royal Gold'

Leguminosae Dyer's greenweed
ZONES 6–10   SHRUB

Height: 45–60 cm (1½–2 ft), **Flowers:** bright yellow, early – late summer, **Foliage:** deep green, longish, deciduous, **Position:** sun, **Soil:** suits most normal well-drained soils, not too rich, **Habit:** bushy and compact, **Propagation:** by heeled cuttings of side shoots in late summer, or from seed sown in a garden frame in early spring.
☐ Suitable for a hot dry bank or larger rock garden.

Right: *Genista lydia*

Gentiana acaulis

Gentianaceae Trumpet gentian
ZONES 5–9   ROCK PLANT

Height: 8 cm (3 in), **Flowers:** vivid, deep blue, spring, **Foliage:** shiny oval leaves, deciduous, **Position:** sun or partial shade, **Soil:** fairly rich alkaline soil, **Habit:** mat-forming, spreading up to 45 cm (1½ ft), **Propagation:** by division of clumps in early summer, or from basal cuttings in mid – late spring and inserted in sandy peat in a garden frame.
☐ Excellent rock-garden plant.

Gentiana × macaulayi

Gentianaceae Gentian
ZONES 5–9   ROCK PLANT

Height: 15 cm (6 in), **Flowers:** dark blue, early – mid-autumn, **Foliage:** light to medium green, **Position:** sun or partial shade, **Soil:** deep, fairly rich, lime-free soil, **Habit:** prostrate, **Propagation:** by division of clumps in spring, or by basal cuttings in mid – late spring and inserted in sandy peat in a garden frame.
☐ A superb plant for the rock garden.

Geranium 'Ballerina'

Geraniaceae Crane's bill
ZONES 5–10   ROCK PLANT

Height: 15–23 cm (6–9 in), **Flowers:** pink, streaked deeper pink, early summer – early autumn, **Foliage:** greyish-green, lobed, deciduous, **Position:** full sun or semi shade, best in full sun, **Soil:** any well-drained soil, **Habit:** low-growing, spreads to 30 cm (1 ft), **Propagation:** by division of clumps in autumn or spring.
☐ Suitable for a rock garden.

Geranium dalmaticum

Geraniaceae Crane's bill

ZONES 4–10   ROCK PLANT

Height: 15 cm (6 in), **Flowers:** pale pink, early – late summer, **Foliage:** medium green, shiny, tinged with red in autumn, deciduous, **Position:** full sun or semi-shade, best in full sun, **Soil:** most well-drained soils, **Habit:** compact low mound, **Propagation:** by dividing plants early autumn – early spring.

☐ Excellent rock-garden plant.

Geranium endressii

Geraniaceae Crane's bill

ZONES 4–10   HERBACEOUS PERENNIAL

Height: 30–45 cm (1–1½ ft), **Flowers:** rose-pink, late spring – late summer, **Foliage:** medium green, lobed, deciduous, **Position:** full sun or semi-shade, **Soil:** any well-drained soil, **Habit:** clump-forming and spreading perennial, **Propagation:** by dividing plants mid-autumn – early spring.

☐ Useful ground-cover for semi-shaded places.

Right: *Geranium dalmaticum*

Geranium pratense 'Johnson's Blue'

Geraniaceae Meadow crane's bill

ZONES 4–10   HERBACEOUS PERENNIAL

Height: 45–75 cm (1½–2½ ft), **Flowers:** pale blue, mid summer – early autumn, **Foliage:** deep green, much divided, deciduous, **Position:** full sun or semi-shade, **Soil:** any well-drained soil, **Habit:** bushy and free-flowering, **Propagation:** by dividing clumps mid-winter – early spring.

☐ Excellent for planting among shrubs.

Geranium sanguineum 'Lancastriense'

Geraniaceae Bloody crane's bill

ZONES 4–10   HERBACEOUS PERENNIAL

Height: 15–23 cm (6–9 in), spreads 45 cm (18 in) or more, **Flowers:** light pink with pink veining, early summer – early autumn, **Foliage:** deep green, lobed, deciduous, **Position:** full sun or semi-shade, **Soil:** any well-drained soil, **Habit:** mat-forming perennial, **Propagation:** by dividing clumps mid-autumn – early spring.

☐ Good ground cover plant.

Geum chiloense 'Lady Stratheden'

Rosaceae Avens

ZONES 6–9   HERBACEOUS PERENNIAL

Height: 30–60 cm (1–2 ft), **Flowers:** yellow, double, late spring – early autumn, **Foliage:** mid green, deciduous, **Position:** full sun or semi-shade, **Soil:** suits most soils, add plenty of peat, **Habit:** forms dense clumps, **Propagation:** by division, early – mid-spring.

☐ 'Mrs Bradshaw' is a fine semi-double scarlet, 'Prince of Orange' is orange.

Ginkgo biloba
Ginkgoaceae Maidenhair tree
ZONES 4–9   TREE
Height: ultimately 20 m (65 ft) or more,
Flowers: flowers insignificant; fleshy part
of fruit evil smelling but rarely produced
unless both male and female trees grow
close, **Foliage:** pale green, fan-shaped,
turning darker green then yellow in
autumn, deciduous, **Position:** full sun,
Soil: any reasonably humus-rich soil,
Habit: varied in shape, usually tall slender
pyramid, branches droop at tips. **Propagation:** from seed in a garden frame.
☐Only living species of a very ancient
group of trees. Tolerant of atmospheric
pollution. Excellent specimen tree for a
lawn.

Right: *Ginkgo biloba*

Gleditsia triacanthos 'Sunburst'
Leguminosae Honey locust
ZONES 3–9   TREE
Height: 6–9 m (20–30 ft), **Flowers:** insignificant, brown seed pods, **Foliage:** young
foliage bright yellow turning greener as it
matures, very attractive long pinnate
leaves, deciduous, **Position:** full sun, **Soil:**
any fertile, well drained soil, **Habit:** quick
growing, round-headed tree, branches
bear stout spines, **Propagation:** by seeds
sown in spring in seed compost and placed
in a garden frame.
☐Ideal as a specimen tree in a lawn – good
choice for modern gardens.

Griselinia littoralis
Cornaceae
ZONES 7–10   SHRUB
Height: 3–5 m (10–16 ft) or more,
Flowers: inconspicuous, green in spring,
Foliage: shiny yellowish-green, thick, evergreen, **Position:** full sun or shade, maritime, **Soil:** tolerates poor but well-drained
soils, including chalk, **Habit:** upright and
bushy, **Propagation:** by cuttings 5–8 cm
(2–3 in) long of side-shoots with a heel
taken in late summer – early autumn.
☐Will withstand sea winds in warmer
districts. Excellent hedging plant. Hedges
should be trimmed in mid-summer.

Griselinia littoralis 'Bantry Bay'
Cornaceae
ZONES 8–10   SHRUB
Height: 1.8–3 m (6–10 ft), **Flowers:** insignificant, **Foliage:** leaves beautifully
splashed with yellow, evergreen, **Position:** sun, shelter from wind and frosts,
Soil: tolerates most soils, including lime
and chalk, **Habit:** erect and bushy, **Propagation:** by 5–8 cm (2–3 in) cuttings of
lateral shoots taken with heel in late
summer – early autumn.
☐Not as hardy as the species. Foliage good
for flower arranging.

Gypsophila paniculata

Caryophyllaceae Baby's breath, chalk plant

ZONES 4–10 HERBACEOUS PERENNIAL

Height: 1 m (3 ft), **Flowers:** white, in large sprays, early – late summer, **Foliage:** thin greyish green, deciduous, **Position:** sunny, **Soil:** suits most well-drained soils, preferably with lime, **Habit:** a free flowering plant with slender flower stems, **Propagation:** by seeds sown in spring outdoors, or by cuttings of basal shoots inserted in sandy peat in a garden frame, mid – late spring.

☐Associates well with coreopsis, erigerons, heleniums and phlox. 'Flamingo' is pink with double flowers. Suits seaside gardens.

Gypsophila repens 'Fratensis'

Caryophyllaceae Baby's breath

ZONES 5–10 ROCK PLANT

Height: 15 cm (6 in), **Flowers:** clear pink, summer, **Foliage:** bluish-green, **Position:** sunny, **Soil:** suits most well-drained soils, **Habit:** prostrate mats, spreading to 60 cm (2 ft), **Propagation:** by cuttings in early summer.

☐Ideal plant for rock garden or paving. 'Rosea' has rose-pink flowers.

Right: *Gypsophila paniculata*

Halesia carolina

Styracaceae Snowdrop tree

ZONES 5–10 TREE

Height: 6 m (20 ft), **Flowers:** white, pendulous, cup-shaped, in profusion in late spring, **Foliage:** green, deciduous, **Position:** sun or partial shade, slightly sheltered, **Soil:** humus-rich, acid, **Habit:** tall and wide spreading, **Propagation:** by layering in early autumn, or from ripe seed in mid-autumn.

☐Winged, pear-shaped fruits follow the flowers. Superb tree for woodland gardens.

× Halimiocistus 'Ingwersenii'

Cistaceae

ZONES 7–10 SHRUB

Height: 45 cm (1½ ft), **Flowers:** white, early summer – early autumn, **Foliage:** green, evergreen, **Position:** warm and full sun, **Soil:** light and dry, **Habit:** free growing shrub, spreading, dwarf, **Propagation:** by heeled cuttings of side shoots in mid – late summer.

☐Recommended for dry sunny banks, in association with brooms. Suitable for seaside gardens.

Halimium lasianthum

Cistaceae

ZONES 7–10 SHRUB

Height: 45 cm–1 m (1½–3 ft), **Flowers:** deep yellow petals with basal purplish blotch, late spring – mid-summer, **Foliage:** greyish-green, evergreen, **Position:** sun and shelter, **Soil:** sandy, well-drained, **Habit:** bushy and rounded, **Propagation:** by heeled cuttings of side shoots in mid – late summer.

☐An excellent shrub for dry situations, like banks, and coastal districts. Good companions are the various kinds of broom.

Hamamelis mollis

Hamamelidaceae Chinese witch hazel

ZONES 5–9   SHRUB

Height: 1.8–2.5 m (6–8 ft), **Flowers:** yellow, spidery, fragrant, mid-winter – early spring, **Foliage:** green, roundish hazel-like leaves, deciduous, good autumn colour, **Position:** sun or partial-shade, **Soil:** lime-free, moist, humus rich, **Habit:** open-branched and twiggy, **Propagation:** layering in early autumn.

☐ Perfect shrub for a small garden or a winter border. Try growing winter-flowering heathers around it.

Hebe albicans

Scrophulariaceae

ZONES 5–10   SHRUB

Height: 60 cm (2 ft), **Flowers:** white, early and mid-summer, **Foliage:** bluish, evergreen, **Position:** sunny and warm, **Soil:** suits most soils with good drainage, including alkaline, **Habit:** a bushy, rounded hardy shrub, **Propagation:** by cuttings 4–5 cm (about 2 in) long of side shoots taken mid – late summer.

☐ Attractive both in and out of flower. Excellent for coastal planting. Dwarf habit makes it ideal for small mixed borders.

Hebe × andersonii

Scrophulariaceae

ZONES 7–10   SHRUB

Height: 1.8 m (6 ft), **Flowers:** soft lavender-blue, fading to white, late summer – early autumn, **Foliage:** green, evergreen, **Position:** sunny and warm, **Soil:** suits most soils with good drainage, including alkaline, **Habit:** vigorous, bushy, **Propagation:** by cuttings 4–5 cm (about 2 in) long of side shoots in mid – late summer.

☐ Cut back leggy growth in mid-spring. Old wood then produces new shoots. 'Variegata' (ZONE 8) is a pretty form (above) with leaves margined and splashed white. Good in maritime conditions.

Hebe 'Autumn Glory'

Scrophulariaceae

ZONES 6–10   SHRUB

Height: 1 m (3 ft), **Flowers:** deep violet-blue from mid-summer to mid-autumn, **Foliage:** deep green, attractive purple shoots, evergreen, **Position:** sunny and warm, **Soil:** suits most well-drained soils, including alkaline, **Habit:** loose, **Propagation:** by cuttings of side shoots taken mid – late summer.

☐ Ideal for seaside gardens.

Hebe brachysiphon

(**syn.** *H. traversii*)

Scrophulariaceae

ZONES 5–10   SHRUB

Height: 1.8 m (6 ft), **Flowers:** white, early and mid-summer, **Foliage:** shiny, deep green, evergreen, **Position:** sun or partial shade, **Soil:** suits most well-drained soils, including alkaline, **Habit:** bushy, sturdy shrub, **Propagation:** by cuttings of side shoots taken mid – late summer.

☐ Makes an excellent hedge in coastal areas. Very hardy.

Left: *Hebe brachysiphon* is very hardy and makes an excellent hedge in coastal gardens

Above: *Hebe* 'Great Orme'
Right: *Hebe* macrantha

Hebe buchananii
Scrophulariaceae
ZONES 6–10   SHRUB
Height: 30 cm (1 ft), **Flowers:** white, early and mid-summer, **Foliage:** green, tiny, rounded and leathery, evergreen, **Position:** sun or partial shade, **Soil:** tolerates most well-drained soils, including alkaline, **Habit:** dwarf and compact, **Propagation:** by cuttings of side shoots, mid – late summer.
☐ Good for seaside gardens.

Hebe 'Carl Teschner'
Scrophulariaceae
ZONES 6–10   SHRUB
Height: 30 cm (1 ft), **Flowers:** violet-blue with a white throat, early to late summer, **Foliage:** greyish-green, evergreen, **Position:** sunny and warm, **Soil:** suits most well-drained soils, including alkaline, **Habit:** dense and spreading, spreads 60 cm–1 m (2–3 ft), **Propagation:** by cuttings of side shoots in summer.
☐ A very useful evergreen for ground cover. Suits seaside gardens.

Hebe × *franciscana* 'Blue Gem'
Scrophulariaceae
ZONES 6–10   SHRUB
Height: 1.2 m (4 ft), **Flowers:** bright blue throughout summer, **Foliage:** green, evergreen, **Position:** sun or partial shade, **Soil:** suits most well-drained soils, including alkaline, **Habit:** compact and dome-shaped, **Propagation:** by cuttings of side shoots taken mid – late summer.
☐ One of the hardiest hebes and suitable for exposed seaside gardens. Will form an attractive low hedge.

Hebe 'Great Orme'
Scrophulariaceae
ZONES 7–10   SHRUB
Height: 1.5–2 m (5–6 ft), **Flowers:** pink flowers from late spring to early summer, **Foliage:** green, evergreen, **Position:** sun, **Soil:** suits most well-drained soils, including chalk, **Habit:** upright and bushy, **Propagation:** by cuttings of non-flowering growths taken mid – late summer.
☐ Prune back old flowering stems in mid-spring. Readily produces new shoots from base. Suitable for seaside gardens.

Hebe hulkeana
Scrophulariaceae
ZONES 9–10   SHRUB
Height: up to 1.2 m (4 ft), **Flowers:** long panicles of pale blue, late spring and early summer, **Foliage:** green, glossy with toothed edges, evergreen, **Position:** sun, best against a south-facing wall, **Soil:** suits most fertile soils, including alkaline, **Habit:** erect and loose, **Propagation:** by cuttings of side shoots taken mid – late summer.
☐ Widely acclaimed as the most beautiful species of hebe in cultivation. Suits seaside gardens. But only suited to very mild areas inland.

Hebe macrantha
Scrophulariaceae
ZONES 7–10   SHRUB
Height: 60 cm (2 ft), **Flowers:** white, large, carried in short racemes, early summer, **Foliage:** pale green, glossy, with jagged edges, evergreen, **Position:** sun and maximum shelter or wall-protection, **Soil:** suits most well-drained soils, including alkaline, **Habit:** erect and bushy, **Propagation:** by cuttings of side shoots taken mid – late summer.
☐ Well worth while in milder districts and by the sea.

Hebe 'Midsummer Beauty'
Scrophulariaceae
ZONES 7–10   SHRUB
Height: 1.5–1.8 m (5–6 ft), **Flowers:** lavender-blue, long, in racemes, **Foliage:** green, evergreen, **Position:** preferably sunny, **Soil:** suits most well-drained soils, including alkaline, **Habit:** bushy and dense, **Propagation:** by cuttings 8–10 cm (3–4 in) long of non-flowering growths mid – late summer.
☐ Prune back old flowering shoots and straggly stems in mid-spring to keep shrub compact.

Hebe ochracea
Schrophulariaceae

ZONES 5–10   SHRUB

Height: 45 cm (1½ ft), **Flowers:** white, mid – late summer, **Foliage:** gold, very small, evergreen, **Position:** sun, **Soil:** suits most well-drained soils, including alkaline, **Habit:** dwarf, very bushy, with yellow shoots, **Propagation:** by cuttings of side shoots taken mid – late summer.

☐ Not to be confused with *Hebe armstrongii* which, while similar, has greener stems and leaves. Suits seaside gardens.

Hebe pimeleoides 'Glaucocaerulea'
Schrophulariaceae

ZONES 5–10   SHRUB

Height: 30 cm (1 ft), **Flowers:** light lavender-blue, early and mid-summer, **Foliage:** deep grey-green, evergreen, **Position:** sun, **Soil:** suits most well-drained soils, including alkaline, **Habit:** dwarf, bushy and compact, **Propagation:** by cuttings of side shoots taken mid – late summer.

☐ Ground-cover plant, suits seaside gardens.

Hebe pinguifolia 'Pagei'
Scrophulariaceae

ZONES 5–10   SHRUB

Height: 15–23 cm (6–9 in), **Flowers:** white, profuse in late spring and sometimes later, **Foliage:** grey, evergreen, **Position:** preferably sunny, **Soil:** suits most well-drained soils, including alkaline, **Habit:** wide, mat-forming, spreading to 1 m (3 ft), **Propagation:** by cuttings of side shoots taken mid – late summer.

☐ Excellent groundcover, suits maritime gardens. Try it around purple-leaved shrubs.

Hebe salicifolia
Scrophulariaceae

ZONES 7–10   SHRUB

Height: 1.8–2.5 m (6–8 ft), **Flowers:** white, tinged with mauve, early – late summer, **Foliage:** slender, light green, evergreen, **Position:** sun, **Soil:** suits most well-drained soils, including alkaline, **Habit:** dense and bushy, **Propagation:** by cuttings of side shoots taken mid – late summer.

☐ A reasonably hardy hebe, excellent for coastal gardens.

Hebe speciosa hybrids
Scrophulariaceae

ZONES 7–10   SHRUB

Height: 1.5 m (5 ft), **Flowers:** shades of pink, red, purple and blue, mid-summer onwards, **Foliage:** shiny and leathery, evergreen, **Position:** sun and maximum protection from frost and wind, **Soil:** suits most well-drained soils, **Habit:** sturdy, bushy and compact, **Propagation:** by cuttings of side shoots taken mid – late summer.

☐ Prune back old flowered growths and straggly stems in mid-spring. These shrubs readily produce new shoots from the base, keeping them compact and sturdy. All good in seaside gardens.

Recommended hybrids of *Hebe speciosa*

'*Gauntlettii*' – pink flowers; dark green foliage.

'*Purple Queen*' – purple; purple-green foliage.

'*Simon Deleaux*' – red flowers; green foliage; looser habit and less hardy than other hybrids.

'*Veitchii*' – bright blue flowers, green foliage.

Top left: *Hebe* 'Midsummer Beauty'
Top right: *Hebe pinguifolia* 'Pagei'
Left: *Hebe speciosa* 'Veitchii'

Hedera canariensis 'Gloire de Marengo' (syn. 'Variegata')

Araliaceae   Canary Island ivy

ZONES 5–10 — CLIMBER

Height: 4.5–6 m (15–20 ft), **Flowers:** of no decorative merit, **Foliage:** large leaves with green centres blending through grey to white margins, attractively red tinted in winter, evergreen, **Position:** sun or partial shade, **Soil:** suits most soil types, **Habit:** climbs by its aerial roots, **Propagation:** by layering at any time, by inserting cuttings of firm shoots of runner growths in a shady sheltered place in autumn, or by tip cuttings in mid – late summer in a closed propagator or frame.
□ Tolerates atmospheric pollution. A good companion plant is *Vitis coignetiae*. Can be used as ground cover.

Right: *Hedera canariensis* 'Gloire de Marengo' is an excellent ground-cover plant

Hedera colchica 'Dentata Variegata'

Araliaceae   Persian ivy

ZONES 5–10 — CLIMBER

Height: 6–9 m (20–30 ft), **Flowers:** of no decorative merit, **Foliage:** large leaves with shining green centres shading to cream-yellow margins, evergreen, **Position:** sun or partial shade, **Soil:** any type of soil, **Habit:** climbs by its aerial roots, **Propagation:** as for *H. canariensis*.
□ Tolerates atmospheric pollution. 'Paddy's Pride' has leaves with a bold central splash of yellow merging through pale to dark green margins.

Hedera helix 'Chicago'

Araliaceae   Ivy

ZONES 5–10 — CLIMBER

Height: 4.5 m (15 ft) or more, **Flowers:** of no decorative merit, **Foliage:** deep green marked with bronzy-purple, small, evergreen, **Position:** sun, partial or full shade, **Soil:** suits most soil types, **Habit:** climbs by its aerial roots, **Propagation:** as for *H. canariensis*.
□ Tolerates atmospheric pollution. 'Glacier' (shown above) has green-grey leaves with narrow white margins, 'Goldheart' has dark green glossy leaves with a central golden blotch. Good ground cover.

Helenium autumnale 'Wyndley'

Compositae   Sneezeweed

ZONES 5–9 — HERBACEOUS PERENNIAL

Height: 1–1.2 m (3–4 ft), **Flowers:** yellow and bronze daisies, late summer – mid-autumn, **Foliage:** green, deciduous, **Position:** sun or partial shade, **Soil:** suits most well-drained soils, **Habit:** easy to grow, upright stems, **Propagation:** by division of clumps in autumn or spring.
□ 'Moerheim Beauty' is red flushed bronze, 'Butterpat' is pure yellow. Flowers deteriorate, becoming smaller as plant ages, so divide every few years, discarding the old centre sections. Good for cutting.

Helianthemum nummularium
Cistaceae Rock rose
ZONES 5–10   SHRUB
Height: 30 cm (1 ft), **Flowers:** yellow, single, freely produced, summer, **Foliage:** small, dark green, evergreen, **Position:** full sun, **Soil:** well-drained, neutral or alkaline, **Habit:** shrubby growth rapidly covers bare areas, **Propagation:** by seeds sown in light soil in a cool greenhouse or garden frame in spring; named hybrids only from cuttings of firm young shoots in sandy soil in a propagator in summer.
☐ Named hybrids range in colour from cream to deep red. Excellent for covering sunny banks or for rock gardens. When flowering is over, trim back.

Helianthus decapetalus
Compositae Sunflower
ZONES 5–10   HERBACEOUS PERENNIAL
Height: 1.2–1.8 m (4–6 ft), **Flowers:** pale yellow, mid-summer – early autumn, **Foliage:** medium green, rather rough texture, deciduous, **Position:** sunny, **Soil:** suits most soils that are well drained, **Habit:** tall and erect perennial needing support, **Propagation:** by seeds sown outdoors, or under glass in mid-spring, or by division of clumps in autumn or spring.
☐ The best double-flowered cultivar is 'Loddon Gold'.

Helichrysum serotinum
  (syn. *H. angustifolium*)
Compositae Curry plant
ZONES 7–10   SHRUB
Height: 30–60 cm (1–2 ft), **Flowers:** yellow, mid – late summer, **Foliage:** silvery grey-green, smelling of curry, evergreen, **Position:** sun, **Soil:** suits most soils as long as drainage is good, **Habit:** compact, bushy, **Propagation:** by cuttings of side shoots taken from mid-spring – mid-summer.
☐ Not too hardy, but suitable for mild areas, especially if planted against a warm wall.

Heliopsis scabra
Compositae
ZONES 5–9   HERBACEOUS PERENNIAL
Height: 1–1.2 m (3–4 ft), **Flowers:** single yellow daisies, mid – late summer, **Foliage:** medium green, lanceolate, deciduous, **Position:** sunny, **Soil:** suits most soil types, **Habit:** compact and bushy perennial, **Propagation:** by dividing roots autumn – spring.
☐ Cut down to ground level after flowering. Good companions are border plants with spikes of flowers, such as delphiniums.

Helleborus corsicus
  (syn. *H. argutifolius*)
Ranunculaceae Corsican hellebore
ZONES 6–9   HERBACEOUS PERENNIAL
Height: 60 cm (2 ft), **Flowers:** greeny yellow, bowl-shaped, early – mid-spring, **Foliage:** medium green with three distinct lobes, thick with spiny margins, evergreen, **Position:** partial or full shade, **Soil:** tolerant even of poor soils, ideally moisture-retentive, **Habit:** forms bushy clumps, **Propagation:** by dividing overcrowded clumps in spring.
☐ Lovely planted with shrubs in a mixed border or with bulbs.

Helleborus foetidus
Ranunculaceae Stinking hellebore
ZONES 4–9   HERBACEOUS PERENNIAL
Height: 60 cm (2 ft), **Flowers:** greenish purple, late winter – mid spring, **Foliage:** dark green, deeply lobed, evergreen, **Position:** ideal for a shaded spot, **Soil:** moist but well drained, **Habit:** fairly upright stems, **Propagation:** by dividing overcrowded clumps in spring, or by ripe seeds sown in seed compost in a garden frame.
☐ Lovely planted with shrubs or in a mixed border.

Helleborus niger
Ranunculaceae   Christmas rose
ZONES 4–9   HERBACEOUS PERENNIAL
Height: 30–45 cm (12–18 in), **Flowers:** white, like single roses, early winter – early spring, **Foliage:** deep green, distinctively lobed, evergreen, **Position:** partial or full shade, **Soil:** any moist but well drained soil, **Habit:** clump-forming, branching stems, **Propagation:** by division of over-crowded clumps in spring.
☐ Lovely flowers need protection from the weather to remain unsullied; cover with a cloche or pane of glass.

Helleborus orientalis
Ranunculaceae   Lenten rose
ZONES 5–9   HERBACEOUS PERENNIAL
Height: 45–60 cm (18–24 in), **Flowers:** cream, pink, purple or reddish, bowl shaped, late winter – early spring, **Foliage:** deep green, evergreen, **Position:** partial or full shade, **Soil:** tolerates most moist but well-drained soils, **Habit:** clump forming, **Propagation:** by dividing over-crowded roots in spring.
☐ Looks lovely in a shrub border, especially in association with snowdrops.

Hemerocallis hybrids
Liliaceae   Day lily
ZONES 4–9   HERBACEOUS PERENNIAL
Height: 75 cm–1 m (2½–3 ft), **Flowers:** shades of red, yellow or pink, lily-like, early – late summer, **Foliage:** light to medium green, grassy, deciduous, **Position:** sun or partial shade, **Soil:** deep and fertile, moist, **Habit:** forming clumps of long, narrow leaves, **Propagation:** by dividing clumps in autumn or spring.
☐ Excellent perennials for grouping around shrubs. Ideal, too, for ornamental containers.

Hibiscus syriacus 'Blue Bird'
Malvaceae   Rose mallow, tree hollyhock
ZONES 5–10   SHRUB
Height: 1.8–3 m (6–10 ft), **Flowers:** single blue, red in centre, mid-summer – mid-autumn, **Foliage:** green, deciduous, **Position:** full sun, **Soil:** suits most well-drained, rich soils, **Habit:** profusely-branched and upright, **Propagation:** cuttings of side shoots, with heel, in mid-summer.
☐ Shorten long growths in mid-spring. 'Hamabo', white, red 'eye', 'William R. Smith' white, and 'Woodbridge', deep crimson, are other recommended cultivars.

Hippophae rhamnoides
Elaeagnaceae   Sea buckthorn
ZONES 3–9   SHRUB
Height: 3–4 m (10–13 ft) or more, **Flowers:** yellow, of no significance, male and female on separate plants; orange berries produced in autumn on female plants; grow a male, too, to ensure pollination, **Foliage:** narrow, silver, deciduous, **Position:** open situation in sun or partial shade, **Soil:** suits most well-drained soils, **Habit:** dense and spiny, **Propagation:** seeds, when ripe.
☐ This useful hedging or screening shrub resists drought and is immune to salt spray. Plant both male and female plants to ensure the showy orange berries.

Hoheria glabrata
Malvaceae
ZONES 6–9   SHRUB
Height: 3–5 m (10–16 ft), **Flowers:** white, highly fragrant, early – mid-summer, **Foliage:** green, deciduous, **Position:** full sun or semi-shade, good against south facing walls, **Soil:** suits most well-drained soils, **Habit:** upright, **Propagation:** sow seeds in early – mid-spring, or layering in early autumn.
☐ A good wall shrub. Suitable only for mild parts of the country. If necessary, thin out growths in early spring.

Hoheria sexstylosa
Malvaceae

ZONES 8–9   SHRUB

Height: 3–5 m (10–16 ft), **Flowers:** white, mid – late summer, **Foliage:** glossy, thick, greyish-green, evergreen, **Position:** full sun or semi-shade, **Soil:** suits most well-drained soils, **Habit:** erect, **Propagation:** sow seeds in early – mid-spring, or layering in early autumn.

☐ A good wall shrub. If necessary thin out growths in early spring.

Hosta fortunei
Liliaceae Plantain lily

ZONES 4–9   HERBACEOUS PERENNIAL

Height: 60 cm–1 m (2–3 ft), **Flowers:** lilac-blue spikes in mid-summer, **Foliage:** greyish-green, strong veining, **Position:** full sun or semi-shade, best in semi-shade, **Soil:** moist and humus-rich, **Habit:** clump-forming perennial with large ornamental foliage, **Propagation:** by division in autumn or spring.

☐ 'Albopicta' (above) has pale green foliage, variegated with light yellow. All hostas make excellent ground cover in shrub borders. Also recommended for poolside planting.

Hosta sieboldiana
(syn. *H. glauca*)
Liliaceae Plantain lily

ZONES 4–9   HERBACEOUS PERENNIAL

Height: 60 cm (2 ft), **Flowers:** pale violet spikes, late summer, **Foliage:** glaucous green, large, heart-shaped and boldly veined, deciduous, **Position:** full sun or shade, best in semi-shade, **Soil:** moist and humus-rich, **Habit:** clump-forming perennial with ornamental foliage, **Propagation:** division, autumn/spring.

☐ Hostas combine well with hydrangeas. 'Elegans', with grey foliage, is an excellent cultivar of *H. sieboldiana*.

Hosta undulata 'Medio-variegata'
Liliaceae Plantain lily

ZONES 4–9   HERBACEOUS PERENNIAL

Height: 60 cm (2 ft), **Flowers:** lilac, arranged in spikes, late summer, **Foliage:** mid green, yellow variegation, wavy-edged, deciduous, **Position:** full sun or semi-shade, **Soil:** moist and humus rich, **Habit:** clump-forming perennial with ornamental foliage, **Propagation:** by dividing clumps in autumn or spring.

☐ Hostas provide ideal ground cover in shrub borders. Good for poolside plantings or in bog gardens.

Hydrangea arborescens
'Grandiflora'
Hydrangeaceae

ZONES 5–9   SHRUB

Height: 1.2–2 m (4–6 ft), **Flowers:** white, in big rounded heads, mid-summer – early autumn, **Foliage:** oval, green, deciduous, **Position:** full sun or semi-shade, **Soil:** fertile, moist, high in humus, **Habit:** open, bushy, **Propagation:** by cuttings 10–15 cm (4–6 in) long of side shoots in late summer – early autumn.

☐ Cut off dead blooms, preferably in early spring, also cutting out spindly or dead shoots. Excellent for the shrub border.

Hydrangea aspera
Hydrangeaceae

ZONES 7–10   SHRUB

Height: 2.5 m (8 ft), **Flowers:** pale blue inner florets, pink outer, early and mid-summer, **Foliage:** deep matt green above, grey undersides, deciduous, **Position:** full sun or semi-shade, protect from late-spring frosts, **Soil:** fertile, moist, high in humus, **Habit:** much-branched and spreading, **Propagation:** by cuttings 10–15 cm (4–6 in) long of side shoots during late summer or early autumn.

☐ Remove dead flower heads. Ideal for the sheltered shrub border.

Above: *Hydrangea macrophylla* 'Hamburg'
Right: *Hydrangea macrophylla* 'Veitchii'

Hydrangea integerrima
(syn. *H. serratifolia*)
Hydrangeaceae
ZONES 7–10   SHRUB
Height: 6 m (20 ft), **Flowers:** cream, small, massed in panicles, late summer, **Foliage:** deep green, shiny, evergreen, **Position:** full sun or semi-shade, in colder districts best against south or south-west wall, **Soil:** fertile, moist, high in humus, **Habit:** climbs by its aerial roots, **Propagation:** cuttings of side shoots in early – mid-summer inserted in sandy peat in a garden frame.
□Good companion plants are climbing roses.

Hydrangea macrophylla
Hortensia Group
Hydrangeaceae   Common or mop-headed hydrangea
ZONES 5–9   SHRUB
Height: 1.2–1.8 m (4–6 ft), **Flowers:** white or shades of pink or blue according to cultivar and soil, mid-summer to mid-autumn, **Foliage:** glossy, pale green, deciduous, **Position:** full sun or semi-shade, **Soil:** fertile, moist, high in humus, **Habit:** rounded and bushy, **Propagation:** by cuttings 10–15 cm (4–6 in) long of side shoots during late summer and early autumn.
□Pink- or red-flowered cultivars turn various shades of blue in acid soils. Blueing powders can be used to blue hydrangeas in alkaline soils of pH 7.5 or more. Attractive dead flower heads can be left on bushes and removed in early spring. Excellent seaside shrub. Cut out very old shoots early spring.

Recommended Hortensia cultivars
'Altona' – large rose-pink florets; blues well when treated; best in shade.
'Deutschland' – deep pink or medium blue; good foliage colour in autumn.
'Europa' – very large heads of dark pink or light blue.
'Hamburg' – deep pink or blue; bracts remain colourful all winter.
'Holstein' – pink, sky-blue in acid soil.
'La France' – bright pink or mid-blue in huge heads.
'Madame Emile Moullière' – white, pink or blue eye.
'Miss Belgium' – rosy-red, dwarf growing.
'Niedersachsen' – light pink or blue.

Hydrangea macrophylla 'Blue Wave'
Hydrangeaceae   Lacecap hydrangea
ZONES 5–9   SHRUB
Height: 1.2–1.5 m (4–5 ft), **Flowers:** pink (blue in acid soil), sterile florets surrounding fertile flowers, mid-summer – early autumn, **Foliage:** green, deciduous, **Position:** best in partial shade, **Soil:** fertile, moist, high in humus, **Habit:** vigorous, bushy, **Propagation:** cuttings 10–15 cm (4–6 in) long of side shoots late summer – early autumn.
□Excellent seaside shrub. Cut out very old shoots in early spring.

Hydrangea macrophylla 'Mariesii'
Hydrangeaceae   Lacecap hydrangea
ZONES 5–9   SHRUB
Height: 1.2–1.5 m (4–5 ft), **Flowers:** deep pink or blue sterile florets surrounding fertile flowers, mid-summer – early autumn, **Foliage:** green, deciduous, **Position:** best in partial shade, **Soil:** fertile, moist, high in humus, **Habit:** compact, bushy, **Propagation:** cuttings 10–15 cm (4–6 in) long of side shoots in late summer – early autumn.
□Excellent seaside shrub. Cut out very old shoots in early spring.

Hydrangea macrophylla 'Veitchii'
Hydrangeaceae   Lacecap hydrangea
ZONES 5–9   SHRUB
Height: 1.2–1.5 m (4–5 ft), **Flowers:** white, sterile florets, fading to pink, surround fertile blue flowers, mid-summer – early autumn, **Foliage:** dark green, deciduous, **Position:** best in partial shade, **Soil:** fertile, moist, high in humus, lime tolerant, **Habit:** loose, bushy, **Propagation:** cuttings 10–15 cm (4–6 in) long of side shoots late summer – early autumn.
□A very hardy lacecap, ideal for seaside gardens. Cut out very old shoots in early spring.

Hydrangea paniculata
'Grandiflora'
Hydrangeaceae
ZONES 5–9   SHRUB
Height: 3.5–4.5 m (12–15 ft), **Flowers:** white panicles up to 25 cm (10 in) long, late summer – early autumn, **Foliage:** medium green, deciduous, **Position:** full sun or semi-shade, **Soil:** fertile, moist, high in humus, **Habit:** large arching shrub, **Propagation:** cuttings 10–15 cm (4–6 in) long of side shoots, late summer – early autumn.
☐ Prune back hard (by about half) in early spring. Ideal for the large shrub border.

Hydrangea petiolaris
Hydrangeaceae   Japanese climbing hydrangea
ZONES 4–9   CLIMBER
Height: up to 18 m (60 ft) when grown up a wall or coarse-barked tree, **Flowers:** white in flat heads, early summer, **Foliage:** deep green above, paler on the underside, ovate, with serrated edges, deciduous, **Position:** full sun or shade, a good climber for north-facing walls, **Soils:** fertile, moist, high in humus, **Habit:** vigorous, self-clinging by its aerial roots, **Propagation:** cuttings of side shoots, early – mid-summer inserted in sandy peat under glass.
☐ Good companion plants are climbing roses.

Hydrangea quercifolia
Hydrangeaceae
ZONES 7–10   SHRUB
Height: 1.8 m (6 ft), **Flowers:** white, mid-summer, **Foliage:** deep green, lobed, good autumn colour, deciduous, **Position:** full sun or semi-shade, **Soil:** fertile, moist, high in humus, **Habit:** open upright bush, **Propagation:** cuttings 10–15 cm (4–6 in) long of side shoots, late summer – early autumn.
☐ Excellent for grouping with other shrubs which have autumn interest.

Hydrangea serrata 'Blue Bird'
Hydrangeaceae
ZONES 5–9   SHRUB
Height: up to 1 m (3 ft), **Flowers:** blue fertile inner florets surrounded by purplish-red sterile florets on chalk soils, blue on acid, mid-summer – mid-autumn, **Foliage:** green, deciduous, **Position:** full sun or semi-shade, **Soil:** fertile, moist, high in humus, **Habit:** dwarf and bushy, **Propagation:** cuttings 10–15 cm (4–6 in) long of side shoots, late summer – early autumn.
☐ 'Grayswood' has blue fertile flowers surrounded by white sterile florets changing to rose and finally deep crimson. Cut out very old shoots periodically.

Hydrangea serrata 'Preziosa'
Hydrangeaceae
ZONES 5–9   SHRUB
Height: up to 1.5 m (5 ft), **Flowers:** pink deepening to purplish-red, mid-summer – mid-autumn, **Foliage:** young leaves flushed with red, deciduous, **Position:** full sun or semi-shade, **Soil:** fertile, moist, high in humus, **Habit:** bushy, very handsome, **Propagation:** cuttings 10–15 cm (4–6 in) long of side shoots, taken late summer – early autumn.
☐ Cut out very old shoots periodically.

Hydrangea villosa
Hydrangeaceae
ZONES 4–9   SHRUB
Height: 1.8–2.5 m (6–8 ft), **Flowers:** light purple, late summer onwards, **Foliage:** matt green, hairy above, greyish below, deciduous, **Position:** full sun or semi-shade, **Soil:** fertile, moist, high in humus, **Habit:** round bushy habit, **Propagation:** cuttings 10–15 cm (4–6 in) long of side shoots, late summer – early autumn.
☐ A distinctive shrub, associating well with purple-leaved shrubs and red roses.

Above left: *Hydrangea paniculata* 'Grandiflora'
Above right: *Hydrangea petiolaris*
Left: *Hydrangea villosa*

Hypericum calycinum
Guttiferae   Rose of Sharon
ZONES 5–9   SHRUB
Height: 30 cm (1 ft), spreading indefinite-ly, **Flowers:** large yellow, early summer – early autumn, **Foliage:** green, evergreen, **Position:** full sun or shade, flowers better in sun, **Soil:** well-drained, even dry, but reasonably rich, **Habit:** very vigorous, forming dense carpets, **Propagation:** division in mid-autumn – mid-spring.
☐ Useful ground cover for awkward places such as steep banks, but plant with care – it can take over. About every two years, shear all growth to ground level in early spring to maintain a neat habit.

Hypericum 'Hidcote'
Guttiferae   St John's wort
ZONES 5–9   SHRUB
Height: 1.8 m (6 ft), **Flowers:** large yellow, mid-summer – mid-autumn, **Foliage:** green, evergreen, **Position:** sun or partial shade, **Soil:** rich, with good drainage, **Habit:** compact and bushy, **Propagation:** heeled cuttings of side shoots, mid-summer – mid autumn.
☐ Highly recommended for the shrub or mixed border. Prune back last year's shoots in early spring.

Hypericum × *moseranum* 'Tricolor'
Guttiferae
ZONES 8–10   SHRUB
Height: 30–45 cm (1–1½ ft), **Flowers:** yellow with reddish anthers, mid-summer – mid-autumn, **Foliage:** green with white variegation and a red margin, deciduous, **Position:** sunny and sheltered, **Soil:** good drainage, well cultivated, **Habit:** low-growing shrub with reddish arching stems, **Propagation:** 5 cm (2 in) long basal cuttings in late spring or early summer.
☐ Good ground cover plant.

Hypericum × *inodorum*
(syn. *H. elatum*) 'Elstead'
Guttiferae   St John's wort
ZONES 5–9   SHRUB
Height: 1–1.2 m (3–4 ft), **Flowers:** yellow, small, mid-summer – mid-autumn, followed by red fruits, **Foliage:** green, semi-evergreen, **Position:** full sun or semi shade, **Soil:** rich, with good drainage, **Habit:** erect-growing, dense shrub, **Propagation:** heeled cuttings of side shoots, mid-summer – early autumn.
☐ Can be pruned back hard in early spring to ensure better flowering.

Ilex × *altaclarensis* 'Golden King'
Aquifoliaceae   Holly
ZONES 6–9   SHRUB
Height: 5–8 m (16–26 ft), **Flowers:** insignificant, white, mid – late spring, followed by red berries in autumn and winter, (surprisingly it's a female cultivar), **Foliage:** virtually spineless, green with yellow edge, evergreen, **Position:** full sun or partial shade, **Soil:** suits most humus-rich garden soils, **Habit:** pyramidal, profusely branched, **Propagation:** heeled cuttings of half-ripened side shoots in a propagator in summer.
☐ Reasonably tolerant of atmospheric pollution and seaside conditions. Makes an excellent lawn specimen.

Left: *Ilex* × *altaclarensis* 'Golden King'

Ilex aquifolium

Aquifoliaceae Common holly
ZONES 5–9   SHRUB
Height: 4–6 m (13–20 ft) or more,
Flowers: insignificant white, mid – late
spring, followed by red berries on female
trees in winter, **Foliage:** glossy, deep
green, wavy-edged, edged with prickles,
evergreen, **Position:** full sun or shade,
Soil: suits most humus-rich soils, **Habit:**
pyramidal, profusely-branched shrub,
sometimes forming a small tree, **Propagation:** heeled cutting of half-ripened side
shoots in a propagator in summer.

☐ Very hardy. Excellent for hedging. Tolerates atmospheric pollution and seaside
conditions.

Recommended cultivars of *Ilex aquifolium*

'*Argenteo-marginata*' – variable white margins on foliage; female plants carry red
berries in autumn.
'*Bacciflava*' ('Fructuluteo') – wavy-edged
foliage with spines; yellow berries in
autumn into winter.
'*J.C. van Tol*' – glossy green foliage, almost
spineless; red fruited, free-berrying female
form.

Left: *Ilex aquifolium*
Centre: *Ilex aquifolium* 'Argento-marginata'
Right: *Ilex aquifolium* 'Pyramidalis'

'*Pyramidalis*' – bright green stems and
leaves, varying in their spinyness; red
berries borne freely on conical bush.
'*Pyramidalis Fructuluteo*' – similar to
'Pyramidalis' but with yellow fruits.
'*Silver Queen*' – purplish shoots, handsome
silver-edged leaves; male form so no
berries.

Incarvillea delavayi

Bignoniaceae Chinese trumpet flower
ZONES 5–9   HERBACEOUS PERENNIAL
Height: 60 cm (2 ft), **Flowers:** dark pink,
late spring – early summer, **Foliage:** deep
green, fern-like, deciduous, **Position:** sunny, **Soil:** suits most fertile well-drained
soils, **Habit:** tuberous rooted perennial,
disappears completely below ground after
flowering, **Propagation:** by seeds sown
thinly in shallow drills outdoors in early or
mid-spring. Or divide in autumn.
☐ Unusual plant for herbaceous or shrub
border, or edge of woodland garden.

Indigofera gerardiana
(syn. *I. heterantha*)

Leguminosae
ZONES 4–10   SHRUB
Height: 1–1.5 m (3–5 ft), **Flowers:** bright
carmine-rose, mid-summer – mid-
autumn, **Foliage:** very elegant, greyish,
pinnate, deciduous, **Position:** sunny,
preferably with wall shelter, **Soil:** well-
drained, suitable for poor dry conditions,
Habit: gracefully arching, **Propagation:**
seeds in early – mid-spring.
☐ Prune back vigorous growth in mid-
spring. Excellent wall shrub.

Inula hookeri

Compositae
ZONES 5–9   HERBACEOUS PERENNIAL
Height: 45–60 cm (1½–2 ft), **Flowers:**
light yellow, scented daisies, late summer –
early autumn, **Foliage:** green, lanceolate,
deciduous, **Position:** full sun, **Soil:** fairly
rich, moist, **Habit:** very bushy, **Propagation:** by division, mid-autumn – early
spring.
☐ An aristocratic plant for the herbaceous
or mixed border.

Iris foetidissima

Iridaceae Stinking iris, gladwin
ZONES 5–9   HERBACEOUS PERENNIAL
Height: 75 cm–1 m (2½–3 ft), **Flowers:** light purple, early summer, followed by attractive and conspicuous orange-red seeds held in pods, **Foliage:** green, strap-like, deciduous, **Position:** full sun or semi-shade, **Soil:** suits most moist soils, **Habit:** clump forming perennial, spreading by rhizomes, **Propagation:** division in early summer after flowering.
☐ Excellent iris for the wild or woodland garden, for planting under trees or for the shrub border.

Iris kaempferi

Iridaceae Japanese iris
ZONES 5–9   HERBACEOUS PERENNIAL
Height: 60 cm–1 m (2–3 ft), **Flowers:** butterfly-like in shades of blue or purple, plus white, mid – late summer, **Foliage:** green, strap-like, deciduous, **Position:** full sun or semi-shade, **Soil:** requires a damp acid soil, **Habit:** floppy but decorative perennial, many-stemmed, **Propagation:** divide after flowering or in spring, sow seeds as soon as ripe in sandy soil under glass.
☐ Some cultivars bear white flowers. Good for pondside planting and bog gardens.

Iris laevigata

Iridaceae
ZONES 5–9   HERBACEOUS PERENNIAL
Height: 60 cm (2 ft), **Flowers:** blue-purple, early – mid-summer, **Foliage:** green, strap-like, deciduous, **Position:** full sun or partial shade, **Soil:** requires a damp soil, **Habit:** erect stemmed perennial, **Propagation:** divide after flowering or in spring, sow seeds as soon as ripe in sandy soil under glass.
☐ Some cultivars bear white flowers. Ideal for permanent planting in water, for pond margins or bog bardens.

Iris pallida 'Variegata'

Iridaceae Border iris
ZONES 5–9   HERBACEOUS PERENNIAL
Height: 60 cm–1 m (2–3 ft), **Flowers:** pale lavender, fragrant, early summer, **Foliage:** two forms, pale blue-green, striped either white or gold, deciduous, **Position:** full sun or partial shade, **Soil:** suits most well-drained soils with lime, **Habit:** fans of sword-like leaves, flowers above, **Propagation:** by division after flowering.
☐ An excellent border plant, contrasting well with purple foliage shrubs.

Iris pumila

Iridaceae Dwarf bearded iris, rockery iris
ZONES 4–9   ROCK PLANT
Height: 10–15 cm (4–6 in), **Flowers:** yellow, blue, purple or white, mid – late spring, **Foliage:** green, broadly linear, deciduous, **Position:** full sun or partial shade, **Soil:** any well-drained, but moist soil, with lime, **Habit:** clumpy and spreading, **Propagation:** by division after flowering.
☐ Many varieties and cultivars to choose from. Ideal for the front of a border or for rock gardens.

Iris sibirica

Iridaceae
ZONES 4–9   HERBACEOUS PERENNIAL
Height: 75 cm–1 m (2½–3 ft), **Flowers:** blue, early summer, **Foliage:** green, slender, turning brown in autumn, deciduous, **Position:** full sun or partial shade, **Soil:** permanently moist, acid or neutral, **Habit:** clump-forming, **Propagation:** divide after flowering.
☐ Numerous cultivars and varieties to choose from. Excellent for herbaceous or shrub border, flowers good for cutting.

Iris unguicularis
(syn. *I. stylosa*)
Iridaceae Algerian iris
ZONES 5–9   HERBACEOUS PERENNIAL
Height: 30 cm (1 ft), **Flowers:** blue with central gold markings, fragrant, winter to early spring, **Foliage:** green, grassy, longer than flowering stems, evergreen, **Position:** full sun, **Soil:** suits most well-drained, even poor soils, lime-tolerant, **Habit:** clump-forming, **Propagation:** by division in early autumn.
□Lovely planted around winter-flowering shrubs. Flowers suitable for cutting.

Iris (tall bearded)
Iridaceae Bearded iris
ZONES 5–9   HERBACEOUS PERENNIAL
Height: 75 cm–1 m (2½–3 ft), **Flowers:** many cultivars with red, pink, blue, purple, white, yellow or bicolor flowers, late spring – early summer, **Foliage:** blue-green, sword-like in fans, deciduous, **Position:** full sun, **Soil:** well-drained, neutral or alkaline, **Habit:** upright perennial, spreading by rhizomes, **Propagation:** by division of rhizomes after flowering.
□Tall stems may need support. Good companion plants are peonies and lupins.

Right: *Iris unguicularis*

Itea ilicifolia
Iteaceae
ZONES 5–10   SHRUB
Height: 2.5–3 m (8–10 ft), **Flowers:** white, fragrant, long pendulous racemes, mid – late summer, **Foliage:** green, holly-like, evergreen, **Position:** full sun or partial shade, **Soil:** moist, loamy, lime-free, **Habit:** lax in growth, **Propagation:** by suckers removed in autumn, or by cuttings in summer.
□Prune when flowers have faded, cutting away old wood but keeping young growths. The attractive foliage makes this a good background shrub for other plants.

Itea virginica
Iteaceae Virginian sweetspire
ZONES 5–10   SHRUB
Height: 1–1.2 m (3–4 ft), **Flowers:** cream upright racemes, scented, mid – late summer, **Foliage:** green, deciduous, **Position:** full sun or partial shade, **Soil:** moist, loamy, lime-free, **Habit:** bushy, **Propagation:** from suckers removed in autumn, or cuttings in summer.
□Can thin out old wood after flowering.

Jasminum mesnyi
(syn. *J. primulinum*)
Oleaceae Primrose jasmine
ZONES 8–10   CLIMBER
Height: 3 m (10 ft), **Flowers:** yellow, semi-double, early – late spring, **Foliage:** deep green, trifoliate, nearly evergreen, **Position:** sunny, warm and sheltered, against a south- or south-west-facing wall, **Soil:** suits most well-drained soils, **Habit:** tall thin stems requiring support and training, **Propagation:** cuttings of side shoots 8–15 cm (3–6 in) long inserted in sandy soil in a garden frame in autumn, or by layering in spring or autumn.

Jasminum nudiflorum

Oleaceae Winter-flowering jasmine

ZONES 5–10   SHRUB

Height: 3 m (10 ft), **Flowers:** yellow, single or in small clusters, late autumn – mid-spring, **Foliage:** small deep green, trifoliate, deciduous on green stems, **Position:** sun or shade, thrives even on cold north walls, **Soil:** suits most well-drained soils, **Habit:** tall thin stems requiring support, **Propagation:** cuttings of side shoots 8–15 cm (3–6 in) long inserted in sandy soil in a garden frame in autumn, or by layering in spring or autumn.

□ Old flowered stems can be pruned back immediately after flowering. Ideal for training against walls, planting on banks, or up pillars.

Ideal companion plant on a wall is *Garrya elliptica*.

Jasminum officinale

Oleaceae Common white jasmine, summer jasmine

ZONES 6–10   CLIMBER

Height: about 9 m (30 ft), **Flowers:** white, in clusters, highly scented, early summer – mid-autumn, **Foliage:** green, compound, deciduous, **Position:** sunny, warm and sheltered, **Soil:** suits most well-drained soils, **Habit:** fast-growing climber, **Propagation:** cuttings of side shoots 8–15 cm (3–6 in) long inserted in sandy soil under glass in autumn, or layer in spring or autumn.

□ Excellent for growing with red or pink climbing roses. When flowering is over cut out some of the oldest stems to prevent a tangled mass of growth.

Jasminum humile 'Revolutum'

Oleaceae Himalayan jasmine

ZONES 8–10   SHRUB

Height: 1.8–2.5 m (6–8 ft), **Flowers:** yellow, slightly scented, early – late summer, **Foliage:** green, evergreen, **Position:** sunny and sheltered, **Soil:** suits most well-drained soils, **Habit:** a shrubby jasmine, **Propagation:** partially ripe, 8–10 cm (3–4 in) long cuttings in late summer – early autumn.

□ Can be grown in the shrub border or against a wall (it does not climb). Occasionally cut out old stems.

Jasminum polyanthum

Oleaceae Jasmine

ZONES 9–10   CLIMBER

Height: 6 m (20 ft), **Flowers:** white, buds pink, extremely fragrant, mid-spring – early summer, **Foliage:** deep green, pinnate, partially evergreen, **Position:** sunny, warm and sheltered, **Soil:** most well-drained soils, **Habit:** climber, for mild districts only, **Propagation:** cuttings of side shoots, 5–8 cm (2–3 in) long inserted in sandy soil in a warm propagator.

□ Makes an excellent conservatory plant and is extensively used as a house plant.

Jasminum × *stephanense*

Oleaceae

ZONES 5–10   CLIMBER

Height: 3–4.5 m (10–15 ft), **Flowers:** pink, scented, in clusters, early – mid-summer, **Foliage:** matt green, simple or pinnate, partially evergreen, **Position:** sunny, warm and sheltered, **Soil:** most well-drained soils, **Habit:** a twining climber, **Propagation:** cuttings of side shoots, 8–15 cm (3–6 in) long, inserted in sandy soil in a garden frame in autumn, or by layering in spring or autumn.

□ Grow on walls, fences, pergolas, etc – perhaps with climbing roses or clematis.

Left: *Jasminum polyanthum*

Juniperus chinensis 'Aurea'

Cupressaceae Young's golden juniper
ZONES 5–10   CONIFER
Height: about 1 m (3 ft) after 10 years, ultimately 7.5 m (25 ft), **Flowers and cones:** insignificant, **Foliage:** brilliant yellow in full sun, evergreen, **Position:** full sun or partial shade, colours best in full sun although foliage may scorch, **Soil:** most well-drained soils, **Habit:** conical, leaves small and closely packed, **Propagation:** by cuttings (see p. 70).
□ Use as a specimen plant. Good for town and city gardens. Like all junipers, foliage is aromatic.

Below left: *Juniperus chinensis* 'Kaizuka'
Below right: *Juniperus chinensis* 'Kuriwao Gold'
Bottom: *Juniperus communis* 'Depressa Aurea'

Juniperus chinensis 'Japonica'

Cupressaceae Chinese juniper
ZONES 4–10   CONIFER
Height: about 60 cm (2 ft) after 10 years, ultimately 1.8 m (6 ft), **Flowers and cones:** insignificant, **Foliage:** pale green, evergreen, **Position:** full sun or partial shade, **Soil:** most well-drained soils, **Habit:** compact and rounded, long leaders emerge with age, **Propagation:** by cuttings (see p. 70).
□ Useful for the heather garden or containers.

Juniperus chinensis 'Kaizuka'

Cupressaceae Hollywood juniper
ZONES 4–10   CONIFER
Height: about 1 m (3 ft) after 10 years, ultimately 7.5 m (25 ft), **Flowers and cones:** insignificant, **Foliage:** brilliant green, evergreen, **Position:** full sun or partial shade, **Soil:** most well-drained soils, **Habit:** spreading and distinctive, **Propagation:** by cuttings (see p. 70).
□ Suitable subject for the heather garden. 'Kaizuka Aurea' has golden foliage.

Juniperus chinensis 'Kuriwao Gold'

Cupressaceae Chinese juniper
ZONES 5–10   CONIFER
Height: about 60 cm (2 ft), ultimately 1.5 m (5 ft), **Flowers and fruits:** insignificant, **Foliage:** yellow green on slender branches, evergreen, **Position:** full sun or partial shade, **Soil:** most well-drained soils, **Habit:** erect habit, spreading to about 1.5 m (5 ft), hardy, **Propagation:** by cuttings (see p. 70).
□ Looks good planted with greyish junipers.

Juniperus chinensis 'Pyramidalis'

Cupressaceae Chinese juniper
ZONES 5–10   CONIFER
Height: 2.2 m (7 ft) after 10 years, ultimately 3.6 m (12 ft), **Flowers:** insignificant, **Foliage:** blue, very prickly, evergreen, **Position:** sunny and open preferred, light shade tolerated, **Soil:** most well-drained soils, **Habit:** vigorous, pyramidal, **Propagation:** by cuttings (see p. 70).
□ Use as a lawn specimen.

Juniperus communis 'Compressa'

Cupresaceae Common juniper
ZONES 4–10   CONIFER
Height: up to 45 cm (1½ ft) after 10 years, ultimately 75 cm (2½ ft), **Flowers:** insignificant, **Foliage:** bluish grey, evergreen, **Position:** open and sunny preferred, light shade tolerated, **Soil:** most well-drained soils, including chalk, **Habit:** forms a tight cone-shaped bush, **Propagation:** by cuttings (see p. 70).
□ Excellent for rock and sink gardens – the smallest conical juniper available.

Juniperus communis 'Depressa Aurea'

Cupressaceae Canadian juniper
ZONES 4–10   CONIFER
Height: a low prostrate juniper, **Flowers:** insignificant, **Foliage:** rich-yellow leaf tips in summer, turning bronzy yellow in winter, evergreen, **Position:** open and sunny preferred, light shade tolerated, **Soil:** most well-drained soils, including chalk, **Habit:** prostrate, spreading to about 3 m (10 ft), **Propagation:** by cuttings (see p. 70).
□ Beautiful golden conifer during summer.

Excellent juniper for the larger heather or rock garden.

Juniperus communis 'Hibernica'
Cupressaceae   Irish juniper
ZONES 4–10   CONIFER
Height: 1.8 m (6 ft) after 10 years, ultimate height 6 m (20 ft), **Flowers:** insignificant, **Foliage:** blue-grey, prickly, evergreen, **Position:** open and sunny preferred, light shade tolerated, **Soil:** most well-drained soils, including chalk, **Habit:** forms a thin column, **Propagation:** by cuttings (see p. 70).
☐ Excellent as a focal point in the garden. Ideal for giving height in small gardens.

Juniperus communis 'Repanda'
Cupressaceae
ZONES 4–10   CONIFER
Height: about 30 cm (1 ft), **Flowers:** insignificant, **Foliage:** matt green, turning a little bronzy in winter, evergreen, **Position:** prefers sunny, open situation, **Soil:** most well-drained soils, including chalk, **Habit:** prostrate, forming a dense mat, ultimately spreading to about 3 m (10 ft), **Propagation:** by cuttings (see p. 70).
☐ Good ground coverer. Recommended for banks.

Juniperus conferta
Cupressaceae   Shore juniper
ZONES 5–10   CONIFER
Height: about 60 cm (2 ft), **Flowers:** insignificant, **Foliage:** bright lime-green, very prickly, evergreen, **Position:** prefers sunny situation, **Soil:** most well-drained soils, including chalk, **Habit:** prostrate, spreading to 1.8 m (6 ft), **Propagation:** seeds early – mid-autumn, in a garden frame, or by cuttings (see p. 70).
☐ Will hang down over walls, good ground cover. Excellent for banks.

Juniperus × *davurica* 'Expansa Aureospicata'
Cupressaceae
ZONES 5–10   CONIFER
Height: 30–75 cm (1–2½ ft), **Flowers:** insignificant, **Foliage:** bright green splashed with yellow, evergreen, **Position:** prefers open, sunny situation, **Soil:** most well-drained soils, including chalk, **Habit:** more or less prostrate, eventually spreading to about 2.5 m (8 ft), **Propagation:** by cuttings taken early – mid-autumn.
☐ Good ground cover plant.

Juniperus horizontalis 'Bar Harbor'
Cupressaceae   Creeping juniper
ZONES 4–10   CONIFER
Height: 15–30 cm (6–12 in), **Flowers:** insignificant, **Foliage:** blue-grey in summer, purplish tints in winter, evergreen, **Position:** sunny situation preferred, **Soil:**

Above: *Juniperus* × *media* 'Pfitzerana Aurea'

most well-drained soils, including chalk, **Habit:** very prostrate, spreading to 4 m (13 ft) or more, **Propagation:** by cuttings (see p. 70).
☐ Excellent ground cover. Highly recommended for banks.

Other recommended cultivars of *Juniperus horizontalis*
'*Douglasii*' – (Waukegan juniper) greyish-green with a tinge of purple in winter; spreading to 1.8 m (6 ft); prostrate but some branches may grow up to 60 cm (2 ft).
'*Glauca*' – (Creeping juniper) very rich blue foliage; spreads to 1.8 m (6 ft); initially prostrate but stacking up new growth as it ages to 50 cm (20 in).
'*Montana*' – closely-packed, rich blue foliage; spreads to 1.8 m (6 ft), prostrate but long thin branches may reach 50 cm (20 in) high.
'*Plumosa*' – greyish-green, feathery foliage, tinged purple in winter, spreads up to 3 m (10 ft); may reach 60 cm (2 ft) in height. All make excellent evergreen ground cover; especially recommended for steep difficult banks.

Juniperus × *media* 'Blaauw'
Cupressaceae
ZONES 4–10   CONIFER
Height: about 1.2 m (4 ft) after 10 years, eventually reaching 3.6 m (12 ft), **Flowers and fruit:** insignificant, **Foliage:** dark greyish-green, colour maintained year round, evergreen, **Position:** sun or partial shade, **Soil:** most well-drained soils, including chalk, **Habit:** an upright juniper, unusual in appearance with growth tips curving outward, **Propagation:** by cuttings (see p. 70).

Other recommended cultivars of *Juniperus* × *media* ZONES 5–10.
'*Hetzii*' – greyish-green, vigorous and hardy, eventually reaching 2.4 m (8 ft) in height and spread.
'*Old Gold*' – golden yellow throughout the year; eventually reaching 2 m (6 ft) in height and spread.
'*Pfitzerana Aurea*' – golden yellow, becoming greener in winter, best colour in full sun, thick semi-erect branches, eventually 1.2 m (4 ft) high, and 3 m (10 ft) wide.
'*Plumosa Aurea*' – yellowish-green, turning bronzy-yellow in winter, long upright arching branches up to 3 m (10 ft) in height and spread.

Juniperus procumbens 'Nana'
Cupressaceae   Creeping juniper
ZONES 5–10   CONIFER
Height: eventually 15 cm (6 in), **Flowers and fruits:** insignificant, **Foliage:** bright green throughout the year, evergreen, **Position:** prefers it open and sunny, tolerates light shade, **Soil:** most well-drained soils, including chalk, **Habit:** prostrate and very procumbent, ultimately spreading to 3 m (10 ft), **Propagation:** by cuttings (see p. 70).
☐ Excellent ground cover. Recommended for steep and difficult banks.

Juniperus recurva 'Embley Park'
Cupressaceae   Drooping juniper
ZONES 4–10   CONIFER
Height: will reach 30 cm (1 ft) eventually, **Flowers and fruit:** insignificant, **Foliage:** deep green, evergreen, **Position:** full sun or light shade, **Soil:** most well-drained soils, including chalk, **Habit:** spreading semi-upright branches, spreads 75 cm (2½ ft) after 10 years, **Propagation:** by cuttings (see p. 70).
☐ Can be used as ground cover or combined with heathers.

Juniperus sabina 'Tamariscifolia'
Cupressaceae   Savin
ZONES 5–10   CONIFER
Height: eventually 30 cm (1 ft), **Flowers and fruits:** insignificant, **Foliage:** grey-green, evergreen, **Position:** full sun or light-shade, **Soil:** most well-drained soils, including chalk, **Habit:** gradually builds up height as new branches overlap older ones, spreading to 1 m (3 ft) after 10 years, **Propagation:** by cuttings (see p. 70).
☐ 'Blue Danube' has greyish-green foliage, grows up to 1.5 m (5 ft) high, a vigorous ground coverer with a spread of about 3 m (10 ft) eventually.

Above left: *Juniperus virginiana* 'Skyrocket.
Above right: *Juniperus sabina* 'Tamariscifolia'

Juniperus sargentii
Cupressaceae   Sargent's juniper
ZONES 5–10   CONIFER
Height: 30–45 cm (1–1½ ft), ultimate height 75 cm (2½ ft), **Flowers:** insignificant, followed by blue fruits, **Foliage:** pale green, evergreen, **Position:** full sun or light shade, **Soil:** most well-drained soils, including chalk, **Habit:** mat-forming, eventually spreading 3 m (10 ft) or more, **Propagation:** by cuttings (see p. 70).
☐ Excellent ground cover.

Juniperus squamata 'Meyeri'
Cupressaceae   Scaly-leaved Nepal juniper
ZONES 5–10   CONIFER
Height: 1.5 m (5 ft) after 10 years, eventually reaching 4.5 m (15 ft), **Flowers:** insignificant, fruits reddish brown, turning deep blue, **Foliage:** rich blue, evergreen, **Position:** open and sunny or light shade, **Soil:** most well-drained soils, including chalk, **Habit:** semi-erect branches with drooping tips, **Propagation:** by cuttings (see p 70).
☐ Prune annually to maintain an attractive bush. An excellent specimen plant for a lawn. 'Blue Star' has rich blue foliage; dense, low growing to 60 cm (2½ ft) or so, with a spread of 60 cm (2 ft) after 10 years.

Juniperus virginiana 'Skyrocket'
Cupressaceae   Rocky mountain juniper, pencil cedar
ZONES 5–10   CONIFER
Height: 2.5 m (8 ft) after 10 years, eventually reaching 6 m (20 ft), **Flowers:** insignificant, **Foliage:** dark grey-blue, evergreen, **Position:** prefers it open and sunny, tolerates light shade, **Soil:** most well-drained soils including chalk, **Habit:** tall, slender like a pencil, fairly quick growing, **Propagation:** cuttings (see p. 70).
☐ Ideal for giving height. 'Blue Heaven' forms more of a pyramid.

Juniperus virginiana 'Grey Owl'
Cupressaceae
ZONES 4–10   CONIFER
Height: eventually about 1.2 m (4 ft), **Flowers:** insignificant, **Foliage:** bright greyish-blue, evergreen, **Position:** open and sunny or light shade, **Soil:** most well-drained soils, including chalk, **Habit:** vigorous, good ground cover, spreading to 2.5 m (8 ft) or so after 10 years; associates well with other prostrate conifers, **Propagation:** by cuttings (see p. 70).
☐ Prune occasionally to make more dense. Looks good in conjunction with other prostrate conifers. 'Burkii', with bluish-grey foliage, flushed purple in winter, makes a 2.5 m (8 ft) compact conical bush after 10 years.

Kalmia angustifolia 'Rubra'
Ericaceae Sheep laurel
ZONES 3–9   SHRUB
Height: 1–1.2 m (3–4 ft), **Flowers:** pinkish-red, early summer, **Foliage:** dark green, evergreen, **Position:** best in dappled shade, **Soil:** acid, moisture-retentive, peaty, **Habit:** erect, bushy and compact, **Propagation:** cuttings 8–10 cm (3–4 in) long of ripening side shoots in late summer, or layer young shoots late summer – early autumn.
☐Beautiful shrub, ideal for growing with rhododendrons and azaleas.

Kalmia latifolia
Ericaceae Calico bush, mountain laurel
ZONES 4–9   SHRUB
Height: 1.8–2.5 m (6–8 ft), **Flowers:** sugar icing pink, in clusters, early summer, **Foliage:** deep green and shiny, evergreen, **Position:** best in dappled shade, **Soil:** acid, moisture-retentive, peaty, **Habit:** erect and bushy, **Propagation:** cuttings 8–10 cm (3–4 in) long, of ripening side shoots in late summer, or layer young shoots late summer – early autumn.
☐Associates well with rhododendrons (including azaleas).

Kalmia latifolia 'Ostbo Red'
Ericaceae Calico bush, mountain laurel
ZONES 4–9   SHRUB
Height: 1.8–3 m (6–10 ft), **Flowers:** rich red, early summer, **Foliage:** deep green and shiny, evergreen, **Position:** best in dappled shade, **Soil:** acid, moisture-retentive, peaty, **Habit:** erect and bushy, **Propagation:** cuttings 8–10 cm (3–4 in) long, of ripening side shoots in late summer, or layer young shoots.
☐Associates well with rhododendrons (including azaleas).

Kerria japonica 'Pleniflora'
Rosaceae Batchelor's buttons
ZONES 4–9   SHRUB
Height: 3 m (10 ft), **Flowers:** yellow, double, mid – late spring, **Foliage:** fresh green on slender green stems, deciduous, **Position:** sun or shade, **Soil:** most soils, **Habit:** erect, suckering, **Propagation:** cuttings 5–8 cm (2–3 in) long of side shoots, late summer – early autumn, or by removing and replanting rooted suckers in autumn or winter.
☐Try an underplanting of muscari or grape hyacinths. Cut back old flowered stems when flowering is over.

Kerria japonica 'Variegata' (**syn.** 'Picta')
Rosaceae Batchelor's buttons
ZONES 4–9   SHRUB
Height: 1.2 m (4 ft), **Flowers:** yellow, single, mid – late spring, **Foliage:** prettily variegated with cream, deciduous, **Position:** sun or partial shade, **Soil:** most soils, **Habit:** erect, suckering, **Propagation:** cuttings of side shoots in late summer – early autumn, or by removing rooted suckers in autumn or winter.
☐An attractive dwarf shrub associating well with purple-leaved shrubs. Ideal for planting against a warm wall.

Kniphofia caulescens
Liliaceae Red hot poker, torch lily
ZONES 7–10   HERBACEOUS PERENNIAL
Height: 1–1.2 m (3–4 ft), **Flowers:** salmon-red, tubular, in fat spikes, mid-summer – early autumn, **Foliage:** greyish green, broad, grass-like, semi-evergreen, **Position:** full sun, **Soil:** very well-drained, including poor, **Habit:** clump forming perennial, **Propagation:** divide overcrowded clumps in spring; seeds sown in spring in a garden frame.
☐This is one of the most spectacular kniphofias, with superb foliage which contrasts well with shrubs. Good for seaside.

Kniphofia galpinii

Liliaceae Red hot poker, torch lily
ZONES 7–10   HERBACEOUS PERENNIAL
Height: 45–60 cm (1½-2 ft), **Flowers:**
orange-red, tubular, in dense spikes, slender stems, mid-summer – early autumn,
Foliage: deep green, grassy, semi-evergreen, **Position:** sunny and open, **Soil:**
very well drained including poor, **Habit:**
clump-forming perennial, **Propagation:**
division of overcrowded clumps in spring;
seeds sown in spring under glass.
□ Best associated with autumn-colouring
shrubs. Suitable for seaside gardens.

Kolkwitzia amabilis

Caprifoliaceae Beauty bush
ZONES 4–9   SHRUB
Height: 1.8–2.5 m (6–8 ft), **Flowers:**
pink, yellow centre, early summer, **Foliage:** deep green, deciduous, **Position:**
full sun, **Soil:** most soils, **Habit:** graceful
and arching, **Propagation:** heeled
cuttings of ripening side shoots, mid – late
summer.
□ A good companion for philadelphus, in
the shrub border. Prune out oldest stems
after flowering.

Laburnum anagyroides
(syn. *L. vulgare*)

Leguminosae Common laburnum
ZONES 5–9   TREE
Height: 4–6 m (13–20 ft), **Flowers:** yellow in pendulous trusses, 15–25 cm (6–
10 in) long, slightly scented, late spring,
Foliage: green, trifoliate, deciduous, **Position:** sunny, **Soil:** most reasonably deep
soils, **Habit:** erect branched, **Propagation:** seed sown in spring outdoors or
under glass.
□ The seeds, carried in pea-like pods, are
highly poisonous – as are all parts of the
plant. Often grown with lilac.

Laburnum × *watereri* 'Vossii'

Leguminosae Laburnum
ZONES 5–9   TREE
Height: 6–9 m (20–30 ft), **Flowers:**
bright yellow in trusses up to 30 cm (1 ft)
long, slightly scented, late spring, **Foliage:**
green, glossy, trifoliate, deciduous, **Position:** sunny, **Soil:** most reasonably deep
soils, **Habit:** erect branched, **Propagation:** by grafting.
□ Seeds are poisonous as are all parts of the
plant. A good companion for lilac.

Lapageria rosea

Liliaceae Chilean bellflower
ZONES 8–10   CLIMBER
Height: 4.5 m (15 ft), **Flowers:** large
waxy rose-red bells, mid-summer – mid-autumn, **Foliage:** thick, deep green, evergreen, **Position** very warm and sheltered,
semi-shade, **Soil:** moist yet well-drained,
humus-rich, lime-free, **Habit:** a twining
slender climber, **Propagation:** seed sown
in early – mid-spring, or layer long shoots
in late spring or late autumn. Can take two
years to root.
□ Tender, only suited to mildest areas.
Otherwise grow in a conservatory.

Larix decidua

Pinaceae European larch, common
larch
ZONES 2–9   CONIFER
Height: 6 m (20 ft) after 10 years, ultimately reaching 24 m (80 ft), **Flowers:**
light green or red, cones brown, **Foliage:**
pale green, changing to yellow in autumn,
deciduous, **Position:** full sun, **Soil:** moisture-retentive, **Habit:** loosely conical
when young, but becoming more irregular
in shape with age, **Propagation:** seed
sown outdoors in early spring.
□ Often used as a specimen tree in a lawn
but only for large gardens.

Laurus nobilis
Lauraceae Sweet bay, bay laurel
ZONES 5–10 SHRUB
Height: 3–6 m (10–20 ft) if left unpruned, **Flowers:** greeny yellow, male and female on separate plants, spring, **Foliage:** long, deep green and shiny, pleasant smell when crushed, evergreen, **Position:** full sun, sheltered from wind, **Soil:** most soils, good on chalk, **Habit:** very adaptable shrub, can be grown as a clipped standard or hedge, **Propagation:** heeled cuttings of side shoots late summer – early autumn, or layering mid – late summer.
☐ Female plants have blackish fruits. Ideal tub plant, can be clipped or trained.

Lavandula angustifolia
(syn. L. spica)
Labiatae Old English lavender
ZONES 5–10 SHRUB
Height: 60 cm–1 m (2–3 ft), **Flowers:** lavender-blue in spikes, fragrant, mid-summer – early autumn, **Foliage:** grey, aromatic, evergreen, **Position:** sun, **Soil:** most well-drained soils, including alkaline, **Habit:** rather lax and eventually woody if not clipped back after flowering every year, **Propagation:** cuttings of young side shoots, late summer.
☐ Discard and replace plants that become straggly and ugly. Cut back dead flower heads and a little of the current year's

Left: *Lavandula angustifolia* 'Hidcote'. **Right:** *L. a.* 'Loddon Pink'

growth after flowering. Ideal for seaside gardens.

Recommended cultivars of Lavandula angustifolia ZONES 6–10.
'Hidcote' – dark purplish-blue; grey foliage; compact and bushy habit; a fine cultivar.
'Loddon Pink' – pale pink; grey foliage; compact.
'Munstead' – dark blue; foliage grey-green; neat, bushy and compact habit.
'Vera' – (Dutch lavender) light blue; wide grey leaves, vigorous plant.

Lavandula stoechas
Labiatae French lavender
ZONES 5–10 SHRUB
Height: 30–45 cm (1–1½ ft), **Flowers:** deep purple, late spring – mid-summer, **Foliage:** grey-green, evergreen, **Position:** warm, dry and sunny, **Soil:** most well-drained to dry soils, including alkaline, **Habit:** dwarf, intensely aromatic, **Propagation:** cuttings of young side shoots, late summer.
☐ Good companion for roses. Suitable for a low-growing hedge. Ideal for seaside gardens.

Lavatera olbia 'Rosea'
Malvaceae Mallow
ZONES 5–10 SHRUB
Height: 1.8 m (6 ft), **Flowers:** rose pink, similar to those of the hibiscus, mid – late summer, **Foliage:** grey-green and downy, deciduous, **Position:** sunny, sheltered from wind, **Soil:** any well-drained soil, on the poor side, **Habit:** erect and bushy sub-shrub, **Propagation:** seed, or by cuttings of firm young shoots in a propagator in summer.
☐ Tender, requiring some winter protection. Good for seaside planting.

Ledum palustre
Ericaceae Wild rosemary
ZONES 5–9 SHRUB
Height: up to 1 m (3 ft), **Flowers:** white, in clusters, mid – late spring, **Foliage:** green, evergreen, **Position:** best in partial shade, **Soil:** moist, acid, **Habit:** dense and broad, **Propagation:** seeds, cuttings or layering.
☐ There is a superior form called *dilatatum*. Can be grown with dwarf rhododendrons.

Leiophyllum buxifolium
Ericaceae

ZONES 5–9   SHRUB

Height: 30–60 cm (1–2 ft), **Flowers:** white, pink in bud, early summer, **Foliage:** small, like those of box (buxus), evergreen, **Position:** partial shade, **Soil:** moist, acid, **Habit:** neat, rounded, compact, **Propagation:** seed, cuttings or layering.

□Unusual but easy plant for a peat garden, in association with dwarf rhododendrons.

Leontopodium alpinum
Compositae   Edelweiss

ZONES 3–8   ROCK PLANT

Height: 10–15 cm (4–6 in), **Flowers:** silvery white in flat heads on short stalks, early – mid-summer, **Foliage:** greyish-green, narrow, deciduous, **Position:** full sun, **Soil:** most well-drained soils, **Habit:** tufty perennial, **Propagation:** seeds sown in early spring under glass.

□Suitable for rock gardens, Interesting rather than attractive.

Leptospermum cunninghamii
Myrtaceae

ZONES 9–10   SHRUB

Height: 1.8 m (6 ft) or more in mild coastal localities, **Flowers:** white, mid-summer, **Foliage:** red stems carry grey leaves, evergreen, **Position:** sunny and sheltered from cold winds, **Soil:** light, good drainage, acid or neutral, **Habit:** bushy, erect and twiggy, **Propagation:** by cuttings of ripening shoots in early – mid-summer.

□Remove unwanted or untidy branches in mid-spring. Good wall shrub. Don't attempt to grow outdoors in cold areas.

Leptospermum scoparium
'Album Flore Pleno'

Myrtaceae   South sea myrtle, manuka, New Zealand tea tree

ZONES 9–10   SHRUB

Height: 1.8–3 m (6–10 ft), **Flowers:** white, double, late spring – early summer, **Foliage:** green, evergreen, **Position:** sunny wall sheltered from cold winds, **Soil:** light, good drainage, acid or neutral, **Habit:** compact and erect, **Propagation:** cuttings early – mid-summer.

□Not reliably frost hardy. 'Burgundy Queen' (above) has single red flowers, 'Nichollsii', single crimson, 'Red Damask', very double, dark red. Suitable for the seaside.

Lespedeza thunbergii
Leguminosae   Bush clover

ZONES 5–10   SHRUB

Height: 1.2–1.5 m (4–5 ft), **Flowers:** purplish pink pea-like flowers, early autumn, **Foliage:** green, trifoliate, deciduous, **Position:** full sun, **Soil:** most soils, **Habit:** lax branches bow down with weight of flowers, **Propagation:** seeds or cuttings.

□Unusual shrub which could be grown on a bank with other sun lovers like cistus and cytisus.

Leucothoe fontanesiana
'Rainbow'

Ericaceae

ZONES 6–9   SHRUB

Height: 60 cm (2 ft), **Flowers:** pure white, early summer, **Foliage:** variegated pink, cream and yellow, turning redder in autumn, evergreen, **Position:** sun or partial shade, **Soil:** humus-rich and lime-free, **Habit;** graceful shrub with elegant arching shoots, **Propagation:** layering in autumn.

□Colourful shrub for ground cover or front of border.

171

Leycesteria formosa

Caprifoliaceae Himalayan honeysuckle, flowering nutmeg

ZONES 7–10   SHRUB

Height: 1.8 m (6 ft), **Flowers:** white with purple-red bracts, followed by red-purple berries, mid – late summer, **Foliage:** rounded, medium green, deciduous, **Position:** sun or partial shade, flowers better in sun, **Soil:** suits most fertile soils, **Habit:** hollow-stemmed, erect growing shrub, **Propagation:** seeds under glass or hardwood cuttings autumn.

□A good plant for seaside districts. Stems attractive in winter. Cut out completely in early spring all of last year's flowered stems.

Liatris pycnostachya

Compositae Button snake-root, Kansas gay feather

ZONES 5–9   HERBACEOUS PERENNIAL

Height: 1–1.2 m (3–4 ft), **Flowers:** purplish crimson, held in dense erect spikes, opening from top of spike first, midsummer – early autumn, **Foliage:** green, grass-like, deciduous, **Position:** sunny and open, **Soil:** light and fairly rich, moist but well-drained, **Habit:** closely packed stiff spikes of flowers, **Propagation:** by dividing clumps in autumn or spring.

□Useful for contrasting with daisy-like flowers in herbaceous or mixed border. Good for cutting.

Ligustrum lucidum 'Excelsum Superbum'

Oleaceae Privet

ZONES 6–9   SHRUB

Height: 3–4 m (10–13 ft), **Flowers:** creamy, tubular, in long panicles, late summer – early autumn, **Foliage:** green margined and splashed with yellow and creamy white, evergreen, **Position:** sun or partial shade, sheltered from cold winds, **Soil:** suits most soils, **Habit:** tall and erect, **Propagation:** hardwood cuttings 10–15 cm (4–6 in) long in early – mid-autumn and inserted in a garden frame.

□Will make a handsome small tree with its strikingly variegated leaves.

Ligustrum lucidum 'Tricolor'

Oleaceae Privet

ZONES 6–9   SHRUB

Height: 3–4 m (10–13 ft), **Flowers:** cream, late summer – early autumn, **Foliage:** narrow, with an irregular white border, young leaves flushed pink, evergreen, **Position:** sun or partial shade, **Soil:** suits most soils, **Habit:** tall and erect, **Propagation:** hardwood cuttings 10–15 cm (4–6 in) long in early – mid-autumn and inserted in a garden frame.

□Handsome plant for shrub border.

Ligustrum ovalifolium

Oleaceae Oval-leaf privet

ZONES 5–9   SHRUB

Height: 3–5 m (10–16 ft) when unrestricted, **Flowers:** creamy-white, scented, mid-summer, black fruits, **Foliage:** shiny, medium green, evergreen in all but the coldest districts, **Position:** sun or shade, **Soil:** suits most soils, **Habit:** tall and erect, **Propagation:** hardwood cuttings 30 cm (1 ft) long inserted outdoors in mid-autumn.

□Excellent hedging plant; clip established hedges several times a year from late spring to early-autumn. Fast growing.

Left: *Ligustrum ovalifolium*, an excellent, fast-growing hedging plant

Ligustrum ovalifolium 'Aureum'
Oleaceae   Golden privet

ZONES 5–9   SHRUB

Height: 3–4 m (10–13 ft), **Flowers:** creamy, scented, mid-summer, black fruits, **Foliage:** green in the centre with an irregular border of rich golden yellow, semi-evergreen, **Position:** sun or partial shade, **Soil:** suits most soils, **Habit:** tall and erect, **Propagation:** hardwood cuttings 30 cm (1 ft) long inserted outdoors in mid-autumn.

□ Widely used for hedges; clip when established several times a year from late spring to early autumn.

Linum narbonense
Linaceae   Perennial flax

ZONES 6–10   HERBACEOUS PERENNIAL

Height: 45 cm (1½ ft), **Flowers:** blue petals with white centres, early–late summer, **Foliage:** green, narrow, on wiry flower stems, deciduous, **Position:** best in full sun, **Soil:** suits most well-drained soils, **Habit:** forms an attractive clump, but a short-lived perennial, **Propagation:** seeds sown in spring or early summer, outdoors in well-drained soil, or in a garden frame, by division in spring, or by basal cuttings in a frame in late spring.

□ Useful for mixed or herbaceous border.

Lippia citriodora
Verbenaceae   Lemon-scented verbena

ZONES 8–10   SHRUB

Height: 3–4 m (10–13 ft) when unrestricted in warm districts, **Flowers:** lilac, late summer, **Foliage:** light to medium green, lanceolate, strongly lemon-scented when bruised, deciduous, **Position:** sun and protected from wind, **Soil:** suits most well-drained soils, **Habit:** loose, bushy, **Propagation:** cuttings about 7 cm (3 in) long of side shoots in mid-summer, root in propagator.

□ Prune away all frost-damaged or dead growth each spring. A pleasing wall shrub.

Lithospermum diffusum
  'Heavenly Blue'
Boraginaceae   Gromwell

ZONES 7–9   ROCK PLANT

Height: 15 cm (6 in), **Flowers:** rich gentian-blue, summer, **Foliage:** dull green, ovate, evergreen, **Position:** sunny, **Soil:** humus-rich, moist and neutral to acid, **Habit:** low and spreading to 60 cm (2 ft), **Propagation:** soft cuttings of heeled side shoots during mid-summer and inserted in sandy peat in a garden frame.

□ For rock or peat gardens.

Lomatia myricoides
Proteaceae

ZONES 7–10   SHRUB

Height: 1.5–2.5 m (5–8 ft), **Flowers:** white, scented, mid-summer, **Foliage:** green, long and narrow, evergreen, **Position:** succeeds best in partial shade, **Soil:** soil tolerant except for shallow chalky soils, **Habit:** profusely branched and wide spreading, **Propagation:** cuttings taken in late summer – early autumn.

□ A very useful shrub for the flower arranger; deserves to be better known.

Lomatia tinctoria
Proteaceae

ZONES 7–10   SHRUB

Height: 1–1.5 m (3–5 ft), **Flowers:** soft-yellow fading to cream white, summer, **Foliage:** green, feathery, evergreen, **Position:** best in partial shade, **Soil:** soil-tolerant except for shallow chalk soil, **Habit:** suckering, forming a dense thicket, **Propagation:** by removing rooted suckers in autumn.

□ Flowers also suitable for arranging.

Lonicera × américana
Caprifoliaceae   Honeysuckle
ZONES 5–10 CLIMBER
Height: 9 m (30 ft), **Flowers:** yellow, flushed with purple, buds white, scented, summer, **Foliage:** green, deciduous, **Position:** full sun or semi-shade, **Soil:** most well-drained, humus-rich soils, **Habit:** a vigorous twining climber, **Propagation:** cuttings of firm young shoots in summer in a propagator; cuttings of ripe wood in autumn outdoors or in a garden frame; or layer in spring or autumn.
☐ Prune out old stems as necessary, when flowering is over. Try growing this honeysuckle with climbing roses or clematis.

Lonicera × brownii 'Fuchsioides'
Caprifoliaceae   Scarlet trumpet honeysuckle
ZONES 5–10 CLIMBER
Height: 3–4.5 m (10–15 ft), **Flowers:** orangy-red, in clusters, fragrant, summer, **Foliage:** blue-green, partially evergreen, **Position:** full sun or semi-shade, **Soil:** well-drained, humus-rich, **Habit:** twining climber, **Propagation:** cuttings of firm young shoots in summer in a propagator; cuttings of ripe wood in autumn outdoors or in a garden frame; or layer in spring or autumn.
☐ Pruning/uses as for *L.* × *americana*.

Lonicera fragrantissima
Caprifoliaceae   Shrubby honeysuckle
ZONES 5–10 SHRUB
Height: 1.8 m (6 ft), **Flowers:** cream-coloured, highly scented, early winter – early spring, followed by red berries in late spring, **Foliage:** green, semi-evergreen in warm districts, **Position:** full sun or semi shade, protect from cold wind, **Soil:** suits most soils, **Habit:** rounded bush, **Propagation:** take 10 cm (4 in) long cuttings in mid – late summer, or 23–30 cm (9–12 in) long hardwood cuttings in early – mid-autumn, and insert in garden frame; or layer in autumn.
☐ One of the best winter-flowering shrubs for scent. Underplant with winter-flowering heathers.

Lonicera × heckrotii
Caprifoliaceae   Honeysuckle
ZONES 5–10 CLIMBER
Height: 3–3.6 m (10–12 ft), **Flowers:** yellow, blended with purplish-red, scented, summer, **Foliage:** green, greyish beneath, deciduous, **Position:** full sun or semi-shade, **Soil:** well-drained, humus-rich, **Habit:** hardy climbing shrub, needs support, **Propagation:** cuttings of firm young shoots in summer in a propagator; cuttings

of riper wood in autumn outdoors or in a garden frame; or layer in spring or autumn.
☐ Prune out old stems as necessary when flowering is over.

Lonicera involucrata
Caprifoliaceae   Shrubby honeysuckle
ZONES 5–10 SHRUB
Height: 1.8–3 m (6–10 ft), **Flowers:** yellow, with red bracts, early summer, followed by shiny black fruits, **Foliage:** green, deciduous, **Position:** full sun or semi-shade, **Soil:** suits most soils, **Habit:** vigorous, spreading, robust, **Propagation:** 10 cm (4 in) long cuttings in mid – late summer; or 23–30 cm (9–12 in) long hardwood cuttings in early – mid-autumn, and insert in garden frame; layer in autumn.
☐ Good for seaside conditions.

Top left: *Lonicera* × *heckrotii*
Top right: *Lonicera japonica* 'Aureoreticulata'
Above: *Lonicera* × *americana*

Lonicera japonica 'Aureoreticulata'
Caprifoliaceae   Japanese honeysuckle
ZONES 7–10 CLIMBER
Height: 7.5–9 m (25–30 ft), **Flowers:** white or light yellow, scented, early summer – mid-autumn, **Foliage:** green, netted with gold, evergreen, **Position:** full sun or semi-shade, best foliage colour in full sun, **Soil:** well-drained, humus rich, **Habit:** twining climber, **Propagation:** cuttings of firm young shoots in summer in a propagator; cuttings of ripe wood in autumn outdoors or in a garden frame.
☐ Grown for its foliage. Looks good with clematis or climbing roses. Prune as for *L.* × *americana*.

Lonicera japonica 'Halliana'

Caprifoliaceae Japanese honeysuckle
ZONES 5–9   CLIMBER
Height: 7.5–9 m (25–30 ft), **Flowers:** white to yellow, highly scented, prolific, early summer – mid-autumn, **Foliage:** green, evergreen, **Position:** full sun or semi-shade, **Soil:** well-drained, humus-rich, **Habit:** very vigorous twining climber, **Propagation:** cuttings of firm young shoots in summer in a propagator; cuttings of riper wood in autumn outdoors or in a garden frame.
☐ Excellent for quickly covering walls, fences, etc. Prune as for *L.* × *americana*.

Lonicera japonica var. repens

   (**syn.** 'Flexuosa')
Caprifoliaceae Japanese honeysuckle
ZONES 5–9   CLIMBER
Height: 4.5–6 m (15–20 ft), **Flowers:** yellow, tinged with purple, scented, early summer – mid-autumn, **Foliage:** green tinged with purple, evergreen, **Position:** full sun or semi-shade, **Soil:** suits most well-drained, humus-rich soils, **Habit:** a twining climber, less vigorous than *L. halliana*, **Propagation:** cuttings of firm young shoots in summer in a propagator; cuttings of ripe wood in autumn outdoors or in a garden frame.
☐ Prune as for *L.* × *americana*.

Lonicera korolkowii

Caprifoliaceae Shrubby honeysuckle
ZONES 5–9   SHRUB
Height: 1.8–3 m (6–10 ft), **Flowers:** pink, early summer, followed by red berries, **Foliage:** pale grey green and downy, deciduous, **Position:** full sun or semi-shade, **Soil:** suits most soils, **Habit:** graceful, arching branches, very attractive and vigorous shrub, **Propagation:** 10 cm (4 in) long cuttings in mid – late summer; or 23–30 cm (9–12 in) long hardwood cuttings in early – mid-autumn, and insert in a garden frame; or layer in autumn.
☐ An eye-catching shrub which deserves to be more widely planted.

Lonicera maackii

Caprifoliaceae Shrubby honeysuckle
ZONES 4–9   SHRUB
Height: 3–4 m (10–13 ft), **Flowers:** white, yellowing with age, fragrant, early summer, followed by dark red berries, **Foliage:** deep green, downy, deciduous, **Position:** full sun or semi-shade, **Soil:** suits most soils, **Habit:** wide and spreading, **Propagation:** 10 cm (4 in) long cuttings in mid – late summer; or 23–30 cm (9–12 in) long hardwood cuttings in early – mid-autumn; or layer in autumn.
☐ Not too well known but worth a place in the larger shrub border.

Above left: *Lonicera maackii*
Top right: *Lonicera korolkowii*
Above: *Lonicera nitida* 'Baggesen's Gold'

Lonicera microphylla

Caprifoliaceae Shrubby honeysuckle
ZONES 5–9   SHRUB
Height: 1 m (3 ft), **Flowers:** pale yellow, late spring, followed by red berries, **Foliage:** dull grey-green, deciduous, **Position:** full sun or shade, **Soil:** suits most soils, **Habit:** stiff, sturdy and neat, **Propagation:** hardwood cuttings autumn.
☐ Not too well known, but suitable for the smaller shrub border.

Lonicera nitida

Caprifoliaceae Shrubby honeysuckle
ZONES 4–9   SHRUB
Height: 1.5–2.5 m (5–8 ft), **Flowers:** greenish, small and insignificant, mid – late spring, **Foliage:** tiny, deep shiny green, evergreen, **Position:** full sun or shade, **Soil:** suits most soils, **Habit:** dense and leafy, quick growing, **Propagation:** cuttings of firm young shoots in summer inserted in a propagator; cuttings of ripe wood outdoors in autumn; or layer in autumn.
☐ Normally used for hedging; trim two or three times a year. 'Baggesen's Gold' has yellow-green foliage in full sun.

Above: *Lonicera periclymenum* 'Belgica'
Right: *Lonicera sempervirens*

Lonicera periclymenum 'Belgica'

Caprifoliaceae   Early Dutch honeysuckle
ZONES 5–9   CLIMBER
Height: 6 m (20 ft), **Flowers:** red purple, ageing to yellow, fragrant, late spring – early summer and again in early autumn, followed by red berries, **Foliage:** matt green above, glaucous beneath, deciduous, **Position:** full sun or semi-shade, **Soil:** well-drained, humus-rich, **Habit:** twining climber, **Propagation:** cuttings of firm young shoots in summer in a propagator; cuttings of ripe wood in autumn outdoors or in a garden frame.
□ 'Serotina' (late Dutch honeysuckle) is similar but flowers mid-summer – mid-autumn. Prune as for *L.* × *americana*.

Lonicera pileata

Caprifoliaceae   Shrubby honeysuckle
ZONES 5–9   SHRUB
Height: 60 cm–1 m (2–3 ft), **Flowers:** yellow-green, insignificant, mid – late spring, followed by blue fruits, **Foliage:** vivid green, partially evergreen, **Position:** full sun or shade, **Soil:** suits most soils, **Habit:** spreading, **Propagation:** by cuttings as *L. nitida*.
□ Makes excellent ground cover.

Lonicera × *purpusii* 'Winter Beauty'

Caprifoliaceae   Shrubby honeysuckle
ZONES 5–9   SHRUB
Height: 1.8 m (6 ft), **Flowers:** cream-yellow, highly scented, early winter – early spring, **Foliage:** green, deciduous, **Position:** full sun or semi-shade, **Soil:** suits most soils, **Habit:** rounded, twiggy bush, **Propagation:** hardwood cuttings in early – mid-autumn, or layer in spring.
□ Excellent for winter flower arrangements. Try grouping winter-flowering heathers around this shrub.

Lonicera sempervirens

Caprifoliaceae   Trumpet honeysuckle
ZONES 5–9   CLIMBER
Height: 9 m (30 ft), **Flowers:** orange-red and yellow during summer, **Foliage:** green, usually partially evergreen, **Position:** sunny, warm and sheltered, **Soil:** well-drained, humus-rich, **Habit:** twining climber of some vigour, but needs wall protection in Britain, **Propagation:** cuttings of firm young shoots in summer in a propagator; cuttings of ripe wood in autumn outdoors, or in a garden frame.
□ Prune as for *L.* × *americana*. A very showy and quick-growing climber.

Lonicera syringantha

Caprifoliaceae   Shrubby honeysuckle
ZONES 4–9   SHRUB
Height: 1.8–2.5 m (6–8 ft), **Flowers:** pink, fragrant, late spring to early summer, **Foliage:** greyish-green, deciduous, **Position:** full sun or shade, **Soil:** suits most soils, **Habit:** upright and very bushy, **Propagation:** cuttings of fully-ripened wood in early – mid-autumn inserted in a garden frame.
□ Philadelphus make good companion plants in the shrub border.

Lonicera tatarica

Caprifoliaceae   Shrubby honeysuckle
ZONES 4–9   SHRUB
Height: 3 m (10 ft), **Flowers:** pink, early summer, followed by red fruits, **Foliage:** ovate, grey-green, deciduous, **Position:** full sun or shade, **Soil:** suits most soils, **Habit:** rounded very bushy habit, **Propagation:** cuttings of fully-ripened wood in early – mid-autumn inserted in a garden frame.
□ A good cultivar is 'Hack's Red' with deep pink blooms. Also very vigorous – ideal for large borders.

Lupinus 'Russell Hybrids'
Leguminosae   Russell lupin
ZONES 5–10   HERBACEOUS PERENNIAL
Height: 1–1.2 m (3–4 ft), **Flowers:** red, pink, yellow, white or blue, pea-like, in dense spikes, summer, **Foliage:** green, hand-shaped, deciduous, **Position:** full sun or semi-shade, **Soil:** prefers a light acid soil, well-drained, **Habit:** short-lived perennial, upright, **Propagation:** seeds sown in sandy soil in a garden frame mid – late spring; hybrids only from basal cuttings in mid-spring.
□May need staking. Excellent companions for peonies and irises in the herbaceous or mixed border.

Right: *Lupinus* 'Russell Hybrids' make excellent companions for peonies and irises in the herbaceous or mixed border.

Lychnis chalcedonica
Caryophyllaceae   Maltese cross, Jerusalem cross
ZONES 4–9   HERBACEOUS PERENNIAL
Height: 1 m (3 ft), **Flowers:** scarlet, grouped closely in flat heads, summer, **Foliage:** green, lanceolate, deciduous, **Position:** full sun or semi-shade, **Soil:** moist and reasonably fertile, **Habit:** clump-forming perennial with erect stems, **Propagation:** seeds sown in spring or early summer, outdoors or in a garden frame, or by division in spring.
□The flowers are suitable for cutting.

Lycium barbarum
Solanaceae   Chinese box thorn, Duke of Argyll's tea tree
ZONES 6–9   SHRUB
Height: 1.8–2.5 m (6–8 ft), **Flowers:** purplish pink in clusters, early summer – early autumn, followed by red or orange fruits, **Foliage:** green, deciduous, **Position:** sun or partial shade, **Soil:** well-drained, **Habit:** vigorous, scrambling with arching branches, quick-growing when young, **Propagation:** heeled cuttings of firm shoots 15–23 cm (6–9 in) long, taken early – mid-autumn and inserted in sandy soil in a shady place.
□Excellent for exposed seaside gardens.

Lyonia ligustrina
Ericaceae
ZONES 4–9   SHRUB
Height: 1–1.5 m (3–5 ft), **Flowers:** white, urn-shaped, mid – late summer, **Foliage:** medium to dark green, deciduous, **Position:** sun or partial shade, **Soil:** moist, with peat added, acid or neutral, **Habit:** compact, bushy, **Propagation:** heeled cuttings taken from shoots that appear beneath the flower panicles.
□Useful for growing with rhododendrons, pieris and other lime haters.

Lythrum salicaria 'Firecandle'
Lythraceae Purple loosestrife
ZONES 3–9   HERBACEOUS PERENNIAL
Height: 1–1.2 m (3–4 ft), **Flowers:** reddish purple in long spikes, early summer – early autumn, **Foliage:** green, lanceolate, deciduous, **Position:** full sun or partial shade, **Soil:** moist and heavyish, **Habit:** very adaptable, clump forming, upright, **Propagation:** division in autumn or spring.
□ Suitable for pondside or herbaceous border.

MAGNOLIAS

This genus of 80 or so hardy evergreen and deciduous trees and shrubs contains some of the most magnificent flowering plants for temperate regions. Magnolias are often passed over as being difficult, but though awe-inspiring and exotic in the size and magnificence of their flowers they are really very easy to grow, provided a few simple rules are followed.

They require a reasonable depth of humus-rich soil, well-drained yet moisture-retentive, and preferably acid or neutral. If it is slightly alkaline, or poor and shallow, prepare each planting position about 60 cm (2 ft) deep and 1 m (3 ft) in diameter and fill with good loam containing plenty of peat and leafmould. Where the soil is more strongly alkaline, magnolias can be grown successfully if the more lime-tolerant kinds are selected, such as *M. × highdownensis* or *M. × loebneri*. Magnolias are quite tolerant of heavy clay, and, despite their exotic appearance, of atmospheric pollution.

It is difficult to give accurate figures for the ultimate height of these magnolias as it varies tremendously according to the conditions in which they are grown. The heights given here are therefore only an approximate guide. Some of the species listed could be classed as trees if grown on a single stem, but are termed shrubs when multi-stemmed from the base.

In exposed districts, the earlier-flowering kinds should be protected from frosts and cold winds. Dappled shade is ideal for most species.

Magnolia denudata
Magnoliaceae Yulan
ZONES 5–9   SHRUB
Height: 6 m (20 ft) or more, **Flowers:** white, scented, early – late spring, free-flowering, **Foliage:** green, deciduous, **Position:** sun or partial shade, protected from cold winds and frost, **Soil:** deep rich loam, moist yet well-drained, acid or neutral, **Habit:** large, tree-like, **Propagation:** by heeled cuttings of firm young growth in a propagator in summer, or by layering in spring.
□ An exceptionally beautiful large shrub when its profusion of pure white flowers is seen on a sunny day.

Magnolia grandiflora
Magnoliaceae Laurel magnolia
ZONES 7–10   SHRUB
Height: 6–10 m (20–33 ft), **Flowers:** very large, white, scented, mid-summer – early autumn, **Foliage:** large, oval, deep shiny green, brown undersides, evergreen, **Position:** full sun or partial shade, **Soil:** well-drained, loamy, acid or neutral, **Habit:** massive, round-headed, **Propagation:** by heeled cuttings of ripening shoots in mid summer, inserted in a propagator, or layer in spring.
□ 'Exmouth' flowers at an earlier age than the species. Both excellent wall shrubs.

Magnolia × highdownensis
Magnoliaceae
ZONES 5–9   SHRUB
Height: 4 m (13 ft) or more, **Flowers:** large, pendent, white with purple centre, fragrant, late spring, **Foliage:** mid green, deciduous, **Position:** sun or partial shade, **Soil:** succeeds on chalk soils, **Habit:** open, tree-like, **Propagation:** layer in spring; cuttings of firm young growth with a heel taken in summer and inserted in a propagator.
□ Excellent for woodland garden in combination with rhododendrons.

Left: *Magnolia grandiflora* makes an excellent wall shrub, provided there is plenty of space for it to spread.

Magnolia liliiflora 'Nigra'
(syn. *M. × soulangiana* 'Nigra')
Magnoliaceae

ZONES 5–9   SHRUB

Height: up to 3 m (10 ft), **Flowers:** reddish purple, cup-shaped, mid-spring – mid-summer, **Foliage:** shiny and dark green, deciduous, **Position:** sun or partial shade, **Soil:** acid or neutral, good drainage, **Habit:** forms a compact upright bush, **Propagation:** layer in spring; cuttings of firm young growth taken with a heel in summer and inserted in a propagator.
□Makes an attractive lawn specimen.

Magnolia 'Jane'
Magnoliaceae

ZONES 5–9   SHRUB

Height: up to 3 m (10 ft), **Flowers:** dark purple, upright, conical, scented, mid-spring – mid-summer, **Foliage:** green, deciduous, **Position:** sun or partial shade, protect from cold winds, **Soil:** well-drained, moisture-retentive, humus-rich loam, **Habit:** multi-stemmed, rounded, strong and compact, **Propagation:** layer in spring; cuttings of firm young growth taken with a heel in summer and inserted in a propagator.
□'Susan' has flowers purple outside, paler within. 'Susan' and 'Jane' are *liliiflora × stellata* hybrids. Both make excellent lawn specimens.

Magnolia × loebneri 'Leonard Messel'
Magnoliaceae

ZONES 5–9   SHRUB

Height: 4–6 m (13–20 ft), **Flowers:** mauve-pink, slightly darker colour in bud, even young plants are covered in blossom, mid – late spring, **Foliage:** green, deciduous, **Position:** sun or partial shade, **Soil:** well-drained but moist, humus-rich, tolerates lime, **Habit:** open-branched and spreading, **Propagation:** layer in spring; cuttings of firm young growth taken with a heel in summer and inserted in a propagator.
□This variable hybrid combines the best qualities of its parents, *M. kobus* and *M. stellata*.

Magnolia × loebneri 'Merrill'
Magnoliaceae

ZONES 5–9   SHRUB

Height: 4–6 m (13–20 ft), **Flowers:** huge white scented blooms, mid-spring – mid-summer, **Foliage:** green, deciduous, **Position:** sun or partial shade, **Soil:** well-drained but moisture-retentive, humus-rich, lime tolerant, **Habit:** open branched and spreading, **Propagation:** layer in

spring; cuttings of firm young growth taken with a heel in summer and inserted in a propagator.
□A very free-flowering magnolia.

Magnolia sieboldii
(syn. *M. parviflora*)
Magnoliaceae

ZONES 5–9   SHRUB

Height: 5–6 m (16–20 ft), **Flowers:** white, waxy with purple stamens, scented, cup-shaped, carried horizontally or hanging down, late spring – late summer, followed by clusters of spectacular orange crimson fruits, **Foliage:** long-stalked, green, deciduous, **Position:** sun or partial shade, **Soil:** well-drained, moist, lime-free, humus-rich, **Habit:** large and spreading, **Propagation:** layer in spring; cuttings of firm young growth taken with a heel in summer an inserted in a propagator.
□Superb magnolia for the woodland garden, or as a lawn specimen. Needs to become established before flowering.

Top left: *Magnolia × loebneri* 'Leonard Messel'
Top right: *Magnolia × soulangiana*
Above: *Magnolia sieboldii*

Magnolia × soulangiana
Magnoliaceae

ZONES 5–9   SHRUB

Height: 4–6 m (13–20 ft), **Flowers:** white, flushed pinky purple, mid-spring before leaves appear, **Foliage:** green, deciduous, **Position:** sun or partial shade, protect from frost and cold winds, **Soil:** well-drained but moist, humus-rich, lime-free, **Habit:** large shrub with several wide-spreading stems, **Propagation:** layering in spring; cuttings of firm young growth, taken with a heel in summer and inserted in a propagator.
□'Lennei' has soft red-purple flowers, white within. 'Rustica Rubra' has rose-red flowers – both are outstanding clones.

Young plants flower freely. Excellent for use as lawn specimens; can also be grown against a wall, or in light woodland conditions.

Magnolia stellata
Magnoliaceae
ZONES 5–9   SHRUB
Height: 2.0–2.5 m (6–8 ft), **Flowers:** starry white scented blooms, early – mid-spring, **Foliage:** light green, deciduous, **Position:** sun or partial shade, protect from frost and cold wind, **Soil:** well-drained but moisture-retentive, humus-rich and lime-free with added peat, **Habit:** compact and rounded, usually wider than tall, **Propagation:** layer in spring; take heeled cuttings of firm young growths in summer and insert in a propagator.

☐Charming free-flowering magnolia: looks spectacular when underplanted thickly with blue grape hyacinths (*Muscari*). The cultivar 'Rubra' has pink-tinged blooms.

Right: *Magnolia stellata* is one of the best species for a small garden and flowers freely.

Below: *Mahonia aquifolium*, an excellent evergreen ground-cover plant which blooms in spring.

Mahonia aquifolium
Berberidaceae   Oregon grape
ZONES 5–9   SHRUB
Height: 1–1.5 m (3–5 ft), **Flowers:** bright yellow in dense racemes, scented, early – mid-spring, followed by clusters of dark blue berries which are edible, **Foliage:** compound, shiny, deep green, evergreen, often turns red in autumn, **Position:** full sun or shade, tolerates exposed windy sites, **Soil:** suits most soils including shallow chalk soils, **Habit:** suckering and dense, **Propagation:** sow seeds when ripe; 10 cm (8 in) cuttings of side shoots in mid-summer, or remove rooted suckers in autumn.

☐The leaves of 'Atropurpurea' turn purple-red in autumn.

Excellent ground cover. Cut back hard in mid-spring each year when used as ground cover.

Mahonia bealei
Berberidaceae
ZONES 6–9   SHRUB
Height: 2–2.5 m (6–8 ft), **Flowers:** yellow, upright racemes, fragrant, winter, **Foliage:** large, compound, greyish-green above, evergreen, **Position:** full sun or shade, **Soil:** suits most soils including chalk, **Habit:** erect and vigorous shrub, **Propagation:** sow seeds when ripe; leaf-bud cuttings in mid – late autumn in a heated propagator.

☐Good with coloured-stemmed dogwoods.

Mahonia 'Charity'
Berberidaceae
ZONES 6–9   SHRUB
Height: 2–2.5 m (6–8 ft), **Flowers:** rich yellow in arching racemes up to 30 cm (1 ft) long, scented, late autumn – late winter, **Foliage:** large compound leaves, deep green and spiny, evergreen, **Position:** sun or shade, **Soil:** suits most soils including chalk **Habit:** upright and stately shrub, **Propagation:** leaf-bud cuttings in mid – late autumn in a heated propagator.
☐Good companion plants are the coloured-stemmed dogwoods (cornus).

Mahonia japonica
Berberidaceae
ZONES 6–9   SHRUB
Height: 2–2.5 m (6–8 ft), **Flowers:** pale yellow in arching racemes, scented, mid-winter – early spring, **Foliage:** large compound leaves, deep green and shiny, evergreen, **Position:** sun or shade, **Soil:** suits most soils including chalk, **Habit:** stiff, sturdy and erect, **Propagation:** leaf-bud cuttings in mid – late autumn in a heated propagator.
☐Good companion plants are the coloured-stemmed dogwoods (cornus).

Malus floribunda
Rosaceae   Japanese crab apple
ZONES 4–9   TREE
Height: 5–7.5 m (16–25 ft), **Flowers:** red buds opening light pink, single, numerous, late spring, followed in autumn by small yellow crab apples, **Foliage:** medium green, deciduous, **Position:** full sun or semi-shade, **Soil:** most well-drained soils, including clay, **Habit:** forms a rounded head of branches, **Propagation:** seeds sown outdoors, or grafting in spring.
☐Excellent as a lawn specimen.

Malus 'John Downie'
Rosaceae   Crab apple
ZONES 4–9   TREE
Height: 7.5–9 m (25–30 ft), **Flowers:** pink buds opening white, single, slightly scented, late spring followed by edible yellow fruits generously marked with red, **Foliage:** medium green, deciduous, **Position:** full sun or semi-shade, **Soil:** most well-drained soils, including clay, **Habit:** upright when young, later the head spreads, **Propagation:** grafting in spring or budding in summer.
☐The best fruits for crab apple jelly. Generally grown as a lawn specimen.

Malus × robusta 'Yellow Siberian'
Rosaceae   Crab apple
ZONES 4–9   TREE
Height: 4–5 m (13–16 ft), **Flowers:** single white, from pink buds, late spring, followed by yellow crab apples that remain well into winter, **Foliage:** green, deciduous, **Position:** full sun or semi-shade, **Soil:** most well drained soils, including clay, **Habit:** broad, with branches arching informally, **Propagation:** grafting or budding, layering is sometimes possible.
☐'Red Siberian' is similar in habit but bears red fruit. Both are often used as lawn specimens.

Meconopsis betonicifolia
Papaveraceae   Blue poppy
ZONES 5–10   HERBACEOUS PERENNIAL
Height: 60 cm–1 m (2–3 ft), **Flowers:** medium blue, poppy-shaped, early – midsummer, **Foliage:** green, deciduous, **Position:** partial shade, sheltered from wind, **Soil:** well-drained yet moist, acid to neutral, **Habit:** plant and flower both short-lived, **Propagation:** seeds sown under glass as soon as they are ripe.
☐Remove any flower buds that appear in the first year to encourage plant to establish. Superb plant for woodland garden or shrub border in association with primulas.

Menziesia ciliicalyx

Ericaceae

ZONES 8–10   SHRUB

Height: 1–1.8 m (3–6 ft), **Flowers:** pink to light purple, pendulous, bell-shaped, early summer, **Foliage:** light to medium green, deciduous, **Position:** full sun or semi-shade, **Soil:** peaty and acid, topdress with peat, **Habit:** slow-growing, bushy, **Propagation:** seed sown in sandy peat during spring, in heated propagator; cuttings of current season's side shoots, with heel, during summer in sandy soil in a heated propagator; or layer in spring or autumn.

☐ Combine with rhododendrons.

Metasequoia glyptostroboides

Taxodiaceae   Dawn redwood

ZONES 5–9   CONIFER

Height: 6 m (20 ft) or so after 10 years, eventually reaching 35 m (115 ft), **Flowers:** female strobili red or pale green, cones pendulous on long stalks, cylindrical, dark brown, **Foliage:** rich medium green in summer changing through bronzy-pink to rust-red in autumn, deciduous, **Position:** best in open sunny situations, **Soil:** any moist but well-drained soil, slower growing on chalk, **Habit:** vigorous, conical when young, **Propagation:** cuttings from tips of shoots in early – mid-summer and inserted in

Above left: *Metasequoia glyptostroboides*
Above: The foliage of *metasequoia*

sandy peat in a heated propagator, or slightly longer cuttings inserted in a garden frame in late autumn.

☐ Superb specimen tree, for the larger garden. Attractive orange-brown bark.

Mitraria coccinea

Gesneriaceae

ZONES 9–10   CLIMBER

Height: 30 cm (1 ft), spreads 3 m (10 ft) or more, **Flowers:** orange-scarlet, tubular, early summer, **Foliage:** small, green, shiny, evergreen, **Position:** best in partial shade, shelter from frost and wind, **Soil:** moisture-retentive, unsuitable for thin chalky soils, **Habit:** prostrate or climbing, slender-stemmed, **Propagation:** by cuttings at any time.

☐ Suitable only for the mildest districts, but where it can be grown makes an excellent groundcover or climbing plant. In cold areas grow in a frost-free conservatory.

Monarda didyma

Labiatae   Sweet bergamot, bee balm, Oswego tea

ZONES 4–9   HERBACEOUS PERENNIAL

Height: 60 cm–1 m (2–3 ft), **Flowers:** red, pink, white or purple, in whorls, early summer – early autumn, **Foliage:** green, oval, pleasantly scented, deciduous, **Position:** full sun or semi-shade, **Soil:** suits most moisture-retentive, well-drained soils, **Habit:** clump-forming perennial, **Propagation:** divide clumps in autumn or spring.

☐ Attractive to bees hence common name. Leaves used in teas and infusions.

Myrtus apiculata
(syn. *M. luma*)

Myrtaceae   Myrtle

ZONES 9–10   SHRUB

Height: 3–5 m (10–16 ft), **Flowers:** white, scented, early autumn, red and black edible fruits sometimes follow, **Foliage:** deep green, elliptic, aromatic when crushed, evergreen, **Position:** full sun, sheltered from wind, such as against a south- or west-facing wall, unsuitable for cold districts, **Soil:** suits most well-drained soils, **Habit:** dense and bushy, decorative reddish-brown peeling bark, **Propagation:** heeled cuttings early – mid-summer.

☐ 'Glenleam Gold' has golden variegated foliage.

Myrtus communis

Myrtaceae Myrtle
ZONES 8–10   SHRUB
Height: 2.5–3 m (8–10 ft), **Flowers:**
white with conspicuous stamens, scented,
early – late summer, **Foliage:** shiny dark
green, aromatic when crushed, evergreen,
Position: sun, sheltered position essential,
best grown as a wall shrub, **Soil:** suits most
well-drained soils, **Habit:** bushy, **Propagation:** heeled cuttings of side shoots in
early – mid-summer, inserted in a heated
propagator.
□ 'Variegata' has cream-variegated foliage (ZONE 8–10). Grows well by the sea.

Nandina domestica

Berberidaceae Sacred bamboo
ZONES 8–10   SHRUB
Height: 1.2–1.8 m (4–6 ft), **Flowers:**
white, in large pyramidal heads, summer,
may be followed by red berries, **Foliage:**
pinnate, light green, tinted red when
young, turning reddish purple in autumn,
evergreen, **Position:** full sun, sheltered
from cold winds, **Soil:** humus-rich, moist
yet well-drained, **Habit:** bamboo-like,
Propagation: heeled cuttings of side
shoots inserted in a peat and sand mix in a
propagator in summer (slow to root).
□ Gives foliage contrast.

Nepeta × faassenii
(syn. N. mussinii)

Labiatae Catmint
ZONES 4–9   HERBACEOUS PERENNIAL
Height: 30 cm (1 ft), **Flowers:** pale purple, in loose upright spikes, late spring –
early autumn, **Foliage:** greyish-green, deciduous, **Position:** best in full sun, **Soil:**
suits most well-drained soils, **Habit:**
rounded, clump-forming perennial,
Propagation: by dividing clumps in
spring, or basal cuttings in spring in
garden frame.
□ Useful edging plant. May need protection from cats! They love this plant.

Nyssa sinensis

Nyssaceae Chinese tupelo, Chinese sour
gum
ZONES 6–10   SHRUB
Height: up to 6 m (20 ft) as a shrub,
Flowers: insignificant, **Foliage:** dull dark
green, turning brilliant orange and scarlet
in autumn, deciduous, **Position:** open
and sunny, **Soil:** acid, fertile and fairly
moist, **Habit:** pyramidal, **Propagation:**
layer in autumn, or sow seeds in mid-
autumn in a garden frame.
□ Superb as a lawn specimen. A good
companion is pampas grass (cortaderia).

Nyssa sylvatica

Nyssaceae Tupelo
ZONES 6–10   TREE
Height: 10.5 m (35 ft) or more, **Flowers:**
insignificant, **Foliage:** dark glossy green,
roughly oval but variable in shape, colouring shades of red, orange and yellow in
autumn, **Position:** sunny and open, **Soil:**
acid, fertile and fairly moist, **Habit:** pyramidal when young, becoming broadly
columnar, slow growing, **Propagation:**
layer in autumn, or sow seed sown in mid
autumn in a garden frame.
□ Outstanding autumn colour. Often
used as a specimen tree in a largish lawn.

Oenothera missouriensis
(syn. O. macrocarpa)

Onagraceae Evening primrose
ZONES 4–10   HERBACEOUS PERENNIAL
Height: 15–23 cm (6–9 in), **Flowers:**
large yellow, opening in the evening, early
– late summer, **Foliage:** longish, medium
green, deciduous, **Position:** full sun, **Soil:**
any soil with good drainage, **Habit:** trailing perennial, **Propagation:** seeds sown
in mid-spring in a garden frame.
□ Attractive perennial for the rock garden
or front of border.

Top left: *Olearia × haastii*
Top right: *Olearia × scilloniensis*
Below: *Olearia stellulata* 'Master Michael'

Olearia × haastii

Compositae Daisy bush
ZONES 7–10   SHRUB
Height: 1.8–2.5 m (6–8 ft), **Flowers:** white daisies in mid – late summer, **Foliage:** shiny green above with greyish-white undersides, evergreen, **Position:** sun or partial shade, good for exposed maritime gardens, **Soil:** suits most well-drained soils, including chalk, **Habit:** bushy, sturdy and rounded, **Propagation:** cuttings of ripening side shoots in late summer, in frame.
☐ This is one of the hardiest of the daisy bushes. Withstands polluted air. Useful as an informal hedge.

Olearia ilicifolia

Compositae Daisy bush, Maori holly
ZONES 8–10   SHRUB
Height: 3 m (10 ft) or more, **Flowers:** white daisies, scented, early summer, **Foliage:** hard, leathery, holly-like, grey-green above with white undersides, evergreen, **Position:** sun or partial shade, good for seaside planting, **Soil:** suits most well-drained soils, including chalk, **Habit:** bushy and spreading, **Propagation:** cuttings of ripening side shoots in the summer.
☐ Also a hardy species for seaside and town conditions. Will make an attractive informal hedge.

Olearia macrodonta

Compositae Daisy bush, New Zealand holly
ZONES 7–10   SHRUB
Height: up to 4 m (13 ft), **Flowers:** white daisies in clusters, early – mid-summer, **Foliage:** medium green, like those of holly, white beneath, evergreen, **Position:** sun or partial shade, good for exposed seaside conditions, **Soil:** suits most well-drained soils, including chalk, **Habit:** strong-growing, upright, **Propagation:** cuttings of ripening side shoots in late summer, in a garden frame.
☐ Good screening plant. Takes sea winds in its stride.

Olearia mollis

Compositae Daisy bush
ZONES 9–10   SHRUB
Height: 1–1.2 m (3–4 ft), **Flowers:** white daisies, **Foliage:** grey leaves with crinkled edges, evergreen, **Position:** sunny and sheltered, **Soil:** suits most well-drained soils, including chalk, **Habit:** rounded and compact, **Propagation:** cuttings of ripening side shoots in late summer.
☐ Not as hardy as other species. Suitable for the seaside.

Olearia × scilloniensis

Compositae Daisy bush
ZONES 9–10   SHRUB
Height: 1.2–1.5 m (4–5 ft), **Flowers:** white daisies in great profusion, late spring – early summer, **Foliage:** brightly silver, evergreen, **Position:** sunny and sheltered, **Soil:** suits most well-drained soils, including chalk, **Habit:** compact, rounded and bushy, **Propagation:** cuttings of ripening side shoots in late summer in a garden frame.
☐ Ideal for a smallish sheltered border.

Olearia stellulata 'Master Michael'

Compositae Daisy bush
ZONES 9–10   SHRUB
Height: 1.5–1.8 m (5–6 ft), **Flowers:** violet-blue daisies, early summer, **Foliage:** dull-green, toothed, evergreen, **Position:** sunny and sheltered, **Soil:** suits most well-drained soils, including chalk, **Habit:** bushy and rounded, **Propagation:** cuttings of ripening side shoots in late summer, in a garden frame or propagator.
☐ A blue daisy bush – something a bit different for mild districts.

Osmanthus delavayi
(syn. *Siphonosmanthus delavayi*)
Oleaceae

ZONES 7–10   SHRUB

Height: 1.8 m (6 ft), **Flowers:** white, scented, mid-spring, **Foliage:** small shiny and deep green, evergreen, **Position:** full sun or semi-shade, **Soil:** suits most soils with good drainage, **Habit:** rather wider than tall, bushy and dense, growth is rather slow, **Propagation:** cuttings of ripening shoots in mid-summer in a heated propagator, or layer in early autumn. □ One of the best scented shrubs.

Osmanthus heterophyllus
(syn. *O. ilicifolius*) 'Variegatus'
Oleaceae

ZONES 8–10   SHRUB

Height: 1.8–2.5 m (6–8 ft), **Flowers:** white, scented, early – mid-autumn, **Foliage:** shiny, deep green, edged with cream, evergreen, **Position:** full sun and shelter, protect from cold winds, **Soil:** suits most soils with good drainage, **Habit:** slow-growing, holly-like shrub, **Propagation:** cuttings of ripening shoots in mid-summer, in a heated propagator. □ Looks good with fuchsias.

Right: *Osmanthus heterophyllus* 'Variegatus'

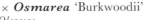

× Osmarea 'Burkwoodii'
Oleaceae

ZONES 6–10   SHRUB

Height: 1.8–3 m (6–10 ft), **Flowers:** white, scented, tubular, in clusters, mid – late spring, **Foliage:** shiny deep green, leathery with toothed edges, evergreen, **Position:** full sun or semi-shade, **Soil:** any, suitable for thin chalky types, **Habit:** compact, rounded and dense, **Propagation:** cuttings of ripening shoots, late summer – early autumn, inserted in sandy peat, shaded and under glass. □ Makes a good hedge. Trim when flowering is over.

Oxydendrum arboreum
Ericaceae   Sorrel tree

ZONES 5–9   SHRUB

Height: 4–6 m (13–20 ft), **Flowers:** small, white, in long pendulous racemes, late summer, **Foliage:** green, lanceolate, up to 15 cm (6 in) long, deciduous, turning brilliant scarlet in autumn, **Position:** open and sunny, or shady, **Soil:** lime-free loam, **Habit:** tree-like, **Propagation:** seeds sown as soon as ripe. □ Makes an impressive lawn specimen.

Ozothamnus ledifolius
(syn. *Helichrysum ledifolium*)
Compositae

ZONES 8–10   SHRUB

Height: 1–1.2 m (3–4 ft), **Flowers:** buds red, opening to white flowers, fragrant seed heads, early – mid-summer, **Foliage:** lime-green above with recurving margins, yellow undersides, evergreen, **Position:** full sun, **Soil:** well-drained, **Habit:** dense and bushy, **Propagation:** cuttings of firm young shoots inserted in a heated propagator in summer. □ Unusual shrub for a sunny border.

Pachysandra procumbens
Buxaceae Allegheny spurge
ZONES 4–10   SHRUB
Height: 15–25 cm (6–10 in), **Flowers:** greenish white or purplish, early – mid-spring, **Foliage:** mid green, evergreen, **Position:** partial or full shade, **Soil:** moist, preferably lime-free, **Habit:** dense and prostrate, sub-shrub, **Propagation:** take cuttings of nearly ripe growths in summer and insert in sandy soil in a propagator, or divide early spring.
□Excellent ground coverer for shade.

Pachysandra terminalis
Buxaceae
ZONES 4–10   SHRUB
Height: 15–25 cm (6–10 in), **Flowers:** greenish white, sometimes purple-tinted, late winter – mid-spring, **Foliage:** glossy, medium green, evergreen, **Position:** partial or full shade, **Soil:** moist, preferably lime-free, **Habit:** prostrate and spreading to 60 cm (2 ft), **Propagation:** take cuttings of nearly ripe growths in summer and insert in a sandy soil in a propagator, or lift, divide and replant in early spring.
□'Variegata' has leaves marked with white and is less vigorous and less hardy. (ZONES 5–10).
Excellent ground cover for a shady spot.

Top right: *Pachysandra terminalis*
Left and above: Pink and white cultivars of *Paeonia lactiflora*

Paeonia lactiflora
(syn. *P. albiflora*)
Paeoniaceae Paeony
ZONES 3–9   HERBACEOUS PERENNIAL
Height: 60–75 cm (2–2½ ft), **Flowers:** red, white or shades of red and pink, single and double, some are scented, early – mid-summer, **Foliage:** dark green with reddish tint, irregularly divided, deciduous, **Position:** sun or partial shade, avoid early morning sun, **Soil:** well-drained, fertile, **Habit:** strong growing perennials forming a rounded clump, **Propagation:** divide in autumn or spring, but only if absolutely necessary. Better to buy new plants from a garden centre. Seeds can be sown but will not come true from named varieties.
□Some cultivars are more scented than others. Long-lived once established, best left undisturbed once planted.
Paeonies make excellent companions for bearded irises.

Paeonia mlokosewitschii
Paeoniaceae Paeony
ZONES 3–9   HERBACEOUS PERENNIAL
Height: 60 cm (2 ft), **Flowers:** yellow, single, mid – late spring, followed by red and blue seedpods in autumn, **Foliage:** grey-green, pinkish when young, turns orange and yellow in autumn, deciduous, **Position:** sun or partial shade, **Soil:** well drained, fertile, **Habit:** strong-growing, rounded perennial, **Propagation:** seeds sown in early autumn in a garden frame, or by division, if necessary, in early autumn.
□Flowers, foliage and seedpods all very attractive.

Paeonia suffruticosa
(syn. *P. moutan*)

Paeoniaceae Moutan paeony, tree paeony
ZONES 6–9   SHRUB
Height: 1.5–1.8 m (5–6 ft), **Flowers:** large, white, single, with variable rose-purple blotch in centre, late spring or early summer, **Foliage:** light green, deciduous, **Position:** sun or partial shade, protect from early morning sun, **Soil:** moist but well-drained, **Habit:** stiff-branched, luxuriant in leaf, gaunt when leafless, **Propagation:** seed sown in early autumn, or by layering early spring.
□ Superb paeony for the shrub border.

Papaver orientale

Papaveraceae Oriental poppy
ZONES 7–10   HERBACEOUS PERENNIAL
Height: 60 cm–1 m (2–3 ft), **Flowers:** huge red, orange, pink or white flowers, late spring – early summer, **Foliage:** green, deeply cut, rough and hairy, deciduous, **Position:** full sun, **Soil:** suits most well-drained soils, **Habit:** clump forming perennial, **Propagation:** division in spring, or root cuttings late autumn – early spring in garden frame.
□ Untidy after flowering so grow a lowish border plant in front of it.

Parrotiopsis jacquemontiana

Hamamelidaceae
ZONES 7–10   SHRUB
Height: 3–5 m (10–16 ft), **Flowers:** flower clusters surrounded by white bracts in similar manner to *Cornus florida* (see page 120), mid – late spring and intermittently in summer, **Foliage:** green turning to yellow in autumn, deciduous, **Position:** sun or partial shade, **Soil:** humus-rich, preferably acid or neutral, but moderately lime-tolerant, **Habit:** erect, **Propagation:** cuttings of firm young growths in a heated propagator in summer.

Parthenocissus henryana

Vitaceae Chinese Virginia creeper
ZONES 6–10   CLIMBER
Height: up to 9 m (30 ft), **Flowers:** yellowy green, very small, followed in hot dry summers by blue berries, **Foliage:** hand-shaped, deep green, with white and pink variegation, autumn colouring red, deciduous, **Position:** sun or partial shade, foliage colours best in partial shade, **Soil:** reasonably moist, humus-rich, **Habit:** beautiful self-clinging climber, slightly tender, **Propagation:** cuttings of ripening shoots in late summer – early autumn in sandy soil in a heated propagator; hardwood cuttings outdoors in late autumn; layer in autumn.
□ Excellent for walls, fences, pergolas.

Parthenocissus quinquefolia

Vitaceae Virginia creeper
ZONES 5–10   CLIMBER
Height: up to 21 m (70 ft), **Flowers:** inconspicuous, yellow-green, followed by small black berries, **Foliage:** green, hand-shaped, bright red in autumn, deciduous, **Position:** sun or shade, **Soil:** reasonably moist, humus-rich, **Habit:** hardy, self-clinging, branching, **Propagation:** layering in spring or autumn; cuttings of firm young growth in a heated propagator in summer; or cuttings of ripe wood in autumn in open ground or a garden frame.
□ Young plants with bare roots do not transplant readily.
    Ideal for growing up tall trees and walls. Thin out if necessary in summer.

Parthenocissus tricuspidata
'Veitchii'

Vitaceae Boston ivy
ZONES 5–10   CLIMBER
Height: up to 21 m (70 ft), **Flowers:** inconspicuous, greeny yellow, followed by dark blue berries, **Foliage:** green, vary in shape from broadly ovate and toothed to lobed, turn brilliant red in autumn, deciduous, **Position:** sun or shade, **Soil:** reasonably moist, humus-rich, **Habit:** a vigorous self-clinging vine, **Propagation:** layering in spring or autumn; cuttings of firm young growths in a heated propagator in summer; or cuttings of ripe wood in autumn in open ground or garden frame.
□ Young plants with bare roots do not transplant readily. Uses as for *P. henryana*.

Passiflora caerulea

Passifloraceae   Passion flower

ZONES 8–10   CLIMBER

Height: up to 9 m (30 ft), **Flowers:** blue and white, exotic-looking, early summer – early autumn, orange-yellow fruits, **Foliage:** green, palmate, evergreen, **Position:** full sun or semi-shade, sheltered, **Soil:** well-drained, **Habit:** vigorous and rampant, **Propagation:** seeds under glass in spring, or cuttings of young shoots in a heated propagator in summer.

☐Recommended only for mild areas. Thin out old growths in early spring.

Paulownia tomentosa (syn. *P. imperialis*)

Scrophulariaceae

ZONES 6–10   TREE

Height: 9–12 m (30–40 ft), **Flowers:** pale heliotrope blue on mature trees only, appearing before the leaves, fragrant, late spring, **Foliage:** medium green, large, heart-shaped, deciduous, **Position:** full sun, sheltered, **Soil:** deep and fertile, **Habit:** rounded head of branches, **Propagation:** seeds sown in sandy soil under glass when ripe or in spring, or heeled cuttings of side shoots in a garden frame in summer.

☐Winter flower buds are easily damaged by frosts. Magnificent lawn specimen for a large garden.

Pernettya mucronata

Ericaceae   Prickly heath

ZONES 5–10   SHRUB

Height: 60 cm–1 m (2–3 ft), taller in shady positions, **Flowers:** white, early summer, followed by cherry-sized fruits in red, pink or white; plant a male to ensure pollination of female plants, **Foliage:** deep green and shiny, evergreen, **Position:** sun or shade, more berries in sun, **Soil:** moist, with peat added, acid or neutral, **Habit:** erect, dense foliage, **Propagation:** cuttings in early – mid-autumn, inserted in sandy peat in a garden frame; sow seed in mid-autumn in a garden frame.

☐Can be used as ground cover around rhododendrons and azaleas.

Perovskia atriplicifolia 'Blue Spire'

Labiatae

ZONES 7–10   SHRUB

Height: 1–1.2 m (3–4 ft), **Flowers:** dark blue in spikes, late summer – early autumn, **Foliage:** grey-green, feathery and slightly downy, deciduous, **Position:** full sun, thrives in coastal gardens, **Soil:** suits most well-drained soils, including chalk, **Habit:** long branched, stiffly erect, **Propagation:** heeled cuttings of side shoots in mid-summer inserted in sandy peat in a garden frame.

☐An excellent companion for red or pink shrub roses. Stems should be pruned hard back in early spring.

Left: *Perovskia atriplicifolia* 'Blue Spire'

Petteria ramentacea

Leguminosae

ZONES 5–10   SHRUB

Height: 1.8–2.5 m (6–8 ft), **Flowers:** yellow, fragrant, late spring – early summer, **Foliage:** green, trifoliate, deciduous, **Position:** sun or partial shade, **Soil:** suits most soils, **Habit:** tree-like, stiffly erect, **Propagation:** sow seeds when ripe.

☐ Similar to laburnum, seeds are poisonous, deserves to be better known.

Below: *Philadelphus* 'Manteau d'Hermine'
Right, above: *Philadelphus* 'Belle Etoile'
Right, below: *P. coronarius* 'Aureus'

Philadelphus 'Belle Etoile'

Philadelphaceae   Mock orange

ZONES 5–9   SHRUB

Height: 1.8–2.5 m (6–8 ft), **Flowers:** white, flushed maroon at centre, single, highly scented, early – mid-summer, **Foliage:** green, deciduous, **Position:** sun or semi-shade, **Soil:** suits most soils, even poor chalk, **Habit:** rounded bush, **Propagation:** cuttings of ripening side shoots in mid – late summer in a garden frame, or hardwood cuttings autumn.

☐ This and the following philadelphus are invaluable for early summer colour in the shrub border, and all should be pruned immediately after flowering by cutting back the flowered stems to young shoots growing lower down.

Philadelphus coronarius 'Aureus'

Philadelphaceae   Mock orange

ZONES 7–9   SHRUB

Height: 1.8–2.5 m (6–10 ft), **Flowers:** white, scented, cup-shaped, single, early – mid-summer, **Foliage:** rich yellow, turning greeny yellow, deciduous, **Position:** sun or semi-shade, colours best in partial shade, **Soil:** tolerates most soils, particularly suitable for dry situations, **Habit:** rounded bush, **Propagation:** cuttings of ripening side shoots in mid – late summer in a garden frame, or hardwood cuttings 30 cm (1 ft) long, outdoors, mid – late autumn.

☐ Grown for its foliage.

Philadelphus × lemoinei

Philadelphaceae   Mock orange

ZONES 5–9   SHRUB

Height: up to 1.8 m (6 ft), **Flowers:** white, highly fragrant, early – mid-summer, **Foliage:** green, deciduous, **Position:** sun or semi-shade, **Soil:** suits most soils, **Habit:** compact and bushy, **Propagation:** cuttings of ripening side shoots in mid – late summer in a garden frame, or hardwood cuttings 30 cm (1 ft) long, outdoors, mid – late autumn.

Philadelphus 'Manteau d'Hermine'

Philadelphaceae   Mock orange

ZONES 5–9   SHRUB

Height: 75 cm–1.2 m (2½–4 ft), **Flowers:** cream, double, highly scented, early – mid-summer, **Foliage:** green, deciduous, **Position:** sun or semi-shade, **Soil:** suits most soils, including alkaline, **Habit:** compact and bushy, **Propagation:** cuttings of ripening side shoots in a garden frame, or hardwood cuttings outdoors.

☐ Excellent choice for the small border.

Philadelphus 'Sybille'
Philadelphaceae   Mock orange
ZONES 5–9   SHRUB
Height: 1.2 m (4 ft), **Flowers:** single, white with purple basal blotch, highly scented, early – mid-summer, **Foliage:** green, deciduous, **Position:** sun or semi-shade, **Soil:** suits most soils, including alkaline, **Habit:** small with arching branches, **Propagation:** cuttings of ripening side shoots under glass, or hardwood cuttings outdoors.
□ Also suitable for the small border.

Philadelphus 'Virginal'
Philadelphaceae   Mock orange
ZONES 5–9   SHRUB
Height: up to 3 m (10 ft), **Flowers:** white, double, highly scented, early – mid-summer, **Foliage:** green, deciduous, **Position:** sun or semi-shade, **Soil:** suits most soils, including chalk, **Habit:** strong-growing, erect branched, **Propagation:** cuttings of ripening side shoots under glass, or hardwood cuttings outdoors.
□ Possibly the best double-flowered cultivar. Ideal for large borders.

Right: *Philadelphus* 'Virginal', with a large-flowered purple clematis as an attractive companion

Philesia magellanica
(**syn. *P. buxifolia***)
Philesiaceae
ZONES 8–10   SHRUB
Height: 45–60 cm (1½–2 ft), **Flowers:** 5 cm (2 in) long, tubular, crimson, mid-summer – mid-autumn, **Foliage:** long, shiny, deep green, evergreen, **Position:** semi-shade and shelter, **Soil:** well drained yet moist, acid, peaty, **Habit:** thickets of thin stems, **Propagation:** suckers in spring, or cuttings in summer inserted in sandy peat in a heated propagator.
□ One of the most beautiful dwarf evergreen shrubs.

Phlomis fruticosa
Labiatae   Jerusalem sage
ZONES 7–10   SHRUB
Height: 1–1.2 m (3–4 ft), **Flowers:** yellow, early – mid-summer, **Foliage:** grey-green, ovate, evergreen, **Position:** sun, good for coastal planting, **Soil:** light, with good drainage, even rather dry, **Habit:** sturdy and bushy, **Propagation:** cuttings in late summer – early autumn inserted in sandy peat under glass.
□ Creates contrast in herbaceous or shrub border. Cut back straggly stems in autumn.

Phlox amoena
Polemoniaceae   Dwarf phlox
ZONES 5–9   ROCK PLANT
Height: 15–23 cm (6–9 in), **Flowers:** pink to purplish pink, late spring – early summer, **Foliage:** green, small and somewhat leathery, deciduous, **Position:** full sun, **Soil:** suits most well-drained soils, **Habit:** ground covering perennial, **Propagation:** basal cuttings under glass in summer.
□ For rock gardens, paving and raised beds.

Phlox douglasii
Polemoniaceae Alpine phlox
ZONES 5–9   ROCK PLANT
Height: 5–10 cm (2–4 in), **Flowers:** lavender-mauve but variable, profuse, late spring – early summer, **Foliage:** green, small, deciduous, **Position:** sun or partial shade, **Soil:** suits most well-drained but moisture-retentive soils, **Habit:** mat forming perennial, spreading to about 45 cm (1½ ft), **Propagation:** basal cuttings in mid-summer.
□'Snow Queen' is white. For rock gardens, paving and raised beds.

Phlox paniculata
(**syn. P. decussata**)
Polemoniaceae
ZONES 4–9   HERBACEOUS PERENNIAL
Height: 60 cm–1.2 m (2–4 ft), **Flowers:** predominantly red, white, pink, blue, mauve or purple according to cultivar, in crowded panicles, fragrant, summer, **Foliage:** mid green, deciduous, **Position:** sun or semi-shade, **Soil:** moist, yet well-drained, fairly rich, **Habit:** clump-forming perennial with erect flowering stems, **Propagation:** division, or root cuttings in late winter – early spring.
□Cut down in mid-autumn. Good companion plant is the ornamental grass, *Phalaris arundinacea* 'Picta'.

Photinia × fraseri 'Red Robin'
Rosaceae
ZONES 8–10   SHRUB
Height: 3–4 m (10–13 ft), **Flowers:** white, produced in mild areas only, spring, **Foliage:** deep green, shiny and leathery, vivid red young growths, evergreen, **Position:** sun or partial shade, **Soil:** light, rich, well-drained, including moderate lime, **Habit:** rounded bush, **Propagation:** cuttings of nearly-ripe side shoots inserted in a heated propagator.
□A good alternative to the red-leaved pieris if you do not have acid soil.

Photinia glabra 'Variegata'
Rosaceae
ZONES 8–10   SHRUB
Height: 1.8–2.5 m (6–8 ft), **Flowers:** white, produced in mild areas only, spring, **Foliage:** pink young growth, turns green with white edges, evergreen, **Position:** sun or partial shade, sheltered, **Soil:** light, rich, well-drained, preferably lime-free, **Habit:** rounded bush, **Propagation:** cutting of nearly ripe side shoots inserted in a heated propagator.
□Spectacular in the shrub border.

Phygelius capensis
Scrophulariaceae Cape fuchsia
ZONES 8–10   SHRUB
Height: 60 cm–1 m (2–3 ft) or up to 1.8 m (6 ft) against a wall, **Flowers:** red, narrowly tubular, mid-summer – mid-autumn, **Foliage:** medium to deep green, evergreen, **Position:** sunny and sheltered, even rather dry, against a wall, **Soil:** suits most soils, drainage must be good, **Habit:** erect, **Propagation:** easily increased by cuttings taken in late summer, or by division in early – mid-spring.
□Can be cut down by frosts.
  Suitable only for very mild areas. Best planted against a warm sunny wall. Cut back dead growth in spring.

Physostegia virginiana 'Vivid'
Labiatae Obedient plant
ZONES 6–9   HERBACEOUS PERENNIAL
Height: 60 cm–1 m (2–3 ft), **Flowers:** rose-pink, tubular in upright spikes, summer, **Foliage:** medium-green, lanceolate, deciduous, **Position:** sun or partial shade, **Soil:** suits most soils, **Habit:** clump-forming perennial, **Propagation:** division of clumps in spring, cuttings of soft shoots in spring under glass.
□Cut to near ground level in late autumn. 'Summer Snow' is white. Flowers excellent for cutting.

Picea abies
(syn. *P. excelsa*)

Pinaceae Common spruce, Christmas tree, Norway spruce

ZONES 4–9   CONIFER

Height: up to 3 m (10 ft) after 10 years growth, eventually reaching 30 m (100 ft), **Flowers:** insignificant, brown cones, pendulous, cylindrical, on mature trees only, **Foliage:** dark green with brown buds in winter, evergreen, **Position:** full sun or semi-shade, **Soil:** deep, moisture-retentive, acid or alkaline, **Habit:** a large conical tree, crown broadening with age, **Propagation:** seeds sown in spring in a garden frame.

☐ Many smaller-growing cultivars to choose from.

Recommended cultivars of *Picea abies*

Heights are estimated after 10 years growth. For rock garden and heather beds.

'*Acrocona*' – bright green foliage on pendulous branches; rust red cones when young; 1.8–2.5 m (6–8 ft); large and spreading bush.

'*Clanbrassiliana*' – mid green with red dormant buds in winter; 30–75 cm (1–2 ft); slow-growing globular bush.

'*Gregoryana*' – greyish-green; 15–20 cm (6–8 in); compact cushion-like plant, wider than tall.

'*Nidiformis*' – deep green, enlivened by light green new growth in early summer; 30–45 cm (1–1½ ft); flat topped.

'*Pumila*' – bright green, 23–30 cm (10–12 in); low, rounded.

Picea glauca var. *albertiana*
'Conica'

Pinaceae Alberta white spruce

ZONES 4–9   CONIFER

Height: up to 1 m (3 ft) after 10 years, eventually reaching 2 m (6½ ft), **Flowers and cones:** insignificant, **Foliage:** bright green, evergreen, **Position:** full sun or semi-shade, **Soil:** deep, moisture-retentive, acid, **Habit:** develops a regular cone shape if a single leader is retained when young, **Propagation:** grafting.

☐ Ideal for rock gardens and heather beds.

Picea mariana 'Nana'

Pinaceae Dwarf black spruce

ZONES 2–9   CONIFER

Height: about 10 cm (4 in) after 10 years, eventually reaching 30 cm (1 ft), **Flowers:** insignificant, cones reddish brown, freely borne, **Foliage:** blue-grey, evergreen, **Position:** full sun or semi-shade, **Soil:** moist, acid, **Habit:** forming a rounded shrub with a very tightly packed foliage spreading to 45 cm (1½ ft), **Propagation:** grafting.

☐ Ideal for rock gardens and heather beds.

Picea pungens var. *glauca*

Pinaceae Blue spruce

ZONES 2–9   CONIFER

Height: about 2.5 m (8 ft) after 10 years growth, eventually reaching about 25 m (80 ft), **Flowers:** insignificant, cones brown but only produced when the tree is about 20 years old, **Foliage:** stiff, grey-blue, needle-like, evergreen, **Position:** full sun or semi-shade, **Soil:** deep, moisture-retentive, acid, **Habit:** very varied, but informally conical, leaves held on horizontal, rather rigid branches, **Propagation:** seed, seedlings selected for foliage colour, or by cuttings (see p. 70).

☐ Superb specimen tree for the large lawn.

Recommended cultivars of *Picea pungens* (Colorado spruce) ZONES 2–8.

Heights are estimated after 10 years growth. Propagate by grafting, or cuttings (see p. 70).

Top left: *Picea abies* 'Pumila'
Top right: *Picea pungens* var. *glauca*
Above: *Picea pungens* 'Globosa'

'*Globosa*' – intense bright blue foliage throughout the year; up to 60 cm (2 ft); slow-growing dense rounded bush.

'*Hoopsii*' – very rich blue; brown cones only after 20 years growth; about 2.5 m (8 ft); conical, essential to train from an early age to maintain a vertical leader.

'*Koster*' – (Koster's blue spruce) silver-blue throughout the year; brown cones after 20 years growth; around 2.5 m (8 ft); conical, training is essential from an early age to maintain a vertical leader.

'*Procumbens*' – silver-blue throughout the year; prostrate ground cover, spreading to 3 m (10 ft); variable in form; prune off any unwanted developing vertical leaders.

Pieris floribunda
Ericaceae
ZONES 5–9   SHRUB
Height: 1.2–1.8 m (4–6 ft), **Flowers:** white, in upright trusses, early – mid-spring, **Foliage:** shiny, deep green, lanceolate, evergreen, **Position:** semi-shade, sheltered from cold winds, **Soil:** acid, moist and peaty, **Habit:** large, bushy and rounded, well furnished to the ground, **Propagation:** cuttings of ripening shoots in late summer, placed in sandy peat under glass.
□Beautiful shrub for border or woodland garden, particularly in association with rhododendrons.

Pieris 'Brouwer's Beauty'
Ericaceae
ZONES 5–9   SHRUB
Height: 1.2–1.8 m (4–6 ft), **Flowers:** white, in very long lax racemes, early – mid-spring, **Foliage:** very shiny, deep green, copper-tinged when young, evergreen, **Position:** semi-shade and sheltered, **Soil:** acid, moist and peaty, **Habit:** bushy and rounded, **Propagation:** cuttings of ripening shoots in late summer, placed in sandy peat under glass.
□Suitable for planting against a wall.

Right: *Pieris floribunda*

Pieris 'Forest Flame'
Ericaceae
ZONES 5–9   SHRUB
Height: 3 m (10 ft) or more, **Flowers:** white in pendulous trusses, mid – late spring, **Foliage:** young growth bright red, changing to pink then cream, eventually to green, evergreen, **Position:** semi-shade and shelter, **Soil:** acid, moist and peaty, **Habit:** vigorous, tall and bushy, **Propagation:** cuttings of ripening shoots in late summer, placed in sandy peat under glass.
□Spectacular foliage plant. Remove old flower heads after flowering and trim back any straggly shoots. Mulch with peat.

Pieris forrestii 'Wakehurst'
Ericaceae
ZONES 5–9   SHRUB
Height: 2.5 m (8 ft) or more, **Flowers:** white in abundant trusses, mid – late spring, **Foliage:** young growth brilliant red, held for a long period before turning green, evergreen, **Position:** semi-shade and shelter, **Soil:** acid, moist and peaty, **Habit:** erect and bushy, **Propagation:** cuttings of ripening shoots in late summer, placed in sandy peat under glass.
□Another spectacular foliage shrub combining well with other members of the *Ericaceae* like rhododendrons.

Pieris japonica
Ericaceae
ZONES 5–9   SHRUB
Height: 2–3 m (6–10 ft), **Flowers:** white, sweetly scented in slender pendulous trusses, early – mid-spring, **Foliage:** dark glossy green, paler beneath, bronzy-red when newly emerged, evergreen, **Position:** semi-shade and shelter, **Soil:** acid, moist and peaty, **Habit:** erect and bushy, **Propagation:** cuttings of ripening shoots in mid-summer, placed in sandy peat under glass.
□'Variegata' has foliage variegated with cream, pink when young (ZONES 6–10).

Pileostegia viburnoides
Hydrangeaceae
ZONES 5–9   CLIMBER
Height: up to 6 m (20 ft), **Flowers:** cream, freely produced in large trusses, late summer – mid-autumn, **Foliage:** green, prominently veined, evergreen, **Position:** shade or partial shade, cool, **Soil:** reasonably good, moist, **Habit:** hardy, climbs by its aerial roots, **Propagation:** layer in spring or autumn, take cuttings in mid-summer – early autumn and insert in sandy soil under glass.
☐ Useful for growing up large trees and covering unsightly walls or outbuildings.

Pinus aristata
Pinaceae Bristlecone pine
ZONES 5–9   CONIFER
Height: about 1.8 m (6 ft) after 10 years growth, ultimately reaching 4.5 m (15 ft), **Flowers:** insignificant, **Foliage:** grey green, lying flat long the branches, evergreen, **Position:** open and sunny, **Soil:** well drained, lime-free, **Habit:** informally conical, **Propagation:** seed during spring in seed compost under glass.
☐ Very long lived. Interesting rather than beautiful.

Pinus cembra
Pinaceae Arolla pine
ZONES 4–9   CONIFER
Height: 1–1.8 m (3–6 ft) after 10 years, eventually reaching 15 m (50 ft), **Flowers:** insignificant, green cones turning purplish-brown on old trees, **Foliage:** deep green on the outside and bluish-white inside, evergreen, new growth in spring is very attractive, **Position:** open and sunny, **Soil:** well drained, lime-free, **Habit:** slow growing, dense foliage, columnar, **Propagation:** seed during early spring in seed compost under glass.
☐ Makes a good lawn specimen.

Pinus contorta
Pinaceae Beach pine, shore pine
ZONES 7–10   CONIFER
Height: up to 3 m (10 ft) after 10 years, will reach 6 m (20 ft), **Flowers:** insignificant, cones yellow-brown, usually in pairs, **Foliage:** yellow green, twisted, evergreen, **Position:** open and sunny, excellent for seaside planting, **Soil:** well-drained, lime-free, suitable for stony or sandy soils, **Habit:** fast growing, irregular shaped tree, **Propagation:** seed during early spring in seed compost under glass.
☐ Good for shelter and screening. A useful pine for creating windbreaks.

Pinus densiflora 'Umbraculifera'
Pinaceae Japanese red pine
ZONES 4–9   CONIFER
Height: about 75 cm (2½ ft) after 10 years, ultimately reaching 2.5 m (8 ft), **Flowers and cones:** insignificant, **Foliage:** deep green, dense, evergreen, **Position:** open and sunny, **Soil:** well drained and lime-free, **Habit:** slow growing with umbrella-shaped crown, **Propagation:** by grafting.
☐ An appealing pine suitable for heather gardens.

Pinus leucodermis
(**syn. *P. heldreichii* var. leucodermis**)
Pinaceae Bosnian pine
ZONES 5–9   CONIFER
Height: 2.5–3 m (8–10 ft) after 10 years, eventually 20 m (65 ft), **Flowers:** insignificant, young cones are blue, **Foliage:** very deep green, young shoots more bluey green, evergreen, **Position:** open and sunny, **Soil:** excellent for dry thin soils over chalk, **Habit:** slender, conical, loose branched, **Propagation:** seed during early spring in seed compost under glass.
☐ 'Compact Gem' is a cultivar with a height and spread of only about 1.8 m (6 ft), worth seeking out.

Pinus mugo 'Gnom'
Pinaceae Mountain pine
ZONES 2–9   CONIFER
Height: no more than 75 cm (2½ ft) after 10 years, ultimate height 2 m (6 ft), **Flowers:** insignificant, cones brown, **Foliage:** deep green, evergreen, **Position:** open and sunny, **Soil:** suits most soils, including lime, **Habit:** dwarf, shrubby bush, ultimately about 1.8 m (6 ft) across, **Propagation:** by grafting.
☐ Delightful pine for the rock garden or heather garden. Suitable for seaside gardens.

Left: *Pinus aristata* is a small, long-lived species.

Left: *Pinus pinea*
Top: *Pinus parviflora*
Above: *Pinus pumila*

Pinus mugo var. *pumilio*
Pinaceae Dwarf mountain pine
ZONES 2–9   CONIFER
Height: prostrate and of varied height up to 1.5 m (5 ft), **Flowers:** insignificant, cones small, brown, oval, **Foliage:** deep green with conspicuous winter buds of lighter colour, evergreen, **Position:** sunny and open, **Soil:** suits most soils, including lime, **Habit:** short upright branches on a generally prostrate plant, spreading up to 3 m (10 ft), **Propagation:** by grafting.
□ Good for ground cover. Tolerates maritime conditions.

Pinus nigra
   (**syn.** *P. nigra* var. **austriaca**)
Pinaceae Austrian pine
ZONES 4–9   CONIFER
Height: about 3 m (10 ft) after 10 years, eventually reaching 20 m (65 ft) or so, **Flowers:** insignificant, brown cones carried singly or in clusters, **Foliage:** deep green, young shoots yellowish brown, evergreen, **Position:** open and sunny, excellent for coastal planting, **Soil:** suits most soils, including lime, **Habit:** conical when young, umbrella-headed later, **Propagation:** seed during early spring in seed compost under glass; seedlings differ considerably.
□ Good windbreak or lawn specimen.

Pinus nigra 'Pygmaea'
Pinaceae
ZONES 4–9   CONIFER
Height: about 60 cm (2 ft) after 10 years, eventually 2.5 m (8 ft), **Flowers:** insignificant, cones small and brown, **Foliage:** deep green changing to a fascinating shade of yellow in winter, evergreen, **Position:** open and sunny, good for seaside gardens, **Soil:** suits most soils, lime included, **Habit:** forming a dense round bush, **Propagation:** by grafting.
□ 'Hornibrookiana' has deep green foliage, yellowish brown young shoots and is compact with ascending branches. Useful for heather gardens.

Pinus parviflora
Pinaceae Japanese white pine
ZONES 5–9   CONIFER
Height: 3 m (10 ft) or so after 10 years, eventually reaching some 10 m (33 ft), **Flowers:** insignificant, clusters of greeny blue cones, **Foliage:** pale blue green, silvery inside, evergreen, **Position:** open and sunny, **Soil:** moist but well drained, lime-free, **Habit:** conical in early life but becoming wide-spreading and flat-topped, **Propagation:** seed during early spring in seed compost under glass.
□ 'Glauca' has striking blue foliage, propagated by grafting.

Pinus pinea
Pinaceae Umbrella pine, Italian stone pine
ZONES 8–10   CONIFER
Height: 3 m (10 ft) or so after 10 years, may reach 15 m (50 ft), **Flowers:** insignificant, shiny light-brown cones on stalks, **Foliage:** green, with grey-green young shoots, evergreen, **Position:** open and sunny, excellent for maritime gardens, **Soil:** suits most, including sandy soils, **Habit:** rounded, eventually umbrella-shaped, **Propagation:** seed during early spring in seed compost under glass.
□ Achieves tree proportions in mild areas. Gives a Mediterranean atmosphere to gardens, especially when maturing.

Pinus pumila
Pinaceae Dwarf Siberian pine, Japanese stone pine
ZONES 3–9   CONIFER
Height and spread: very varied, can reach 2.5 m (8 ft), **Flowers:** insignificant, green cones turning purplish-brown on old trees, **Foliage:** pale green, bluish inside, evergreen, **Position:** open and sunny, **Soil:** moist but well drained, and lime-free, **Habit:** dwarf and spreading bush, **Propagation:** seed during early spring in seed compost under glass.
□ Very effective with heathers.

195

Pinus strobus 'Nana'
Pineaceae Weymouth pine
ZONES 3–9 CONIFER
Height: about 60 cm (2 ft) after 10 years, eventually reaching 2.5 m (8 ft), **Flowers:** insignificant, long, pendent cones, **Foliage:** green tinged blue, evergreen, **Position:** open and sunny, **Soil:** moist but well drained and lime-free, **Habit:** slow-growing, usually rather broader than tall, **Propagation:** by grafting.
☐ Excellent pine for the heather garden.

Pinus sylvestris
Pineaceae Scots pine
ZONES 3–9 CONIFER
Height: 4 m (13 ft) or so after 10 years, may reach 35 m (115 ft), **Flowers:** insignificant, light brown cones, **Foliage:** bluish-green needles, grouped in pairs, evergreen, **Position:** open and sunny, **Soil:** any soil, **Habit:** conical in early life, becoming a flat-topped tree, **Propagation:** seed during early spring in seed compost under glass.
☐ Only suitable for large gardens.

Right: *Pinus strobus* 'Nana', the Weymouth pine, is highly recommended for planting in heather gardens.

Pinus sylvestris 'Beuvronensis'
Pinaceae Dwarf Scots pine
ZONES 3–9 CONIFER
Height: about 75 cm (2½ ft) after 10 years, eventually 2 m (6 ft) or so, **Flowers and cones:** insignificant, **Foliage:** blue-green, evergreen, striking brown winter buds, **Position:** sunny and open, **Soil:** suits most humus-rich soils, **Habit:** forms a dwarf, dense, dome-shape shrub, spreading to 1 m (3 ft) or more, **Propagation:** by grafting.
☐ 'Watereri' makes a cone-shaped bush, about 1.8 m (6 ft) high, eventually it assumes a more rounded shape.

Pittosporum tenuifolium
Pittosporaceae
ZONES 7–10 SHRUB
Height: up to 5 m (16 ft), **Flowers:** small, brownish purple, scented, spring, **Foliage:** light green with undulating edges, blackish stems, evergreen, **Position:** sun or partial shade, **Soil:** good drainage, fairly rich, including chalk, **Habit:** dense and bushy, **Propagation:** sow seeds in early spring and germinate under glass; take heeled cuttings of ripening side shoots and insert in a heated propagator.
☐ An excellent hedging plant. Suitable only for mild areas. Trim hedges in spring.

Recommended cultivars of *Pittosporum tenuifolium*
'*Abbotsbury Gold*' – green foliage with central yellow-green variegation; up to 5 m (16 ft) high. (ZONES 7–10).
'*Garnettii*' – foliage variegated with white, flushed pink; up to 5 m (16 ft) high. (ZONES 7–10). Illus. above right.
'*Irene Paterson*' – foliage strikingly mottled white and green; up to 4 m (13 ft) high. (ZONES 8–10). Illus. above left.
'*Purpureum*' – young foliage light green, turning purple with age, 2–4 m (10–13 ft) high. (ZONES 7–10).

Pittosporum tobira
Pittosporaceae
ZONES 8–10   SHRUB
Height: 2.5–4 m (8–13 ft), **Flowers:** pale
yellow, scented, early summer, **Foliage:**
thick, deep green, evergreen, **Position:**
sun and maximum shelter, **Soil:** good
drainage, fairly rich, including chalk,
Habit: stiff and bushy, **Propagation:**
heeled cuttings of ripening side shoots in
mid-summer, inserted in a heated
propagator.
□ Only suited to very mild areas. Best
grown against a warm sunny wall.

Podocarpus nivalis
Podocarpaceae   Alpine totara
ZONES 6–9   CONIFER
Height: about 30 cm (1 ft) after 10 years,
eventually around 1 m (3 ft), **Flowers
and cones:** insignificant, **Foliage:** dark
green, evergreen, **Position:** sun or partial
shade, **Soil:** suits most soils, acid or
alkaline, **Habit:** variable, often spreading,
Propagation: by seed.
□ Excellent groundcover or rock garden
plant.

Polemonium caeruleum
Polemoniaceae   Jacob's ladder, Greek
valerian
ZONES 4–9   HERBACEOUS PERENNIAL
Height: 60 cm (2 ft), **Flowers:** blue, cup
shaped, mid spring – late summer, **Foliage:** rich green, arching, feathery, deciduous, **Position:** full sun or semi-shade,
Soil: any reasonably rich soil, **Habit:**
clumps of arching decorative leaves,
Propagation: seeds sown outdoors when
ripe or in spring; or by division mid
autumn – early spring.

Polygonum affine 'Darjeeling Red'
Polygonaceae   Knotweed
ZONES 4–10
HERBACEOUS PERENNIAL OR ROCK PLANT
Height: 15–23 cm (6–9 in), **Flowers:** red,
on long spikes, summer – autumn but still
decorative when dead, **Foliage:** deep
green, lanceolate, bronzy-red in autumn,
deciduous, **Position:** full sun or semi-
shade, **Soil:** suits most soils, not too rich,
Habit: carpeting, spreads vigorously and
can be invasive, **Propagation:** division in
autumn or spring.
□ Can be used as a ground cover plant
where space permits.

Polygonum baldschuanicum
Polygonaceae   Russian vine, mile-a-
minute vine
ZONES 5–10   CLIMBER
Height: up to 12 m (40 ft), **Flowers:**
white, tinged pink, in large sprays, mid-
summer – mid-autumn, **Foliage:** light
green, ovate or heart shaped, deciduous,
Position: full sun or semi-shade, **Soil:**
any, excellent on chalk, **Habit:** rampant
hardy twining climber, **Propagation:**
semi-ripe heeled cuttings in mid – late
summer, under glass, or hardwood
cuttings rooted outdoors.
□ Clip back hard to keep under control.
Capable of quickly covering a shed, fence
or other unsightly object.

Populus nigra 'Italica'
Salicaceae   Lombardy poplar
ZONES 2–10   TREE
Height: 30 m (100 ft) or more, **Flowers:**
insignificant, **Foliage:** light green, deciduous, **Position:** full sun, **Soil:** most types
including heavy clay, but not shallow
chalk, **Habit:** fastigate with upward
pointing branches, **Propagation:** hardwood cuttings about 30 cm (1 ft) long
inserted in the garden mid-autumn – early
winter; or by lifting suckers.
□ Tolerant of atmospheric pollution and
salt-laden winds. Avoid planting close to
buildings or walls.
    Makes a striking specimen tree in the
large garden, or windbreak.

Top left: *Potentilla arbuscula*
Top right: *Potentilla atrosanguinea* 'Gibson's Scarlet'
Below: *Potentilla fruticosa* 'Goldfinger'

Potentilla arbuscula
Rosaceae Shrubby potentilla
ZONES 6–10   SHRUB
Height: 60 cm (2 ft), spreads up to 1.5 m (5 ft), **Flowers:** yellow, like single roses, **Foliage:** light green, deeply cut, deciduous, **Position:** sunny, **Soil:** light, with good drainage, **Habit:** twiggy and spreading, **Propagation:** heeled cuttings of ripening side shoots, early – mid-autumn inserted under glass.
☐ Prune in mid-spring by cutting out weak growths and shortening others by about two-thirds. All the potentillas are very free flowering and should be in every shrub border.

Potentilla arbuscula 'Beesii'
Rosaceae Shrubby potentilla
ZONES 6–10   SHRUB
Height: 45 cm (1½ ft), **Flowers:** yellow, early summer – early autumn, **Foliage:** greenish silver, deciduous, **Position:** sunny, **Soil:** light with good drainage, **Habit:** compact and bushy, **Propagation:** heeled cuttings of ripening side shoots in early – mid-autumn, inserted under glass.
☐ Prune in mid-spring by cutting out weak growths and shortening others by about two-thirds.

Potentilla atrosanguinea 'Gibson's Scarlet'
Rosaceae Cinquefoil
ZONES 4–10   HERBACEOUS PERENNIAL
Height: 30–45 cm (1–1½ ft), **Flowers:** bright red, single, summer, **Foliage:** attractive greyish-green, deciduous, **Position:** sunny, **Soil:** reasonably fertile, well-drained, **Habit:** semi-prostrate, **Propagation:** division in autumn or spring.
☐ Useful for cutting.

Potentilla davurica 'Abbotswood'
Rosaceae Shrubby potentilla
ZONES 6–10   SHRUB
Height: 60 cm (2 ft), **Flowers:** white, freely produced, and long lasting, early summer – late autumn, **Foliage:** deep green, deciduous, **Position:** sunny, **Soil:** light, good drainage, **Habit:** compact shrub spreading to 1.5 m (5 ft), **Propagation:** heeled cuttings of ripening side shoots in early – mid-autumn, inserted under glass.
☐ Prune in mid-spring, cutting out weak shoots and shortening others by about two-thirds. 'Manchu' is more compact and lower growing.

Potentilla 'Dart's Goldigger'
Rosaceae Shrubby potentilla
ZONES 6–10   SHRUB
Height: 45–60 cm (1½–2 ft), **Flowers:** dark yellow, large, early summer – early autumn, **Foliage:** light grey-green, deciduous, **Position:** sunny, **Soil:** light with very good drainage, **Habit:** dense and compact, **Propagation:** heeled cuttings of ripening side shoots, early – mid-autumn inserted under glass.
☐ Prune in mid-spring, cutting out weak shoots and shortening others by about two-thirds.

Potentilla fruticosa 'Goldfinger'
Rosaceae Shrubby potentilla
ZONES 6–10   SHRUB
Height: 1–1.5 m (3–5 ft), **Flowers:** deep yellow, early summer – early autumn, **Foliage:** medium green, deciduous, **Position:** sunny, **Soil:** light with very good drainage, **Habit:** dense and bushy, **Propagation:** heeled cuttings of ripening side shoots in early – mid-autumn, inserted under glass.
☐ Prune in mid-spring by cutting out weak growths and shortening others by about two-thirds. 'Princess' is pink, 'Red Ace' flame red, 'Royal Flush' deep pink.

Potentilla nitida 'Rubra'
Rosaceae   Rock cinquefoil
ZONES 4–9   ROCK PLANT
Height: 8 cm (3 in), **Flowers:** deep pink, summer, **Foliage:** silvery green, hairy, lobed, **Position:** best in full sun, **Soil:** suits most soils, **Habit:** clumpy, mat-forming alpine, spreading to about 30 cm (1 ft), **Propagation:** division in autumn.
☐ An attractive rock-garden or ground-cover plant.

Potentilla 'Tangerine'
Rosaceae   Shrubby potentilla
ZONES 6–10   SHRUB
Height: 45–60 cm (1½–2 ft), **Flowers:** deep orange, early summer – early autumn, **Foliage:** medium green, divided into five to seven leaflets, deciduous, **Position:** sunny, **Soil:** light with very good drainage, **Habit:** dense bushy shrub, spreading up to 1 m (3 ft), **Propagation:** heeled cuttings of ripening side shoots, early – mid-autumn inserted under glass.
☐ Prune in mid-spring by cutting out weak growth and shortening others by about two-thirds. Looks good when combined with silver-foliage shrubs.

Right: *Potentilla nitida* 'Rubra'

Primula denticulata
Primulaceae   Drumstick primrose
ZONES 3–9   ROCK PLANT
Height: 23–30 cm (9–12 in), **Flowers:** mauve, purple, red or white, in rounded heads, early – late spring, **Foliage:** light green, deciduous, **Position:** ideally dappled shade, **Soil:** moist and peaty, **Habit:** forms a rosette of foliage, **Propagation:** divide after flowering, sow seed when ripe late spring – early autumn.
☐ Excellent and easy primula for shrub borders and woodland garden.

Primula × pruhoniciana 'Wanda' (syn. P. × juliae)
Primulaceae
ZONES 4–9   ROCK PLANT
Height: 15 cm (6 in), **Flowers:** purple-red, late winter – mid-spring, **Foliage:** dark green, deciduous, **Position:** partial shade, **Soil:** permanently moist, but well-drained and acid, **Habit:** forms a flat mat, spreads rapidly, **Propagation:** divide after flowering.
☐ Often used for edging beds and borders.

Prunus 'Accolade'
Rosaceae   Ornamental cherry
ZONES 5–9   TREE
Height: 6–9 m (20–30 ft), **Flowers:** pink, semi-double, abundant, early spring, **Foliage:** medium green, deciduous, **Position:** sunny, **Soil:** well-drained, slightly alkaline, **Habit:** spreading, branched tree, **Propagation:** grafting in early spring, or budding in mid-summer.
☐ Shallow rooted so do not plant too deeply. Stake securely. Good lawn specimen.

Prunus 'Amanogawa'

Rosaceae Japanese flowering cherry
ZONES 5–9   TREE
Height: 4.5–7.5 m (15–25 ft), **Flowers:** pale pink, semi-double, scented, **Foliage:** green, bronze-tinted when young, deciduous, **Position:** sunny, **Soil:** well-drained, preferably slightly alkaline, **Habit:** narrow, fastigiate, flowering from ground level, **Propagation:** grafting in early spring or budding in mid-summer.
☐ Ideal tree for planting in a small garden due to narrow habit.

Prunus cerasifera 'Pissardii' (syn. 'Atropurpurea')

Rosaceae Purple-leaved plum
ZONES 3–9   TREE
Height: 6 m (20 ft), **Flowers:** pink, single, spring, **Foliage:** dark reddish purple, deciduous, **Position:** sun or semi-shade, **Soil:** suits most well-drained soils, **Habit:** round-headed tree with twiggy branches, **Propagation:** grafting in spring or budding in summer.
☐ Very popular as a specimen tree in town gardens.

Prunus × *cistena*

Rosaceae Purple-leaf sand cherry
ZONES 3–9   SHRUB
Height: 1.2–1.5 m (4–5 ft), **Flowers:** white, early – mid-spring, followed by black-purple fruits, **Foliage:** purple-red, deciduous, **Position:** sun or semi-shade, **Soil:** well-drained, preferably slightly alkaline, **Habit:** erect and bushy, ideal for low hedging, **Propagation:** heeled cutting of ripening shoots in mid-summer inserted in sandy peat in a heated propagator.
☐ When grown as a hedge, prune or trim immediately after flowering. Foliage and flowers make a pleasing contrast: excellent as a specimen in the shrub border, planted with shrubby potentillas. Can be grown as a small standard tree.

Prunus glandulosa 'Albiplena'

Rosaceae Chinese bush cherry
ZONES 4–9   SHRUB
Height: 1–1.5 m (3–5 ft), **Flowers:** white, double, mid-spring, **Foliage:** green, deciduous, **Position:** sun or semi-shade, **Soil:** suits most well-drained soils, preferably slightly alkaline, **Habit:** upright and bushy, **Propagation:** heeled cuttings of ripening shoots in mid-summer, inserted in sandy peat in a heated propagator.
☐ Cut back flowered shoots as soon as flowering is over. 'Sinensis' has double pink flowers. Forsythias make good companions.

Prunus laurocerasus 'Otto Luyken'

Rosaceae Cherry laurel
ZONES 6–9   SHRUB
Height: 60 cm–1 m (2–3 ft), **Flowers:** white in erect racemes, mid-spring, followed by red fruits which turn black, **Foliage:** glossy, deep green, narrow, evergreen, **Position:** sun or shade, **Soil:** suits most soils, **Habit:** low and compact, wider than it is high, **Propagation:** cuttings in a heated propagator in summer, or cuttings of riper growth in a garden frame in autumn.
☐ Prune large misshapen plants hard back in early–mid-spring. Excellent ground-cover shrub.

Prunus laurocerasus 'Rotundifolia'

Rosaceae Cherry laurel, common laurel
ZONES 6–9   SHRUB
Height: 4–6 m (13–20 ft) if not trimmed to shape, **Flowers:** white, held erect like candle-sticks, mid-spring, followed by red berries, **Foliage:** large shiny medium green, evergreen, **Position:** sun or shade,

Above: *Prunus* × *cistena*, the purple-leaf sand cherry, can also be grown as a hedge.

Soil: suits most soils, **Habit:** very bushy, **Propagation:** cuttings inserted in a heated propagator in summer, or of riper growth under glass in autumn.
☐ An excellent hedging plant. Overgrown misshapen specimens can be cut back hard in early – mid-spring; trim hedges with secateurs in summer.

Prunus laurocerasus 'Zabeliana'

Rosaceae Cherry laurel
ZONES 5–9   SHRUB
Height: 60 cm–1 m (2–3 ft), **Flowers:** white, abundant, mid-spring, **Foliage:** long, narrow, willow-like, medium green, evergreen, **Position:** sun or shade, **Soil:** suits most soils, **Habit:** low growing with horizontal branches, **Propagation:** cuttings inserted in a heated propagator in summer, or riper wood under glass in autumn.
☐ Trim as necessary with secateurs in summer. An excellent ground-cover shrub, even under trees.

Prunus lusitanica
Rosaceae   Portugal laurel
ZONES 5–9   TREE
Height: 4–6 m (13–20 ft) if unrestricted, **Flowers:** creamy white, fragrant, in long sprays, followed by red berries which turn black, early summer, **Foliage:** shiny, dark green, pointed, held on red stalks, evergreen, **Position:** sun or shade, **Soil:** suits most soils, good for chalky soils, **Habit:** erect and very bushy, **Propagation:** cuttings inserted in a heated propagator in summer, or cuttings of riper wood under glass in autumn.

Below left: *Prunus persica* 'Clara Meyer'
Below right: *Prunus sargentii*

☐ Can be used for hedging. Trim as necessary with secateurs in summer. 'Variegata' has white variegated foliage and is rather less vigorous (ZONES 6–8).

Prunus padus 'Watereri'
Rosaceae   Bird cherry
ZONES 3–9   TREE
Height: 4.5–6 m (15–20 ft), maybe more, **Flowers:** white, single, carried in long tassels, fragrant, late spring, fruits black tinged crimson, **Foliage:** mid green, deciduous, **Position:** sunny, **Soil:** well-

Bottom: *Prunus subhirtella* 'Autumnalis', the winter-flowering cherry

drained, preferably slightly alkaline, **Habit:** rounded head of branches, **Propagation:** grafting in early spring or budding in mid-summer.
☐ A very attractive specimen tree.

Prunus persica 'Clara Meyer'
Rosaceae   Ornamental peach
ZONES 3–9   TREE
Height: 4.5–7.5 m (15–25 ft), **Flowers:** pink, double, early spring, followed by green rather insignificant fruits, **Foliage:** medium green, lanceolate, toothed, deciduous, **Position:** sunny, sheltered in cold areas, **Soil:** well-drained, fertile, preferably slightly alkaline, **Habit:** fast growing, round headed, **Propagation:** grafting in early spring or budding in mid-summer.
☐ An attractive small tree for a lawn.

Prunus pumila depressa
Rosaceae   Sand cherry
ZONES 5–9   SHRUB
Height: prostrate, **Flowers:** white, in profusion, late spring, **Foliage:** green, deciduous, colouring bright red in autumn, **Position:** sun or partial shade, **Soil:** suits most soils, preferably slightly alkaline, **Habit:** spreading shrub much wider than it is high, **Propagation:** heeled cuttings of ripening shoots in mid-summer inserted in sandy peat in a heated propagator.
☐ An unusual ground-cover plant.

Prunus sargentii
Rosaceae   Ornamental cherry
ZONES 5–9   TREE
Height: 6–12 m (20–40 ft), **Flowers:** pink, single, spring, **Foliage:** green, bronze when young, magnificent autumn colour, deciduous, **Position:** sunny, **Soil:** suits most well-drained soils, preferably slightly alkaline, **Habit:** round-headed, **Propagation:** grafting in early spring or budding in mid-summer.
☐ One of the best ornamental cherries for specimen planting in lawns, shrub borders or woodland edge.

Prunus subhirtella 'Autumnalis'
Rosaceae   Winter flowering cherry
ZONES 3–9   TREE
Height: 6–9 m (20–30 ft), **Flowers:** pale pink buds opening white, semi-double, produced on and off throughout late autumn and winter, **Foliage:** mid-green, small, ovate, deciduous, **Position:** sunny, **Soil:** well-drained, preferably slightly alkaline, **Habit:** twiggy, erect branches, **Propagation:** take heeled cuttings of semi-ripe wood.
☐ 'Autumnalis Rosea' is a pale pink form. Best grown against a dark background, with winter-flowering shrubs.

Prunus tenella 'Firehill'
Rosaceae Dwarf Russian almond
ZONES 5–9   SHRUB
Height: 1–1.2 m (3–4 ft), **Flowers:** bright
pinky red, smothering upright stems in
mid-spring, **Foliage:** shiny, green, deciduous, **Position:** sun or partial shade, **Soil:**
suits most soils, preferably slightly
alkaline, **Habit:** upright, long stems,
suckering, **Propagation:** lift and replant
rooted suckers in early autumn.
□ 'Alba' has white flowers. Highly recommended for the small shrub border.

Prunus triloba
Rosaceae
ZONES 5–9   SHRUB
Height: 3–4 m (10–13 ft), **Flowers:** pink,
double, covering the stems, early – mid-
spring, **Foliage:** mid green, deciduous,
Position: sun or partial shade, **Soil:** suits
most soils, preferably slightly alkaline,
Habit: dense, partially upright, **Propagation:** heeled cuttings of ripening shoots
in mid-summer, inserted in sandy peat in a
heated propagator.
□ Prune back old flowered shoots almost
to their bases, immediately after flowering.
Can be grown as a small standard tree.

Right: *Prunus tenella* 'Firehill'

Prunus × *yedoensis*
Rosaceae Yoshino cherry
ZONES 5–9   TREE
Height: 6–7.5 m (20–25 ft), **Flowers:**
white, single, well scented, spring, **Foliage:** mid green, ovate, slender pointed
and toothed, deciduous, **Position:** sunny,
Soil: well-drained, preferably slightly
alkaline, **Habit:** attractive arching habit,
rounded head, **Propagation:** grafting or
budding.
□ A pleasing lawn specimen.

Pseudotsuga menziesii
Pinaceae Douglas fir
ZONES 5–9   CONIFER
Height: up to 6 m (20 ft) after 10 years,
but may eventually reach 30 m (100 ft),
Flowers: insignificant, pendulous brown
cones, **Foliage:** green, aromatic, young
shoots yellowish, evergreen, **Position:**
open, full sun, **Soil:** deep, moist but well
drained, humus-rich, lime-free, **Habit:**
broadly conical in early life, becoming a
flat-topped tree, rapid growth, **Propagation:** by seed.
□ Far too large for all but the largest
gardens as a feature tree.

Pseudotsuga menziesii 'Fletcheri'
Pinaceae
ZONES 5–9   CONIFER
Height: 60 cm (2 ft) or so after 10 years,
ultimately 3.6 m (12 ft), **Flowers:** insignificant, pendulous brown cones, **Foliage:**
bluish green, aromatic, evergreen, **Position:** open, full sun, **Soil:** moist but well
drained, humus-rich and lime-free,
Habit: flat-topped, slow-growing, **Propagation:** by grafting.
□ Ideal for the heather garden.

Punica granatum 'Flore Pleno'
Punicaceae Double pomegranate
ZONES 8–10   SHRUB
Height: 1.8–2.5 m (6–8 ft), **Flowers:**
scarlet, double, early summer – early
autumn, followed by edible orange-red
fruits, **Foliage:** glossy, fairly light green,
deciduous, **Position:** sun, sheltered,
against a south-facing wall, **Soil:** suits
most soils with good drainage, **Habit:**
bushy, slightly tender, **Propagation:**
cuttings of ripening side shoots in a heated
propagator in summer, or of ripe wood in a
garden frame in autumn.
☐ Can form an attractive small tree if
conditions are favourable. But only recommended for mild areas.

Pyracantha atalantioides
Rosaceae Firethorn
ZONES 5–10   SHRUB
Height: 3–4 m (10–13 ft), **Flowers:**
white, in clusters in early summer, red
berries all winter, **Foliage:** dark green,
shiny, evergreen, **Position:** sun or semi-
shade, excellent for north-facing walls,
Soil: suits most well-drained soils, including chalk, **Habit:** bushy, or train against a
wall, suitable for hedging, **Propagation:**
cuttings of side shoots in mid – late summer, in heated propagator.
☐ Trim any unwanted growths from wall-
trained plants late spring – late summer.
Hedges can also be clipped to shape then.
Favoured by birds.

Pyracantha coccinea 'Lalandei'
Rosaceae Firethorn
ZONES 5–10   SHRUB
Height: 3–4 m (10–13 ft), **Flowers:**
white, early summer, followed by reddish
orange berries, **Foliage:** shiny, dark
green, evergreen, **Position:** sun or semi-
shade, **Soil:** suits most well-drained soils,
including chalk, **Habit:** strong upright
grower, **Propagation:** cuttings of side
shoots in mid – late summer, in heated
propagator.
☐ Trim any unwanted growths from wall-
trained plants and trim hedges late spring
– late summer. Excellent shrub for a shady
wall.

Pyracantha 'Orange Glow'
Rosaceae Firethorn
ZONES 5–10   SHRUB
Height: 3–4 m (10–13 ft), **Flowers:**
white, early summer, followed by abundant orange berries which last well into
winter, **Foliage:** glossy, dark green, evergreen, **Position:** sun or semi-shade, **Soil:**
suits most well-drained soils, including
chalk, **Habit:** vigorous and dense, **Propagation:** cuttings of side shoots in summer.
☐ Trim any unwanted growths from wall-
trained specimens and trim hedges late
spring – late summer. Ideal for north-
facing wall.

Pyracantha rogersiana 'Flava'
Rosaceae Firethorn
ZONES 5–10   SHRUB
Height: 3–4 m (10–13 ft), **Flowers:**
white, early summer, followed by yellow
berries, **Foliage:** shiny dark green, evergreen, **Position:** sun or semi-shade, **Soil:**
suits most well-drained soils, including
chalk, **Habit:** vigorous and erect-growing
shrub, **Propagation:** cuttings of side
shoots in summer, heated propagator.
☐ Trim unwanted growths late spring –
late summer. Also good against a wall,
north-facing or otherwise.

Left: *Pyracantha rogersiana* 'Flava'

Pyrus salicifolia 'Pendula'
Rosaceae   Weeping or willow-leaved pear
ZONES 5–9   TREE
Height: 4.5–6 m (15–20 ft), **Flowers:** white, spring, **Foliage:** silvery-grey, narrow and willow-like, deciduous, **Position:** sunny, **Soil:** suits most well-drained soils, **Habit:** small weeping tree, **Propagation:** by layering.
☐Delightful specimen tree for a small garden. Hardy and tolerant of atmospheric pollution.

Quercus coccinea
Fagaceae   Scarlet oak
ZONES 4–10   TREE
Height: 18–24 m (60–80 ft), **Flowers:** insignificant, followed by acorns, **Foliage:** medium green, lobed, magnificent red autumn foliage, deciduous, **Position:** sunny and open, **Soil:** deep, moist and fertile, **Habit:** starts as a narrow tree, then becomes wider, fast growing, **Propagation:** sow seeds (acorns) as soon as ripe in a garden frame.
☐Only for the largest of gardens. Magnificent lawn specimen.

Quercus ilex
Fagaceae   Holm oak, evergreen oak
ZONES 7–10   TREE
Height: 15–18 m (50–60 ft), **Flowers:** greeny yellow, rather insignificant, early summer, followed by acorns, **Foliage:** deep green, greyish-green undersides, thick and tough, evergreen, **Position:** full sun or semi-shade, **Soil:** suits most well-drained soils, **Habit:** large rounded head of branches, ribbed bark, **Propagation:** seed (acorns) sown outdoors.
☐Makes an excellent thick evergreen hedge for seaside gardens. Tolerates atmospheric pollution. Trim hedges in spring.

Raoulia australis
Compositae
ZONES 7–10   ROCK PLANT
Height: 1 cm ($\frac{1}{2}$ in), **Flowers:** yellow, minute and insignificant, mid – late spring, **Foliage:** bright silver, very small, evergreen, **Position:** sunny, **Soil:** any, with good drainage, **Habit:** forms a flat mat, spreading to 30 cm (1 ft) or so, **Propagation:** divide in mid-summer – early autumn.
☐Excellent for rock and sink gardens and for paving.

Raphiolepis × *delacourii*
Rosaceae
ZONES 8–10   SHRUB
Height: 1.5 m (5 ft), **Flowers:** pink, in upright panicles, summer, **Foliage:** shiny green, evergreen, **Position:** warm, sunny and sheltered, **Soil:** well-drained, fertile, **Habit:** slow-growing rounded shrub, slightly tender, **Propagation:** cuttings of firm shoots inserted in a compost of equal parts sand, peat and loam under glass.
☐Best grown against a warm wall in full sun. An unusual shrub but well worth growing. 'Coates Crimson' has deeper flowers.

Rheum palmatum
Polygonaceae   Ornamental rhubarb
ZONES 3–9   HERBACEOUS PERENNIAL
Height: 1.5–1.8 m (5–6 ft), **Flowers:** red, numerous, tiny, held in upright panicles, early summer, **Foliage:** opening purpled-red, grandly ornamental, loses colour after flowering, lobed, deciduous, **Position:** full sun, **Soil:** best in moist, fertile soils, **Habit:** large, herbaceous, **Propagation:** sow seeds in spring outdoors or under glass; divide in autumn or spring.
☐Highly decorative foliage plant. Best used as a lawn specimen but impressive, too, in a shrub border.

RHODODENDRONS

There are hundreds of rhododendron species and hybrids hardy enough to plant almost anywhere and many more suitable for milder districts. Azaleas also belong to this genus, but as most amateur and professional gardeners think of them as a separate group, I have described them under their own name on p. 91.

Rhododendrons vary tremendously in height from small shrubs to giants which grow to 18 m (60 ft) in their natural habitats. Many are sensitive to full sun, so should be planted in dappled shade. Some require protection from cold winds and early frosts, which can damage their young flower buds.

Remember that rhododendrons are shallow rooters and need to be watered copiously in prolonged spells of dry weather. With few exceptions they demand an acid soil and will not thrive where there is even a hint of lime.

Rhododendrons can also be grown in tubs filled with ericaceous compost. To ensure success, be extra careful with feeding and watering. Tapwater in chalk districts is likely to be alkaline so rainwater is to be preferred. Use sequestered iron in these areas and feed with a proprietary compound fertilizer such as Maxicrop-plus Sequestered Iron applied according to the manufacturer's instructions.

Rhododendron hardy hybrids
ZONES 5–9

'*Pink Pearl*' – rose-pink flowers fading with age in late spring and early summer; shiny dark green leaves; forms a round, bushy shrub 2.5–4.5 m (8–15 ft) tall.

'*Purple Splendour*' – dark purple flowers in late spring – early summer; dark green foliage; forms a rounded bushy shrub up to 4.5 m (15 ft).

'*Sappho*' – white flowers with a dark purple blotch, in late spring and early summer; dark green leaves; forms a rounded bush up to 4.5 m (15 ft) high.

'*Temple Belle*' – pale pink bell-shaped flowers which hang down; dark green leaves; forms a rounded bush about 1.5 m (5 ft) high and wide.

'*Unique*' – cream flowers spotted with deep red on insides, spring; dark green leaves; dense bush up to 2.5 m (8 ft) high.

Rhododendron augustinii
Ericaceae

ZONES 5–9   SHRUB

Height: 1.8–3 m (6–10 ft), **Flowers:** in varying shades of mauve and blue; try to obtain a good shade of blue; mid – late spring, **Foliage:** deep green, evergreen, **Position:** partial shade preferable, sheltered, **Soil:** moist but well-drained, light, peaty, lime-free, **Habit:** upright, **Propagation:** layering or cuttings (see p. 71).

Rhododendron cinnabarinum
Ericaceae

ZONES 5–9   SHRUB

Height: 1.8–2.5 m (6–8ft), **Flowers:** orange-red in clusters, late spring – early summer, **Foliage:** hazy blue when young turning greyish-green, evergreen, **Position:** partial shade preferred, sheltered, **Soil:** moist but well drained, light, peaty, lime-free, **Habit:** compact and bushy, **Propagation:** layering or cuttings (p. 71).

☐ Excellent for woodland or shrub border.

Rhododendron falconeri
Ericaceae

ZONES 5–9   SHRUB

Height: can reach 10 m (33 ft) or more, **Flowers:** pale yellow with purple markings, fragrant, mid – late spring, **Foliage:** large, deep veined, deep green above, felted reddish-brown undersides, evergreen, **Position:** best in shady woodland protected from winds, **Soil:** moist, but well-drained, light, peaty, lime-free, **Habit:** large shrub or even small tree, **Propagation:** layering or cuttings (see p. 71).

☐ A truly magnificent rhododendron best suited to mild parts of the country.

Left: *Rhododendron cinnabarinum*
Below: *Rhododendron augustinii*
Bottom: *Rhododendron falconeri*

Top: *Rhododendron sinogrande*
Above: *Rhododendron williamsianum*
Right: *Rhododendron wardii*

Rhododendron rubiginosum
Ericaceae
ZONES 5–9   SHRUB
Height: 1.8–3 m (6–10 ft), spread rather less, **Flowers:** pale pink, abundant, early – late spring, **Foliage:** elliptic, matt green above, reddish scales beneath, evergreen, **Position:** partial shade, **Soil:** moisture-retentive, may even tolerate a little lime, **Habit:** very hardy, erect-growing shrub, **Propagation:** layering or cuttings (see p. 71).
☐ Ideal for small shrub borders.

Rhododendron sinogrande
Ericaceae
ZONES 6–9   SHRUB
Height: 10 m (33 ft), **Flowers:** creamy white to pale yellow, bell-shaped, in enormous trusses, mid – late spring, **Foliage:** largest leaves of all rhododendrons, smooth and green above, grey to creamy buff on the undersides, evergreen, **Position:** partial shade, sheltered, **Soil:** moist, but well-drained, peaty, lime-free, **Habit:** tall shrub with magnificent flowers and foliage, may reach tree-like proportions, **Propagation:** layering or cuttings (see p. 71).
☐ For woodland gardens in mild parts of the country.

Rhododendron wardii
Ericaceae
ZONES 5–9   SHRUB
Height: 2.5–4 m (8–13 ft), **Flowers:** yellow, held in loose trusses, late spring – early summer, **Foliage:** green, varying somewhat in shape, evergreen, **Position:** prefers partial shade, **Soil:** moist but well-drained, peaty, lime-free, **Habit:** rounded, bushy, compact, **Propagation:** layering or cuttings (see p. 71).
☐ Needs sheltered conditions.

Rhododendron williamsianum
Ericaceae
ZONES 5–9   SHRUB
Height: 1.2–1.8 m (4–6 ft), **Flowers:** red buds, opening pale pink, wide bell-shaped, mid – late spring, **Foliage:** bronze when young, turning deep green, bluish undersides, evergreen, **Position:** prefers partial shade, shelter from frosts, **Soil:** moist, but well-drained, peaty, lime-free, **Habit:** forms a rounded dome, **Propagation:** layering or cuttings (see p. 71).
☐ Susceptible to frost damage in the spring.

Rhododendron yakushimanum
Ericaceae
ZONES 5–9   SHRUB
Height: 1.2 m (4 ft), **Flowers:** pink buds, fading to white, bell-shaped, late spring – early summer, **Foliage:** very attractive, deep green above, buff felted on the undersides, evergreen, **Position:** prefers partial shade, **Soil:** moist but well-drained, peaty, lime free, **Habit:** compact, rounded, **Propagation:** layering or cuttings (see p. 71).
☐ This species has been used to produce a number of attractive and hardy hybrids in various colours.

Rhus typhina
Anacardiaceae   Stag's-horn sumach
ZONES 3–9   TREE
Height: 3–4.5 m (10–15 ft), **Flowers:** pale red, individually very small, but arranged densely in upright 'cones' in summer, deep red berries on female plants, **Foliage:** large, pinnate, green, turning brilliant red and orange in early autumn, deciduous, **Position:** full sun, **Soil:** suits most soils, **Habit:** suckering, flat topped small tree, **Propagation:** lift and replant rooted suckers in autumn or late winter; take cuttings of firm shoots, insert in a garden frame in autumn.
☐ Excellent for town and city gardens. Makes a good lawn specimen. Can be pruned hard in late winter each year if a more bushy plant is required.

Ribes sanguineum 'Brocklebankii'
Grossulariaceae   Flowering currant
ZONES 5–10   SHRUB
Height: 1–1.5 m (3–5 ft), **Flowers:** pink, early – late spring, followed by black berries, **Foliage:** deep yellow, deciduous, **Position:** best in partial shade as tends to scorch in full sun, **Soil:** any soil with good drainage, **Habit:** low and shrubby, ultimately rather wider than tall, **Propagation:** hardwood cuttings about 30 cm (1 ft) long inserted in the garden in mid – late autumn.
☐ Prune out old shoots in late spring.

Ribes sanguineum 'King Edward VII'
Grossulariaceae   Flowering currant
ZONES 5–10   SHRUB
Height: 1.5–2.5 m (5–8 ft), **Flowers:** intense crimson in racemes, mid – late spring, followed by black berries in autumn, **Foliage:** green, deciduous, **Position:** sun, partial or full shade, **Soil:** any soil with good drainage, **Habit:** vigorous shrub, ultimately rather wider than tall, **Propagation:** hardwood cuttings in the garden in mid – late autumn.
☐ Prune out old shoots in late spring. Ribes make good companions for forsythia. Suitable for an informal hedge.

Ribes sanguineum 'Pulborough Scarlet'
Grossulariaceae   Flowering currant
ZONES 5–10   SHRUB
Height: 1.8–3 m (6–10 ft), **Flowers:** dark red in racemes, at first drooping, then more upright, mid – late spring, followed by black berries, early – mid autumn, **Foliage:** green, deciduous, **Position:** sun, partial shade or full shade, **Soil:** any soil with good drainage, **Habit:** wide-spreading, **Propagation:** hardwood cuttings about 30 cm (1 ft) long inserted in the garden in mid or late autumn.
☐ Prune out old shoots in late spring.

Ribes speciosum
Grossulariaceae
ZONES 5–10   SHRUB
Height: 1.8–3 m (6–10 ft), **Flowers:** stamens protruding beyond the red narrow petals, held in drooping clusters, midspring – early summer, fruits red and bristly, **Foliage:** glossy green, semi-evergreen, **Position:** grow against a warm south-facing wall, especially in cold districts, **Soil:** any soil with good drainage, **Habit:** tall and bushy, spiny, very showy, **Propagation:** hardwood cuttings about 30 cm (1 ft) long inserted in the garden in mid or late autumn.
☐ This shrub is closer to a gooseberry than a currant.

Robinia pseudoacacia 'Frisia'
Leguminosae   False acacia, black locust
ZONES 3–9   TREE
Height: 9–12 m (30–40 ft), **Flowers:** creamy white, highly fragrant, on mature trees only, early summer, **Foliage:** bright yellow, pinnate with oval leaflets, deciduous, **Position:** full sun, sheltered, tolerant of city conditions, **Soil:** suits most soils with good drainage, **Habit:** suckering, spiny, rather brittle stems, open branched tree, **Propagation:** remove and replant rooted suckers late autumn – early spring, or graft on to the species in spring.
☐ Excellent in association with red foliaged shrubs, and often used as a specimen tree in town and city gardens.

ROSES

Climbing and rambling roses

Contrary to popular belief, roses do not necessarily do better on clay soils; indeed, these are only made acceptable by the addition of plenty of humus. A well-drained, slightly acid loam enriched with plant foods and humus is best. A high lime content is harmful. Since plenty of air is necessary for the production of healthy growth, both above and below ground, it is essential that the soil is well prepared. Double digging is recommended to aerate the topsoil and loosen up the subsoil to improve drainage. Peat or well-rotted compost should be incorporated as digging proceeds.

One rose should never replace another in the same spot unless fresh soil is supplied, otherwise a condition known as rose sickness will affect the new rose.

In spite of the container revolution it is still best to plant roses in the autumn when they are bare-rooted, rather than container-grown subjects, as the soil will still be sufficiently warm to encourage some new root growth before winter sets in. It is also beneficial to spread out the roots and not leave them twisted round as they are likely to be in a container. However, container-grown roses can be planted at any time of the year just so long as there is no disturbance to the root system when planting during the summer months. Choose an open, sunny situation where possible although some climbing roses thrive well enough against north-facing walls.

To get the best results apply a specially formulated rose fertilizer twice a year. Once in spring before the leaves are fully open and again in mid summer at the recommended rate.

Pruning

Newly-planted climbing roses should not be pruned at all as it can cause them to revert to a bush form. However any dead

tips should be cut out and weak shoots shortened or removed. On established plants remove any dead or weak twiggy growth and shorten small lateral branches to about 23–30 cm (9–12 in). It is important to maintain a graceful habit with adequate, but not too abundant growth or too much old wood. Train the new growths horizontally, or even slightly downwards to encourage flowering low down.

Ramblers should be pruned back to between 60 cm–1 m (2–3 ft) when first planted. With the most vigorous ramblers, cut out canes which have produced flowers

Above: *Rosa banksiae* 'Lutea', the yellow Banksian rose

to ground level in the autumn and tie in new stems. Some old wood can be retained in seasons when insufficient young growth is produced or if the plant is less vigorous. In these cases branches should be reduced to about 23–30 cm (9–12 in).

Rosa

Rosaceae Climbing rose
ZONES 5–9 CLIMBER
Height: up to 8 m (26 ft), **Flowers:** white and shades of pink, red, yellow and bi-color, summer through to autumn, often fragrant, **Foliage:** green, matt or glossy, often tinted red when young, deciduous with a few exceptions, **Position:** generally sunny, against a wall, pillar or pergola, **Soil:** well drained but not prone to drying out, rich and preferably slightly acid, **Habit:** climbing, requires training, keep framework open, best fanned out laterally, **Propagation:** budding or cuttings in summer.
□ Many uses in the garden including training against walls and fences, over pergolas, old tree stumps and sheds, up pillars and tripods. Long flowering season and source of cut flowers.

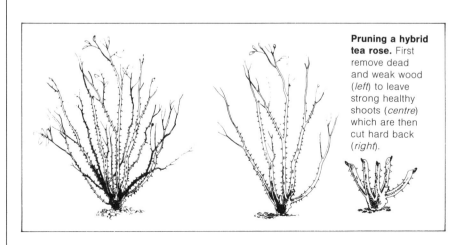

Pruning a hybrid tea rose. First remove dead and weak wood (*left*) to leave strong healthy shoots (*centre*) which are then cut hard back (*right*).

Recommended climbing roses

(A small selection from the vast choice available.) ZONES 7–10.

RED-FLOWERED

'Altissimo' – rich red, single with golden anthers, produced in clusters throughout summer.

'Climbing Ena Harkness' – crimson, double, near perfect in form, gloriously fragrant, produced from early to late summer; flowers droop to look down.

'Climbing Etoile de Hollande' – crimson, double/semi-double, produced throughout summer, sweetly fragrant; suitable for north- or east-facing wall.

'Parkdirektor Riggers' – rich red, semi-double, free-flowering in clusters; recommended for its show rather than its perfume. (ZONE 5).

'Sympathie' – dark red, double, produced in clusters from early summer until autumn; vigorous; disease-resistant; suitable for a north-facing wall.

PINK-FLOWERED

'Aloha' – warm pink, double, large, fragrant; produced throughout summer; attractive foliage.

'Compassion' – warm yellow-based pink, double, very fragrant.

'New Dawn' – pale creamy pink, small, semi-double/double, fragrant, produced in clusters intermittantly throughout summer (strictly speaking a rambler, but treat as a climber).

'Pink Perpétue' – pink with carmine underpetals, double, moderately scented, free flowering, produced in many headed clusters throughout summer.

'Zéphirine Drouhin' – carmine, semi-double, gloriously fragrant, produced in clusters on thornless stems; prone to mildew so routine spraying with a systemic fungicide is advised. This variety is over 100 years old. (ZONE 5).

WHITE-FLOWERED

'Climbing Iceberg' – white, double, abundantly produced in large, many-headed clusters from early summer into autumn; attractive foliage, not too many thorns. (ZONE 5).

'Swan Lake' – white, double, near-perfect in shape, throughout summer; not readily damaged by wet weather; prone to black spot and mildew so routine spraying with a systemic fungicide is advised.

'White Cockade' – white, well-formed, delicately fragrant, produced throughout the summer; glossy, mid green foliage; lower growing than most climbers so unsuitable for planting against high walls.

Below left: Rose 'Climbing Etoile de Hollande'. **Below right:** The climber 'Golden Showers'. **Bottom left:** 'Aloha', fragrant climber. **Bottom right:** 'Climbing Iceberg'.

YELLOW-FLOWERED

'Climbing Lady Hillingdon' – apricot-yellow, double, richly scented, produced throughout the summer; needs protection from the worst winter weather. (ZONE 7).

'Golden Showers' – bright golden yellow, double, moderately fragrant, produced from early summer until well into autumn; good for north- or east-facing walls.

'Maigold' – apricot-yellow, large, double, very fragrant, produced from late spring through to mid summer; attractive foliage, very prickly stems; suitable for north- or east-facing walls.

'Mermaid' – sulphur yellow, large single with a central boss of golden stamens; produced throughout summer; slow to get going, eventually covering a large area; purchase container-grown specimens as root disturbance will not be tolerated.

'Schoolgirl' – orange-apricot, large double, well shaped, very fragrant, produced throughout summer.

Recommended rambling roses

ZONES 7–10.

'Albéric Barbier' – yellow buds open to creamy white, double, fragrant, produced from early to mid summer; shiny dark green foliage, almost evergreen; a good pillar rose able to withstand adverse weather conditions without damage.

'Albertine' – salmon-red buds open pink, free-flowering, fragrant, produced in abundance in early summer and sometimes rather less so again in early autumn.

'Crimson Shower' – deep red flowers turn dull purple with age, double, fragrant, prolific flowerer; excellent pillar rose.

'Emily Gray' – fawny yellow, semi-double, well scented; glossy dark green foliage, red when young, is almost evergreen.

Below: Rambling rose 'Albertine'

Above: *Rosa centifolia.* **Above centre:** *Rosa filipes* 'Kiftsgate'. **Above right:** *Rosa foetida* 'Bicolor'. **Below right:** *Rosa gallica* var. *officinalis.* **Below far right:** *Rosa moyesii* 'Geranium'

Rosa banksiae 'Lutea'
Rosaceae   Yellow Banksian rose
ZONES 5–9   CLIMBER
Height: 6 m (20 ft) or more, **Flowers:** double yellow, lightly scented, late spring – early summer, does not flower when young, **Foliage:** glossy, fresh green, three to five leaflets, semi-evergreen, **Position:** full sun against a warm wall, **Soil:** well-drained, humus-rich and fertile, **Habit:** tall climbing shrub with slender stems, **Propagation:** cuttings.
☐ A lovely companion for early-flowering clematis.

Rosa centifolia
Rosaceae   Cabbage rose, Provence rose
ZONES 5–9   SHRUB
Height: 1.5 m (5 ft), **Flowers:** pink, large and double, highly scented, early – midsummer, **Foliage:** green, five to seven oval leaflets, deciduous, **Position:** full sun, **Soil:** well-drained, humus-rich and fertile, **Habit:** very thorny shrub rose of open habit, **Propagation:** cuttings.
☐ Charming rose for the shrub border and cottage gardens.

Rosa chinensis 'Mutabilis'
Rosaceae   China rose
ZONES 5–9   SHRUB
Height: 1.2–1.8 m (4–6 ft), **Flowers:** orange buds open fawn-yellow turning coppery pink, eventually deep red, very fragrant, summer, **Foliage:** copper coloured when young, turning green, deciduous, **Position:** sun, **Soil:** well-drained, humus-rich and fertile, **Habit:** slender stemmed shrub, **Propagation:** cuttings.
☐ For the shrub border or cottage garden.

Rosa filipes 'Kiftsgate'
Rosaceae
ZONES 5–9   CLIMBER
Height: 6 m (20 ft) or more, **Flowers:** white, single, fragrant, borne in large trusses, early – mid-summer, followed by decorative round red hips, **Foliage:** copper colour when young turning light green, deciduous, **Position:** sun, **Soil:** well-drained humus-rich and fertile, **Habit:** very strong-growing and rambling, **Propagation:** cuttings.
☐ Vigorous rose for training up a large mature tree; needs plenty of space.

Rosa foetida 'Bicolor'
Rosaceae   Austrian copper briar
ZONES 5–9   SHRUB
Height: 1–1.5 m (3–5 ft) or more, **Flowers:** startling copper-red with yellow reverse, single, early – mid-summer, **Foliage:** bright green, deciduous, **Position:** full sun, **Soil:** good, rich, well-drained, **Habit:** erect growing shrub with very prickly stems, **Propagation:** cuttings.
☐ Well worth growing in the shrub border.

Rosa gallica var. officinalis
Rosaceae   Apothecary's rose, red rose of Lancaster
ZONES 5–9   SHRUB
Height: 1–1.2 m (3–4 ft), **Flowers:** crimson, semi-double, well scented, early – mid-summer, followed by red hips, **Foliage:** green, formed of three to seven leaflets, deciduous, **Position:** full sun, **Soil:** well-drained, humus-rich and fertile, **Habit:** upright, very prickly, **Propagation:** cuttings or by removing and replanting suckers.
☐ Ideal choice for cottage gardens.

Rosa gallica 'Versicolor'
Rosaceae   Rosa Mundi
ZONES 5–9   SHRUB
Height: 1–1.2 m (3–4 ft), **Flowers:** red, marked white, semi-double, well scented, early – mid-summer, red hips, **Foliage:** green, formed of several leaflets, deciduous, **Position:** full sun, **Soil:** well-drained, humus-rich and fertile, **Habit:** suckering, upright habit, **Propagation:** cuttings or by removing and replanting suckers.
☐ Can be grown as a hedge.

Rosa moyesii 'Geranium'
Rosaceae
ZONES 5–9   SHRUB
Height: 1.8–2.5 m (6–8 ft), **Flowers:** deep red, single, early – mid-summer, large bright-red hips, **Foliage:** green, numerous leaflets, deciduous, **Position:** sun, **Soil:** well-drained, humus-rich, fertile, **Habit:** fairly compact shrub with upright branches, **Propagation:** cuttings.
☐ As impressive in fruit as in flower.
   Marvellous for grouping with autumn-colouring shrubs.

Rosa omeiensis var. pteracantha
Rosaceae
ZONES 5–9   SHRUB
Height: 2–4 m (7–13 ft), **Flowers:** white, single, late spring – early summer, red and yellow hips, **Foliage:** green, numerous leaflets, deciduous, **Position:** sun, **Soil:** well-drained, humus-rich, fertile, **Habit:** forms a dense shrub, **Propagation:** cuttings.
☐ The showy crimson thorns are the main attraction. These are best on the young basal shoots, so it pays to prune out old wood annually or every second year to encourage new growth.

Rosa rubrifolia
Rosaceae
ZONES 5–9   SHRUB
Height: 2.5 m (8 ft), **Flowers:** purplish pink, single, in small clusters, early summer, round red hips, **Foliage:** purple grey, deciduous, **Position:** sun, **Soil:** suits most well drained, fertile soils, **Habit:** upright shrub with purplish stems, fairly wide spreading to 1.5 m (5 ft), **Propagation:** budding or cuttings.
☐ A good companion for purple-leaved shrubs.

Rosa rugosa 'Blanc Double de Coubert'
Rosaceae   Ramanas rose
ZONES 5–9   SHRUB
Height: 1.5–2 m (5–7 ft), **Flowers:** pink tinged buds opening white, semi-double, scented, summer, followed by large scarlet hips, **Foliage:** green, deciduous, **Position:** sun, **Soil:** well-drained, humus-rich, fertile, **Habit:** strong-growing shrub with stout, extremely prickly and bristly stems, **Propagation:** cuttings.
☐ Good hedging plant. Or impressive in the shrub border. Suitable for seaside gardens.

Rosa rugosa 'Frau Dagmar Hastrup'
Rosaceae   Ramanas rose
ZONES 5–9   SHRUB
Height: up to 1.8 m (6 ft), **Flowers:** light pink, single, early summer – early autumn, large deep red hips, **Foliage:** deep green, deciduous, **Position:** sun, **soil:** well-drained, humus-rich, fertile, **Habit:** strong-growing shrub with stout, extremely prickly and bristly stems, **Propagation:** cuttings.
☐ Excellent for hedging. Suitable for seaside gardens.

Rosa rugosa 'Roseraie de L'Hay'
Rosaceae   Ramanas rose
ZONES 5–9   SHRUB
Height: 1.5–2 m (5–7 ft), **Flowers:** pointed buds open to display purplish red flowers, double, early summer – early autumn, large red hips, **Foliage:** dark green, deciduous, **Position:** sun, **Soil:** well-drained, humus-rich, fertile, **Habit:** very strong grower, **Propagation:** cuttings.
☐ Makes an excellent hedge. Suitable for seaside gardens.

Top left: *Rosa omeiensis* var. *pteracantha*
Top right: *Rosa rugosa* 'Frau Dagmar Hastrup'
Left: *Rosa gallica* 'Versicolor'

Rosmarinus lavandulaceus
Labiatae

ZONES 7–10   SHRUB

Height: 15 cm (6 in), **Flowers:** blue, late spring – early summer, **Foliage:** linear, green above and white beneath, aromatic, evergreen, **Position:** sun, **Soil:** suits most well-drained soils, **Habit:** low-growing, forming dense prostrate carpets, spreading 1–2 m (3–6 ft), **Propagation:** cuttings of ripening shoots in mid- or late summer inserted in a garden frame.

☐ Useful for ground cover, planting on walls and banks. Suited only to mild areas.

Rosmarinus officinalis
Labiatae Rosemary

ZONES 7–10   SHRUB

Height: 1–1.8 m (3–6 ft), **Flowers:** light blue, late spring – early summer, **Foliage:** linear, green, whitish underneath, aromatic, evergreen, **Position:** sun, sheltered from cold winds, **Soil:** suits most well-drained soils, **Habit:** upright and bushy, **Propagation:** cuttings of ripening shoots in mid- or late summer and inserted in a garden frame, or cuttings of mature shoots in early autumn outdoors.

☐ Makes an attractive low hedge, tolerates clipping and seaside conditions.

Rosmarinus officinalis
'Fastigiatus'

Labiatae Rosemary Miss Jessup's variety

ZONES 7–10   SHRUB

Height: 1–1.5 m (3–5 ft), **Flowers:** violet-blue, late spring – early summer, **Foliage:** as for *R. officinalis*, **Position:** sun, **Soil:** suits most well-drained soils, **Habit:** upright, strong growing, **Propagation:** as for *R. officinalis*.

☐ Makes an attractive low hedge and tolerates clipping. In early spring prune out dead growth and untidy shoots. Suitable for seaside conditions.

Rubus tridel
Rosaceae

ZONES 5–10   SHRUB

Height: up to 3 m (10 ft), **Flowers:** white, single, late spring, **Foliage:** light green, deciduous, **Position:** full sun or semi-shade, **Soil:** suits most well-drained soils, **Habit:** strong growing, upright shrub with peeling spineless stems, **Propagation:** division mid-autumn – early spring, or ripening cuttings in late summer or early autumn inserted in peat and sand in a garden frame.

☐ A lovely subject for the shrub border. Cut out old flowered stems after flowering.

Rudbeckia fulgida 'Deamii'
Compositae Coneflower

ZONES 3–9   HERBACEOUS PERENNIAL

Height: 60 cm (2 ft), **Flowers:** yellow, with dark brown, almost black centres, mid-summer – early autumn, **Foliage:** medium green, deciduous, **Position:** sun or partial shade, **Soil:** suits most fertile soils, **Habit:** clump-forming, **Propagation:** division of clumps in autumn or spring.

☐ Cut to near ground level in late autumn. Good for cutting, lasts well in water.

Ruta graveolens
Rutaceae Rue

ZONES 8–10   SHRUB

Height: 60 cm–1 m (2–3 ft), **Flowers:** bright-yellow, early to late summer, **Foliage:** ferny, greeny blue, unpleasantly aromatic, evergreen, **Position:** full sun, **Soil:** suits most well-drained soils, **Habit:** bushy, rounded sub-shrub, **Propagation:** seed sown in early – mid-spring under glass, or cuttings of side shoots in late summer under glass.

☐ 'Jackman's Blue' is smaller and of better foliage colour. Makes a good companion for roses.

Salix alba 'Chermesina' (syn. 'Britzensis')

Salicaceae Scarlet willow

ZONES 2–10   TREE

Height: 3–4.5 m (10–15 ft) if cut back regularly, up to 24 m (80 ft) if left unpruned, **Flowers:** greenish catkins, late spring, **Foliage:** greyish green, lanceolate, deciduous, **Position:** sun or partial shade, **Soil:** moist, or even wet, **Habit:** an upright wind-resistant tree if left unpruned, a shrubby thicket if cut almost down to ground regularly, **Propagation:** hardwood cuttings outdoors in autumn.

□ Prune hard every, or every other, spring to encourage the bright orange-scarlet young shoots. Ideal for waterside planting.

Salix caprea 'Pendula'

Salicaceae Kilmarnock willow

ZONES 4–9   TREE

Height: rarely more than 2.5 m (8 ft), **Flowers:** yellow (male) or silver catkins (female) borne on separate plants, early spring, **Foliage:** medium green, oval, deciduous, **Position:** sunny, **Soil:** preferably moist, thrives on chalk soils, **Habit:** small tree with weeping branches, **Propagation:** grafting in spring on the species *S. caprea.*

□ Excellent specimen for lawns, including small gardens.

Salix × chrysocoma (syn. *S. alba* 'Vitellina Pendula', *S. alba* 'Tristis')

Salicaceae Golden weeping willow

ZONES 2–10   TREE

Height: 6–9 m (20–30 ft), **Flowers:** yellow catkins, spring, **Foliage:** light green, lanceolate, deciduous, **Position:** sun or partial shade, **Soil:** any type of moist or wet soil, **Habit:** strong growing weeping tree with yellow shoots, **Propagation:** cuttings of young stems in summer under glass, or hardwood cuttings in autumn outdoors, or layer in autumn.

□ Excellent lawn specimen for large gardens only. Keep well away from buildings.

Salix 'Fuiji-Koriangi'

Salicaceae Dwarf Japanese willow

ZONES 4–9   SHRUB

Height: 60 cm–1 m (2–3 ft), **Flowers:** silver-grey catkins, spring, **Foliage:** shrimp pink when young, turning white then green, deciduous, **Position:** sun or partial shade, **Soil:** suits most moist soils, **Habit:** compact and bushy, **Propagation:** hardwood cuttings mid-autumn and early spring, inserted in a moist spot in the garden.

Salix hastata 'Wehrhahnii'

Salicaceae

ZONES 4–9   SHRUB

Height: 1.2–1.8 m (4–6 ft), **Flowers:** silvery catkins which become yellow, early–mid-spring, **Foliage:** green above, greyish-green undersides, deciduous, **Position:** sun or partial shade, **Soil:** suits most moist soils, **Habit:** slow-growing, spreading shrub, **Propagation:** hardwood cuttings mid-autumn–early spring outdoors.

□ Useful tall ground cover, especially for large areas that need covering.

Left: *Salix hastata* 'Wehrhahnii', useful for covering large areas of ground.

Salix lanata
Salicaceae Woolly willow
ZONES 5–9   SHRUB
Height: 60 cm–1.2 m (2–4 ft), **Flowers:** yellowish male catkins early – mid-spring, **Foliage:** roundish, grey and woolly, deciduous, **Position:** sun, **Soil:** suits most moist soils, **Habit:** low, slow-growing shrub, **Propagation:** hardwood cuttings mid-autumn – early spring outdoors.
☐Can be used on rock gardens or as ground cover on banks.

Salix matsudana 'Tortuosa'
Salicaceae Corkscrew willow
ZONES 4–9   SHRUB
Height: 4–6 m (13–20 ft), **Flowers:** greenish catkins, spring, **Foliage:** narrow, greyish undersides, deciduous, **Position:** sun or partial shade, **Soil:** suits most moist soils, **Habit:** upright, slow grower, twisted stems and shoots, **Propagation:** hardwood cuttings mid-autumn – early spring outdoors.
☐Unusual lawn specimen; shoots often used by flower arrangers.

Right: *Salix lanata*, the woolly willow, makes good ground cover on banks.

Salix moupinensis
Salicaceae
ZONES 5–9   SHRUB
Height: 1.8–2.5 m (6–8 ft), **Flowers:** 15 cm (6 in) long yellow female catkins, spring, **Foliage:** shiny bright green 15 cm (6 in) long, borne on red brown stems, deciduous, **Position:** sun or partial shade, **Soil:** suits most moist soils, **Habit:** rather open shrub with stout shoots, can form a small tree, **Propagation:** hardwood cuttings mid-autumn – early spring, outdoors.
☐Extremely ornamental throughout the year.

Salix sachalinensis 'Sekka'
Salicaceae Japanese fan-tail willow
ZONES 4–9   SHRUB
Height: 4–6 m (13–20 ft), **Flowers:** large, showy male catkins, yellow, spring, **Foliage:** glossy green, lanceolate, deciduous, **Position:** sun or partial shade, **Soil:** suits most moist soils, **Habit:** wide-spreading and vigorous shrub, **Propagation:** hardwood cuttings mid-autumn – early spring, outdoors.
☐Interesting flattened (fasciated) stems are encouraged by the severe pruning necessary to keep this shrub in trim. Useful for flower arrangements.

Sambucus nigra 'Pulverulenta'
Caprifoliaceae Common elder
ZONES 5–9   SHRUB
Height: over 4 m (13 ft), **Flowers:** cream, scented, early summer, glossy black berries, **Foliage:** dramatically marked white and green, deciduous, **Position:** full sun or semi-shade, **Soil:** most fairly rich soils, **Habit:** tall upright and vigorous shrub, **Propagation:** hardwood cuttings in mid – late autumn outdoors.
☐Contrasts beautifully with purple-leaved shrubs. Can be pruned hard back in late winter for more striking foliage.

Sambucus racemosa 'Plumosa Aurea'

Caprifoliaceae

ZONES 5–9   SHRUB

Height: 2.5–3 m (8–10 ft), **Flowers:** yellow in pyramidal terminal panicles, mid – late spring, sometimes followed by red fruits ripening in early – mid-summer, **Foliage:** golden yellow, compound leaves composed of five leaflets, deciduous, **Position:** full sun or semi-shade, colouring earlier in sun but retaining it for longer in cool moist shade, **Soil:** most fairly rich moist soils, **Habit:** slow-growing, upright and bushy, as wide as it is tall, **Propagation:** hardwood cuttings in mid – late autumn, outdoors.

□ 'Sutherland' has golden foliage which is more resistant to bright sunlight.

Santolina chamaecyparissus (syn. *S. incana*)

Compositae   Cotton lavender

ZONES 6–10   SHRUB

Height: 45–60 cm (1½–2 ft), **Flowers:** yellow, mid-summer, **Foliage:** silver, woolly, feathery, on white stems, aromatic, evergreen, **Position:** full sun, **Soil:** suits most soils with good drainage, **Habit:** forming a thick mound if clipped back every year after flowering, **Propagation:** cuttings of ripening side shoots mid-summer – early autumn under glass.

□ Looks good planted with bush roses or purple-leaved shrubs.

Below: *Sarcococca hookerana* var. *digyna*

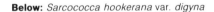

Sarcococca confusa

Buxaceae   Christmas box

ZONES 5–9   SHRUB

Height: 1–1.2 m (3–4 ft), **Flowers:** white, sweetly fragrant, mid-winter – early spring, followed by black berries, **Foliage:** shiny, dark green, evergreen, **Position:** partial or full shade, **Soil:** moist, humus-rich, ideally alkaline, **Habit:** dense and spreading shrub, **Propagation:** cuttings of firm young growth inserted in a heated propagator in mid – late summer, or by riper cuttings in autumn and put in a garden frame.

□ Excellent shrub for the woodland garden or shrub border.

Sarcococca hookerana var. *digyna*

Buxaceae   Christmas box

ZONES 5–9   SHRUB

Height: 1–1.2 m (3–4 ft), **Flowers:** white, scented, mid-winter – early spring, followed by black berries, **Foliage:** shiny, dark green, long and narrow, evergreen, **Position:** partial or full shade, **Soil:** moist, humus-rich, ideally alkaline, **Habit:** slender and erect growing, **Propagation:** cuttings of firm young growth inserted in a heated propagator in mid – late summer, or by riper cuttings in autumn in a garden frame.

□ Excellent shrub for woodland garden or shrub border, valued for its scented flowers.

Sarcococca humilis

Buxaceae   Christmas box

ZONES 5–9   SHRUB

Height: 30–60 cm (1–2 ft), **Flowers:** white, scented, mid-winter – early spring, black berries, **Foliage:** glossy green above, paler beneath, evergreen, **Position:** partial or full shade, **Soil:** moist, humus-rich, preferably alkaline, **Habit:** suckers freely, very dense growth, **Propagation:** cuttings of firm young growth, inserted in a heated propagator in mid – late summer, or by riper cuttings in autumn in a frame.

□ Excellent ground-cover shrub for woodland or shrub border.

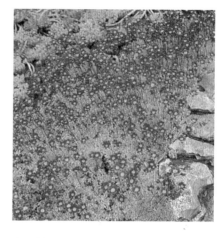

Saxifraga 'Elizabethae' (Kabschia section)

Saxifragaceae
ZONES 5–9   ROCK PLANT
Height: 8 cm (3 in), **Flowers:** light yellow, single, early – mid-spring, **Foliage:** matt green, narrow pointed, evergreen, **Position:** partial shade, protect from hot sun, **Soil:** moist but well drained, **Habit:** forms a low green cushion, spreading 30 cm (1 ft), **Propagation:** divide after flowering, or detach young rosettes in late spring – early summer, rooting them under glass.
☐ Good for planting in crevices.

Saxifraga fortunei (Diptera section)

Saxifragaceae
ZONES 5–9   HERBACEOUS PERENNIAL
Height: 30–36 cm (12–15 in), **Flowers:** white, star-like, mid – late autumn, **Foliage:** dark green with red undersides, round, evergreen, **Position:** partial shade, cool, **Soil:** suits most reasonably humus-rich soils, **Habit:** forms clumps of leaves from which the branching flower-stems arise, **Propagation:** division or offsets in spring.
☐ Ideal for a peat garden or woodland edge.

Saxifraga moschata 'Atropurpurea' (Dactyloides (mossy) section)

Saxifragaceae
ZONES 5–9   ROCK PLANT
Height: 5–8 cm (2–3 in), **Flowers:** dark pink, saucer-like, mid – late spring, **Foliage:** vivid green, evergreen, **Position:** partial shade, **Soil:** suits most reasonably humus-rich soils, **Habit:** forms a soft dense mat, spreading to 30–45 cm (12–18 in), **Propagation:** division or offsets in spring.
☐ Plant on cool side of rock garden.

Saxifraga umbrosa var. *primuloides* (Robertsonia section)

Saxifragaceae Dwarf form of London pride
ZONES 5–9   ROCK PLANT
Height: 10–15 cm (4–6 in), **Flowers:** clouds of tiny pink starry flowers, late spring – early summer, **Foliage:** medium green, rather succulent, in rosettes, evergreen, **Position:** partial or full shade, **Soil:** suits most reasonably humus-rich soils, **Habit:** spreads by new rosettes, **Propagation:** division or by offsets.
☐ For shady side of rock garden.

Scabiosa caucasica

Dipsacaceae Scabious, Pincushion flower
ZONES 4–9   HERBACEOUS PERENNIAL
Height: 45–60 cm (1½–2 ft), **Flowers:** mauvy-blue, summer – early autumn, **Foliage:** green, lanceolate, deeply cut, deciduous, **Position:** full sun, **Soil:** ideally chalky, well drained, fairly rich, **Habit:** clump-forming hardy perennial, **Propagation:** division in spring; seed sown in a garden frame in spring; or cuttings of basal shoots under glass in spring.
☐ Cut down to the ground in late autumn. Excellent cut flower.

Sedum cauticola

Crassulaceae Stonecrop
ZONES 3–9   ROCK PLANT
Height: 10–15 cm (4–6 in), **Flowers:** rose-crimson in flattish panicles, late summer – early autumn, **Foliage:** greyish-green, deciduous, **Position:** plenty of sun, **Soil:** suits most soils with good drainage, **Habit:** low spreading habit to 30 cm (1 ft) or more, **Propagation:** sow seed in seed compost in early – mid-spring under glass, or divide in mid-autumn – early spring.
☐ For rock gardens and gaps in paving. Suitable, too, for hot dry banks and seaside gardens.

Sedum spathulifolium 'Cappa Blanca'

Crassulaceae Stonecrop
ZONES 3–9   ROCK PLANT
Height: 5–10 cm (2–4 in), **Flowers:** yellow, on red stems, late summer – mid-autumn, **Foliage:** whitish grey, succulent, in rosettes, evergreen, **Position:** plenty of sun, **Soil:** suits most soils with good drainage, **Habit:** forms low mounds, **Propagation:** division or offsets mid-autumn – early spring.
☐ Ground cover and suitable for planting in crevices. 'Purpureum' is similar but with purplish rosettes. Seaside gardens.

Sedum spectabile

Crassulaceae Stonecrop
ZONES 3–10   HERBACEOUS PERENNIAL
Height: 30–45 cm (1–1½ ft), **Flowers:** small, pink, arranged in wide flat heads, summer – mid-autumn, **Foliage:** grey-green, succulent, partially evergreen, **Position:** plenty of sun, **Soil:** well-drained, suitable for hot, dry chalk soils, **Habit:** somewhat rigid and formal, unbranched hardy perennial, **Propagation:** divide in mid-autumn – early spring.
☐ Valuable late-flowerer for front of a border, attracts bees and butterflies. Grow it with shrubs noted for autumn colour.

Sedum spurium 'Schorbusser Blut'

Crassulaceae Stonecrop
ZONES 6–10   ROCK PLANT
Height: 10 cm (4 in), **Flowers:** small dark red arranged in flat heads, mid-summer – early autumn, **Foliage:** medium green on red stalks, evergreen, **Position:** plenty of sun, **Soil:** suits most soils if drainage is good, **Habit:** mat-forming, rather invasive, spreads to 30 cm (1 ft) or more, **Propagation:** division mid autumn – early spring.
☐ Attracts bees and butterflies. Grows well by the sea.

Sempervivum arachnoideum

Crassulaceae Cobweb houseleek
ZONES 3–9   ROCK PLANT
Height: 2–5 cm (1–2 in), **Flowers:** dark rose-pink held on 15 cm (6 in) stems, early – mid-summer, **Foliage:** green, often red-tinted, webbed with grey hairs, evergreen, **Position:** plenty of sun, **Soil:** suits most soils if drainage is good, **Habit:** rosette-forming evergreen succulent, **Propagation:** offsets, or sow seeds under glass in spring.
☐ Suitable for seaside gardens, planting on walls, in crevices, containers and, traditionally, on roofs where they bring good luck.

Sempervivum montanum

Crassulaceae Houseleek
ZONES 5–9   ROCK PLANT
Height: 2–5 cm (1–2 in), **Flowers:** pink, in large clusters on sturdy stem 15–23 cm (6–9 in) tall, summer, **Foliage:** green, semi-succulent rosettes, variable in size, evergreen, **Position:** sunny, **Soil:** well-drained, even very dry, **Habit:** rosette-forming; these multiply to cover the ground, **Propagation:** offsets, or sow seeds under glass in spring.
☐ Ideal for dry cracks and crevices in sun and seaside gardens.

Left: *Sempervivum montanum*

217

Senecio 'Sunshine' (syn. *S. greyi*)

Compositae

ZONES 5–9   SHRUB

Height: 1–1.2 m (3–4 ft), **Flowers:** yellow, single, daisy-like in loose clusters during summer, **Foliage:** light grey, oval, evergreen, **Position:** sun or partial shade, **Soil:** suits most well-drained soils, **Habit:** forms a dense, low-growing mound, **Propagation:** cuttings of ripening side shoots in late summer, inserted in peaty sand in a garden frame.

☐ Makes an attractive low informal hedge. Suitable for planting by the seaside. Contrasts well with bush roses and purple-leaved shrubs. Good ground-covering habit.

Sequoiadendron giganteum (syn. *S. wellingtonia*)

Taxodiaceae Big tree, mammoth tree, Wellingtonia

ZONES 6–10   CONIFER

Height: up to 7 m (23 ft) after 10 years, ultimate height 70 m (230 ft), **Flowers:** these and the cones are not particularly showy, **Foliage:** deep green, evergreen, **Position:** sunny and sheltered, **Soil:** needs a good depth of moisture-retentive soil, **Habit:** the largest living tree, bulkier though not so tall as the Californian redwood, soft brownish red bark, **Propagation:** sow seed in early spring in a garden frame.

☐ Thinking to the future, this is well worth planting but only where space permits.

Sidalcea malvaeflora

Malvaceae

ZONES 4–9   HERBACEOUS PERENNIAL

Height: 75–90 cm (2½–3 ft), **Flowers:** pink, in slender spikes, early – late summer, **Foliage:** medium green, deciduous, **Position:** sun or partial shade, sheltered, **Soil:** suits most moist but well-drained soils, **Habit:** clump-forming perennial, **Propagation:** divide clumps in autumn or spring, or sow seeds under glass in mid-spring.

☐ There are several excellent pink and crimson cultivars, but these do not come true from seed. Lovely subject for cottage-garden borders.

Silene alpestris

Carophyllaceae Alpine catchfly

ZONES 5–9   ROCK PLANT

Height: 15 cm (6 in), **Flowers:** starry white blooms, late spring – late summer, **Foliage:** green, evergreen, **Position:** full sun or semi-shade, **Soil:** suits most well-drained soils, **Habit:** forms a loose mat, **Propagation:** sow seeds in spring under glass; cuttings of young shoots in garden frame in summer; or divide in spring.

☐ For rock gardens and gaps in paving.

Skimmia japonica 'Foremanii'

Rutaceae

ZONES 5–9   SHRUB

Height: 1.2–1.5 m (4–5 ft), **Flowers:** white, female, scented, early – mid-spring, followed by large crops of bright red fruits, **Foliage:** deep green, broad oval, evergreen, **Position:** full sun or semi-shade, **Soil:** suits most well-drained soils, acid or alkaline, but best in the former, **Habit:** slow growing, neat rounded bush, **Propagation:** heeled cuttings of ripening side shoots under glass in mid – late summer.

☐ Plant with *S. japonica* 'Fragrans', a male form, to ensure berries.

Skimmia japonica 'Fragrans'

Rutaceae

ZONES 5–9   SHRUB

Height: 1–1.5 m (3–5 ft), **Flowers:** white, in panicles, highly scented, early – mid-spring, no fruits (male form), **Foliage:** light green, evergreen, **Position:** full sun or semi-shade, **Soil:** suits most well-drained soils, acid or chalk, though best in acid soils, **Habit:** rounded bushy shrub, **Propagation:** heeled cuttings of ripening side shoots in mid – late summer under glass.

☐ This is a male form and tolerates atmospheric pollution and maritime situations.

Skimmia japonica 'Rubella'
Rutaceae
ZONES 5–9   SHRUB
Height: 45 cm–1 m (1½–3 ft), **Flowers:** deep red buds, white flowers, early – mid-spring, **Foliage:** deep green, lanceolate, evergreen, **Position:** full or semi-shade, **Soil:** acid or neutral, well-drained, **Habit:** compact and rounded, **Propagation:** heeled cuttings of ripening side shoots in mid – late summer under glass.
☐ This is a male form, grown for its profusion of flowers.

Skimmia reevesiana
(syn. *S. fortunei*)
Rutaceae
ZONES 5–9   SHRUB
Height: 45 cm–1 m (1½–3 ft), **Flowers:** cream, fragrant, hermaphrodite, early – mid-spring, deep red fruits ripening in late summer, **Foliage:** deep green, lanceolate, evergreen, **Position:** full sun or semi-shade, **Soil:** acid or neutral, well-drained, **Habit:** compact and rounded, **Propagation:** heeled cuttings of ripening side shoots in mid – late summer under glass.

Right: *Skimmia reevesiana* is a free-berrying species

Solanum crispum 'Glasnevin'
Solanaceae   Chilean potato tree
ZONES 8–10   CLIMBER
Height: 4.5–6 m (15–20 ft), **Flowers:** purplish blue with a cluster of yellow stamens in the centre, mid-summer – early autumn, **Foliage:** deep green, oval, semi-evergreen, **Position:** grow against a sunny wall, **Soil:** suits most soils if well drained, including chalk, **Habit:** very vigorous, rambling habit, **Propagation:** cuttings of young shoots in mid – late summer inserted in sandy peat in a heated propagator; or layer in spring or autumn.
☐ Looks marvellous in combination with red climbing roses. In early spring, reduce last year's stems to 15 cm (6 in).

Solanum jasminoides 'Album'
Solanaceae   Jasmine nightshade
ZONES 8–10   CLIMBER
Height: 4.5–9 m (15–30 ft), **Flowers:** white, early summer – mid-autumn, **Foliage:** light green, shiny, semi-evergreen, **Position:** grow against a sunny wall. **Soil:** suits most soils if well drained, **Habit:** twining climber, **Propagation:** by cuttings of young shoots in mid – late summer and inserted in sandy peat in a heated propagator, or by layering in spring or autumn.
☐ Thin out spindly growths in early spring.

Solidago virgaurea
Compositae   Golden rod
ZONES 3–9   HERBACEOUS PERENNIAL
Height: 75 cm–1 m (2½–3 ft), **Flowers:** yellow, small and daisy-like in branched sprays, late summer – mid-autumn, **Foliage:** light greeny yellow, lanceolate, deciduous, **Position:** full sun or partial shade, **Soil:** suits most soils, **Habit:** clump-forming, somewhat invasive, **Propagation:** division between mid-autumn – early spring.
☐ Tall stems need some support; cut back to near ground level after flowering. There are several rather less invasive cultivars of different heights. Excellent for cutting.

Sorbaria aitchisonii
Rosaceae
ZONES 5–9 SHRUB
Height: 1.8–3 m (6–10 ft), **Flowers:** plumes of tiny white flowers, late summer – early autumn, **Foliage:** pinnate, green, deciduous, **Position:** full sun or partial shade, **Soil:** suits most well-drained soils, **Habit:** quick growing, bushy, **Propagation:** remove and replant rooted suckers mid-autumn – early spring, or take heeled cuttings of ripening sideshoots in mid – late summer and root under glass.
☐ Cut down almost to the ground in early spring.

Sorbus aria 'Lutescens'
Rosaceae Whitebeam
ZONES 2–9 〉TREE
Height: 7.5–12 m (25–40 ft), **Flowers:** cream, similar to those of crataegus in late spring – early summer, followed in autumn by globular deep red berries, **Foliage:** young leaves silvery white turning greyish green above and grey beneath with age, deciduous, **Position:** sun or semi-shade, **Soil:** at its best on chalk, **Habit:** upright and broadly pyramidal, **Propagation:** grafting in spring or budding in summer.
☐ An excellent tree tolerant of atmospheric pollution and salt-laden air.

Sorbus aucuparia
Rosaceae Mountain ash, rowan
ZONES 2–9 TREE
Height: 9–15 m (30–50 ft), **Flowers:** cream, similar to those of crataegus, late spring, followed in autumn by shiny red berries, **Foliage:** medium green, pinnate, variable autumn colour, deciduous, **Position:** sun or semi-shade, **Soil:** good, deep and well drained, will not live long in shallow chalky soils, but very tolerant of extremely acid conditions, **Habit:** upright branched with a head of roughly oval shape, **Propagation:** seeds sown outdoors as soon as ripe.
☐ Berries are attractive to birds. Often grown in small gardens.

Sorbus hupehensis
Rosaceae
ZONES 4–9 TREE
Height: 6–9 m (20–30 ft), **Flowers:** white, early summer on purplish branches, followed by white or pale pink berries in autumn, **Foliage:** grey-green, pinnate, brilliant autumn colour, deciduous, **Position:** sun or semi-shade, **Soil:** suits most well-drained soils, **Habit:** forms a compact head, **Propagation:** seeds sown outdoors as soon as ripe.
☐ A far better choice than the ubiquitous *S. aucuparia*.

Spartium junceum
Leguminosae Spanish broom
ZONES 7–10 SHRUB
Height: 2.5–3 m (8–10 ft), **Flowers:** bright yellow, scented, early – late summer, **Foliage:** green leaves are small and insignificant but stems give an evergreen effect, **Position:** sun, **Soil:** suits most soils if well drained, **Habit:** rather gaunt if left unpruned, **Propagation:** sow seed in early – mid-spring under glass.
☐ Good plant for the seaside. Dead flowers should be removed. Prune back *lightly* in autumn. Excellent for hot dry places.

Spiraea × arguta
Rosaceae Bridal wreath
ZONES 4–9 SHRUB
Height: 1.8–2.5 m (6–8 ft), **Flowers:** masses of tiny white flowers, mid – late spring, **Foliage:** medium green, deciduous, **Position:** full sun, **Soil:** fairly rich, well drained, **Habit:** arching stems, **Propagation:** cuttings of ripening side shoots in mid – late summer in a garden frame.
☐ Branches smothered in flowers. *S. × vanhouttei* is similar and flowers in early summer. Prune out older stems when flowering is over.

Spiraea × *billiardii* 'Triumphans'
Rosaceae

ZONES 4–9   SHRUB

Height: 1.2–1.8 m (4–6 ft), **Flowers:** rose-pink in long panicles mid- to late summer, **Foliage:** light or medium green, deciduous, **Position:** full sun or semi-shade, **Soil:** fairly rich, well drained, avoid thin chalky soils, **Habit:** twiggy, bushy, suckering shrub, **Propagation:** cuttings of ripening side shoots in mid – late summer, in a garden frame.

☐ Cut off dead blooms and thin out old stems after flowering.

Spiraea × *bumalda*
Rosaceae

ZONES 4–9   SHRUB

Height: 60 cm–1 m (2–3 ft), **Flowers:** carmine-pink in flat panicles, mid – late summer, **Foliage:** medium green, lanceolate, deciduous, **Position:** full sun or semi-shade, **Soil:** fairly rich, well drained, **Habit:** erect and bushy shrub, compact if cut back annually, **Propagation:** cuttings of ripening side shoots in mid – late summer under glass.

☐ 'Anthony Waterer' often produces some foliage variegated with pink and white. Cut back to 10–15 cm (4–6 in) from ground annually in spring. A good companion for shrubby potentillas.

Spiraea × *bumalda* 'Goldflame'
Rosaceae

ZONES 5–9   SHRUB

Height: 60 cm–1 m (2–3 ft), **Flowers:** carmine-pink in flat panicles, mid – late summer, **Foliage:** young leaves are brilliant yellow and orange, deciduous, **Position:** full sun for best colour, **Soil:** prefers reasonably rich soils, **Habit:** upright and bushy, compact if cut back annually, **Propagation:** cuttings of ripening side shoots in mid – late summer under glass.

☐ Outstanding foliage plant.

Spiraea japonica 'Alpina'
Rosaceae

ZONES 4–9   SHRUB

Height: 45–60 cm (1½–2 ft), **Flowers:** bright pink, individually very small in tight clusters, mid – late summer, **Foliage:** medium green, deciduous, **Position:** full sun or semi-shade, **Soil:** suits most reasonably rich soils, **Habit:** forms a dense and compact mound, slightly wider than it is tall, **Propagation:** cuttings of ripening side shoots in mid – late summer in a garden frame.

☐ 'Golden Princess' has orange-red foliage turning yellow (ZONES 5–9). Excellent for small borders.

Spiraea japonica 'Shirobana'
Rosaceae

ZONES 5–9   SHRUB

Height: 30–45 cm (1–1½ ft), **Flowers:** clusters of pinky red and white flowers, mid – late summer, **Foliage:** medium green, deciduous, **Position:** full sun or semi-shade, **Soil:** suits most reasonably rich soils, **Habit:** forms a dense and compact mound, spread rather greater than height, **Propagation:** cuttings of ripening side shoots in mid – late summer in a garden frame.

☐ Cut back to 10 cm (4 in) from ground level annually in early spring. An unusual and colourful spiraea ideal for small borders.

Spiraea nipponica var. *tosaensis* (syn. 'Snowmound')
Rosaceae

ZONES 4–9   SHRUB

Height: 1–1.5 m (3–5 ft), **Flowers:** white, smothering the plant in early summer, **Foliage:** medium green, deciduous, **Position:** full sun or semi-shade, **Soil:** suits most reasonably rich soils, **Habit:** forms a

Above: *Spiraea japonica* 'Shirobana' is a colourful and unusual cultivar suitable for small borders.

dense mound with arching shoots, **Propagation:** cuttings of ripening side shoots in mid – late summer under glass.

☐ One of the most floriferous spiraeas. Thin out old wood after flowering.

Spiraea prunifolia 'Plena'
Rosaceae

ZONES 4–9   SHRUB

Height: 1.5–1.8 m (5–6 ft), **Flowers:** white, double, in tight clusters along the branches, mid – late spring, **Foliage:** medium green, ovate with finely toothed margins, colouring orange and red in autumn, deciduous, **Position:** full sun or semi-shade, **Soil:** suits most reasonably rich soils, **Habit:** arching, forming a dense bush, **Propagation:** cuttings of ripening side shoots in mid – late summer under glass.

☐ Thin out old wood after flowering.

Spiraea thunbergii
Rosaceae
ZONES 4–9   SHRUB
Height: 1.5–2.5 m (5–8 ft), **Flowers:** white, all along the stems, early – mid-spring, **Foliage:** medium green, deciduous, **Position:** full sun or semi-shade, **Soil:** suits most reasonably rich soils, **Habit:** forms a very dense bush, **Propagation:** cuttings of ripening side shoots in mid – late summer under glass.
☐ Generally the earliest spiraea to flower. Thin out old wood when flowering is over.

Stachys lanata
Labiatae   Lamb's ears, lamb's tongue
ZONES 4–9   HERBACEOUS PERENNIAL
Height: 30–45 cm (1–1½ ft), **Flowers:** pale purple, mid – late summer, **Foliage:** grey-green and covered with white hairs, evergreen, **Position:** full sun or semi-shade, **Soil:** suits most soils if well drained, **Habit:** spreading perennial, **Propagation:** division mid-autumn – early spring.
☐ Cut back in late autumn. Grown for its foliage. Gives good ground cover. Better for ground cover is the cultivar 'Silver Carpet' which does not flower.

Stachyurus praecox
Stachyuraceae
ZONES 5–9   SHRUB
Height: 1.8–2.5 m (6–8 ft) or more, **Flowers:** light yellow, in hanging clusters, early spring, **Foliage:** green, deciduous, **Position:** full sun or semi-shade, sheltered, **Soil:** best on peaty soils but tolerates some lime, **Habit:** large spreading shrub, **Propagation:** heeled cuttings of fairly firm wood in mid-summer and placed in gentle heat; or layer in spring.
☐ 'Rubriflora' is a new introduction from Japan with red buds whose outer petals retain a flush.

Stephanandra incisa
Rosaceae
ZONES 5–10   SHRUB
Height: 1.2–1.8 m (4–6 ft), **Flowers:** greenish, not particularly attractive, early summer, **Foliage:** green, turning yellow in mid-autumn, fern-like, deciduous, **Position:** full sun or semi-shade, **Soil:** suits most soils if drainage is good, **Habit:** slender arching stems, **Propagation:** lift, remove and replant rooted suckers mid-autumn – early spring; or hardwood cuttings in mid-autumn in the garden.
☐ Prune untidy plants in winter.

Stephanandra tanakae
Rosaceae
ZONES 5–10   SHRUB
Height: 1.5–2.2 m (5–7 ft), **Flowers:** creamy white, early – mid-summer, **Foliage:** medium green, rich golden-orange in autumn, deciduous, **Position:** full sun or semi-shade, **Soil:** suits most soils if drainage is good, **Habit:** twiggy with gracefully arching branches, **Propagation:** lift, remove and replant rooted suckers mid-autumn – early spring; or take hardwood cuttings in mid-autumn and insert in the garden.
☐ Attractive over a very long period.

Stokesia laevis
Compositae   Stokes's aster
ZONES 5–9   HERBACEOUS PERENNIAL
Height: 30–45 cm (12–18 in), **Flowers:** blue, late summer – mid-autumn, **Foliage:** green, lanceolate, deciduous, **Position:** full sun or (preferably) partial shade, **Soil:** ideally sandy with good drainage, **Habit:** clump-forming herbaceous perennial, **Propagation:** division in mid-spring, seeds under glass in early spring.
☐ Cut back in late autumn. Very useful for late colour in the border.

Stranvaesia davidiana
Roseaceae
ZONES 5–10   SHRUB
Height: 4–5 m (13–16 ft), **Flowers:** white, in clusters, early summer, followed by deep red berries, **Foliage:** deep green, lanceolate, the oldest leaves colour red in autumn, contrasting with the younger ones which remain green, evergreen, **Position:** full sun or semi-shade, **Soil:** suits most reasonably good soils, **Habit:** large and upright, can form a small tree, **Propagation:** seeds sown in mid – late autumn in a garden frame, or by heeled cuttings of ripening side shoots in mid-summer, inserted in a heated propagator.
☐ Tolerates polluted air. 'Prostrata' is low-growing and makes good ground cover. 'Fructuluteo' has yellow berries.

Right: *Stranvaesia davidiana* is grown mainly for its crop of deep red berries.

Stranvaesia davidiana 'Palette'
Roseaceae
ZONES 6–10   SHRUB
Height: 1.8–2.5 m (6–8 ft), **Flowers:** white, in clusters, early summer, followed by red berries, **Foliage:** variegated with pink, orange, white, cream and green, evergreen, **Position:** full sun or semi-shade, **Soil:** suits most reasonably good soils, **Habit:** upright shrub, can develop a tree-like habit, **Propagation:** heeled cuttings of ripening side shoots in summer, rooted in a heated propagator.
☐ Extremely showy small tree or shrub.

Stuartia malacodendron
Theaceae
ZONES 6–9   SHRUB
Height: 4–6 m (13–20 ft), **Flowers:** white, single, with prominent purple stamens, mid – late summer, **Foliage:** green, oval to ovate, colouring gold and crimson in autumn, deciduous, **Position:** sun or semi-shade, **Soil:** lime-free, well-drained but moisture-retentive, with added peat or leaf-mould, **Habit:** erect shrub, can form a small tree, **Propagation:** seed sown as soon as ripe in garden frame, or cuttings of ripening side shoots in late summer in a garden frame.
☐ Magnificent in flower and autumn colour. Also has attractive bark. Superb for woodland garden.

Symphoricarpos × doorenbosii 'Magic Berry'
Caprifoliaceae
ZONES 3–9   SHRUB
Height: 1.2–1.5 m (4–5 ft), **Flowers:** pink, insignificant, early – mid-summer, followed by masses of bright pink berries in autumn and winter, **Foliage:** green, deciduous, **Position:** anywhere – sun, partial or full shade, **Soil:** suits most soils, **Habit:** spreading and suckering shrub, **Propagation:** remove and replant rooted suckers mid-autumn – early spring; or take hardwood cuttings during autumn and insert in the garden.
☐ Makes an attractive hedge, trim as necessary in summer. Useful to flower arrangers. Also good ground cover.

223

Symphoricarpos rivularis
(**syn. *S. albus* var. laevigatus**)

Caprifoliaceae Snowberry

ZONES 3–9   SHRUB

Height: 1.5–1.8 m (5–6 ft), **Flowers:** pink, insignificant, early – mid-summer, white berries, **Foliage:** green, deciduous, **Position:** anywhere – sun, partial or full shade, **Soil:** almost any, **Habit:** suckering, forming a dense mass of erect slender stems, **Propagation:** remove and replant rooted suckers, or take hardwood cuttings during autumn and insert in the garden.

☐About the least fussy shrub there is. Much used by flower arrangers. Suitable for hedging, which can be clipped as necessary in summer. Useful for quickly filling large areas.

Syringa × *josiflexa* 'Bellicent'
Oleaceae Lilac

ZONES 3–9   SHRUB

Height: 3–5 m (10–16 ft), **Flowers:** bright pink, scented, enormous panicles, late spring – early summer, **Foliage:** deep green, deciduous, **Position:** full sun or semi-shade, **Soil:** suits most reasonably rich soils, excellent on chalk, **Habit:** upright, sturdy and bushy, **Propagation:** heeled cuttings of ripening side shoots in mid – late summer inserted in sandy peat in a heated propagator.

☐Remove dead flowers. Thin out weak shoots in winter and remove suckers from grafted plants.

Below: *S. vulgaris* 'Katherine Havemeyer'

Syringa microphylla 'Superba'
Oleaceae Small-leaved lilac

ZONES 4–9   SHRUB

Height: 1.2–1.8 m (4–6 ft), **Flowers:** bright pink, scented, late spring intermittently to mid-autumn, **Foliage:** green, smaller leaves than other lilacs, deciduous, **Position:** full sun or semi-shade, **Soil:** suits most reasonably rich soils, excellent on chalk, **Habit:** very bushy habit, downy young shoots, **Propagation:** heeled cuttings of ripening side shoots in mid – late summer and inserted in sandy peat in a heated propagator; or by lifting and replanting rooted suckers from plants growing on their own roots (not grafted).

☐One of the most suitable lilacs for small borders, beautiful when grown with philadelphus.

Syringa velutina
(**syn. *S. palibiniana***)

Oleaceae Korean lilac

ZONES 4–9   SHRUB

Height: 1.2–1.8 m (4–6 ft), **Flowers:** mauve–pink, scented, early summer, **Foliage:** deep green, velvety, deciduous, **Position:** full sun or semi-shade, **Soil:** suits most reasonably rich soils, does well on chalk, **Habit:** neat rounded habit, **Propagation:** heeled cuttings of ripening side shoots in mid – late summer and inserted in sandy peat in a heated propagator.

☐A lovely species for small gardens.

Syringa vulgaris
Oleaceae Common lilac

ZONES 3–9   SHRUB

Height: 2.5–4 m (8–13 ft), **Flowers:** lilac, scented, late spring and early summer, **Foliage:** green, deciduous, **Position:** full sun or semi-shade, **Soil:** suits most reasonably rich soils, excellent on chalk, **Habit:** strong and erect, very bushy and wide spreading, **Propagation:** heeled cuttings of ripening side shoots in mid – late summer and inserted in sandy peat in a heated propagator.

☐There are a number of cultivars, all best suited to the larger shrub border.

Above: *Syringa vulgaris* 'Primrose'

Recommended cultivars of *Syringa vulgaris*

'*Charles Joly*' – deep red-purple, double, scented.

'*Katherine Havemeyer*' – bluish-purple fading to pale mauve-pink, double, fragrant.

'*Madame Lemoine*' – cream buds opening to white, double, fragrant.

'*Primrose*' – light yellow, single, moderately fragrant.

'*Souvenir de Louis Späth*' – deep red, single, fragrant.

Tamarix pentandra
Tamaricaceae Tamarisk
ZONES 4–10　　　　　　　SHRUB
Height: 3–4 m (10–13 ft), **Flowers:** bright pink, in long racemes, late summer, **Foliage:** greyish green on red-brown stems, deciduous, **Position:** full sun, **Soil:** suits most soils except thin chalky types, **Habit:** straggly by nature, so pruning is necessary to keep shrubs bushy, **Propagation:** hardwood cuttings about 23 cm (9 in) long in mid-autumn outdoors.

□ Excellent for seaside planting. Makes a good screen or hedge. Cut back all new growth by about half in winter.

Tamarix tetrandra
Tamaricaceae Tamarisk
ZONES 5–10　　　　　　　SHRUB
Height: 2.5–3.5 m (8–12 ft), **Flowers:** pink, in feathery sprays, on last year's shoots, late spring, **Foliage:** light green, deciduous, **Position:** full sun, **Soil:** suits most soils except thin chalky types, **Habit:** a large rather shapeless shrub, **Propagation:** hardwood cuttings about 25 cm (10 in) long in mid-autumn outdoors.

□ An excellent plant for seaside planting. Cut back flowered stems when flowering is over. Useful windbreak or informal hedge.

Taxodium distichum
Taxodiaceae Swamp cypress
ZONES 4–9　　　　　　　TREE
Height: up to 6 m (20 ft) after 10 years, but will eventually reach 30 m (100 ft), **Flowers:** insignificant, round cones, purple when young, **Foliage:** lime green, colouring red-bronze in autumn, deciduous, **Position:** full sun or semi-shade, sheltered, **Soil:** suitable for wet places or any reasonably moist soils, **Habit:** pyramidal, **Propagation:** sow seeds in spring, or take hardwood cuttings in autumn, both under glass.

□ Specimen tree for the large garden

Taxus baccata
Taxaceae Common yew, English yew
ZONES 6–9　　　　　　　CONIFER
Height: up to 10 m (33 ft), **Flowers:** male and female on separate plants, red succulent fruits on female trees contain poisonous seeds, **Foliage:** narrow, very deep green, yellowish undersides, evergreen, **Position:** sun, partial or full shade, **Soil:** suits most, at their best on chalk, **Habit:** small tree or large shrub, wide spreading, **Propagation:** sow seed in mid-autumn under glass, or take heeled cuttings of side shoots in early and mid-autumn and root under glass.

□ Excellent for hedging and topiary work.

Taxus baccata 'Fastigiata'
Taxaceae Irish yew
ZONES 6–9　　　　　　　CONIFER
Height: up to 2.5 m (8 ft) after 10 years, may eventually reach 4.5 m (15 ft), **Flowers:** this is a female clone, red succulent fruits contain poisonous seeds, **Foliage:** deep green, evergreen, **Position:** sun or partial shade, **Soil:** suits most soils, excellent on chalk, **Habit:** upright, forming a dense column, **Propagation:** sow seed or take cuttings as *T. baccata*.

□ Excellent as a focal point even in very small gardens.

Above: *Taxus baccata* 'Repandans'
Right: *Taxus baccata* 'Repens Aurea'

Taxus baccata 'Fastigiata Aurea'
Taxaceae   Golden Irish yew
ZONES 6–9   CONIFER
Height: about 1.8 m (6 ft) after 10 years,
eventually reaching 4 m (13 ft), **Flowers:**
this is female, red succulent fruits contain
poisonous seeds, **Foliage:** dark gold green
leaves, the gold being most pronounced in
early summer and best in full sun, evergreen, **Position:** sun or partial shade,
Soil: suits most well-drained even dry
soils, excellent on chalk, **Habit:** upright,
columnar, **Propagation:** cuttings as *T.
baccata*.
□ A most attractive yew, suitable for most
gardens as a specimen plant.

Taxus baccata 'Repandans'
Taxaceae   Yew
ZONES 6–9   CONIFER
Height: up to 50 cm (20 in), **Flowers:**
female, red succulent fruits contain poisonous seeds, **Foliage:** bright mid green,
drooping branches, evergreen, **Position:**
does equally well in sun or shade, **Soil:**
suits most well-drained soils, including
chalk, **Habit:** flat habit, spreading to
1.5 m (5 ft), **Propagation:** cuttings as *T.
baccata*.
□ Excellent ground cover.

Taxus baccata 'Repens Aurea'
Taxaceae   Yew
ZONES 6–9   CONIFER
Height: up to 45 cm (1½ ft), **Flowers:** a
female, **Foliage:** variegated with gold,
turning cream, evergreen, **Position:** sun
or partial shade, colours best in sun, **Soil:**
suits most well-drained soils, including
chalk, **Habit:** low flat habit and wide-
spreading, **Propagation:** cuttings as *T.
baccata*.
□ Good ground cover.

Taxus baccata 'Semperaurea'
Taxaceae   Evergold English yew
ZONES 6–9   CONIFER
Height: about 75 cm (2½ ft) after 10 years,
ultimately 2.5 m (8 ft), **Flowers:** insignificant, **Foliage:** the best golden yew, holding its colour the year round, evergreen,
Position: best planted in full sun, **Soil:**
suits most well-drained soils, including
chalk, **Habit:** spreads widely, some
branches are partially upright, **Propagation:** cuttings as *T. baccata*.
□ Brings a bright splash of colour to the
shrub border.

Taxus cuspidata 'Densa'
Taxaceae   Cushion Japanese yew
ZONES 5–9   CONIFER
Height: up to 60 cm (2 ft), **Flowers:**
insignificant, **Foliage:** deep green, yellow
green beneath, evergreen, **Position:** sun
or partial shade, **Soil:** suits most well-
drained soils, including chalk, **Habit:**
dwarf, variable, compact but branching
irregularly with age, **Propagation:**
cuttings as *T. baccata*.
□ Very hardy, requires occasional pruning to maintain compact shape.

Tellima grandiflora
Saxifragaceae
ZONES 4–9 HERBACEOUS PERENNIAL
Height: 45–60 cm (1½–2 ft), **Flowers:** yellowy green in spikes, mid-spring – early summer, **Foliage:** mid green, lobed, hairy, ground-hugging, evergreen, **Position:** full sun or semi-shade, **Soil:** suits most soils, **Habit:** low-growing perennial, **Propagation:** divide in mid-autumn – early spring.
☐ Useful ground cover.

Thalictrum aquilegifolium
Ranunculaceae Meadow rue
ZONES 5–10 HERBACEOUS PERENNIAL
Height: up to 1 m (3 ft), **Flowers:** mauve-purple in fluffy panicles, late spring – mid-summer, **Foliage:** shiny greyish-blue, leaves similar to those of the aquilegia, deciduous, **Position:** full sun or partial shade, **Soil:** suits most soils, but best where fertile and moisture-retentive, **Habit:** clump forming perennial, **Propagation:** seeds sown in early spring under glass, or divide in early – mid-spring, though it can take a long time to re-establish.
☐ Decorative in both flower and foliage.
Several cultivars, with white or purple flowers.

Thalictrum dipterocarpum
Ranunculaceae Meadow rue
ZONES 5–10 HERBACEOUS PERENNIAL
Height: up to 1.5 m (5 ft), **Flowers:** mauve-purple in feathery sprays, early – late summer, **Foliage:** green, blue-tinted, deciduous, **Position:** full sun or partial shade, **Soil:** best in fertile, moist soil, though most soils are tolerated, **Habit:** clump-forming perennial, **Propagation:** as for *T. aquilegifolium*.
☐ Decorative in flower and foliage. 'Hewitt's Double' has double flowers.

Thuja occidentalis 'Danica'
Cupressaceae Arbor-vitae, white cedar
ZONES 4–9 CONIFER
Height: may eventually reach 1 m (3 ft), **Flowers:** insignificant, **Foliage:** medium green, slightly bronzed in winter, evergreen, **Position:** sun or partial shade, **Soil:** suits most moisture-retentive soils, **Habit:** slow-growing dwarf and rounded, **Propagation:** take cuttings in early or mid-autumn and root under glass.
☐ Useful conifer for the heather garden. Like all thujas this has aromatic foliage.

Other recommended cultivars of Thuja occidentalis
'*Holmstrup*' – reddish male strobili in spring, small brown cones; dense green foliage; strong-growing, ultimately 2.5 m (8 ft); forms a neat cone. (ZONES 4–9).
'*Lutea Nana*' – reddish male strobili in spring; gold foliage, best in sunny position; ultimately reaches about 2.5 m (8 ft); upright and bushy cone. (ZONES 5–9)
'*Rheingold*' – reddish male strobili in spring; gold foliage, best in sunny position; reaches about 1.2 m (4 ft) or so; slow

Left: *Thuja occidentalis* 'Danica'
Centre: *Thuja occidentalis* 'Rheingold'
Right: *Thuja occidentalis* 'Smaragd'

growing, compact, forming a broad cone. (ZONES 4–9)
'*Smaragd*' – reddish male strobili in spring, small brown cones; emerald green foliage; reaches about 2.5 m (8 ft) or more; forms a neat cone; excellent for hedging as responds well to clipping. (ZONES 4–9)

Right: *Thuja orientalis* 'Aurea Nana'

Thuja orientalis 'Aurea Nana'
Cupressaceae
ZONES 5–9   CONIFER
Height: up to 2 m (6 ft), **Flowers:** reddish male strobili in spring, small brown cones, **Foliage:** deep yellow held in flat upright sprays, turning bronze in winter, evergreen, **Position:** best in full sun, **Soil:** suits most moisture-retentive soils, **Habit:** compact rounded bush, **Propagation:** tip cuttings in early or mid-autumn, rooted under glass.
☐ An excellent small conifer.

Thuja orientalis 'Conspicua'
Cupressaceae
ZONES 5–9   CONIFER
Height: about 1.8 m (6 ft) after 10 years, eventually reaching 4.5 m (15 ft), **Flowers:** reddish male strobili in spring, small brown cones, **Foliage:** deep yellow, evergreen, **Position:** best in full sun, **Soil:** suits most moisture-retentive soils, **Habit:** forms medium-sized, compact cone, **Propagation:** tip cuttings in early or mid-autumn, rooted under glass.
☐ Makes a superb lawn specimen.

Thuja plicata
(syn. *T. lobbii*)
Cupressaceae   Western red cedar
ZONES 5–9   CONIFER
Height: up to 6 m (20 ft) after 10 years, ultimately 30 m (100 ft) or more, **Flowers:** reddish male strobili in spring, small brown cones, **Foliage:** bright green and shiny, pleasantly scented when crushed, evergreen, **Position:** sun or partial shade, **Soil:** suits most moisture-retentive soils, tolerates lime, **Habit:** quick growing tree, cone-shaped, **Propagation:** seed in spring in a garden frame, or tip cuttings in early or mid-autumn, rooted under glass.
☐ Good plant for hedging.

Thuja plicata 'Aureovariegata'
(syn. 'Zebrina')
Cupressaceae
ZONES 6–9   CONIFER
Height: about 4 m (13 ft) after 10 years, ultimately 15 m (50 ft), **Flowers:** reddish male strobili in spring, small brown cones, **Foliage:** green banded with yellow, evergreen, **Position:** best in full sun, **Soil:** suits most moisture-retentive soils, tolerates lime, **Habit:** will form a broad cone-shaped tree if left unclipped, **Propagation:** tip cuttings in early or mid-autumn, rooted under glass.
☐ One of the best variegated conifers. Good hedging plant.

Thuja plicata 'Rogersii'
Cupressaceae
ZONES 5–9   CONIFER
Height: may eventually reach little more than 1.2 m (4 ft), **Flowers:** insignificant, **Foliage:** deep green with yellowy bronze tips, evergreen, **Position:** best in full sun, **Soil:** suits most moisture-retentive soils, tolerates lime, **Habit:** rounded or globe-shaped, **Propagation:** tip cuttings in early or mid-autumn, rooted under glass.
☐ Good formal conifer for a tub. Slow growing.

Thymus serpyllum
Labiatae   Wild thyme
ZONES 5–9   ROCK PLANT
Height: 5 cm (2 in), **Flowers:** deep pink, prolifically produced, early – late summer, **Foliage:** green, fragrant, evergreen, **Position:** full sun, **Soil:** any with good drainage, **Habit:** prostrate sub-shrub spreading to 60 cm (2 ft) or more, **Propagation:** division of mats in autumn or spring.
☐ Good for planting in cracks in paving. Cultivars include 'Alba', white and 'Coccineus', deep red.

Trachelospermum asiaticum (syn. *T. divaricatum*)
Apocynaceae

ZONES 7–10 CLIMBER

Height: up to 6 m (20 ft), **Flowers:** white, turning pale yellow, scented, mid – late summer, **Foliage:** deep green and shiny, oval, evergreen, **Position:** full sun, against a south- or west-facing wall, **Soil:** lime-free, very good drainage, **Habit:** climber, self-clinging, dense growth, **Propagation:** cuttings of ripening shoots taken in summer and placed in a heated propagator.

☐ Not recommended for very cold parts of the country. Valued for its delightful scent.

Trachelospernum jasminoides
Apocynaceae Chinese jasmine

ZONES 7–10 CLIMBER

Height: up to 3.5m (12 ft), **Flowers:** white, scented, mid – late summer, **Foliage:** deep green, thick and tough, evergreen, **Position:** full sun, against a south- or west-facing wall, **Soil:** lime-free, very good drainage, **Habit:** climber, self-clinging, dense growth, **Propagation:** cuttings of ripening shoots taken in summer and placed in a heated propagator.

☐ Not recommended for very cold parts of the country.

Trollius europaeus 'Superbus'
Ranunculaceae Globe flower

ZONES 3–9 HERBACEOUS PERENNIAL

Height: 45–60 cm (1½–2ft), **Flowers:** lemon-yellow, large and buttercup-like, late spring – early summer, **Foliage:** deep green, deciduous, **Position:** full sun or semi-shade, **Soil:** moist and humus-rich, **Habit:** clump forming perennial, **Propagation:** sow seeds in a shady situation outdoors in spring; or divide in autumn or spring.

☐ Cut flower stems down after flowering to encourage further blooms in late summer.

Good for boggy ground and pondside or moist borders.

Tsuga canadensis
Pinaceae Eastern Hemlock

ZONES 4–9 CONIFER

Height: 4 m (13 ft) after 10 years, ultimately 30 m (100 ft), **Flowers:** insignificant, small pendulous greeny purple cones turning brown, **Foliage:** narrow, mid green with two white bands on the undersides, evergreen, **Position:** sun or semi-shade, best in semi-shade and sheltered, **Soil:** moist, yet well drained, including alkaline, **Habit:** broad pyramid shape, **Propagation:** sow seed in early or mid-spring under glass.

☐ Superb lawn specimen, but for large gardens only.

Tsuga canadensis 'Bennett'
Pinaceae

ZONES 4–9 CONIFER

Height: 30 cm (1 ft) after 10 years, may ultimately reach 1.2 m (4 ft) or more, **Flowers:** insignificant, **Foliage:** medium green with two white bands on underside, evergreen, **Position:** best in semi-shade, **Soil:** moist, yet well drained, including alkaline, **Habit:** slow-growing, dense and spreading at least 2 m (6 ft), **Propagation:** heeled cuttings of side shoots in early autumn under glass.

☐ A distinctive conifer which looks good adjacent to a patio.

Tsuga canadensis 'Pendula'
Pinaceae

ZONES 5–9 CONIFER

Height: about 45 cm (1½ ft), after 10 years, ultimately 2.5 m (8 ft), **Flowers:** insignificant, **Foliage:** medium green with two white bands on undersides, evergreen, **Position:** sun or semi-shade, **Soil:** moist, yet well drained, including alkaline, **Habit:** forms a low mat, with layers of branches, spreading to 1 m (3 ft) or more, **Propagation:** heeled cuttings of side shoots in early autumn under glass.

☐ Looks good planted on a bank or overhanging a wall.

Vaccinium corymbosum

Ericaceae Swamp blueberry, high bush blueberry

ZONES 3–9   SHRUB

Height: 1.2–1.8 m (4–6 ft), **Flowers:** white, with pink flush, late spring and early summer, followed by edible black berries, ripening in late summer, **Foliage:** green, colouring red in early autumn, deciduous, **Position:** full sun, **Soil:** acid, moist, with peat added, **Habit:** a dense thicket of upright branching stems, **Propagation:** layer in early autumn; sow seeds in moist sandy peat in spring; or take semi-ripe cuttings in summer, and insert in moist sandy peat in a propagator in shade.
☐ Well worth growing, perhaps with rhododendrons, for its superb autumn leaf colour.

Right: *Vaccinium corymbosum*

Vaccinium vitis-idaea

Ericaceae Cowberry, mountain cranberry

ZONES 3–9   SHRUB

Height: up to 15 cm (6 in), **Flowers:** light pink or white in summer, deep red edible berries retained well into winter, **Foliage:** shiny deep green, evergreen, **Position:** full sun, **Soil:** acid, moist, with peat added, **Habit:** more or less prostrate, spreading up to 45 cm (1½ ft), **Propagation:** layer in early autumn; sow seeds in moist sandy peat in spring; take semi-ripe cuttings in summer, insert in propagator in shade.
☐ Makes good ground cover.

Veronica incana

Scrophulariaceae Speedwell

ZONES 5–9   HERBACEOUS PERENNIAL

Height: 30–45 cm (1–1½ ft), **Flowers:** blue, held in long narrow spikes, early – mid-summer, **Foliage:** grey-green, lanceolate, deciduous, **Position:** sun or semi-shade, **Soil:** suits most well-drained soils, **Habit:** clump-forming perennial, **Propagation:** divide clumps in autumn or spring.
☐ Cut back to near ground level in late autumn. Suitable for an herbaceous or mixed border.

Veronica spicata

Scrophulariaceae Speedwell

ZONES 4–9   HERBACEOUS PERENNIAL

Height: 15–45 cm (6–18 in), **Flowers:** different shades of blue held in long narrow spikes in early – late summer, **Foliage:** green, lanceolate, deciduous, **Position:** sun or semi-shade, **Soil:** suits most well-drained soils, **Habit:** clump-forming perennial with upright flower spikes, **Propagation:** divide clumps in autumn or spring.
☐ Cut down to the ground late in autumn. Suitable for an herbaceous or mixed border.

Right: *Viburnum carlesii*

Viburnum × *bodnantense*
Caprifoliaceae
ZONES 5–9   SHRUB
Height: 2.5–3 m (8–10 ft), **Flowers:** pale
rose-pink, fragrant, in clusters on bare
stems in early – late winter, **Foliage:**
young leaves bronzy green, deciduous,
Position: protect from cold winds and
morning sun, sun or partial shade, **Soil:**
moist, fertile, including chalk, **Habit:**
strong upright-growing shrub, **Propagation:** heeled cuttings of side shoots in early
– mid-summer inserted in sandy soil under
glass; layer in early autumn.
☐ 'Dawn' is the best form, with deeper
pink flowers. A good companion plant is
Mahonia japonica.

Viburnum × *burkwoodii*
Caprifoliaceae
ZONES 5–9   SHRUB
Height: 1.8–2.5 m (6–8 ft), **Flowers:**
white from pink buds, extremely fragrant,
early – late spring, **Foliage:** deep green,
evergreen, **Position:** sun or partial shade,
Soil: moist, fertile, including chalk,
Habit: erect and bushy shrub, **Propagation:** heeled cuttings of side shoots in early
– mid-summer inserted in sandy soil under
glass; or layer in early autumn.

Viburnum × *carlcephalum*
Caprifoliaceae
ZONES 5–9   SHRUB
Height: 1.8–2.5 m (6–8 ft), **Flowers:**
cream in spherical corymbs, highly scented, mid – late spring, **Foliage:** mid-green,
deciduous, colours well in autumn, **Position:** sun or partial shade, **Soil:** moist,
fertile, including chalk, **Habit:** upright
and bushy, **Propagation:** heeled cuttings
of ripening side shoots in mid-summer
inserted in sandy soil in a propagator.

Viburnum carlesii
Caprifoliaceae
ZONES 5–9   SHRUB
Height: 1.2–1.8 m (4–6 ft), **Flowers:**
pink in bud, opening white, in rounded
heads, highly scented, mid – late spring,
followed by black fruits, **Foliage:** matt
green above, greyish green undersides,
often good autumn colour, deciduous,
Position: sun or partial shade, **Soil:**
moist, fertile, including chalk, **Habit:**
rounded and bushy, **Propagation:** heeled
cuttings of ripening side shoots, summer,
in à propagator.
☐ 'Aurora' has attractive red buds opening to pink flowers. Highly scented.

Viburnum davidii
Caprifoliaceae
ZONES 7–10   SHRUB
Height: 60–90 cm (2–3 ft), **Flowers:**
heads of small white flowers, early summer; female plants carry turquoise berries
if planted near a male plant, **Foliage:** deep
green, leathery and strongly veined, evergreen, **Position:** sun or partial shade,
Soil: moist, fertile, including chalk,
Habit: compact, forming a low mound,

Above left: *Viburnum* × *bodnantense*
Above right: *Viburnum davidii*

spreading up to 1.5 m (5 ft), **Propagation:** half-ripe cuttings in mid-summer
inserted in sandy soil in a propagator; or
layer in spring or autumn.
☐ Male and female flowers on separate
plants so it is necessary to plant in mixed
groups to ensure pollination. Good for
ground cover.

Viburnum farreri
(syn. *V. fragrans*)
Caprifoliaceae
ZONES 6–9   SHRUB
Height: 2.2–2.5 m (7–8 ft), **Flowers:** pink in bud, opening white, sweetly fragrant, late autumn – early spring, **Foliage:** opens bronze, turning green, with conspicuous parallel veins, deciduous, **Position:** sun or partial shade, **Soil:** moist, fertile, including chalk, **Habit:** stiff, erect shrub, becoming broader and rounded with age, **Propagation:** half-ripe cutting in mid-summer inserted in sandy soil in a propagator; or layer in spring or autumn.
☐An 'essential' winter-flowering shrub, which combines well with hamamelis and *Mahonia japonica*.

Viburnum × juddii
Caprifoliaceae
ZONES 5–9   SHRUB
Height: 1.5–2.5 m (5–8 ft), **Flowers:** pink buds opening white, very fragrant, mid–late spring, **Foliage:** deep green, deciduous, **Position:** sun or partial shade, **Soil:** moist, fertile, including chalk, **Habit:** bushy and rounded shrub, **Propagation:** cuttings of ripening side shoots in mid-summer inserted in sandy soil in a propagator; or layer in spring or autumn.

Viburnum opulus
Caprifoliaceae   Guelder rose
ZONES 3–9   SHRUB
Height: 3–4 m (10–13 ft), **Flowers:** white, carried in flattish heads, late spring – early summer, followed by shining red berries, **Foliage:** deep green, lobed, similar to those of maple, good autumn colour, deciduous, **Position:** sun or partial shade, **Soil:** moist, fertile, including chalk, **Habit:** vigorous spreading shrub, **Propagation:** cuttings of ripening side shoots in mid-summer inserted in sandy soil in a propagator; layering in spring or autumn.
☐Best planted in groups for good berrying. 'Xanthocarpum' has yellow berries. 'Notcutt's Variety' has larger berries than the species. Excellent for an autumn group in the shrub border.

Viburnum opulus 'Sterile'
Caprifoliaceae   Snowball tree
ZONES 3–9   SHRUB
Height: 3–4 m (10–13 ft), **Flowers:** white sterile florets in large, almost spherical clusters up to 8 cm (3 in) across, summer, **Foliage:** green, deeply toothed and lobed, good autumn colour, deciduous, **Position:** sun or partial shade, **Soil:** moist, fertile, including chalk, **Habit:** vigorous and spreading shrub, **Propagation:**

cuttings of ripening side shoots in mid-summer inserted in sandy soil in a propagator; or layer in spring or autumn.
☐Makes a large shrub, so needs a fair amount of space.

Viburnum plicatum plicatum
(syn. *V. tomentosum*)
Caprifoliaceae   Japanese snowball
ZONES 4–9   SHRUB
Height: 2.5–3 m (8–10 ft), **Flowers:** white sterile florets in round heads, late spring – early summer, **Foliage:** green, deciduous, **Position:** sun or partial shade, **Soil:** moist, fertile, including chalk, **Habit:** wide spreading, forms a large shrub, **Propagation:** half-ripe cuttings in mid-summer inserted in sandy soil in a propagator; or layer in spring or autumn.
☐'Mariesii' is a superb cultivar whose branches are arranged in tiers and bear numerous flower heads.

Top left: *Viburnum farreri*
Top right: *Viburnum × juddii*
Above: *Viburnum opulus* 'Sterile'

Viburnum rhytidophyllum
Caprifoliaceae
ZONES 5–9   SHRUB
Height: 3–5 m (10–16 ft), **Flowers:** dull-white, spring, red fruits in autumn, **Foliage:** leathery deep green with deep venation, fawn felted beneath, large, oblong, evergreen, **Position:** sun or partial shade, **Soil:** moist, fertile, including chalk, **Habit:** vigorous and erect, **Propagation:** half-ripe cuttings in mid-summer inserted in sandy soil in a propagator; or layer in spring or autumn.
☐Magnificent foliage plant. Plant in a group to ensure pollination and hence good crops of berries.

Viburnum tinus

Caprifoliaceae   Laurustinus
ZONES 7–9   SHRUB
Height: 2.2–3 m (7–10 ft), **Flowers:** pink in bud opening white, in flattened heads, late autumn – late spring, **Foliage:** shiny dark green, oval, evergreen, **Position:** sun or partial shade, **Soil:** moist, fertile, including chalk, **Habit:** very bushy, well clothed with foliage, **Propagation:** half-ripe cuttings in mid-summer inserted in sandy soil in a propagator; or layer in spring or autumn.
☐ Suitable for an informal hedge and for seaside planting. 'Eve Price' is of denser habit and has pink flowers. 'Variegatum' has yellow variegated leaves. Trim or prune all in mid-spring.

Right: *Viburnum tinus*

Vinca major

Apocynaceae   Greater periwinkle
ZONES 4–9   SHRUB
Height: up to 30 cm (12 in), **Flowers:** rich blue, mid-spring – early summer, **Foliage:** shiny deep green, evergreen, **Position:** sun or semi-shade, flowers best in sun, **Soil:** suits most soils, **Habit:** vigorous, trailing, mat forming, spreading to 1.2 m (4 ft), **Propagation:** divide and replant early autumn – mid-spring; the plant also layers itself, rooting at the nodes.
☐ Easy-care, if rampant, ground cover plant. 'Elegantissima' has leaves variegated with white and is not quite so rampant (ZONES 5–10).

Vinca minor

Apocynaceae   Lesser periwinkle
ZONES 4–9   SHRUB
Height: 5–10 cm (2–4 in), **Flowers:** blue, early spring – mid-summer, and on and off until autumn, **Foliage:** shiny deep green, evergreen, **Position:** flowers best in full sun, but tolerates shade, **Soil:** most soils, **Habit:** trailing, **Propagation:** divide and replant early autumn – mid-spring. The plant also layers itself.
☐ Useful ground cover plant, less rampant than *V. major*. 'Variegata' has leaves marked with white.

Left: *Vinca major*

233

Vitis coignetiae
Vitaceae Japanese crimson glory vine
ZONES 5–10   CLIMBER
Height: up to 18 m (90 ft), **Flowers:** insignificant, green, late spring, black berries (inedible), **Foliage:** huge round leaves turning scarlet in autumn, deciduous, **Position:** sun or partial shade, **Soil:** fertile, moisture-retentive, **Habit:** strong grower, clings by tendrils, **Propagation:** seeds sown in late autumn and placed in a heated propagator.
□ Grown for its variable foliage and magnificent autumn colouring. A good companion plant is *Hedera colchica* 'Dentata Variegata'.

Vitis 'Brandt'
Vitaceae
ZONES 6–10   CLIMBER
Height: up to 6 m (20 ft), **Flowers:** insignificant, green, early summer, followed by bunches of sweet red-purple grapes, **Foliage:** green, deeply lobed, colouring orange and scarlet in autumn, deciduous, **Position:** sun or partial shade, **Soil:** fertile, moisture-retentive, **Habit:** hardy, climbing vine clinging by tendrils, **Propagation:** sow seeds in late autumn and place in a heated propagator; cuttings of firm young shoots in summer, raise in a propagator; hardwood cuttings in autumn under glass.
□ Prune back all side shoots in early winter.

Vitis vinifera 'Purpurea'
Vitaceae Teinturier grape
ZONES 6–10   CLIMBER
Height: 6 m (20 ft), **Flowers:** green, early summer, followed by black-purple grapes, **Foliage:** wine-red, becoming purple in autumn, deciduous, **Position:** sun or partial shade, maximum sun to ripen fruit, **Soil:** fertile, moisture-retentive, **Habit:** hardy, climbing vine, **Propagation:** sow seeds in late autumn and place in heated propagator; cuttings of firm young shoots in a propagator in summer; or hardwood cuttings under glass in autumn.
□ An excellent companion for red climbing roses.
   Side shoots can be pruned back in early winter.

Weigela florida 'Foliis Purpureis'
Caprifoliaceae
ZONES 5–9   SHRUB
Height: 1.2–1.8 m (4–6 ft), **Flowers:** pink, tubular, late spring and early summer, **Foliage:** purplish brown, deciduous, **Position:** full sun or semi-shade, **Soil:** reasonably rich, well-drained but moisture-retentive, **Habit:** neat rounded bush, **Propagation:** heeled cuttings of ripening side shoots in sandy soil in a heated propagator, mid – late summer, or hardwood cuttings in a garden frame in autumn.
□ Prune after flowering, shortening shoots that have carried flowers.
   An attractive companion for shrub roses.

Weigela florida 'Variegata'
Caprifoliaceae
ZONES 4–9   SHRUB
Height: 1.2–1.8 m (4–6 ft), **Flowers:** pale pink, tubular, late spring and early summer and sometimes again in autumn, **Foliage:** green edged with cream, deciduous, **Position:** sun or partial shade, **Soil:** reasonably rich, well-drained but moisture-retentive, **Habit:** neat rounded bush, **Propagation:** heeled cuttings of ripening side shoots in mid-summer inserted in sandy soil in a heated propagator, or hardwood cuttings in a garden frame in autumn.
□ Looks good with purple-leaved shrubs.
   Prune after flowering, shortening shoots that have carried flowers.

Weigela 'Bristol Ruby'
Caprifoliaceae
ZONES 4–9   SHRUB
Height: 1.8–2.5 m (6–8 ft), **Flowers:** bright red, tubular, free-flowering, late spring and early summer, often again in autumn, **Foliage:** green, deciduous, **Position:** sun or partial shade, **Soil:** reasonably rich, well-drained but moisture retentive, **Habit:** upright bush, strong grower, **Propagation:** heeled cuttings of ripening side shoots in mid-summer, inserted in sandy soil in a heated propagator, or hardwood cuttings in a garden frame in autumn.
□ Prune after flowering, shortening shoots that have carried flowers. 'Mont Blanc' has white flowers.

Wisteria floribunda
Leguminosae   Japanese wisteria
ZONES 4–10   CLIMBER
Height: up to 6 m (20 ft), **Flowers:** blue, scented, in long trusses, late spring – early summer, **Foliage:** pale to medium green, pinnate, deciduous, **Position:** full sun, south or west wall, **Soil:** any fertile moisture-retentive soil, **Habit:** strong-growing climber, **Propagation:** layer young shoots in spring; cuttings of firm young growth in a heated propagator in summer.
☐ Cut back side shoots in mid-summer, further reduce in late winter. 'Alba' has white flowers.

Wisteria floribunda 'Macrobotrys'
Leguminosae   Japanese wisteria
ZONES 4–10   CLIMBER
Height: 6 m (20 ft), **Flowers:** mauve-blue tinged purple, scented, in very long trusses, late spring – early summer, **Foliage:** pale to medium green, pinnate, deciduous, **Position:** full sun, south or west wall, **Soil:** any fertile moisture-retentive soil, **Habit:** strong-growing climber, **Propagation:** layer young shoots in spring; cuttings of firm young growth in a heated propagator in summer.
☐ Pruning as *W. floribunda*.

Right: *Wisteria floribunda*

Wisteria sinensis
Leguminosae   Chinese wisteria
ZONES 5–10   CLIMBER
Height: 9 m (30 ft) or more, **Flowers:** deep lilac-blue, scented, in long trusses, late spring and early summer, **Foliage:** green, pinnate, deciduous, **Position:** sun, south or west wall, **Soil:** any fertile moisture-retentive soil, **Habit:** very vigorous climber, **Propagation:** layer young shoots in spring; cuttings of firm young growth in a heated propagator in summer.
☐ Pruning as *W. floribunda*. A highly popular species, excellent for growing through large trees.

Yucca filamentosa
Liliaceae
ZONES 8–10   SHRUB
Height: foliage up to 1 m (3 ft), **Flowers:** cream, held in cone-shaped panicles on a 1.8 m (6 ft) stem, mid – late summer, **Foliage:** green, rigid, sword-like, with dangerously spined tips, evergreen, **Position:** very sunny, **Soil:** well-drained, including very poor and dry, **Habit:** foliage in clumps, no stem produced, **Propagation:** remove and replant rooted offsets in early – mid-spring.

The flowers (**left**) and the foliage (**right**) of *Yucca filamentosa*.

☐ 'Variegata' has cream-edged leaves. Marvellous 'architectural' plant for use as a lawn specimen; also effective in and around patios but take due regard of the spine-tipped leaves. Suitable for seaside gardens.

Glossary

Acid (soil) Soil with a pH below 7.0; lacking lime.

Alkaline (soil) Soil with a pH above 7.0; containing lime.

Anther The pollen-bearing tip of a stamen.

Axil The angle between a leaf or lateral branch and a stem.

Bract A modified leaf on a flower stalk.

Calcifuge Lime-hating. Plants that will not succeed on lime soils.

Calyx The outer part of the flower, consisting of sepals fused together.

Catkin A dense spike-like raceme of tiny scaly-bracted flowers.

Cone The fruit of a conifer.

Corolla The inner part of a flower. Normally conspicuous. Petals.

Corymb A flat-topped cluster of flowers with stalks arising one above another from a vertical stem.

Cyme A domed or flat-topped flower head. Flowers opening progressively from the centre.

Deciduous Plants loosing leaves at the end of the growing season.

Dioecious Male or female flowers on separate plants.

Elliptic (leaf). Wide in middle, narrowing to each end.

Evergreen Remaining in leaf throughout all seasons.

Farinose Where foliage, stems or fruits have a covering of white powder.

Fastigate Branches close together and upright.

Floret One of the flowers that make up the head of a composite flower (e.g. daisy).

Glaucous Grey-blue. Covered with a 'bloom' of blue-white or blue-grey.

Heel The expanded base of a side shoot that is pulled away from the main stem when taking a cutting 'with a heel'.

Herbaceous Any plant not forming a persistent woody stem.

Hermaphrodite Where the organs of both sexes are present in a flower.

Hip The fruit of a rose.

Humus The dark brown result of the final breakdown of vegetable matter.

Hybrid A plant derived from crossing two varieties or species.

Inflorescence The flowering part of a plant.

Internode The portion of stem between two joints (nodes).

Inorganic A chemical compound or fertilizer that contains no carbon.

Lanceolate (leaf) A narrow leaf, widest at the base tapering to a point. At least three times longer than wide.

Lateral A stem or shoot at the side of a larger stem.

Leader The main stem that extends existing branch systems.

Linear (leaf) Long and narrow. Roughly parallel margins. At least 12 times longer than wide.

Monoecious A plant that has flowers of two sexes.

Mulch A layer of organic material spread on the soil surface around plants.

Neutral (soil) Soil that is neither acid nor alkaline, with a pH of between 6.5 and 7.0.

Node A stem joint where leaves, buds and side shoots arise.

Oblanceolate (leaf) Reverse of lanceolate.

Oblong (leaf) Three times longer than broad with almost parallel sides.

Obovate (leaf) Egg-shaped, but broadest at the tip. Reverse of ovate.

Organic Any chemical compound of carbon.

Ovate (leaf) Egg-shaped. Broadest at the base.

Palmate (leaf) Hand-shaped.

Panicle A branching flower cluster.

Petal A modified leaf. Separate segment of the corolla, usually coloured and forming part of the flower.

Petiole Leaf stalk.

Pinnate (leaf) Leaflets either side of a central stalk.

Pistil The complete female organ comprising ovary, stigma and style.

Raceme (flower) A simple elongated arrangement of flowers. The individual flowers are stalked and spirally arranged.

Rhizome An underground stem.

Scale A tiny leaf or bract, or an appendage on a leaf shoot or flower.

Sepal One of the leaves forming the calyx.

Shrub A woody plant branching from the base.

Spike (flower) A simple elongated arrangement of flowers that are stalkless and spirally arranged.

Stamen The male reproductive organ of a flower consisting of filament and anther.

Strobilus The flowers of the conifer.

Sucker Growth produced from below the ground. Also shoots growing from stock of a grafted plant.

Tendril A twining modified stem or leaf that enables some plants to climb.

Tree A woody plant that produces a head of branches on a single stem or trunk.

Umbel (flower) An arrangement where all flower stalks arise from one point.

Variegated Leaves or, in some cases, flowers that are marked, streaked or spotted with a contrasting colour.

Whorl Where three or more leaves or flowers arise from one point.

Bibliography

Bean, W.J. *Trees and Shrubs Hardy in the British Isles.* John Murray, London, 4 vols, 8th edn, 1970, 1973, 1976, 1980.

Bloom, A. *Conifers for Your Garden.* Floraprint, Sachets Floraisse, 1972. (dist. Wisbech, Cambs)

Fell, D. *Trees and Shrubs.* H.P. Books, New York, 1986.

Hellyer, A. *The Collingridge Illustrated Encyclopedia of Gardening.* Collingridge, London, 2nd rev. edn, 1982.

Herwig, R. *The Hamlyn Dictionary of House and Garden Plants.* Hamlyn, London, 1985.

Hillier, H.G. *Manual of Trees and Shrubs.* David and Charles, London, 3rd rev. edn, 1981.

Hortus III

Reader's Digest Encyclopedia of Garden Plants and Shrubs. The Reader's Digest Association, London, 3rd rev. edn, 1975.

Index of Common Names

Acknowledgements

Heather Angel, Farnham 126 top centre, 144 left; *A-Z Collection, Dorking* 88 top right, 96 top left, 144 top right, 145 centre left, 163 bottom centre, 214 bottom centre, 227 bottom right; *Pat Brindley, Cheltenham* 74 top and bottom centre, 75 bottom, 78 bottom centre, 79 bottom, 83 bottom left, 84 bottom right, 85 top, 87 bottom left, 88 top left, 89 bottom, 91 top left, 94 right, 96 top right, 98 top centre, 101 top, 102 top centre and top right, 104 right, 105 top and bottom centre, 107 top centre, 111 top left and bottom, 112 top left, bottom centre and bottom right, 114 bottom, 116 bottom, 118 top centre, top right and bottom left, 119 top, 123 bottom centre, 124 top left and top centre, 125 top right, 127 bottom right, 128 bottom centre, 129 bottom centre, 130 top right and bottom left, 131 bottom centre, 132 bottom right, 133 top centre and bottom right, 134 bottom right, 139 top centre, 140 top, 141 top left, 142 top left and top right, 152 left, 154 bottom centre, 158 left, 165 top left and bottom, 171 top right, 179 bottom, 182 top left, 183 top left, 184 bottom, 185 bottom right, 186 top, 189 bottom left, 190 bottom right, 191 bottom right, 192 bottom, 196 top and bottom right, 197 top left, 202 top, 203 top right and bottom, 209 right, 212 bottom left, 215 bottom, 220 top centre, 222 top left, 223 top, 225 top left and top right, 228 top, 229 top left, 235 top; *Derek Gould, Maidstone* 84 top right, 122 top left, 171 bottom right, 173 bottom centre; *Hamlyn Publishing Group Limited/W.F. Davidson* 75 top left, 80 bottom left and bottom right, 84 bottom left, 86 top left and centre, 87 bottom centre, 90 top, 98 bottom left and right, 101 bottom centre, 103 top right and bottom centre, 109 bottom, 115 right, 125 bottom right, 138 top right and bottom right, 148 top, 154 bottom right, 155 bottom right, 157 top centre, 160 top left, 161 top left and bottom right, 169 top right and bottom centre, 171 bottom left, 173 top centre, 180 top, 198 bottom, 206 top left, 214 top, 217 (all four), 230 bottom right; *Hamlyn Publishing Group Limited/Anthony Martin* 80 top centre, 82 bottom left, 92 top left, 100 top, 108 bottom left and bottom right, 109 top left and top right, 126 top left and top right, 136 bottom, 140 bottom right, 180 bottom, 189 bottom right, 192 top left, 202 bottom right, 207 bottom left, 209 top left, top centre, bottom left and bottom centre, 210 top left, 211 bottom, 215 top left, 218 top centre, 226 top left, 228 bottom left, 231 top, 232 right; *Jerry Harpur, Chelmsford* 6–7, 10–11, 58–9, 67, 72–3; *Peter McHoy, Henfield* 142 bottom right; *Brian Mathew, Esher* 103 top centre; *Octopus Books Limited, London* 8 left and right, 76 top left, 77 bottom, 78 bottom right, 86 bottom centre, 88 top left, 91 top right, 95 bottom left, 96 bottom left, 98 bottom centre, 102 bottom, 104 bottom left, 106 top left and bottom right, 107 top left, 117 bottom left, 119 bottom right, 120 bottom, 121 bottom centre, 122 top right and bottom, 125 top left, 127 top, 129 top left and top centre, 130 bottom centre, 132 bottom left, 134 bottom left, 138 bottom centre, 147 top, 149 top, 151 top centre, 157 top left and bottom centre, 162 bottom right, 163 bottom left, 166,

174 bottom, 177 top, 178 bottom, 181 bottom right, 185 bottom left, 186 bottom centre, 188 bottom, 193 bottom left, 207 bottom centre, 212 top centre, 213 bottom, 218 bottom centre, 222 top right, 233 top, 234 bottom left; *Octopus Books Limited/Michael Boys* 83 top left, 86 bottom left, 106 bottom centre, 121 bottom left, 131 bottom right, 159 bottom, 168 bottom left, 171 top centre, 181 top centre, 219 bottom centre; *Octopus Books Limited/Jerry Harpur* 80 bottom centre, 81 bottom centre, 90 bottom right, 94 left, 112 bottom left, 137 bottom right, 145 bottom, 156 top right, 169 top centre; *Octopus Books Limited/George Wright* 90 bottom centre, 107 top right, 140 bottom centre, 161 top right, 220 bottom centre; *Photos Horticultural, Ipswich* 9 left and right, 74 bottom left, 76 bottom, 78 top and bottom left, 79 top centre, 80 top left and top right, 81 top centre and bottom right, 83 bottom right, 84 top centre and bottom centre, 85 bottom, 86 bottom right, 87 bottom right, 90 bottom left, 91 bottom, 92 top right and bottom, 93 top, 95 right, 96 bottom right, 98 top right, 99 bottom right, 101 bottom left, 105 bottom right, 106 top right, 107 bottom, 110 top right, 111 top right, 112 top centre, 113, 116 top right, 117 bottom centre, 121 top, 124 bottom, 125 bottom centre, 128 top right and bottom right, 129 bottom right, 130 top left and top centre, 134 top, 135 top and bottom left, 136 top right, 139 top left, 141 top right, 144 bottom right, 147 bottom right, 148 bottom (all three), 149 bottom centre, 150 (all four), 151 top right and bottom, 152 right, 153 bottom, 154 top, 155 top right and bottom left, 156 bottom left, 157 bottom right, 158 right, 160 bottom, 161 top centre, 163 bottom right, 164 top right and bottom, 165 top right, 167 right, 168 top left and top right, 170 top right and bottom right, 171 bottom centre, 174 top left, 175 left, 176 right, 179 top left, 182 bottom right, 185 top, 189 top, 191 bottom centre, 193 top, 194 bottom, 195 top right, 199 top, 200, 201 bottom, 206 right, 207 top right, 212 top right, 214 bottom left and bottom right, 216 top right, 218 bottom left and bottom right, 221, 222 bottom left, 223 top right, 224 top right, 225 bottom centre, 226 top right, 227 bottom left, 229 bottom left and bottom centre, 232 bottom, 234 top right; *Harry Smith Horticultural Photographic Collection, Chelmsford* 74 bottom right, 75 top left, 76 top centre and top right, 77 top left and top right, 79 top left and top right, 81 top left, top right and bottom left, 82 top, bottom centre and bottom right, 83 top centre, top right and bottom centre, 84 top left, 86 top right, 87 top, 88 top centre, 89 top left and right, 93 bottom left and bottom right, 95 top left, 96 top centre and bottom centre, 97 (all four), 98 top left, 99 top left, top right, bottom left and bottom centre, 100 top left and right, 101 bottom right, 102 top left, 103 top left, bottom left and bottom right, 104 top left, 105 bottom left, 106 top centre and bottom left, 108 top left and top right, 110 top left and bottom, 111 top centre, 112 top right, 114 top left and top right, 115 left, 116 top left, 117 top and bottom right,

118 top left, bottom centre and bottom right, 119 bottom left, 120 top left and top right, 121 bottom right, 122 top centre, 123 top, bottom left and bottom right, 124 top right, 125 top centre and bottom left, 126 bottom, 127 bottom left, 128 top left, top centre and bottom left, 129 top right and bottom left, 130 bottom right, 131 top and bottom left, 132 top and bottom centre, 133 top left, top right, bottom left and bottom centre, 134 bottom centre, 135 bottom centre and bottom right, 136 top left, 137 left and top right, 138 top left, top centre and bottom left, 139 top right and bottom, 140 bottom left, 141 bottom left and bottom right, 142 top centre, bottom left and centre, 143 (all four), 145 top and centre right, 146 (all six), 147 bottom left and bottom centre, 149 bottom left and bottom right, 151 top left, 153 top left and top right, 154 bottom left, 155 top left, top centre and bottom centre, 156 top left, top centre, bottom centre and bottom right, 157 top right and bottom left, 159 top left and top right, 160 top right, 161 top centre and bottom left, 162 top (all three), bottom left and bottom centre, 163 top, 164 top left and top centre, 167 left, 168 top centre, bottom centre and bottom right, 169 top left, bottom left and bottom right, 170 top left, top centre, bottom left and bottom centre, 171 top left, 172 (all four), 173 top left, top right, bottom left and bottom right, 174 top right, 175 top right and bottom right, 176 left, 177 bottom (all three), 178 top, 179 top right, 181 top left, top right, bottom left and bottom centre, 182 top centre, top right and bottom centre, 183 top centre, top right and bottom (all three), 184 top left and top right, 185 bottom centre, 186 bottom left and bottom right, 187 (all six), 188 top (all three), 189 centre right, 190 top, bottom left and bottom centre, 191 top (all three) and bottom centre, 192 top right, 193 bottom centre and bottom right, 194 top, 195 left and bottom right, 196 bottom left and bottom centre, 197 top centre, top right and bottom (all three), 198 top left and top right, 199 bottom (all three), 201 top left and top right, 202 bottom left and bottom centre, 203 top left and top centre, 204 (all six), 205 (all three), 206 bottom left, 207 left, top centre and bottom right, 208, 210 top centre, top right, bottom left and bottom right, 211 top left and top right, 212 top left, bottom centre and bottom right, 213 top, 215 top centre and top right, 216 top left, top centre and bottom (all three), 218 top left and top right, 219 top, bottom left and bottom right, 220 top left, top right, bottom left and bottom right, 222 top centre, bottom centre and bottom right, 223 bottom left and bottom centre, 224 top left, top centre and bottom, 225 top centre, bottom left and bottom right, 226 bottom left and bottom right, 227 top (all three) and bottom centre, 228 bottom right, 229 top right and bottom right, 230 top, bottom left and bottom centre, 231 bottom left and bottom right, 232 top left, 233 bottom, 234 top left, top centre, bottom centre and bottom right, 235 bottom (all three); *David Squire, Hassocks* 229 top centre; *Jane Taylor, London* 182 bottom left.